LIBERTY &
CULTURE

LIBERTY &
CULTURE

Essays on the Idea of a Free Society

Tibor R. Machan

Prometheus Books
Buffalo, New York

To my children—Kate,
Thomas, and Erin

Published 1989 by Prometheus Books
700 East Amherst Street, Buffalo, New York 14215

Copyright © 1989 by Tibor R. Machan

Library of Congress Cataloging-in-Publication Data

Machan, Tibor R.
    Liberty and culture: essays on the idea of a free society / by
Tibor R. Machan.
        p.   cm.
    ISBN 0-87975-524-5
    1. Liberty. 2. Political culture—United States.
3. Individualism. 4. Free enterprise. 5. Capitalism—United
States. 6. Democracy. I. Title.
JC599.U5M264   1989
320′.01′1—dc19   88-32183
                                                                            CIP

Preface

Throughout the last twenty years, I have written a semi-regular column published by one major newspaper and syndicated in several others. Various of these pieces have appeared on the Op-Ed pages of some of America's most prominent papers: the *Orange County Register*, the *New York Times*, and the *Los Angeles Times*. I have also written columns and short articles for various magazines, most notably *Reason*, the *Freeman*, the *Humanist*, the *Lincoln Review*, the *National Review*, *National Forum*, and *Liberty*, among others. Some of these appear here as well.

I wish to thank all the publishers for their permission to reprint these previously published pieces in this work. (I have occasionally made some very minor editorial changes in order to update material.) The reader should note that those essays which lack a source reference are original to this volume.

Only a few of these articles have been strictly topical. Most focus on an event or issue of the day, using it to illustrate a point or principle.

My main concern in these writings has been with moral and political standards for contemporary society. I have stressed the enormous diversity open to each of us as we strive to live a morally proper life. And I champion the preservation of individual liberty, which makes moral conduct possible for everyone in the human community. In what follows, some may hear the note of freedom being played too often. Maybe this is the case because those who strive for freedom first need to voice their cry repeatedly. Even then the masters ignore it.

Contents

1

Marxism

ESCAPE FROM TYRANNY*

During the middle and late 1960s, I was a student at various undergraduate and graduate schools and witnessed, as well as participated in, the various political upheavals. During all that time, one thing struck me as characteristically American and, at once, very fortunate for those concerned. This was the fact that political consciousness came to people in this country at a relatively late age.

For me, the realities and horrible conflicts of political life were an early experience. I was born on the eve of World War II and began my awareness of political affairs at the age of six, when the Germans and Russians were fighting over Budapest, the beautiful capital of Hungary. I spent many hours in various bomb shelters, and, later, I was sent to a White Cross home (set up for children on the outskirts of the city) where I watched the Russians shoot down German planes that were trying (quite successfully) to bomb all the bridges between Buda and Pest. And while watching, night after night, the battles between antiaircraft guns and the bombers, I sat among Russian soldiers who were singing and praying for the German pilots' lives!

In 1948, Hungary was taken over by the Communist forces, after they brutally eliminated all opposing political parties. My great uncle, who worked in a small jewelry store, was beaten up on his way to the polls because it was suspected that he was a counter-revolutionary. From that time on, I lived in a city with a great history and a present filled with terror and fear.

In those days, it was common to hear that one's neighbors had been deported. Near our apartment several people (indeed, entire families) committed suicide rather than submit to being taken to slave labor camps. My own family lived in constant fear, especially because some members had German ancestry, and others could be classed among what the Communist party officials called "the bourgeoisie."

---

*Originally published in *World INK* (January 1977).

Not a day went by without someone giving me a long lecture about how, when I was outside the house, I could not say anything to anyone about my parents: what they did, said, or thought. On numerous occasions I was severely scolded for tuning our radio to some western European radio station.

In school the change from the haphazard, old-fashioned, and diversified educational system to the rigid, dogmatic, and terrifying party indoctrination came swiftly, but with evident destruction. Older teachers were deported or they just disappeared over night. Those with religious inclinations were often turned in by zealots who followed party instructions to the letter. Textbooks were changed to reflect the party line, especially in such courses as history and civics. But biology did not escape Communist influence. Even the physical sciences were touched by the "revolution." The signs of change came through claims about how Aleksandr S. Popov, not Guglielmo Marconi, invented the radio, while in biology the doctrines of Michurin and the dogmas of Trofim D. Lysenko became official educational material.

For me the evidence of politics and its impact on human existence zoomed in on my childhood without the possibility of a calm and gradual development. I must say that from the start I took sides. What this involved can only be hinted at here, partly because I did not have any systematic answers to the Communists, and partly because I just cannot remember all of the risky ventures I undertook.

As an example, I engaged in under-the-counter book purchases, mostly involving Hungarian translations of books by Mark Twain, Max Brand, Karl May, Jonathan Swift, Earl Stanley Gardner, and others. My favorite was Zane Grey, the American western writer. I cannot determine how much impact this reading had on me, but I do know that I was devoted to the spirit of these novels. This devotion was carried further when I began to travel about Budapest as a young student. Sometimes my friends and I would run by the Russian embassy or other official Soviet outposts and yell obscenities to the guards who stood in frozen positions, and whom we thought were therefore of little danger to us. At other times, I played hooky from the Saturday mass marches that all schools, factories, bureaus held in honor of Josef Stalin ("our dear father") and Mátyás Rákosi, Hungary's puppet leader. Yet, at other times, I simply rebelled. For example, during a mass singing performance, I stood—not at attention, but at what is here called "parade rest"—upsetting the uniformity of the performance at which we all sang Russia's revolutionary songs.

My first major confrontation came when I was about twelve. In a class euphemistically called "constitutional government," we were presented with Marx's dictum that in the proper social order of things the principle, "from each according to his ability, to each according to his needs," would be fully implemented. During the ensuing elaborations of this famous point of Marxist ideology, I suddenly raised my hand and asked to be allowed a question. Having gained permission, I pointed to a fellow student, whom I knew to be the son of a state policeman (member of the AVH, the State Protective Authority), and asked whether, if we both started with an equal sum of money and he purchased wood while I bought wine, would he have to share the earnings from a table he could have built and later sold, even though I might end up drunk in the gutter by week's end? (Mind you, I had no training in economics or natural rights theory. I believe I simply thought up the problem, although Marxists will no doubt reason *a priori* that I was infected with class consciousness.) At any rate, I was quickly ordered out of class, my mother was called into school, and I was expelled and later assigned to a trade school that lacked an academic program. My question was, needless to say, never answered. (Which is not to say that Marxists might not be able to give some kind of reply to the case I raised. The teacher was, after all, only reciting dogma, not actually developing the theories of Marx.)

So, obviously, political reality was part and parcel of my life in Hungary. This was not a blessing, however important politics is for human beings. One can sometimes be required to cope with some aspects of reality way before the proper time!

What my early introduction to politics did to me was not all harmful, for in October of 1953, a man came to our house and presented to my mother his credentials as a representative of my father (who escaped from Hungary in 1946) in a mission to smuggle me out of Hungary. My mother's question to me—"Do you want to risk an escape?"—was met with a clear-headed and firm yes.

I had, of course, heard about escape attempts and the fact that some of them succeeded. At one point, my mother had given refuge to someone who had tried to escape and was caught, then escaped from jail; he had slept in my bed for weeks, telling me of his "adventure." The stories from the border of "don't ask questions, just shoot" policies reverberated throughout the city all during my youth. This was, after all, the era of Stalin, and risking life in the face of great odds seemed more sensible to many than a visit to Siberia or being handed over to the firing squad. Where due process of law isn't even pretended, these risks seem quite natural.

My particular escape could read like a relatively exciting novel; but, alas, I am not the one to write it. Still, here are some details.

Everyone, except my mother, was left out of the scheme. My stepfather was told that I was visiting my grandmother who, in turn, was given some other cover story. My friends had to be kept in the dark—a most difficult task for me, as you can imagine. We shipped my bicycle to Gyor, a city about forty miles from the Austro-Hungarian border, and I was supplied with very good forgeries of identification papers for someone supposedly living in a border town.

On a Wednesday morning, I said a very tense but tearless goodbye to my mother and took a streetcar to the downtown bus station, where the smuggler, dressed in laborer fatigues, joined me in boarding a bus for Gyor. I must say, I behaved impeccably, giving this man no trouble at all. In Gyor, we were startled to find three AVH officers coming at us as we disembarked, only to find them walking by us without even a suspicious look. We claimed our bicycles from the baggage department and met our fellow escapees. The smuggler was, after all, earning a living, and he took on five adults besides me as clients for this service.

When the evening came, we biked about eighteen miles toward the border, sometimes taking detours, other times pushing our bicycles because the road required it. The next morning we slept in haystacks, where we also hid our bicycles in preparation for our more than twenty miles of hiking the next night. (My compatriots, incidentally, were the entire staff of the Hungarian Motion Picture Bureau with all the funds along to tide them over when they arrived in the West.)

After a long night's walk, we arrived at the border, quite battered, with bloody feet; all of our personal luggage had been discarded on the way to make the journey easier. We walked in fields, avoiding the roads on which our silhouettes would have been easily visible to any observers. Anyone who has ever tried to walk some distance in street shoes on freshly turned soil will appreciate that the trip is not to be taken for fun!

At the border, our guide left us and we went to prepare the barbed wire fences for crossing. First came spotting the hair-wires embedded in soft soil twenty-five feet in from the barbed wire on the Hungarian side of the border ditch. Spreading the hair-wires that were wrapped around the barbed wires avoided a dangerous explosion; these land mines were meant for unsuspecting escapees who got this far without being caught. Finally, came the actual cutting of the wire. Then each of us was called, and, watching each step, we carefully proceeded across the first barbed wire fence, leaving Hungary behind and preparing for our entry into Austria through the next barbed wire. This last was easier to cross, but now a different obstacle confronted us.

Having crossed both borders—for there are two lines to cross between countries—the adults of our group simply conked out. After we kissed and hugged, expressing our immense joy at having made it across, the "older" folks just wouldn't move. But the dangers had not passed. Austria at that time was divided into several sectors, and we were still within the Soviet part of the country. We had to proceed to Nichelsdorf and meet a train at 7 A.M., which meant another ten-mile trek. At this time, our guide and I undertook what can only be considered a rescue mission. We moved the others forward, one by one, some distance down the road, and, eventually, we got it into their heads that the trip wasn't over yet.

Finally, we reached the station, boarded the train, and found ourselves in the middle of the Soviet armed forces. But we didn't have to worry—every member of the gallant force was drunk. Still, to be on guard, my guide took advantage of my meager ability to speak German, and we walked around the car speaking loud German, aiming to placate any questioning minds that might have been among the soldiers.

We changed trains in Vienna, taking a long taxi drive from station to station, and, finally, we were headed toward the safety of Linz, the headquarters of American forces in Austria at the time, I believe. I had a bottle of beer on this train ride and promptly passed out, only to wake up to the receiving line of American GIs and officials.

We were taken to the United States counterespionage center and debriefed for two weeks, to make sure that we were not sent by the Soviets or Hungarians as spies. Our successful escape engendered understandable suspicion, since not too many groups of seven people came trotting through the Austro-Hungarian border in those days, or even now.

About the escape, there is just one valuable afternote: Back in 1969, I believe, TIME magazine ran a pious article about the greedy smugglers who, for a fee, will attempt to bring people out of eastern European countries. Horrid, horrid! Instead of humanitarianism, it was the profit motive that inspired these "terrible" people to exploit the desires of the enslaved to be liberated. I fired off a letter to TIME, explaining that our own smuggler charged $1,000 for each of us. But he later went back to bring out his fianceé and was promptly shot down when he fired on the Austrian borderguards who spotted him. I won't conclude that professionalism must suffer when deep emotions take over, but I did tell TIME how pleased I was that my smuggler asked me for money and loved me very little. (They published the letter—edited!)

I have dwelled on the escape because this is the only time I have ever written about it, and because it does point to the enormous risks people will take to escape from tyranny. As to what I found upon my arrival and gradual amalgamation within the West—that is another story. Obviously, in contrast, the situation in Germany and the United States is a haven of liberty, but the devotion of the people to this important political value was very disappointing. I began to think through the differences between the freedom that I was aware of only as an abstract possibility and the tyranny that surrounded me. I later immersed myself in the study of this issue full time. It led me to a philosophical study of society, and I am convinced that, concerning the issue of what is best politically for human beings, the right answer comes from theories of natural or human rights. I also realized that politics is insufficient—economics even less comprehensive—for an understanding of why freedom should be protected and preserved in the human community. My studies in these and related areas continue.

Some will say that my only reason for believing that freedom is important is not a reason real at all; I merely claim to have good reasons when, in fact, my personal history has determined my "preference." I have heard this charge often. I have studied it, for instance, in the writing of Nietzsche, who said in his *Beyond Good and Evil* that "the greater part of the conscious thinking of a philosopher is secretly influenced by his instincts, and forced into definite channels. . . ." Marx, too, tried to explain away the force of anti-Communist arguments by consigning them to bourgeois prejudice. Freud, Skinner, and many others advanced similar theses.

But, aside from the bad logic involved in such hypotheses and their self-defeating nature, let me tell of an episode that may better illustrate their futility.

Some years ago, I was asked to attend a lecture by a Hungarian freedom fighter. I am not much of a nationalist, but I was curious, and so I went. To my dismay! The man stood there telling his audience how great an idea Marxist communism is, if only it worked. But people are imperfect, and, shame on us all, we are stuck with our Western-type democracies that are well suited to creatures such as we—beastly, brutish—flops from the start.

That the views of people who have very similar historical backgrounds can differ dramatically is well illustrated by this forgettable event! This "landsman" of mine was saying things diametrically opposed to views that I was gradually developing at the time I heard them.

Personal history can present someone with the numerous facts of life worth paying attention to, and personal historical highlights can accentuate some of these facts. But only the individual can initiate the mental processes, the thought required to understand the nature and implications of these facts. That is why my own history is, perhaps, interesting. But it would only be instructive to someone who studies and reflects upon it beyond having simply lived through it, heard about it, or read about it.

But isn't this, as a matter of fact, an essential point about individualism? I think that it highlights well the crucial difference between what statist regimes think of their citizens, and what the constitution of a free society must express in its legal structure.

What we have now in the United States is creeping fascism. In Hitler's Germany each person had title to his own property; the regime simply told everyone how to use that property. It was a grand deception: People both owned *and* did not own their work, their property, and the like. That is what's happening in the United States now. The doctor appears to be a free agent, yet his work is controlled by the government through wage-controls, red tape, etc. Add this to the burden of coping with numerous phony patients and you'll understand why the profession of medicine, with its difficult prerequisites, is ceasing to attract productive students. Why, the thing to do is to become a bureaucrat: from Washington one can be doctor, philosopher, artist, television broadcaster, meat cutter, or anything else through the mechanism of governmental regulation and controls.

Fascism, here we come!

FREE FROM REALITY*

Today many things divide the people of this country: race, religion, nationality, age, sex, cultural heritage, and other less obvious factors on which society can be seriously divided.

Recently I discussed economics with some people, and during the discussion I noticed that several of those with whom I disagreed had a very peculiar notion of freedom. Whenever I would talk about human freedom and point to instances where I would have thought people were really free, these individuals would contest my claim. For instance, if I would point out that unlike people who cannot travel freely in Iron Curtain countries, we can, more or less, do so in the United States, the reply would be that in point of fact no one is really free to travel in America. Do I really believe that I am free to go anywhere I want? Is it not true, instead, that my various plans, responsibilities, living conditions, and economic circumstances make it impossible for me to leave?

---

*Originally published in the *Orange County Register* (circa 1968).

Of course, I had to answer with a yes. But clearly there was something drastically different between the ways we used the word *freedom*. If it is taken in the way my adversaries used the term, then no one could ever be said to be free. The laws of nature—psychological, physical, meteorological, and the like—do limit us to operations and activities within given boundaries.

To protest that we are not free in this sense would amount to saying that we are forced to eat in order to live. One may wish it to be otherwise, but even such wishing, if not followed by efforts at seeking a scientifically feasible alternative, might be wasteful.

Often, in political and moral discussions, it is unclear just what kind of moral boundaries we must accept: boundaries that we can ignore for a while but that may catch up with us in the end. The limitation on one's "liberty" to be a barbarian or to steal a friend blind can, of course, be overcome, but not without serious consequences. In both cases, at least the victims would suffer adverse consequences from such exercises of "freedom." In the end, the party who acted to overcome the "petty limitation" of morality would also find that reality has caught up with him.

Freedom used to mean (for John Locke and the founders who devised our legal system), one's right to act without interference from others. Freedom, especially in political, economic, and social contexts, did not refer to one's right and ability to behave in any way at all, including breaking of the laws of nature and morality. Granted, we never got very clear on just what the latter are. We did think that whatever they are, they are binding on us, and that if freedom means anything at all, it means acting within these boundaries of human action.

If anyone has doubts as to the relevance of philosophy to our daily lives, maybe he'd like to know that the currently fashionable notion of freedom is one that Marx, and before him Hegel, worked out with the greatest care. And thus far their work has paid off.

GAZING AT THE WORLD THROUGH MARX'S EYES*

A letter writer asked me whether it is true that there are numerous Marxist professors teaching at American universities. He thought that employing such professors was self-destructive, inasmuch as Marxism is committed to the overthrow of the kind of society that the United States tends to be, namely, capitalist.

There are indeed outright Marxist professors at U.S. universities, in sociology, history, and philosophy departments, though some work in economics. My impression is that their number (about 10 percent) is growing. Administrators permit them "to put a Marxist spin on their course content," although this is more likely to occur in sociology and history than in philosophy courses.

All this is quite aboveboard. Marxist teachers are quite openly Marxist.

Sometimes Marxists have their own ideological subgroups in professional

---

*Originally published in the *Orange County Register* (November 30, 1984).

academic organizations. For example, the American Philosophical Association has a subgroup called the Society for the Study of Dialectical Materialism. But most Marxists who give talks and teach at universities are of a different sort from the activist types, though no less hazardous to our health.

Most "Western" Marxists argue that Marx was a democratic socialist who believed that only when socialism is democratic will it turn into communism, to put it as simply as possible.

The dispute centers on whether Marx really would have accepted Lenin's obviously elitist interpretations of Marxism. He would have had to, though he might not have wished to! Marx would probably not have welcomed the Stalinist developments in Russia, but his views are the handiest way to give Stalinism some semblance of intellectual legitimacy.

The central question is whether the "dictatorship of the proletariat" means some kind of single-party dictatorship or a form of communalism in which every-one manages to make decisions respecting all the affairs of a society. The latter is nonsense, but arguably it does not explicitly express a preference for a dicta-torial, totalitarian structure of government.

It is also true that Marx explicitly rejects the need for violent revolutions in countries where there is universal suffrage, where he said the unemployed and alienated masses will express their hatred of the capitalists at the ballot box.

One might argue that some of this is happening in the United States, given the trends toward rent control and extensive limitations on the right to private property. Various coastal commissions, environmental restrictions, wildlife-pres-ervation efforts, government regulations, and numerous planning boards have ushered in the peaceful socialism Marx was predicting.

The right to private property is being eroded, and may be abolished through the ballot box, the courts, and other "democratic" (nonviolent) revolutionary measures, just as Marx envisioned. Thus one can technically claim to be a Marxist and still repudiate violent revolution.

The communism these "democratic" Marxists embrace is a sham, of course (just take note of Nicaragua or Cuba). Still, there is something to the view that Marx is different from Lenin or Stalin. It is a bit like the relationship between Nietzsche and the Third Reich. However Nietzsche might have been horrified by the latter, it was in part his own creation.

The universities and the country are far more "left" than most conservatives believe. The major intellectual magazines—the *New York Review of Books,* the *Nation, Harper's,* the *Atlantic, Saturday Review, Psychology Today*—publish reams of articles reeking with neo-Marxian phrases and concepts.

In my own discipline of philosophy, especially in ethics and political philos-ophy, "Marxian" ideals of what is right and just get far more play than do liber-tarian or conservative concepts.

One can imagine how this strikes someone who in his youth was forced to attend rallies organized for Stalin, "our dear father." Still, there is a kind of justice to it all. Much of corporate America seems to wish to play ball with Marxism rather than mount a vigorous charge agains this utter nonsense.

Instead of funding "Masterpiece Theater," they might do well to pour funds into organizations that mount a philosophically sound and conscious attack on Marxism.

ALIENATION: WAS MARX RIGHT?*

Imagine, if you will, someone laboring away on a flower pot, designing it carefully, making it in a shop somewhere in a basement, then taking it to the market to be sold by a merchant to a buyer who will give it as a wedding present to a friend. As the purchase is made, it is hardly likely that the seller or the buyer will pay much attention to the history of the flower pot's production. The buyer wants something that will serve as a charming gift. The happy couple, in turn, will open the box containing the pot, exclaim with a few oohs and ahs, and shortly the pot will join a dozen other gifts on some shelf.

Has the potmaker's labor been appreciated? Have those who exchanged and eventually received the item treated it with the regard such labors should be afforded? The merchant and the purchaser gave little or no thought to the potmaker's labors, treating the pot as one among many commodities, while the couple, of course, gave no thought to what went into making it.

Working Humans

This is what Karl Marx had in mind when he talked about alienation. Roughly put, Marx believed that alienation arises when an individual worker is divorced from his distinctive human nature, or essence. For Marx, the defining characteristic of human beings is that they are conscious producers—workers with conscious plans triggered by economic factors in their society. And he believed that the failure to take into account the personal element of production in market transactions precipitates widespread alienation in any society where buying and selling occurs.

This was one of his objections to capitalist economic systems. People who buy goods and services disregard the essentially human, personal elements of what they are obtaining. In focusing on the result—the commodity or service—they forget about the process of work. Goods and services are thus objectified, dehumanized, depersonalized, creating a gulf between workers and their nature as conscious producers. And so Marx charged capitalism with widespread alienation of the producing class, the workers or laborers.

Now we all know plenty of unalienated workers—flowerpot makers and workers of all stripes—who claim to have their essential humanity well intact and to enjoy their work in the context of a market economy. Doesn't this prove that Marx didn't have the facts straight?

Marxists will answer that such producers suffer from false consciousness, a deluded belief that they are treated humanely. This false consciousness is created,

---

*Originally published in *Reason* magazine (September 1979).

the Marxists will continue, by the market economy itself; indeed, it is a symptom of alienation. Neo-Marxists such as C. Wright Mills and Herbert Marcuse add to this the contention that a concerted conspiracy is afoot within modern capitalist societies to manipulate the working class into thinking that they are treated humanely. Advertising, for example, creates shallow desires and, because these can be satisfied within a market economy, deludes workers into thinking they are well off.

Today, the theme of the inherently alienating character of capitalism has many variations, heard way beyond Marxist and neo-Marxist circles. Contemporary critics of technology extend the idea when they charge technology with giving us all the impression that we have control over our lives, whereas in fact technocrats have manipulated us so that we are deluded about this. From both the Left and the Right, critics of capitalism and the system's productive capacity aim to convince us that the things we think are of value to us—kitchen gadgets, car accessories, office machinery, etc.—appear to be of value only because we have been taken in by the business folks and bankers who survive entirely as parasites upon our deluded satisfaction with what they sell us. Such critics, who on this count are joined by Alexander Solzhenitsyn, complain that we in the industrialized West are too materialistic. We are too much concerned with things in the marketplace and too little concerned with intangible goods that distinguish human beings from other creatures.

Economic Man

But the question needs to be confronted at its heart: Must the free society, with its market economy, be alienating?

It would be silly to deny that in a free society alienation is a distinct possibility. And this doesn't depend on Marx's definition of human beings as conscious producers. In a free society it is possible to subvert one's humanity, whatever that must ultimately amount to—conscious producer, divinely inspired beast, or rational animal.

But suppose for the moment that one's essential humanity would be undermined by becoming what the Canadian Marxist C. B. Macpherson calls a "possessive individualist"—someone entirely immersed in attempting to obtain gratification through the possession of material things or pleasures. Even so, it is all wrong to maintain that in free societies this sort of life will be widely cherished. Single-minded possessiveness is possible in a free society, but that it is necessary, or even very probable, is extremely doubtful.

Marx, it bears recalling, was committed to economic determinism when he developed his mature theory about alienation. He believed that one's actions, and even one's thought processes, are entirely dictated by the economic aspects of whatever society one lives in. Thus, in a society where the economics of a free market prevail, one's personal life must become subordinate to market factors. And although Engels tried to deny it later, Marxist theory just does not hang together once economic determinism is lifted from it.

So the first point to be made about Marx's view of alienation is that this determinism is ultimately inconsistent with the possibility of any theoretical activity such as Marx engaged in. He appeared to be quite aware of this, since he exempted himself from the all-embracing economic determinism the rest of us are supposedly subject to!

Pride and Creativity

But Marx also forgot about the capacity to keep on oneself a perspective different from that which others hold. A worker, for example, could keep in clear focus his full human nature even as the rest of those involved in trading his product forget about the producer. In short, producers can have personal pride in their work and can easily do without the audience Marx believed everyone requires to keep one's humanity in clear view. Marx, however, being fundamentally an altruist (as is clear in all his writings, starting with letters to his father from high school), refused to give personal pride a serious place in his human psychology.

Marx's idea of alienation also encounters the problem that conscious material production is not what is distinctive about human beings. A historical/dialectical materialist, Marx closed his eyes to the fact that human nature is only partially characterized by productivity (and not necessarily material productivity, at that). Of course, without material production one would neglect some essential features of one's humanity—one's physical, chemical, biological existence. But there is more to human life. The formation of ideas, learning, understanding, artistic creativity and appreciation, emotional exaltation, and so forth, all constitute equally important features of human living. And only by a materialist prejudice can all these be subsumed under material production. Since social life involves all of these in one form or another, a correct conception of human nature must make room for education, the arts and sciences, friendship, and a family life as well as commerce.

Since conscious material production is not the distinctively human characteristic, there is ample opportunity for involvement with the world on other than commercial levels, even while engaged mainly in material labor or the exchange of its product. To regard human beings as incapable of widening the scope of their involvement with one another beyond the narrow material dimensions of some action is unjustifiably pessimistic.

Finally, the Marxist theory of alienation is insulting to workers. Most people do material, even menial, labor at some time in their lives. I was a box-cart packer for a year, and at another point in my life I was a shipping clerk, where all I did was pack and mail machinery. And at still another point I was a welder. I didn't know I would advance past this point in my life, although I never failed to make plans. But quite apart from any long-range hopes, I never failed to create opportunities on the job to make the most of my work.

Those for whom I worked—with whom I engaged in market exchange— "merely" wanted the result of what I did, such as neatly packed box-carts. Yet every day, every hour, I'd improve my packing, eventually learning to throw boxes, with precision, from several yards. In all my jobs as a laborer and as a more skilled worker, I found ample opportunity to improve my work and come up with a better product, and I found the opportunity to discover what I wanted to specialize in, what suited me well.

Many, many people could tell very similar stories. This shows clearly enough that selling one's labor to those who have no personal interest in it—as the economic system of capitalism requires—need not engender alienation for those involved.

No doubt some people stagnate in the sort of labor that does not suit them or box themselves into routine and boring work. But this does not at all reflect badly on the marketplace itself, unless one is a utopian like Marx, who could not accept the fact that individuals might botch their lives on their own, that such failure does not require some metaphysical explanation and, in turn, some revolutionary remedy.

Let us simply admit it: If individuals in a free marketplace are alienated, the problem is usually of their own making, not the result of the inherently alienating feature of the system—contrary to what Marx and many conscious and unconscious followers would have us believe.

SOME STILL WORSHIP THE GOD THAT FAILED*

After the revelations of Aleksandr Solzehnitsyn, in his *The Gulag Archipelago,* it was no longer possible for any person with some measure of self-respect to support Soviet-style socialism. The system was so evidently brutal that no one in his right mind could say anything in its behalf.

But this did not deal the deathblow to socialism itself, not yet even to Marxism. There was, we were told, a humanistic, democratic side to Marxism and we can find it in the old revolutionary himself. We were told that he was in fact a defender of individual liberty—of course, a bit different from the kind prized in the Western political tradition. Marx was a democratic socialist, someone who favored full participation in the whole of social life by every member of society.

The Soviet system is a betrayal of Marxism, we were told. And there was something to this story. The Soviet Union emerged from a revolution not in a capitalist society but one that was barely past Czarist feudalism. Sure, the Czar's Russia had elements found in Western liberal societies, but still, Marx clearly said that society must pass through its capitalist phase before it can change into socialism. So the case for the betrayal is not entirely implausible.

Then Lenin clearly revised Marxist theory to favor the leadership of the revolution by an elite cadre rather than by the mass of workers. This, incidentally, went hand in hand with the earlier point about Russia's unreadiness for a workers' revolution, because of the absence of any capitalist phase in its history. Without a disenchanted, angry, united working class, which by Marxist theory can only arise in a capitalist world, there could be no way to socialism but via a revolutionary cadre.

---

*Originally published in the *Orange County Register* (February 1, 1987).

Of course, if Marxism is wrong, then there will not be some inevitable work-ers' revolution in the first place and those who want it simply will have to grab for power by brute force. That seems to be what is happening throughout all the Marxist national-liberation efforts. And Marxism made provisions for this kind of forceful approach to instituting socialism and communism.

Whatever its affinity to Marx, Soviet-style socialism has faltered lately in its popularity. Too much poverty, too much brutality, too little individuality for anyone.

What are socialists to do? In a recent book, *Arguing for Socialism,* Professor Andrew Levine, of the University of Wisconsin, defends the system on grounds that it most faithfully upholds, and is likely to preserve in practice, traditional moral values. In particular, socialism favors a form of equal opportunity which cannot be found either in capitalist theory or in capitalist practice. Equality of opportunity, understood as genuine similarity in the material starting points for human beings, maintained by public policy, would seem to be something that traditional morality requires. Fairness, equity, even justice would appear to de-mand that we should not leave people helpless. And only government can come close to guaranteeing that this imperative is fully met. Ergo, socialism.

There is, of course, a lot more to Levine's work but the central thesis is not difficult to appreciate. If the moral outlook supports the principle of equal human material opportunity, and socialism offers the best chance of delivering this goal, surely socialism should be preferred to capitalism, which does not even offer this as its main virtue but boasts, instead, of producing prosperity. Clearly some people who favor capitalism talk of its provision of equal opportunity to all, meaning some mythical equal economic starting point for everyone. But clearly this flies in the face of the facts in all Western societies, so dreaming of a better socialist system seems then warranted.

If you think that Professor Levine is impressed with any historical data comparing equal material opportunities for people in, say, the United States of America and the Soviet Union, forget it. Historical accidents account for the economic advantages people enjoy in the U.S. Otherwise even Soviet socialism, one that Professor Levine admits as to harsh for his taste, would have done better on the score of equalizing opportunity than has American capitalism.

What is remarkable about this book is that it has one very good point. If the traditional emphasis on charity, altruism, equity, fairness and the like is ac-cepted as decisive, we cannot dispute Professor Levine's point very easily. Yet despite the temptation to rush to socialism's defense one should remember tthat even charity is impossible if the central capitalist principle of the right to pri-vate property is denied, as socialism of any type must deny it. How can one be charitable, as a matter of a personal moral choice, if one has nothing of one's own—nothing, at least, of significant weight—to bequeath? What is generosity if one has no right to the use and disposal of the products of one's skill, inven-tion, creation, labor, etc.?

But, of course, there is more. For example, one of the cardinal human vir-tues is prudence—the responsibility to secure for oneself and those one holds dear a decent standard of living, a measure of significant prosperity. But under socialism a person cannot practice this virtue since all significant economic decisions are made collectively. The individual just drops out of the picture and humankind takes on the formal characteristics of a beehive or ant colony (losing productivity in the process).

No, equal material opportunity is not a central value in the West, although it is often stressed that persons should be generous and charitable to those less well off. Even the condemnation of wealth is actually more of a caution against greed. Equal opportunity does not mean an equal economic starting point but rather the more realistic legal protection of everyone's quite possibly unequal starting effort to improve on his or her life. It is for that reason that millions of people have come to the United States, not because they sought some guarantee of an equal starting point.

The importance of personal self-development, by individual effort, is far more vital. Capitalism is superior to socialism because it recognizes the diversity of life human beings can live and refuses to regiment anyone, even at the obvious risk of foregoing utopian perfection of the species. Since perfection is a fraudulent promise, it is to capitalism's credit that it avoids making it.

NICARAGUA'S CHIEF IMPORT*

With the debacle of the Reagan administration's deal with Iran and ensuing jubilance of the bulk of the press, which is now helping to draw the whole matter into a maxi-series on the nightly news, the real issues involving Nicaragua have started to fade from attention. I want to call attention to some of the actual problems in connection with Nicaragua.

In an article by "Father" Miguel D'Escoto Brockmann, published some time ago in the *San Diego Tribune,* entitled "Nicaragua denies it threatens region," we are treated to a very interesting rationale for Nicaragua's behavior. The Nicaraguan leader tries to persuade us of Nicaragua's peace-loving nature. He says, among other things, that it would be silly for Nicaragua to invade any neighbor since that would give the Reagan administration the excuse it needs to raise arms against it. Furthermore, it is the United States that is imperialistic, not Nicaragua, and the only reason that country is welcoming Soviet help is that the United States has turned against it.

While some of the points raised in the essay are plausible enough, there is one matter that simply cannot be dismissed. However much D'Escoto attempts to avoid discussing it, it's vital to realize that Nicaragua's leaders are Marxists-Leninsts. And there are certain principles of geopolitics that can be inferred from the self-declared Marxism of Nicaragua's government, regradless of any denials.

In the preface of the Russian edition of *The Communist Manifesto,* Marx wrote that Russia may be turned into a socialist country only "If the Russian

Revolution becomes the signal for a proletarian revolution in the West, so that both complement each other. . . ."

By any reasonable interpretation, this means that a Marxist nation that has not reached the highest stage of capitalism must have a public policy committed to exporting communist revolution. D'Escoto's protests to the country notwithstanding, Nicaragua, just as Cuba and the Soviet Union itself, is obliged to try to instigate revolution within its neighboring countries. This may not involve outright invasions—these measures may indeed be suicidal, as D'Escoto notes, because they may provide the United States with grounds for retaliation. But there are other than direct or even violent means by which reovultions can be supported, such as infiltration, subverison, propaganda, and the like.

The claim that Nicaragua is arming itself only because it fears American invasion is unprovable. It always sounds halfway plausible to say this, but when one considers that this is being said by Marxist-Leninists, the doubts must intensify considerably.

When we recall that Marx believed true-blue socialism can only be built on top of successful capitalism, then the need for such spreading of revoltuion becomes crystal clear. Nicaragua has never been capitalist. It has enjoyed some capitalist incursions by way of Ameircan business. It has never developed the productive capacity that by Marx's own account a society requires in order to be managed collectively, for the benefit of the whole community. For this reason alone, a Marxist country that has not yet gone through a capitalist phase needs to export revolution and eventually capture capitalist institutions within its region. That, by Marxist theory, is the only way to make socialism work.

So, when one reads the words of D'Escoto, one can only be reminded of what Shirley Christian noted in the *Atlantic* not long ago, namely, "Internationalism—the assistance of fellow revolutionaries—is a key element of the faith to Marxist-Leninists and telling them not to practice is like telling priests not to pray."

Of course, none of this implies that the United States has any just grounds for actually invading Nicaragua. The issue there is not whether Nicaragua is becoming a tyranny, which it is. The issue is whether it poses a demonstrable threat to the people of the United States. About that there can be a great deal of disagreement.

What is indisputable is that the government of Nicaragua is committed, philosophically, to spread communism. Without doing that, its Marxism would be but empty rhetoric. And, furthermore, without fostering revolution—in the hope that some of the wealth now owned by private U.S. and South or Central American individuals and firms will be acquired by like-minded tyrannies—Nicaragua has no chance, in Marxist terms, of surviving.

THE SCAPEGOAT OF IDEOLOGY*

American individualism—in terms of which the right to private property has been taken most seriously in the legal systems of the United States as well as many other countries—has been dubbed an *ideology,* in the pejorative sense of that term. In that sense "ideology" refers to a system of ideas serving consciously or subconsciously to rationalize (i.e., make artificially palatable) preexisting wants, interests, or socioeconomic roles.

The term *ideology* has gained much of its currency under the influence of Karl Marx, for whom ideologies were theories of political economy serving the interests of the ruling classes in society. Marx treated most of his serious intellectual adversaries as ideologues with whom argument was pointless. Ideologies are reflections of essential features of a society that involves the oppression of one class by another, with the hidden purposes of legitimizing this oppression. Thus, those who argued for these principles of political economy really were not honest thinkers who could be convinced of their mistakes. They were agents of a class, apologists, mouthpieces of the ruling class, even when others considered them major theorists. According to Marx, Adam Smith, who founded modern economics, really was not a scientist or theorist but merely a man engaged in elaborate, sometimes brilliant, albeit not consciously produced, rationalizations. (In his posthumously published book *Grundrisse,* Marx contrasts Smith, who entertained "insipid illusions" with "Steuart, who . . . escaped with simplicity [sic] of view." He discusses several others whose ideas he attributes to their class membership, not their own thinking.)

Under Marx's influence, but with the support of many non-Marxist views, American individualism has been dubbed an ideology by many social commentators. Some only mean by this that individualism, when expressed in simplistic terms, does not deserve to be called a serious social philosophy. But others really think the doctrine merely serves to rationalize the status quo, especially when there is little evidence that a society actually embodies individualist principles and policies, as is the case in ours at the present time.

For Marxists a system of laws based largely on the "rights of man"—e.g., the right to private property—had a limited function in human history, viz., to facilitate production and technological development. Once this function had been achieved, these principles would be abolished by a new phase, and eventually by the last phase of human history, communism.

> Communism is for us not a state of affairs which is to be established, an ideal to which reality will have to adjust itself. We call communism the real movement which abolishes the present state of things. The conditions of this movement result from the premises now in existence. (*Selected Works* [Moscow: Progress Publishers, 1977], p. 171)

---

*Originally published in the *Orange County Register* (circa 1984).

The movement in question can be viewed as analogous to the way an individual develops from infancy to childhood, then to adolescence and finally to maturity. Marx made clear enough that, "[From] my standpoint . . . the evolution of the economic formation of society is viewed as a process of natural history. . . ." (*Selected Works,* p. 417).

Marx laid claim to having a "God's eye" perspective on humanity, which he saw as a growing "organic body." He spoke of early Western civilization as a stage of childhood when he wrote that "the Greeks were normal children." His method of analysis supposedly entitled him to pinpoint the stages of humanity's development from its beginning through to its full emancipation. And thus for him capitalism was humanity's adolescence. As in adolescence, so in capitalism, we experience joys and sorrows, costs and benefits, all quite unavoidable but only temporarily, with better times to come.

There are immense problems with the Marxian perspective; yet Jean-Paul Sartre was right to regard Marxism as the dominant thought in our age. The reasons for this are complicated but they have to do mainly with Marx's valiant but unsuccessful attempt to merge two indispensable and yet apparently incompatible human concerns, namely, science and values. In the end Marxism fails to be a theoretically successful system. Still, it is the most powerful, intellectually appealing, and widely discussed system of thought in our time.

This is not the place to take on Marxism. I want only to suggest where its major problems lie. This will indicate why his claim that individualism as an ideology should be rejected:

First, Marxism conceives of human beings collectively, as if humanity as a whole, not you and I, were the individual person with purposes, intentions, ideas, health and illness, values, and so on. Marx discounts the importance of individuality and measures all values by reference to an idea of collective human essence. As he says, "The human essence is the true collectivity of man." The foundation of this essence is material production, *ergo,* the labor conception of value and the messianic role of the working class.

But contrary to Marx, human nature appears to be incoherent without admitting the concept of individuality into its understanding. As I have argued earlier, human beings are unique in being self-motivated and thus self-differentiating. The entire Marxist edifice rests on a misunderstanding of human nature, inspired largely by Hegel's dialectical and teleological metaphysics. The error of seeing individuals as merely parts of the larger whole of humanity's "organic body" ultimately infects not only Marxian historical analysis—which is its most influential part—but also the practicability of socialism and communism, which supposes the further development of human nature so that the principles of universal love and nonegoism will eventually become reality.

Second, Marxian characterization of capitalism and its social-philosophical foundation, individualism, are unfounded. If humanity is not what undergoes the developmental process of a biological organism, as Marx suggests, then his understanding of human history on the model of that process is unsupported. In turn, the various arguments about how human society should be organized, the right way for people to live together, cannot be dismissed as mere ideology. Rather, these are serious contenders for the answer to the perennial question of how we should live in one another's company, the central political question from time immemorial. The belief that in tribal societies human beings were at their stage of infancy, whereas in capitalist times they are in their adolescence, is an appealing, progressivist notion, but it turns out to be an unwarranted extrapolation. Human nature is far more stable than this view would have it. One need not deny the possibility of some changes in human nature to accept far greater stability over time than implied in the Marxian analysis. The question is what human nature is and how we must accommodate it, not at what stage of humanity's growth period or maturation we happen to be, as Marx and many of his conscious and unknowing followers suppose. This does not deny that the basic nature of human beings—albeit not likely eternally fixed—lacks stability through time.

Having noted these two problems in Marxism, we can now see that a political theory need not be a mere ideology. It may be much more than the rationalization of class interests. When people like Milton Friedman and F. A. Hayek espouse the free market "ideology," they must, in turn, be dealt with as grown people who know what they are talking about and are not merely passive mouthpieces of their ruling class.

When we talk of ideology apart from the Marxist influence, we are not considering the framework pejoratively. Rather, we are considering it from the point of view of its practical utility as a relatively simple—that is, not philosophically elaborate—public policy-guiding system of ideas. In that sense ideological thinking cannot be avoided. Politicians, bureaucrats, and others are not able to devote themselves to philosophical study. They haven't the luxury to sit around and dispute everything. They must prepare for action. And in this preparation, they must have some guidelines that keep them on the right track. They will, therefore, draw on the ideology that they have come to regard as most appropriate, most successful for guiding public policy. None of this means that they could not take a critical look at this ideology if that is what they chose to do. Anyone who charges them with such a limitation is leveling an unjustified insult and is, moreover, showing an unwarranted elitism, as if he, unlike the poor slob being criticized, had a special facility for seeing things in their true light.

2

Democracy

SENATOR RUDMAN AND DEMOCRACY*

On Monday, July 13, 1987, Lieutenant Colonel Oliver North was subjected to several speeches from members of the Select Congressional Committee on the Iran-Contra affair. Among them was Senator Rudman, Republican of New Hampshire, Vice-Chairman of the Committee. His last remarks were very much on target and deserve serious reflection.

What Senator Rudman said to Colonel North is that even while Oliver North and Co. believed firmly in their own cause—indeed, even while they might have been dead right about the righteousness of their cause—the "American people have a Constitutional right to be wrong. And what Ronald Reagan thinks or what Oliver North thinks or what I think or what anybody else thinks makes not a whit [of difference] if the American people say 'enough.' " In short, once polls showed that a majority of Americans opposed support to the Contras by way of the Boland Amendment, this has to be accepted by those who accept our democratic institutions. Oliver North, a servant of the American people, should realize that when a majority of Americans oppose some policy, that policy must stop.

What are we to say about Senator Rudman's forceful remarks? Of course, there is the initial point that what the polls show isn't always so. Polls are taken by sampling the public and the samples are not always very good. Even election poll-taking cannot be fully trusted, despite improvement on the process since the time when polls showed Thomas Dewey to have become president when in fact Harry Truman had been elected by a majority of Americans once all the votes were finally counted.

Of course Senator Rudman's point does hold independently of the issue about polls. It might be that the Boland Amendment—which Congress tagged onto the final budget bill at the eleventh hour and then forced down President Reagan's

---

*Originally published in the *Orange County Register* (1987).

throat (to give Illinois Republican Senator Henry Hyde's version)—managed to express the will of the majority of Americans. What about that? Is the duty of an official of the government to always heed the will of the majority?

Our society is not in fact a pure representative democracy. Rather it is a *constitutional* democracy, in which the will of the majority is not unlimited. The Bill of Rights seriously limits majority rule, as the U.S. Supreme Court made clear in *West Virginia State Board of Eduction* v. *Barnette* (1943): "Fundamental rights may not be submitted to a vote; they depend on the outcome of no elections."

The issue Senator Rudman raised is whether North was concerned with matters that are "beyond the reach of majorities and officials" or rather with matters subject to majority decision and therefore subject to congressional oversight (from one month to the next). In short, were North's actions in conflict with the American ideal of constitutional democracy?

It is arguable that appropriating moneys for intelligence gathering by the CIA, the Department of Defense, and others is subject to majority rule and, thus, to congressional determination. This follows from the general principle of "No taxation without representation," certainly a cornerstone of the democratic form of government. But it is also arguable that the foreign policy of the United States must be conducted with one goal in mind that cannot be construed as subject to majority decision, namely, protecting the lives of American citizens. The pro-Contra Reagan doctrine certainly could be said to promote this end. It is a measure aimed at defending against continued Soviet incursion into a realm of immediate political concern to our national security.

So we seem to have a conflict here between the central objectives of U.S. foreign policy, which must be treated as beyond the reach of majorities, and matters that are open to majority decision, e.g., the spending of funds for various aspects of foreign policy. Yet it makes sense and is manageable.

In the conduct of foreign affairs the *goal* should be fixed for the long range, as in the case of our judicial system, which is designed to seek justice. The Bill of Rights affirms this when it insists on due process of law without exception.

The fixed foreign policy objective is the protection of the country against all foreign elements that threaten our right to life, liberty, and property. This may extend to supporting opposition to the government of Nicaragua when a real, objective threat exists, i.e., its development of a Soviet beachhead in Central America.

But the means for carrying out this fixed objective cannot themselves be fixed. So the Congress, expressing the majority's wishes, could curb spending in this area—and the Boland Amendment(s) did just this, however obscurely and unreasonably.

Lieutenant Colonel Oliver North has been arguing that the White House should be able to carry out foreign policy even in the face of congressional opposition. And he is partly right: The president's charge is clear and does not depend on repeated expressions of majority support.

But North makes another telling point. When the president can carry out his objective without going against the will of Congress—e.g., spending public monies for the Nicaraguan Democratic Resistance (Contras)—he must do so. In this he is only carrying out his oath of office, according to the U.S. Constitution and subsequent interpretations. He can proceed to urge funds for the Contras even if Congress does not like it! He may, and should at times, partially privatize foreign policy if the Congress will not support him.

It is all well and good to love democracy, but democracy is not an end in itself. Our political system largely recognizes this, although we have in the last century lost sight of the matter and subjected more and more issues to democratic decision making (especially with regard to the right to property, as outlined in the Fifth Amendment). Such full democratization is improper; it may also explain why Senator Rudman loves democracy more than he should.

DEMOCRATS' DILEMMA*

Democrats are, of course, the party of compassion. They certainly pass themselves off as the kind of people who take charity very seriously. Mike Dukakis is bending over backward to make himself out to be a clone of New York Governor Mario Cuomo in the compassion department. His and his party's primary complaint against George Bush is that the Republicans are the party of the rich. In contrast, Democrats are the party of the poor.

All this is often very effective rhetoric. For as long as human beings have thought about such matters, it has been fashionable to show sadness about the poor. And the rich have been denounced roundly in virtually all the philosophies and religions of the world—never mind that the rich are also the group that everyone dreams of joining (other than some who wish to make a point against them). "It is easier for a camel to go through the eye of a needle, than for a rich man to enter into the kingdom of God" (Matthew xix). The bourgeoisie, that group of persons who have felt comfortable about pursuing wealth and a good life here on earth, has had to contend with snide comments from both the aristocrats and the proletarians of the world.

The Democrats are merely cashing in on an old prejudice. The Jews of the world have had to suffer this prejudice everywhere they have lived. They were not allowed to join other cultures because they had an alien religion and they were the only ones allowed to deal professionally in the field of finance. When they succeeded, they were roundly denounced; they eventually paid for the experience with mass extermination at the hands of resentful gentiles.

No doubt, there are rich people with ill-gotten wealth. But there are also poor people who don't deserve any better. The whole thing of dividing people on the basis of their economic well-being to gain undeserved allegiance, is a simplistic trick, which plays on envy and resentment, and is not based on good judgment and substance. Yet this is just what seems to be the central tactic of Mike Dukakis and the Democratic Party.

---

*Originally published in *LP News*.

There is a dilemma, however, that this approach to governing has presented to the Democrats. It became evident recently when the party of "wear your compassion on your shirtsleeve and indulge in it with other people's money" tried to get government to guarantee child care for all working mothers. The federal childcare initiative, a bill that meant to assign $2.5 billion of tax money to childcare, has run aground on the old problem of the relationship of state and church.

Connecticut Democrat Christopher J. Dodd (that friend of Nicaraguan tyrant Daniel Ortega) sponsored the bill in the Senate and Michigan Democrat Dale E. Kildee and Maine Republican Olympia J. Snowe are pushing for it in the House of Representatives. But they did not pay enough attention to the details of their scheme—including the fact that of the two million kids using day care centers, a third utilize church-related facilities. Oops! This poses a problem for the liberal Democrats, does it not? They do not believe in mixing government with religion—they have opposed educational vouchers on the grounds that this would enable parents to send their children to church-run schools. In general, the liberal Democrats—along with a few liberal Republicans—think it horrible to give money to anything not under direct government control, which, of course, includes America's churches.

So funding child care has now run into a snag. Will the Democrats stick by their support of the doctrine of separation of church and state? Or will they stick by their show of compassion so as to impose some perfect vision on us all? They should heed the words of Herbert Spencer: "The ultimate result of shielding men from the effects of folly is to fill the world with fools."

SWISS DEMOCRACY*

The Swiss do it right, according to lots of folks. In addition to a beautiful country, they enjoy internal peace. And they have a long tradition of town-meeting-style government, open to all the people, that larger democratic countries can only eye wistfully. Lately, even Western socialists, casting about for a model, have been looking to Switzerland.

By now, Marxist-style socialism has hardly any support. Even the few notable neo-Marxists—for instance, John Elster, author of *Making Sense of Marx*—have had to recast their leader's doctrines to make them palatable. And Aleksandr Solzhenitsyn's account of the Soviet gulags makes it difficult to associate Soviet socialism with anything but modern barbarianism.

Yet Marxism's decline has not sparked a resurgence of widespread intellectual support for capitalism, the free market, or the basic principle of the right to private property. Although certain segments of the public may once again see hope in a *Reader's Digest* version of capitalism—Reagan's type, unprincipled but capable of producing wealth for almost everyone—the pundits and educators, at least outside economics departments, still don't much like capitalism.

---

*Originally published in *Reason* magazine (July 1986).

The enthusiasm of leftist intellectuals these days is with a new kind of socialism, "economic democracy." Its proponents envision a system in which the decisions of economic significance in a society will be made by *all* members of the community.

In this vein, many economic democrats have turned their attention to the Swiss model of direct participatory democracy. A notable example is Rutgers University political scientist Benjamin R. Barber, who in his book *Strong Democracy* advocates that virtually everything in our midst be open to democratic decision making. In Barber's view only society has rights, not individuals, particularly rights to the means of production. Thus everyone should participate in deciding economically vital matters.

Actually, Americans are becoming familiar with this kind of socialism, as noted in the April 1981 *Reason* article "Socialism . . . On the Street Where You Live." It has to do with collective decision making about matters of relevance to the community. But in America the process is relatively indirect. Decisions are not made directly by the public but by elected and appointed officials.

Switzerland, by contrast, enjoys the kind of political order that leaves small communities with extensive authority to run the affairs of concern to them. These communities—actually called "communes"—pretty much run themsleves in a fashion familiar to Americans via the New England town meetings.

There is, however, an aspect to the Swiss communal experience that has gone largely unnoticed. I came upon it by accident during my two stays in Carona, a small village in Ticino, the Italian canton in southernmost Switzerland. It is directly tied to the participatory democracy that has become the darling of those socialists who are disillusioned with Marx. The phenomenon seems to be duplicated throughout Switzerland.

In essence this Swiss phenomenon embodies the (local) politicization of human existence. All matters of interest to people in these sorts of political organizations are up for consideration at the village meeting. Back yards may be taken from some homeowners; front yards may be transformed into parking lots for the use of the village; the cemetery may be remodeled at public expense; holidays may be changed at the majority's discretion; trees may be removed or planted; wood burning mandated or forbidden; and so on, whatever suits the people as a whole—or at least the majority of politically assertive members in the community.

Now all this is not very new. Swiss communes have experienced it for centuries. What is rarely noticed, however, is that such a political life may well have its casualties—namely, community spirit, cheerfulness, neighborliness, and friendship, not to mention genuine individual liberty.

In the commune of Carona, virtually no one appears to like anyone else. People are persistently suspicious of one another. Everyone appears to be on guard against some forthcoming assault from the rest. These observations are made not by outsiders but by some Swiss themselves, who have come to know the ways of other lands, ways that are free from Swiss direct majoritarianism or, to use Professor Barber's term, "strong democracy."

Genuine friendship is rare in Carona, and it is always under strain. When you add to this the fact that most communes are inhabited by members of various ethnic groups, who in the general European tradition of collectivism tend to be hostile to each other, you can imagine the joy that permeates many Swiss villages.

Now there is, of course, an advantage to all this. The Swiss are generally regarded as very diligent, hard-working, and clean—yes, very clean, cleanliness being the civil religion in Switzerland. They enjoy a certain kind of stability of government unheard of elsewhere.

They may, however, be paying a steep price for this stability. In my experience, it is relatively rare to find Swiss people laughing heartily, enjoying themselves, relaxing and joking, etc. There are exceptions, but the sour side of the Swiss personality is taken for granted in Switzerland.

Just why the Swiss are so morose is somewhat of a mystery. But the hypothesis I wish to put forth is that it has a lot to do with the Swiss system of direct participatory democracy. I base this not just on what seems to be the obvious result of such a political system—how could one be happy with everyone looking over his shoulder all the time, ready to meddle when a sufficiently powerful group has been amassed? It is, instead, based on observation and personal reports from Swiss citizens. They admit that such a political arrangement is depressing, leaving them unfriendly and always on guard.

I may not be taking into account other factors that contribute to Swiss sourness, especially in the commune of Carona. But even this much raises doubts about the virtues of direct democracy. Some years ago, Vladimir Bukovsky wrote an essay in *Commentary* magazine, "The Soul of Man in Socialism," in which he beautifully chronicled the effects of Soviet socialist life on the citizens of that country. Wouldn't it be interesting to do this with other political systems? It may be troublesome to formulate criteria of happiness and flourishing. But I am willing to bet that Swiss direct democracy contributes to neither. My limited experience suggests as much, at least.

DO WE REALLY WANT ECONOMIC DEMOCRACY?*

In contrast to the 1960s and early 1970s, contemporary social reform is urged upon us with less hoopla and excitement. Gone are the calls for the total demolition of the system. We no longer hear about the imprudence of trusting anyone over thirty. The cops aren't all "pigs."

Yet beneath the apparently accommodating facades of the current movements for reform lurks a more serious challenge to the culture than that which was offered up in those seemingly revolutionary years of just a decade ago. What those who made up the movement for revolution lacked, and one main reason for their ultimate failure to accomplish very much, is now with us in full force. I am talking about the frank and open advocacy of the reformation of the American political system.

---

*Originally published in *Santa Barbara New Directions* (1981).

Take, for example, the Campaign for Economic Democracy. This is an effort that no one could fault for lack of respectability. There is very little fanfare associated with it. When their representatives appear at a rally and speak in support of their beliefs, they engage in no worse polemics than we could expect at a union meeting or even the Democratic Party's national convention. Often they are attacked for this by small groups of leftover "radicals" who have by now joined the revolutionary communists or some other hardline Marxist organization.

But in the CED's less rebellious approach we can detect the more mature and determined thought of serious radicals who have resolved to carry on in an effective manner, leaving out the distracting and wasteful shenanigans. The Campaign for Economic Democracy is no flake. It advocates the placing of our economic lives at the disposal of the democratic process. The idea is not really very new. Industrial democracy was at one time the most serious alternative to revolutionary Marxism, adopted by Sidney and Beatrice Webb for the Fabian Society ideology in England. Industrial democracy is the view that since the workers produce everything of value in a society, they should have a hand in the management and distribution of their products. Economic democracy is less directly tied to this view concerning the role of labor in the production of what is valuable, but the affinity between the two movements is not difficult to detect.

What is more interesting than the ideological background of the campaign for economic democracy is its actual content or substance. In effect, economic democracy would require public boards and panels and commissions and committees, growing out of political elections, to administer the way property is used and disposed of throughout our society. In short, economic democracy amounts to the nonrevolutionary abolition of private property rights. Instead of building one's home as one would wish, it would be built as a result of consensus. Permission would have to be obtained each time one engaged in major economic decisions, e.g., investing one's savings, selling one's business, and the like. Indeed, the idea that one owns anything of significance, that an individual or a group of partners or shareholders are entitled to own things of some importance to society, must be abandoned in a system of economic democracy.

The arguments supporting this idea are not at all easy to refute. For one, most institutions in our society are already under political control, including such economic projects as the building of hotels, the development of low-cost housing, the sale of parks, or the construction of high-rise apartments. Local planning commissions, architectural boards, zoning boards, and many other quasi-democratic political bodies have been engaged in a form of economic democracy since about the 1920s, shortly after the U.S. Supreme Court affirmed the authority of local governments to employ police power in order to regulate local land use. Since virtually all economic activities occur in some building and on some land, the tie-in with politics in each case is not difficult to establish. In short, economic democracy is not something new but only something made more explicit and utilized for different purposes.

Initially the various boards, from which permission must be obtained in order to add a swimming pool or build a patio, came about because of a concern for the aesthetics and racial make-up of neighborhoods. Yes, many alleged liberal processes were once employed by conservatives and bigots to achieve their particular restrictions on the use people would make of their property. Today the processes are being extended, strengthened, and redirected. The idea is not so much the attainment of a coordinated architectural environment or safety in building practices. It is, instead, to give power to the people, whatever they might wish to do with this power. And, of course, the people involved tend to be those who have the time and inclination to carry out the administrative duties associated with such property management. The question to be faced in connection with economic democracy is this: Should everyone be involved in the decision of how our labor, our works of art, our scientific inventions, our homes, our shares in some business endeavor, indeed our entire economic lives will be handled? True, there is already a lot of economic democracy about. But perhaps there should not be; perhaps it was a mistake in the first place, a sop to quiet down the revolutionaries who wanted to nationalize economics. The great virtue of the American political tradition is that when consistently implemented it leaves each person the sole authority within a certain sphere. Here an individual is protected from the mob or well-wishing neighbors. Here a person is independent. As William Pitt noted, "But the king of England cannot enter: all his forces dare not cross the threshold" of one's own castle.

While economic democracy sounds like just a benign extension of a good idea, it may in fact be a misapplication of it. Not only would it rob us of our personal realm. It would introduce even more bureaucracy into our lives than we now have and would by no means achieve the hopes of its advocates—namely, justice and the fair distribution of wealth.

SEARCHING FOR THE CHAMPIONS OF DEMOCRACY*

One of the major difficulties faced by Western liberal societies has been that people seem unable to be morally inspired by its philosophy. Since the system is mostly defended by economists—the last several Nobel Prize winners in economics have all been ardent supporters of capitalism—there is a lack of moral support in the intellectual arena.

For the most part, people defend the system because it is a good engine of wealth creation, it produces a lot of goods and services. It is mainly in terms of its instrumental worth, not its moral worth, that capitalism and Western liberal democracy have gained support.

Quentin Skinner of Cambridge University observed not long ago in his Harvard University lecture "The Paradoxes of Political Liberty" that "we are very poor guardians of our own liberties." He referred to liberalism's "minimalist view of civic obligation" and lamented the "dangerous privatization" of certain values of Western civilization. He meant that the kind of defense of capitalism most widely

---

*Originally published in the *Orange County Register* (August 30, 1987).

circulated simply cannot give adequate moral support to it, support that can actually convince people to defend the system, to stand up for it proudly, to think of it as morally inspiring and even noble.

Actually, the main trouble with defending capitalism is the definition of the concept "human being" that the system usually relies on. Most economists hold the view that human behavior always amounts to pursuing self-interest, trying to maximize wealth, seeking to satisfy our desires. Critics argue, however, that this is quite inadequate; false to the fact; and, moreover, quite self-defeating in the end. The assumption that we are all seeking just to satisfy ourselves does not support the conclusion that we should actually stand up for our system. What if liberty and capitalism are under assault? If we are all just desire-satisfiers and pleasure-seekers, then we will not take on the often difficult task of defending our system, advocating it, and supporting educational programs that show its merits. The business community will just concentrate on immediate or longer range profit making, rather than on the uncertain task of spreading the word about capitalism, about how good it is for people. They charge that economic man—homo economicus—has no binding reason for defending the features of his economic system that insure its survival in the long run. Economic man is nonpolitical and nonpatriotic man.

Are the criticisms of the economic arguments for free markets valid? Can we defend freedom based on economic arguments alone?

The critics do make a good point. The defense of free markets cannot rely solely on economic arguments based on crass self-or vested-interest. These arguments imply that people may quite rationally act not to defend their freedom. But any theory that is incapable of self-defense is a self-defeating theory in the face of many competing ones that ask for courage and vigilance in their own support. Communism, socialism, the various theocratic or religiously inspired systems such as Islamic fundamentalism—all call for valiant support from the people, promising moral rewards for such devotion. And while mostly ill-founded, something more potent is needed to reply to these systems than merely saying "You will probably be richer in capitalism."

Human beings do indeed—and often should—act as prudent individuals. Yet this is not all there is to them even in the framework of a sound capitalist outlook. They should also vigorously fight for and pursue certain objective values if they have become convinced of their existence. But this kind of approach to defending the free society involves a different idea of human nature from that used by capitalist economists.

Interestingly, Adam Smith, the "father of scientific economics," recognized the value of an earlier outlook on morality and the moral defense of the free capitalist system when he wrote the following:

In [Greek] philosophy the duties of human life were treated of as subservient to the happiness and perfection of human life. . . . In [that] philosophy, the perfection of virtue was represented as necessarily productive to the person who possessed it, of the most perfect happiness in this life. In the modern philosophy, it was frequently represented as almost always inconsistent with any degree of happiness in this life, and heaven was to be earned by penance and mortification, not by the liberal, generous, and spirited conduct of a man. By far the most important of all the different branches of philosophy became in this manner by far the most corrupted. (*The Wealth of Nations,* Modern Library, p. 726.)

Today it need also be noted that what is good about capitalism, first and foremost, is that it enables its citizens to strive for a noble life on their own— it secures the freedom, independence, and personal sovereignty of its citizens. Capitalism, in short, treats each mature individual as an adult moral agent, unlike other systems that treat people as wards or subjects of the state.

Capitalism accepts that it is indeed morally right for everyone to act so as to maximize personal happiness.

Though one ought to be free to pursue the values one chooses—and this is impossible without economic liberty—one is morally bound (which does not mean one can be forced legally) to pursue some goals ahead of others. Human individual liberty is just such a goal.

DEMOCRACY AND ITS DISCONTENTS*

America has been the world's leading democratic society for more than two hundred years. Yet some people are still very dissatisfied with our system precisely on grounds that it is not democratic enough. And throughout the worldwide political arena, a fight has been brewing about which of the major powers, the United States or the Soviet Union, is really more democratic. Underlying this question is the assumption that democracy is somehow a good in itself. But is it?

The founding fathers of the American republic viewed democracy with suspicion. Thus our system of government assigns only a limited number of topics to democratic processes. Ideally, if one goes by the Declaration of Independence itself instead of the Constitution—the latter being something of a compromise on the original political ideas of the founders—very few matters in society are to be decided democratically. The reason is fairly simple: Human beings are extremely diverse. A society that is pluralistic and in which the only sure thing that all people share is their individual rights to life, liberty, and the pursuit of happiness would perpetrate grave injustice by submitting a great many of the people's concerns to a democratic process.

What is the individualism for which America is so unique? Is it the caricature we often hear about, involving a kind of "dog-eat-dog" approach to social life? Is it the view that Karl Marx took a lot of space to ridicule, namely, that each of us is an isolated atom, separated from everyone else? In short, is the American political tradition of individualism one that really amounts to idealizing hermits, rugged individualists who are actually antisocial?

*Originally published in the *Orange County Register* (February 22, 1987).

In fact, America's individualistic tradition stresses one feature: personal protection by means of a system of individual human rights. This is what the grandfather of our country, the philosopher John Locke, pointed to: Each of us is by nature "free and independent" in being morally responsible to live a good human life. Our form of individualism is one that emphasizes how important it is for each of us to make the effort to live a good life and to act responsibly. This means that only a few matters in our lives may be subjected to a vote, to public authority and majority rule. Being responsible for our own lives means that as a nation we will not permit others to gather into large or powerful groups and impose decisions on us that we do not want—even if those courses of action are right. What is crucial, despite the dangers and risks, is for individuals to cultivate the ability to govern themselves.

But isn't self-government just another way of saying democracy? Some people certainly believe that our limited democracy needs to be expanded precisely in the name of self-government. Yet expanding democracy would accomplish the very opposite. It would make people victims of mass rallies and subject them to unwanted public power. If the "people" had even more political power than they now possess, they would come to suppress individuality and human dignity to a degree currently found only in totalitarian societies and in feudal systems. Democracy in this form is really not self-government.

One reason there is widespread misunderstanding about democracy is that people mistake it for self-government, primarily because "self-government" is an ambiguous term that is open to interpretation. In one sense "self-government" means that a nation is not governed by other nations but by itself. Here self-government is to be contrasted with imposed rule from without. In the past, many nations had been ruled by neighboring empires, and so self-government became an important political objective. one that is still prominent in certain parts of the world: Poland, Hungary, Cuba, and other "socialist" societies. Some countries that America defends also experience too much political rule from without, sometimes based on economic dependence, sometimes outright political pressure.

The other sense of "self-government" has to do with the ideals of individualism. Here what is stressed is that instead of government or a ruling elite imposing its will upon members of society, each person must individually choose how to live, provided he or she does so in peace and respects similar decisions made by their neighbors. Granted, this may be difficult to uphold in a complex society; nevertheless, it is what self-government means when we consider the matter of individual diversity and responsibility.

Democracy is, of course, mainly concerned with the first type of self-government. And to the extent that it prevents arbitrary rule by elites or dictators, from within or without, democracy is a very good thing indeed. But when democracy starts abolishing the second type of self-government, it must itself be restricted. That is how we preserve the kind of individualism that has distinguished America from all other nations of the world.

BLACKS AND REVOLUTION*

Those blacks in America who are opting for revolution are often chided by old Left liberals and socialists for their haste. These establishment people, with their Americans for Democratic Action credentials and FDR buttons, are telling the blacks to cool it. And the blacks are frankly refusing to listen to the desperate advice.

A bit of historical perspective ought to explain this. In the past fifty years the country was led toward our great welfare state society by reformers of the Left. They were the leaders who opened up the avenue for the majoritarianism that prevails today. It is with the political and intellectual aid of these men, such as Walter Lippman, Arthur Schlesinger, Jr., John Kenneth Galbraith, and others that American law began responding not to justice but to the wishes of the mob. The Constitution, which suffered from enough flaws, was now distorted beyond recognition in the interest of "the general welfare" and "the public interest." The rights of life, liberty, and property were sacrificed to the rights to work, to get a "fair" wage, to receive help from the government, to have a job at government expense, and so on. Clearly, if anyone has the right to an education, as an educator, I have no right to liberty, namely the liberty to refuse to give such an education. In like fashion, the original human rights were eliminated in favor of social rights, rights that involved the subjugation of man's rights to life, liberty, and property. (The introduction of conscription—in behalf of the general welfare—eliminated the first, a hundred other laws did away with the second, while thousands, including "eminent domain," knocked out the last.)

But now we must recall that the mob was white throughout these times. So where the original rights were sacrificed to these new ones, only white people had the political power to institutionalize the benefits from them. The legal and economic advantages enjoyed through labor unions, social security legislation, public works projects, state financed schools, welfare—all products of old Left efforts—were gobbled up by the white majority. The black population got little, yet it had to pay the same tax rate as everyone else to support the welfare schemes.

For years this has been going on. Socialists and liberals have been congratulating themselves on their humanitarianism while blacks have failed to perceive it. No wonder. The civil rights of a citizen allow him to exercise his political power in efforts to get a slice of the pie. But few bothered about the civil rights of blacks, who were unable to exercise political power in their own behalf.

Once America's black population had grown beyond containment, the liberal elite decided to throw them some crumbs in the form of civil rights legislation. But it was too late for that. The white population had established a strict control over the benefits to be reaped from the welfare state; this is most evident in education. But the crumbs did tease the appetite of black people who, for the first time, perceived that maybe they too could aspire to the life styles of other human beings in this country.

---

*Originally published in the *Orange County Register* (circa 1969).

Now we see the results. And I hope the old Left gets what it deserves: to be thrown out of all leadership in American life.

CALL FOR VOTER BOYCOTT*

If we are to believe such organizations as the League of Women Voters, voting is our sacred and only political responsibility. It is the end-all and be-all of our nature as political beings. But most people in America could not keep up with political affairs even if they wanted to. Unlike our grocer, doctor, auto mechanic, dance teacher, and other professionals whom we pay to do work for us, our politicians have no definite jobs. They are required to be masters of thousands of issues but in fact have expertise at hardly any. The congressional representative (or the person we elect to the other political bodies) must make decisions that most of us could not know about even if we tried. The various governmental committees must regulate commerce, professions, labor-management negotiations, international treaties, and hundreds of other human affairs. Or if they do not regulate these, they must pass judgments on proposed laws guiding the various regulatory bodies. The policies of the Federal Communications Commission; the Food and Drug Administration; the Civil Aeronautics Board; the Interstate Commerce Commission; the Department of Health, Education and Welfare [now defunct], and other agencies of the federal government must be supervised by the politicians who ask for our vote. Yet hardly any person could inform himself (or herself) about the subject matter of the decisions a candidate must make, let alone learn the rights and wrongs involved.

Nevertheless, we are urged to vote. We are told that our central political responsibility is to make a decision that could only be based on ignorance. Perhaps under these circumstances my suggestion that most people should abstain from voting will appear to be outrageous, even antidemocratic. Certainly no one should be prohibited from voting. What I am urging is that citizens seriously examine their own knowledge or ignorance of the politicians' business, and, if they cannot see their way through to a politically meaningful decision, they should respectfully decline the invitation to vote. Clearly if this approach were adopted by all, the few who would decide to vote would probably make valuable contributions to our political atmosphere.

The objection might be raised that we need to know only the political philosophy of our candidates. If it is the right one, he will most likely be guided correctly while he occupies his seat of government.

Unfortunately, the bulk of our politicians have no political philosophy. The terms, "liberal," "conservative," "Republican," and "Democrat" no longer signify clearly defined political alternatives. Instead vote-gathering proceeds by way of appeal to prejudices, special interests, the ring of popular slogans, and sexual or general aesthetic preferences. Our time is filled with political pragmatism that

---

*Originally published in the *Dunkirk-Fredonia* (New York) *Observer* (September 24, 1974).

rejects a principled approach to conducting government. There simply is no hope for learning about the general framework of the bulk of the politicians. Most wouldn't reveal their political philosophy even if they had one, lest we might predict what they will do, or anticipate something from them and hold them responsible for doing so when the occasion arises. The plain truth is that today's politicians cannot tell what they will do, for most are no more capable of keeping up with their sphere of authority than we are. (Thus when President Ford was asked why he didn't do what he promised when earlier he was asked whether he would pardon his predecessor, he simply told us that he had changed his mind. That is the meaning of being unprincipled in politics.)

Perhaps when voters demonstrate their indecision by staying away from the polls, the politicians will get the message. It may even bring on an effort to be more informative about the multifaceted and unmanageable political business that the politician faces. And perhaps, after a while, the business of politics will be narrowed down to what politicians—who are by the way human beings, not gods— can set out to accomplish. Perhaps.

3

Individual Human Rights

THE STATE OF AMERICAN INDIVIDUALISM*

In recent years there have been renewed attacks on American individualism, the ideology that is closely associated with the political traditions and history of the United States. Most notably, Professor Robert Bellah of the University of California at Berkeley has been engaged in lambasting American individualism, including during a recent talk at the Commonwealth Club of San Francisco, "The Price of American Individualism," which was also broadcast on National Public Radio in mid-October. Earlier this century, the same kind of anti-individualist crusade was conducted by the likes of philosopher John Dewey, but the latter had at least a more constructive tone to it.

Professor Bellah, co-author of the anti-individualist book, *Habits of the Heart: Individualism and Commitment in American Life* (Harper and Row), argues that it is a mistake to link individualism to the ideal of a free society—in fact, quite the contrary. Individualism is a threat to human liberty, argues Professor Bellah, citing Alexis de Tocqueville as the authority in support of his thesis.

But does Professor Bellah tell us what he means by American individualism? Actually, the conception of the individual person he has in mind has little to do with the philosophy of the founding fathers or the framers of the U.S. Constitution, all of whom were concerned to a considerable degree with the political sovereignty of every person and with the protection of individual rights.

What Professor Bellah has in mind is a very different kind of individualism, namely, one that appears in the works of theoretical economists, the individual who is exclusively concerned with advancing on the economic front, who wants only to acquire more goods and services, who is an obsessive acquisitor. This caricature of individualism is the very same idea that Karl Marx took to task and slanderously associated with liberal capitalism.

---

*Originally published in the *Orange County Register* (December 20, 1987).

Now, there is little doubt that many people in America and throughout the world partly fit this characterization. And the fact that many people have spent much time on this objective is also understandable—they recall the not-so-recent periods of history when only a very small and privileged proportion of a country's population had been allowed to gain wealth. The rest were usually held in servitude and lived by the grace of these few.

But even in such a country, is it really true that most people are obsessed with wealth acquisition as such, as the caricature of individualism Professor Bellah would have us endorse? Or are they rather concerned with obtaining some of the benefits attainable in human life that had been denied to their ancestors—home, transportation, entertainment, medical care, education for the kids, etc.?

The economist uses his model of acquisitive human nature for purposes of understanding the way the market works, the place where we do our buying and selling. No wonder then that he does not concentrate on other elements of individualism. But a sociologist would seem to have the responsibility to take seriously different aspects of individualism when he considers its implication.

Consider that American individualism means mainly that persons must make decisions about their lives, that no one may take over that role for them, that whatever associations persons enter, they are responsible for what they have done and cannot defer to God, tradition, or family as the agents who should take the credit or blame for this action. American individualism means, ultimately, moral independence—the responsibility of every person to make the choice between good and evil, right and wrong, and not abdicate one's role as an active agent in one's life.

American individualism is not some arid, callous, and silly idea that we ought to live as hermits and renounce the company of our fellow human beings. Nor does it cut us off from freely chosen responsibilities to our fellows, to our country, to our culture. But it does deny that we are all really just one thing, some totalitarian *Einheit* or "oneness" that swallows us individuals and makes us the subjects of the larger organism, the state.

I am afraid that attacks on individualism are, in fact, mostly attacks on the sovereignty of persons as far as making decisions about their lives is at issue. Those doing the attacking help, willingly or not, the people who would rather have us surrender to them our freedom to decide how we will live and spend our labors.

Of course, every viewpoint has its ridiculous version, including individualism. The real question is which basic social philosophy is more suited to human nature, one that stresses individual responsibility and choice or one that treats people as parts of some larger superior whole? There are clearly those who favor the latter view. And the kind of attacks carried out by Professor Bellah on American individualism seem to me to serve their purposes rather than to help avoid the occasional excesses of the individualism that is at heart the most respectful social philosophy to human beings that has ever been proposed.

THE CORRUPTION OF HUMAN RIGHTS*

These days every wish of some sizable group seems to have earned the status of a basic human right. We are held both by some very prominent philosophers (for example, John Rawls at Harvard and Ronald Dworkin at Oxford) and by innumerable political activists (for example, Tom Hayden, Ralph Nader, and Michael Harrington) to have human rights to be employed, to be provided with vacations, to receive lifetime security against disease and poverty, and even to escape from loneliness, if one is to judge by a recent "public service" ad.

At one time, human rights were taken to encompass but a few central, indispensable conditions of a good and free human community: the rights of life, liberty, and property (or pursuit of happiness). These rights mean that each individual is owed a very wide area of personal discretion—to be guided by conscience and social influence but never by force—as to how his life will be lived, what he will do, and toward what productive and creative activities he will devote himself. Government exists only to see to it that no one intrudes on his sphere of personal authority. Beyond ensuring such respect for the rights of everyone, government is not supposed to be managing the affairs of individuals, families, clubs, firms, schools, churches, theaters, or any other peaceful institutions in society.

The idea underlying natural rights theory is that there are certain definite rights we all possess simply by virtue of our human nature, nothing else. A right is a social condition that human beings are due from others so that they may enjoy some range of conduct as their own jurisdiction. And a natural human right is a social condition that human beings are required to uphold by refraining from interfering with someone's conduct in virtue of someone's being a human being.

Our ordinary popular thinking, however, is permeated with what we learn in colleges, through magazines and television specials, and while in practice we might cling to an idea of human nature, in our thinking, great confusion and lack of self-confidence have resulted. Some of this has led to serious proposals about the "rights" of animals, even trees and mountains, not simply in philosophical speculation but in the chambers of various legislatures.

Many factors influence the day-to-day politics of a large republic such as the United States. Some of these are the most prominent views promulgated by renowned political thinkers. *Time* magazine correctly reported in July 1975 that "The doctrine of natural inalienable rights would be hotly denied by most philosophers." (Ironically this is so even while various scientific and other professional groups engage in protests against violations of human rights of all sorts across the globe.) Instead, they are giving philosophical support to the view that virtually any interests human beings have are fair game for purported human rights. And arguments based on interests ultimately issue in talk of the rights of animals and trees. That our courts and legislatures welcome this trend goes without saying. It casts them in the role of great benefactors of humanity.

---

*Originally published in the *Santa Barbara News-Press* (July 28, 1981).

It isn't justified to reject the concept of human rights because of this abuse, any more than it would be justified to reject the concept of democracy simply because the dictators of Eastern Europe label their political processes democratic, or the concept of a republic simply because the Soviet Union calls itself by that name. Instead, the task is to recover the sensible, precise, and meaningful explication of the concept of human rights.

It is simply incorrect to think that people have human rights to food, medical care, employment, vacations, education, and the rest of life's values and amenities, by virtue of their human nature. Human rights are conditions specifying the most general requirements individuals living together owe to each other. These conditions are required because of one thing alone: the capacity human beings have for intruding upon each other's lives as a matter of choice, of their free will. This is what makes such intrusion morally and politically impermissible and justifies retaliation, and political and legal provisions to thwart it. By contrast, the needs for food, shelter, work, medical care, education, and so forth exist quite apart from other people. Such needs would exist even for those who lived apart from society, and the threat of their going unsatisfied has nothing uniquely to do with the presence of others.

It is complicated to uncover why it has come to be believed that there are human rights to being supplied with what one needs in life. One reason can be found in the idea of determinism: that our life is not under our control and we are not responsible for what we do, let alone responsible to do certain things (for example, support ourselves). Furthermore, if we each have the natural right to education, etc., governments will be responsible to "protect and preserve" these rights, which can, in practical terms, mean only that governments must make some people supply others with what they need. It is only a stone's throw from this to the all-encompassing, planned, totalitarian state.

A serious confusion has been generated in the area of foreign affairs by the corruption of the concept of human rights in America's official rhetoric. Desperately trying to appear both politically and morally neutral (as becomes a state with no clear moral foundations) and at the same time to appear virtuous and worthy of moral respect, the U.S. government under President Jimmy Carter forged a so-called human rights policy. It is unfortunate that as a result of Mr. Carter's perplexing and confused policy, the Reagan foreign policy effort will probably avoid reference to human rights even where this is fully warranted.

The central point is that a confused idea of human rights will not serve to enhance the proper interest of either the United States or the people who suffer hardship and abuse at the hands of dictatorial or authoritarian governments. When the petty dictators of Latin and Central America are lumped together with the massive tyranny of the Soviet Union, with claims that the lawlessness of the latter is equal to the stupidity and irrationality of the former, it shows how much confusion exists concerning human rights.

Also, it is not clear what any government ought to do toward other societies when witnessing bona fide human rights violations. More or less tyrannical societies surround the United States. But what should a government of a society with greater institutional respect for human rights do vis-à-vis societies in which governments ignore these rights?

First, the government of a free or relatively free society is obligated to secure the protection and preservation of the human rights of it own citizens, in whose service, after all, it stands. This is the proper meaning of the concept of national interest.

On the domestic front America's subjugation to the corruption of the concept of human rights is more blatant still. We have "human rights"—"renters' rights," "students' rights," "workers' rights," "women's rights"—all of which express an alleged derivation from human rights, making them at first glance seem quite real, but upon closer inspection they are nothing but perversions of the idea of basic, individual human rights. All of these confusing, obfuscating "rights," of course, governments are supposed to protect and preserve, at taxpayer's expense.

Affirmative action, fair-housing provisions, fair-employment practices, and so forth—these developments all relate in some way to the expanding scope of government, which in turn is largely the result of the corruption of the concept of human rights. Such corruption should be firmly resisted, both in theory and in practice. There is, in fact, a sound notion of human rights, based on a sound conception of human nature. Human nature exists, all the fancy philosophical obfuscation notwithstanding. "Human nature" means the most sensible, rational, consistent, and functional classification of human beings, because we share certain attributes as human beings.

From the point of view of political authority—the legitimate use of force— all of us are equal. This requires that others, including governments, refrain from physically intruding upon us. The law should serve the purpose of making sure that any intrusion is dealt with justly and efficiently. Beyond that, there is much of great concern to us in our lives, in our family relations, work, community, culture, and so forth. But those are not matters of relevance in human rights theory and discourse.

FOR JUSTICE*

In recent years the racial problems which have beset us have culminated in some unfortunate acts on the part of some members of black society. There cannot be a question as to whether there is justification for many of these acts—even on behalf of justice, injustice, and violent attacks on innocent people are without justification.

Unfortunately, what has been obliterated by the notoriety of such actions on the part of many blacks is the real injustice that still prevails in American society and that renders the life of many a black American unbearable.

For years a considerable portion of the white population failed to acknowledge the reality of a major compromise of principle in America's history. In the face

---

*Originally published in the *Goleta Advisor* (circa 1970).

of an emphatic Declaration of Independence and an assertion of the self-evident truth that "All men are created equal," our legal system tolerated the existence of slavery within our borders. It cannot be denied—and those who try to do so are to that extent guilty of moral evasiveness—that a great portion of America's white population simply evaded the evil of slavery, and that another portion not only evaded it but perpetuated it for a significant portion of our history. In the midst of the only country on the face of the earth that has gone so far as to assert in its legal documents that the individual is the most important social element, Americans have allowed other Americans to be slaves. Only after almost a century of slavery did it occur to some people that slavery was a complete contradiction to the principles of our Constitution. Only then did people begin to think about the personal injustices that have been perpetrated on a nationwide scale. Even then, however, the concern was less with injustice to individual black Americans than with the preservation of the Union, a goal characteristic not of a free society but of Nazi or Soviet socialism, places where the state is more important than its citizens.

America is now paying for its "fatal compromise." Our society is suffering—i.e., individual human beings are suffering on a wide scale within our nation—because our legal system allowed the horrifying injustice of slavery to exist in our country. Those who are all so shocked at the activities of black students and people in this country are right to be; but they would do well to reflect on the most important contributor to that kind of action: the tragic history of black Americans in this country. It should be remembered that to throw off the shackles of slavery is not simple. While the tragic consequences of such injustice cannot be eliminated by indicting those who had nothing to do with it (many whites today), neither should it be forgotten that a grandson of a slave cannot be expected to have had the same opportunities for self-improvement as the grandson of a slave owner. And while no one is morally responsible for the crimes of his elders, why not acknowledge that there are consequences to slavery and segregation that affect the welfare of blacks today? This, in turn, should lead to more perceptive thinking about the present crises in our schools and cities.

Black students today reflect the teaching of the bulk of white society: They demand that they should be helped for their misfortune! This is just what the old-aged or the poor demanded when they saw that they had no funds to pay for hospital bills or no money to send their kids to school. The idea that others should pay for one's misfortunes (stemming either from slavery or from other kinds of evils) is very widespread in today's culture. Black people are merely unwilling to wait for the political extortion of their share (which many whites have achieved), so a number of them demand it with threats of violence, with violence itself.

A thorough education in the futility of thinking that others owe us our life and our welfare is needed to correct the present situation once and for all. Such education will take time: Processes of thought cannot be wiped out by force, only by rational argument, and even then only with perseverance. But, unfortunately, nothing else will begin to solve our problems for us. Any other method will merely perpetuate the troubles we have and merely change some rulers into servants, some servants into masters, and make innocent sufferers of the rest. As human beings we deserve and can certainly do much better.

JUSTICE THURGOOD MARSHALL AND REAGAN'S CIVIL RIGHTS RECORD*

Justice Thurgood Marshall of the United States Supreme Court ranked President Ronald Reagan at "the bottom" of U.S. presidents regarding their record on civil rights. From this we learned not only that the the manners of those on the Court are very different from what they used to be. We also learned that some justices have no understanding at all as to the nature of individual rights. What they want is to make people be good, not to protect the rights of persons to be free. And while the zeal behind this is understandable at times, the danger of its coming back to haunt us is considerable.

Now it must be admitted that Ronald Reagan is no champion of individualism. His conservative administration is often guilty of trying to impose on us the regime of a spiritual welfare state. But in civil rights he has been largely on the right tract. He has held, in effect, that governments are not authorized to discriminate unjustly against blacks or any other members of society. But he has also believed that as far as private conduct, including conduct in the marketplace, is concerned, immoral discrimination, however repugnant and vicious, ought not be corrected by law.

Many people, especially American liberals who are eager to acknowledge— sometimes even invent—their collective guilt, find this disagreeable. The point is, however, that the Reagan doctrine is not hostile to civil rights. Those who agree with Reagan are not racists, anti-black, or even insulting. Indeed, they may be on the forefront in giving blacks a fair and respectful shake in various non-public areas, as well as in liberating them from unjust laws. But they disagree with Justice Marshall that government is the proper solution to the problem of black disadvantage in the society. They reject the practice of reverse discrimination. They could well accept affirmative action privately and support helping blacks or other minorities in areas where they have suffered discrimination or other disadvantages. But this ought not to be enforced by government—except where it has been doing the unjust deed.

Is it then just to rank Reagan at "the bottom"? Consider that many presidents reigned over the country during slavery and did not do a whole lot about it! Consider that those who foisted so-called civil rights on us have contributed to the serious demoralization of blacks—making them wards of the state, treating them as if they are inept—unlike Jews or members of other ethnic groups who have also had injustice and misfortune heaped upon them. Blacks are capable of personal sovereignty, self-development, and competence without the repentant white man's help!

No, while Ronald Reagan may be wrong on some issues, he is right about

---

*Originally published in the *Lincoln Review* (Spring 1988).

civil rights. What blacks deserve and have always deserved is equal protection under the law. They should be treated as adults and as equal members of our society as far as the protection of their individual rights are concerned. This phony preaching of special privilege in the name of past injustice may ring generous and compassionate, but in all cases but those where the actual guilty parties who have unjustly benefited from slavery or legal segregation can be punished, this policy of reverse discrimination and coercion for the sake of balance is detestable.

It is also instructive to consider that many who find opposition to "open housing" laws objectionable, even racist, are themselves fervent defenders of the sanctity of the home. If the authorities would wish to intrude on a person's privacy in order to foil some crime, the American Civil Liberties Union would be first in line to argue that such crime prevention measures are unconstitutional because they violate the rights of those who live there. What does such intrusion do that intruding on the right of sellers to decide whom they wish to do business with does not? If the state intrudes on two persons doing business, so that the one is forced to do business with the other, that is certainly no less severe than intruding into a home where people wish to be left alone. The seller of a house may be a racist and bigot, but in a free society all sorts of shady people are protected in their rights. The task is to find a way to change the thinking and behavior of these people that does not intrude upon or deny their sovereignty—i.e., their individual right to be wrong!

Notice how eager a civil libertarian is to defend the rights of communists and even fascists to have their way so long as they do not force others to comply with their views. But why not racists? There is no reason, except perhaps the urgency felt by many to finally eradicate the legacy of slavery from our society. But that simply does not justify stepping over the rights of people, even those who keep this legacy alive.

There are, incidentally, some legal measures that could be taken against people who will not trade with their fellows, measures that do not involve violation of rights. If a merchant announces that he has opened a restaurant but makes no mention of excluding certain types of customers, then when he does try to exclude some he is probably guilty of misrepresentation, a version of breach of contract. The same can be said of sales in homes and anything else.

It is characteristically more difficult to live with yourself if you have to announce to everyone that you are a vicious person—a racist—than if you can hide this and act on it behind closed doors. So let the racists be open and hold them to their position. If they refuse to be racists all the way through, well then they have probably committed themselves to a course of action that is open to legal rebuke.

One of the problems with the early civil rights laws, as well as with equal rights for women, is the hurry in which they were drawn up and the impatience they demonstrated vis-à-vis our legal system. It is a case of throwing out the baby with the bathwater: The very rights blacks and women ought always to have enjoyed and were denied are now violated so as to obtain rectification. But that is just what can help destroy the legal system, to help it disintegrate.

The wonderful thing about the U.S. constitutional system is that it can help correct the injustices that had been left within our society. But not overnight. The civil rights era introduced bogus rights that now keep many from granting to women and to gays the rights they naturally possess, fearing that this implies acceptance of their bogus rights. The gays' freedom to engage in private sexual conduct is struck down in part because it is feared that the next step will be granting gays legal rights to be hired by those who disapprove of them. The right to liberty is packed in with the phony right to employment, and the former suffers.

Justice Marshall may be sentimentally attached to the civil rights era and its laws, having had such a vital role in bringing about so many of the changes, many of which were quite on target. But frankly he would be better off as a defender of the rights of individuals, including blacks, if he would recognize that what he dislikes about Reagan's stance toward blacks is indeed the most respectful attitude to have.

RACIAL PREJUDICE VERSUS HOMOPHOBIA

In a recent issue of the *Journal of the American Medical Association* Professor Gregory Pence, a professor of philosophy at the University of Alabama, Birmingham, recounts that he spoke before a group of Americans who showed strong prejudice against gays. He rightly denounces the hatred that some of these persons showed toward gay men and women. Then, however, he makes a comparison that is extremely dubious. Professor Pence equates dislike of blacks and dislike of homosexuals. It is quite doubtful that the two are the same kind of attitude at all.

When one holds it against someone that he or she has dark skin, this is categorically unjust: It has nothing at all to do with what the person does, his or her character or choices in life. It is plainly irrational and unjustified. When one holds it against someone that he or she is homosexual, there is something plausible about that attitude: Sexually desiring a member of one's own sex and acting on that desire can seem rather peculiar to an ordinary person. And there need be nothing irrational about this.

A homosexual feels and acts in a way that would appear to be out of line with the norm for both humans and nonhumans that have both sexes represented in their species. This will probably remain so for a very long time—as long as both sexes of the species are needed for purposes of reproduction and, in the case of humans, are going to build a family life around themselves and their children.

Of course, this alone does not ultimately justify ill feelings and discriminate action toward homosexuals. Yet it is demeaning toward the plight of blacks to make such prejudice the equal of the thorough racial injustice being perpetrated against them. There is no moral equivalence here at all. Racial condemnation is wholly unjust, while condemning someone who is homosexual can have some plausibility. After all, homosexuality—at least the behavior that goes with it—is a matter of choice, and it runs against the tide (which many people plausibly associate with what is basically healthy and normal).

One would have thought that when a philosopher undertakes to discuss different kinds of human foibles, he or she would not only wag a finger but also point up some relevant distinctions. Discrimination against homosexuals is wrong in many cases, especially if they are in need of our support and help in their failing health. But it is by no means as bad as discriminating against people who simply happened to have been born with a different skin color from ours. They had absolutely nothing to do with this and to hold it against them is plainly wrong. But homosexuality is not something a person cannot help. And it can be viewed as at least a threat to some aspects of normal human existence—e.g., family life and reproduction. The suspicion about homosexuality is at least understandable, which cannot be said about racial prejudice.

If we are going to invoke standards of right and wrong conduct, we need also to keep in mind degrees of culpability. The belief in the moral equivalence of racial prejudice and ambivalence about homosexuality is unfounded.

THE FUTURE OF ADDICTION MANIA*

I read a prominent national daily paper each weekday. I also peek at numerous television talk-shows at least to note what their producers believe will sell as daily sensation for daytime viewers. And I also watch the weekend fare of network interviews—"This Week with David Brinkley" (ABC), "Meet the Press" (NBC), and "Face the Nation" and "60 Minutes" (CBS). From this constant sampling of saleable "facts" and ideas I have come to the conclusion that our culture is in the grips of "addiction mania."

First, there is the tried and true candidate of soft and hard drugs. Since the late 1960s popular culture has toyed with the idea of the inevitability of becoming addicted to marijuana or being lead by the recreational use of this drug to harder drugs such as LSD, cocaine, heroin, and whatnot. While the leaders of the counterculture used to protest this thesis, when they did admit that it had some validity, they quickly turned the tables on the middle class by noting that it is, after all, its fault: Isn't alcohol and tobacco usage a form of drug abuse? And don't millions of respectable American adults indulge in such drug abuse? So who is to blame the young who simply turn to a slightly different drug and follow the lead of the older generation?

Eventually, of course, it became official dogma that liking these various substances a lot amounts to being addicted to them. Addiction is a relationship one has to something whereby it is no longer a matter of choice whether one desires that thing. Drug addiction, then, is not simply wishing to have the drug but the inability to ever change one's mind about whether to take it. One is,

---

*Originally published in the *Orange County Register* (March 5, 1989).

as the saying goes, "hooked." And by now the candidates for addiction have proliferated beyond reason.

There are those who maintain that philandering spouses are sexually addicted. Books are written advising mates of such spouses how to cope with this kind of addiction. The addicts parade themselves on various television talk-shows, confessing their helplessness in the face of this addiction, speculating on cures, and insisting that, of course, their medical insurance covers whatever expenses they incur in the process of coping! (I fancy that Medicaid will go bankrupt not because of rising medical costs but because of the incredible proliferation of diseases such as sexual addiction!)

The other day I glanced through my national daily only to learn of a recent study, conducted at some prominent university by two sociologists. It purported to show how slow, sad country Western music seems to be a contributory cause of alcoholism! You know, those tormenting songs that make for the ballads of the genre! Well, it has been found that listening to such musical fare frequently sends people to the bottle.

This study of course is just one in a million in which a "statistically significant" correlation is established between one factor and another. Then it is concluded that the one causes the other—*post hoc, ergo propter hoc*—since B follows A often enough, A must cause B! This is the basis of virtually all claims about addiction: People will often enough behave in certain ways following having consumed some substance, so they are declared addicts. What is omitted from this analysis is that the people have made a choice to indulge. Smokers may often claim they "want" to quit. But more often than not they only wish they would quit—something akin to how one might wish one had become a pianist, even though one made no effort to learn the instrument. As State University of New York psychiatrist Thomas S. Szasz suggested a long time ago—but has promptly been ignored in this—millions of people intensely like smoking, drinking, taking various dangerous drugs, engaging in various pleasant but risky activities, and they have been conveniently shut out of the human race by being declared mentally ill. Credit is not given them for knowing their own mind and being able to decide what they want to do.

Sure, many people have wishes—they may at some point in their lives be pleased with the vision that they are not doing what they are doing indeed often enough. But what of that? There is also plenty of evidence that when the stakes become high enough and the prospective losses imminent, many people quit smoking, quit drinking, cease other behaviors. Even going to one of those clinics that proclaim that all alcoholics, smokers, drugs users, etc., are sick must ultimately count on a person reaching the conclusion that he or she no longer wants to indulge and wants to follow some tried and true method of discontinuing what has become a difficult habit to shake.

All the pseudomedical mumbo-jumbo will not change the fact that the primary factor in all this is the individual person—except in some very rare cases of brain damage.

Why is all this vital? Because all the claims about our helplessness in the face of all these temptations that surround us, some people are gaining enormous power over us. I do not believe I am paranoid when I fear that soon someone will advocate that country music be government regulated so as to cut down on alcoholism. Sure, in our society the First Amendment has thus far been interpreted by the courts to bar any such move. But the interpretations of courts can change and the U.S. Constitution can be amended. It is not impossible that in the future the addiction mania will lead to outlawing more than just the taking of drugs. These days people who are drug users are having their homes confiscated by the police. (For example, in Santa Barbara, California, Francine Marie Gabel had her home taken by the police because she used drugs in the home, with a percentage of the price of the home going to the local police to fight drugs!) Soon words might be outlawed if their use is correlated with something risky and dangerous. Perhaps the advocacy of drug legalization will be found to correlate positively with some risky activity, so it too must be banned. And then, folks, petty tyrannies will mushroom into the atomic explosion of full-scale statism: national police, prior restrain, abolition of civil liberties, etc.

Addiction mania seems to me to correlate positively with the abolition of individual liberty!

COPING WITH SMOKING?*

Laws forbidding business proprietors from permitting smoking in their offices, cinemas, aircraft, stores, etc. are now legion. But such government-mandated prohibitions ignore the rights of those who don't mind smoking as well as those who wish to live in a tolerant society.

No doubt, smokers can be annoying. They even may be harmful to those around them. One need not dispute these contentions to still be concerned with their rights.

In most cases, anti-smoking ordinances aren't limited to public places such as municipal courts. If the government confined itself to protecting the rights of nonsmokers in bona fide public areas, there would be nothing wrong with the current trend in legislation.

Instead of such a limited approach, however, government has embarked upon the full regimentation of people's choices concerning smoking. The government has decided to bully smokers, regardless of whether they violate anyone's rights or merely indulge with the consent of others.

People suffer many harms willingly. And in a society that respects individual rights, this has to be accepted. Boxers, football players, nurses, doctors, and many other people expose themselves to risks of harm that come from others' behavior. When this exposure is voluntary, in a free society it may not be inter-

*Adapted from *The Freeman* for the *Harrington Journal*, Harrington, Delaware (March 29, 1989).

fered with. The sovereignty of persons may not be sacrificed even for the sake of their physical health.

Individuals' property rights are supposed to be protected by the Fifth Amendment. Not unless property is taken for public use—for the sake of a legitimate state activity—is it properly subject to government seizure. By treating the offices, work spaces, and lobbies of private firms as if they were public property, a grave injustice is done to the owners.

When private property comes under government control, practices may be prohibited simply because those who engage in them are in the minority or waver from preferred government policy. Members of minority groups can easily lose their sphere of autonomy.

There is no need, however, to resort to government intervention to manage the public problems engendered by smoking. There are many cases of annoying and even harmful practices that can be isolated and kept from intruding on others. And they do not involve violating anyone's right to freedom of association and private property.

The smoking issue can be handled quite simply. In my house, shop, or factory, I should be the one who decides whether there will be smoking. This is what it means to respect my individual rights. Just as I may print anything I want on my printing press, or allow anyone to say whatever he or she wants in my lecture hall, so I should be free to decide whether people may smoke on my property.

Those displeased by my decision need not come to my facilities. If the concern is great and the opportunity to work in a given place is highly valued, negotiations or contract talks can ensue in behalf of separating smokers from nonsmokers. In many cases all that's needed is to bring the problem to light. Maybe the firm's insurance costs will be inordinately high where there is smoking, or maybe a change in policy will come about because customers and workers are gradually leaving.

In some cases it may go so far as to involve tort litigation. Exposing employees to serious dangers that are not part of the job description and of which they were not warned may be actionable. But what the company does initially at least must be its decision. And the onus of proof in these cases must be on those who claim to have suffered unjustified harm.

Clearly, smoking isn't universally bad. For some people it may be okay to smoke, just as it could be okay to have a couple of drinks or to run five miles a day. For others, smoking is very harmful to their health. In either case, health may not be the highest good for many people. All things considered, even those whose health suffers may wish to smoke. In a free society, people are free to do what is wrong, so long as they don't violate the rights of others.

In a free and pluralistic society, it isn't necessary to appoint the government as the caretaker of our health and the overseer of our interpersonal negotiations concerning how we best get along with others.

THE STATISM OF C. EVERETT KOOP*

In recent weeks, the Tobacco Institute, a lobbying outfit pleading the case for the tobacco industry, has been placing ads in numerous publications complaining about the harshness with which government is fighting cigarette smoking. It is doubtless that Surgeon General C. Everett Koop has been a vigilant soldier in the government's fight. But it is very probable that he has gone way beyond the call of duty in what he is willing to say and do about many Americans' choice to smoke cigarettes.

Dr. Koop is a good case in point as to why, despite the very attractive rhetoric of former President Ronald Reagan, his kind of conservative administration is far from a true friend of individual freedom. In his farewell message to the American people, President Reagan sounded extremely good to me—as if all he had had in mind throughout his presidency was how to restore the true spirit of America's libertarian heritage to this nation.

Yet Regan's employment of Dr. Koop is clear evidence that much of the talk is nothing more than talk. Indeed, the actual policies endorsed by the Reagan administration toward people who choose to live their lives differently from Dr. Koop's idea of propriety are quite dangerous to the very ideals Ronald Reagan claims to have been championing.

Consider that Dr. Koop is the person who said he "wants a smoke free America by 1990." Now this sounds like an out-and-out threat against the liberty of a great many people who might not choose to quit smoking by that designated year. It is clearly an utterance with dictatorial overtones to it!

But perhaps Dr. Koop allowed himself some hyperbole. He may simply have meant that this is what he wishes would happen by 1990—i.e., that people would have quit smoking cigarettes. No such luck. Dr. Koop does not only sound like a zealous dictator, he seems to be thinking like one as well.

Some time ago, Dr. Koop commented on the Tobacco Institute's ads, which lament all the harshness against smokers. He took the opportunity to respond to the industry's claim that the plan to ban cigarette ads is an unconstitutional attempt at censorship. He said that it was indeed the tobacco industry that engaged in censorship. As evidence he noted that many papers that carry cigarette advertisements refuse to run reports on the hazards of smoking!

Note the sly ploy of this claim by the kindly Dr. Koop. All of a sudden refusing to run ads in papers that carry reports the industry does not like counts as censorship. This is akin to what I have heard defenders of the Soviet Union's government press say about the Western press. They claim that since in the West publishers can influence the editorial content of their papers, they are just as much involved in censorship as in the Soviet government.

That, as well as Dr. Koop's response, is sheer, unadulterated sophistry. Censorship means government banning of the publication or display of human creations for others to freely choose to accept or reject. Censorship can only

---

*Originally published in *Chronicles* (1989).

be carried out two ways: via the state and via a criminal (who might firebomb a newsstand or newspaper plant).

If and when members of the tobacco industry withhold ads from papers that treat them unkindly—and the Tobacco Institute denies that this is a widespread practice or that it even has any impact—they are simply refusing to trade in ways they believe will not be to their advantage. That is no different from my not choosing to eat at a certain restaurant or refusing to purchase a particular coat—perhaps for odd reasons (e.g., I am a vegetarian, I object to the use of animal furs). Such a boycott is the highest example of exercising one's right to a freedom of choice, and in a free society no one with an ounce of understanding of the nature of individual freedom would dare suggest that it constitutes censorship. Are we to regard Cesar Chavez a censor just because he proposes to boycott grapes? What about those Jews who following the Holocaust refused to buy German cars? Or, perhaps even more to the point, what about people who refuse to purchase blasphemous literature or refuse to see *The Last Temptation of Christ?*

It is actually interesting to notice that some knee-jerk liberals did, indeed, claim that the refusal to run or to view that movie amounted to censorship. That was as much nonsense as Dr. Koop's utterly silly remark.

In a free country there is freedom of the press and freedom of choice as to what one reads or which press one hires for purposes of running one's commercials. The paper can reject the ads and the advertiser can refuse to place their ads in it—it is all a matter of free trade. Because all of us have this freedom in such a society, there is a far greater likelihood of all the news and all the various commentary getting fully aired somewhere. No advertiser or any of the publications offering room to run ads is owed cooperation from the others, only full respect of rights.

Ronald Reagan said he regretted the deficit in his administration but the rest was not bad, "not at all bad." Well, I beg to differ. By having Dr. Koop in his administration, he might as well have hired Ralph Nader or Jeremy Rifkin. None of these individuals has a clear enough understanding of the nature of individual liberty to deserve to be in a government sworn to protect it for all of us, smokers and nonsmokers.

HOW TO PROTECT PROPERTY RIGHTS FOR THE FUTURE*

An interesting concern expressed through numerous media outlets has to do with whether we are taking care to enable future generations of people to live on earth. This is not futurism, a somewhat offbeat field where people explore what is likely to be going on in the near future. This concern is more basic. Will our children or grandchildren be well fed, find room to roam and build, have precious metals, minerals, fuels, and other life-supporting materials available to them?

This concern is often identified as one about the rights of future generations.

---

*Originally published in the *Orange County Register* (April 16, 1985).

We assume human beings have certain rights. We are then naturally concerned with whether, in the future, respect for those rights will be possible. If we now poison the atmosphere, it is doubtful that we can sensibly talk about the right to life in the future. Should all the land become thoroughly spoiled, it would seem pointless even to talk about people's right to property.

These days there is much talk about "rights" just recently invented: the right to health, to a job, or to clean air. What should we be talking about when we discuss rights? A right is a social condition that people must maintain and preserve. My right to use my typewriter means that I need no permission, moral or otherwise, from others to use it if I want to, and no one should have legal authority to stop me from using it.

When we discuss the rights of future generations, we must be thinking about such social conditions for them. Will they be possible? How can we do our best to make them possible without making things intolerable for the present population?

Many things that people value have now been christened "rights," such as education, a job, health and safety on the job, social security, a vacation, peace of mind, friendship, or a fair wage. But no one has any right to such things. What we do have a right to is the freedom to do our utmost to achieve these values. To actually have a right to these values would mean to have rights to the lives, efforts, and property of other people who have created these values. What if we really did have a human right to education? This would mean that other people could be forced to educate us (or our children). Their right to freedom would be violated.

What we all have as human beings are those rights the respect of which requires nothing more than for others to abstain from forcibly intruding on us. True, most legal systems no longer pay heed to this crucial point. "Rights," so called, proliferate all around us. But these are rights in the same sense that Soviet-style governments are democracies. What we are witnessing is a corruption of thought and a distortion of reality.

But even if these phony rights are dismissed, there remain sound concerns about basic human rights of members of future generations. The main concern is whether future generations will be able to enjoy any property rights. This concern has been met, mostly, by calls for extensive government regulation, even ownership, of property, especially real estate, wilderness, farm land, and so forth. The idea is that since people can misuse these things, even ruin them for those who might wish to make use of them in the future, government should make sure that this does not happen.

Is this really a sound way to handle the problem? In fact, government is the most susceptible to harmful influences when it comes to how things are to be used. When governments manage the forests, for example, what usually happens is that the forests are leased. But because the lessee has no long-term interest in the forest, the management leaves much to be desired. Similar processes can be expected from other governmental solutions. Governments are the servants of the current generation. Future voters do not vote today.

In democratic regimes governments are bad managers. They serve political interests, vested interests, immediate demands and wants, and cannot be trusted with long-term problems. The most reliable, though still imperfect, way to help future generations is to firm up the private property system. By protecting private property rights, a legal system does the best it can to foster responsible conduct vis-à-vis all that is of value to human life on earth.

SPECIAL PROTECTION FOR ENTERTAINERS?*

Ever since video recorders became relatively cheap and available to the public, a clamor has been heard from the Hollywood community about how this new technology makes it possible to infringe on their rightful earnings.

It is undoubtedly true that the older audio-tape technology makes it possible for viewers to record programs off radio for their own personal use and re-use. And it is also possible that this leads to some losses of potential revenue. Economist Alan Greenspan has studied the matter and claims that the music industry is losing around $1.5 billion in sales every year because of the availability of such taping equipment to the public.

But the crucial question is whether the proposal advanced by the Hollywood creative community—that Congress tax tape equipment and transfer the funds to the industry—is consistent with individual rights. Is this a special case requiring government intervention or is it simply another case of special-interest pleading?

Taping of music has been possible for decades. There has not been anything like the current hoopla about this matter throughout the forty or so years that audio-taping equipment has been available. And the reason is simple. When someone makes one's wares available to the public via some medium that yields to the kind of usage exemplified by taping, it is not the fault of the tapers. It is similar to exposing one's home and one's neighborhood to strollers, tourists, and, indeed, even television or movie cameras using location shots. There's no doubt others could benefit from this exposure, and it would be silly to try to penalize people for that. They did not ask for it but once they receive it, they may well take advantage of it.

Similarly, Hollywood broadcasts its musical compositions, films, or other creative efforts in such a way that others can receive them. The fact that some uses of these broadcasts are made that were not intended is a mere innocent byproduct of the broadcasting technology and industry. So long as the industry is unable to make certain that the benefit of its creations do not go to nonpaying recipients, it is only morally proper that no one be penalized for being able to take advantage of the free good. The proposal that government should tax those of us who purchase tape machines—whether video or audio—is desperate and asks for something quite unjust.

First of all, some who purchase such equipment do not tape the programs whose creators would benefit. Second, many who use taping equipment have

---

*Originally published in the *Washington Times* (September 3, 1984).

only the limited purpose of postponing their viewing or listening to a different, more convenient time, and even those who aim for repeated listening or viewing have no commercial purpose in mind. They are not trying to cash in on the availability of the broadcasts. Third, the commercial marketing of such tapes can be prevented by strict copyright laws. Just as with the publishing world, if a book or magazine article is copyrighted, it puts commercial parties on notice that the right to sell and buy the items involved is restricted. The same applies to anything that is broadcast.

This for the time being still leaves any programs available for taping open to repeated use by private, noncommercial interests. You and I could tape television or radio broadcasts and enjoy them without having to put up with the commercials that usually pay for the production of such programs. Would this not be unfair? No. Because the alternative would be intolerable. Some kinds of creative activity just cannot be confined to select users without establishment of a virtual police state.

And finally there is also the fact that the $1.5 billion figure for the music industry is misleading. It does not consider that may of us are inspired to purchase records and programs upon having had the benefit of enjoying some repeatedly, at our own convenience. It also fails to consider the funds we save through the availability of taping, funds which for those who are enthusiastic about the programs they tape will probably be spent on the industry's other products.

None of this means that the Hollywood creative industry should not try to secure a more efficient way of controlling its products. That is the right of every creator. But they are not justified in enlisting the force of the state to make it difficult for the rest of us to enjoy what is there for us to enjoy. The creators have chosen to beam their programs into our homes despite failing to find a way to restrict their beaming to those who are going to pay them in a fashion they prefer. They must accept the consequence of their actions.

We all know that some of the things we do for ourselves benefit others, sometimes inadvertently. The Hollywood creative industry must simply accept that such a fate can affect its members just as easily as the rest of us.

It should not try to avoid it by seeking special governmental assistance.

LIBERTY AND THE INTELLECTUALS*

It is distressing how infrequently the idea of political liberty is hailed these days. Peace, welfare, charity, and all sorts of other virtues are paid homage to constantly. But just listen to a presidential speech, campaign oratory, or some other form of advocacy. The value of liberty is hardly mentioned. Yet within a political context nothing is more important! Freedom is the only justification for the existence of politics. Welfare can be secured without the use of law. So can peace. But freedom requires that a well-framed legal system specify each man's legitimate

---

*Originally published in the *Orange County Register* (circa 1971).

sphere of authority. And the same law must work out what is to be done when that sphere has been transgressed. All the specifications of the rights of the accused, for example, serve to protect individual liberty: the right of each man to maximum freedom as long as he is innocent. That is, as long as he has not been proved guilty.

That freedom is no longer an important value for most Americans is evident in many ways. Consider that these days when some people, housewives, for instance, are dissatisfied with a grocery item, they immediately call for government action against grocers. If the prices are "too high," the government must cut them; if tomatoes are not red enough, the government must inspect them; if beef is too tough, call in the government again. But more than this. The mere possibility that some toy will hurt some child or that some television program will injure the sensibilities of someone; or that some television commercial may leave someone confused—just the bare possibility sends hordes to their local politicians asking for "immediate action."

With the slightest respect for human freedom, these people would realize that grocers, toymakers, advertisers, butchers, and the like must first be proven guilty of some crime before any limiting actions should be taken against them. To force the lowering of the prices on some goods is to deprive the seller of his liberty to bargain with the buyer. To force the elimination of certain toys is simply to prohibit the toymaker from selling toys that customers will buy. (Practically anything, toy or not, can be misused, broken, distorted, and thereby rendered dangerous. The possibility exists. And at times it will happen.) To force a television program to eliminate certain scenes is to deprive the writers, actors, producers, and others of their liberty to make their living and create their art as best as they can. As if the American public could not reach for the knob and turn off whatever offends! The self-righteousness of this view is staggering.

The bulk of America's intellectuals love to talk of the rights of the defendants, prisoners, the accused, and others. Once a person has been proved guilty, many of these "humanitarians" will rush to his defense—especially if he or she is a criminal of some magnitude. Yet when these same saviors of humanity lash out against business, they don't even wait until the verdict is in. Ralph Nader has never submitted any of his reports to a careful scientific analysis with stringent rules of evidence in effect. And although I, too, am critical of the alphabet-soup agencies in Washington, Nader's claims against them and the firms he claims control their operations need far more than the "reports" of a self-selected group of judges and jurors.

If Americans (in general) had more respect of human rights and liberty, they would not stand still for the massive disregard of these ideals by those who send their children to schools, colleges, and universities. The trouble is that most Americans never acquainted themselves with the philosophy of liberty. They simply enjoy it. Now when it is under severe attack, they are defenseless against the heavy artillery of educated Skinnerians, Marxists, Eastern mystics, and the like. One can only hope and work so that these attacks will wake up instead of defeat the American culture—one born in the spirit of human liberty and dignity.

SORRY PROFESSOR, FREEDOM IS ALSO GOOD FOR THE RICH*

Envy is not one of my vices, but whenever I read something by John Kenneth Galbraith, I have to admit that I see green. I envy his enormous wealth as far as the opportunity for airing his ideas is concerned.

In a recent column for one of this country's preeminent newspapers, the professor emeritus from Harvard University once again unleashes his ire, in his characteristically charming and crafty, not to mention venomous, manner against America's wealthy. He does this by faintly praising the press for not sticking it to the rich after the stock market plunge of October 1987. By the professor's lights, a truly conscientious, as distinct from tactful and kind, press ought to have gone after the rich of the country by, for instance, urging Congress to stop next year's scheduled changes in tax laws. Galbraith went on for about 750 words to indict the press for not hounding the rich far more than they already do.

Now there is nothing terribly new about this rich-baiting in Western culture, not even in the United States, where the rich, along with anyone else, are supposed to have the unalienable right to life, liberty, and the pursuit of happiness. For centuries there have been those leaders of church and state who kept persecuting all those who sought a prosperous life here on earth. The life of the spirit—or the next best thing here on earth, namely, the intellect—had been placed into a position of greater superiority to that of mere worldly enjoyment and prosperity. Indeed, several of the greatest horrors of humankind can be attributed to this attitude of wealth-denunciation. The Nazi extermination of the Jews was largely motivated by the hatred European Christians had toward those who became prosperous and wealthy. In Europe centuries of anti-usury laws and various religious doctrines created prohibitions against the practice of financial investment and speculation for others than Jews, so eventually the few Jews on the continent got to be noticeably more successful at this than those who by law and conviction had abstained. No great surprise in this. But the ensuing resentment against the Jews was largely responsible for what happened to them at the hands of the Nazis, who were willing to make use of it to barbarous ends.

Karl Marx, too, was an anti-Semite because he saw in the Jews the paradigm capitalists, human beings eager to seek prosperity in life. One result of this hatred is the persecution of Jews in the Soviet Union, not to mention the horrors of the liquidation of private entrepreneurs.

Professor Galbraith, then, is following in the footsteps of a notorious tradition. One can only hope that those whom he was addressing and urging to take his message to the rest of us, the American press, resist his call. The last thing we need in this country is a creation of the scapegoat of the nasty rich. There is enough of that in communist, socialist, and similarly utopian ideologies, ones that promise glory in the spiritual realm or the future and hold up high the nobility of going without, of being forever modest in one's desires for wealth and health here and now on earth.

---

*Originally published in the *Orange County Register* (1987).

Unfortunately, the press will not go far enough in rejecting the professor's call. Members of this profession tend, in the main, to be just as resentful toward the wealthy as members of mine are, in the world of academe. There is this idea that we of words ought to rule the minds and hearts of the public, not the sellers of deodorants, pet rocks, soft drinks, water beds, and similar frivolity. Professor Galbraith seems to find it unbearable that although he can get into the pages of the most prestigious newspapers and magazines, not to mention academic journals, he simply cannot get the attention of the masses. They seem to be willing to make those rich who give them less elevated goods than books on the evil of affluence or the glory of building socialism.

And for that the American public is to be commended. I would commend the American press, too, for largely rejecting the witchhunt recommended by Professor Galbraith, only I am afraid the only reason they do this is that they lack courage. They are, unfortunately, no less convinced of the evil of riches than the dear professor.

There is just one more point worth noting here. In terms of stature in the academic world, Professor Galbraith is about as wealthy as anyone. Having enjoyed a position at Harvard University for most of his career put him into the wealthiest class of academics. Anyone familiar with that profession knows that when one is at Harvard, one is at the top of the heap, not unlike commercial success when one reaches the level of a Fortune 500 company.

Yet there is little evidence of John Kenneth Galbraith offering to trade places, even occasionally, with the poor junior college professors out in Montana or Bakersfield, California, in a gesture of altruism and egalitarianism. No sir. Professor Galbraith is perfectly willing to hog his own domain. Yet he is willing to urge that others who happen to have managed to get to the top be cut down to size.

One thing that we should not expect of most persecutors of the rich is that they will sacrifice any of their own riches as a demonstration of sincerity. Of course, even then their hatred of the wealthy would be unjustified.

GUN LAWS AND THE FREE SOCIETY*

I am not a member of the National Rifle Association (NRA). I have never owned a weapon in my life. While serving as an Air Policeman in the U.S. Air Force, I had extensive training in the handling of weapons, including the .45 sidearm, the BAR, the "grease-gun," and the carbine. I do not hunt, nor have I ever had the inclination toward gun collecting or the sport of shooting firearms.

I am in complete opposition to the current craze for federal gun-control legislation and the frequently suggested confiscation of all weapons from the citizens of this country. Let me explain my reasons for my stand: I have done so to my representatives and to the various organizations and people who are urging

---

*Originally published in the *Orange County Register* (circa 1969)

lawmakers to enact strict laws to control the sale, ownership, and use of weapons by the American people.

We must recognize, at the outset, that weapons have a characteristic not possessed by most other tools and instruments used by human beings. Weapons are used to kill or to practice the skill of harming either animals or human beings for various purposes. But killing and hurting living things are not in themselves good or bad; whether killing and hurting are evil or good depends on the context in which they are undertaken. Every legal system humankind has devised recognizes this. The simple fact that the acquisition of food frequently requires the killing of animals proves this point conclusively (even vegetarians kill living things).

This special characteristic of weapon use is necessary to point out in order to avoid the difficulties and confusions that arise when we begin to draw analogies between weapons and, for example, the automobile, knives, and other man-made tools and instruments.

The social use of weapons must be guided by moral principles. The moral principle that underlies our legal system is that each man has an absolute right to his life. Our type of government was built on this principle; our governmental institutions serve the purpose of securing for our citizenry the kind of legal framework within which the right to life is protected at each step of the evolution of human technology. As technology develops, the means of abridgment of human rights, including the right to life, become more and more complex. So must the specification of the securement of these rights become increasingly complex. When we speak of a "flexible legal system," this is what we ultimately refer to. In the process of legal evolution, ever more attention must be paid to the fundamental moral principle that underlies our political system, one in which government is designed to serve the interest of the individual citizens of the society. (This distinguishes the governmental system of the United States, at least in intent, from all other systems of government in the history of the world.)

Because in human history the rights of human beings have most often been threatened by none other than the governments ruling various societies, the founders of our legal system were especially sensitive to the citizen's need for an ultimate recourse to self-protection, in the event that the government, which was intended to protect rights, should gain sufficient power to usurp those rights. Since ours was the first experiment in devising a governmental system that served its people, the framers were aware of the possibility of mistakes that may have been incorporated within the legal system they constructed. To reduce such a possibility, they devised the Bill of Rights, which was aimed at restricting the powers and range of activities of government. The second article of this document makes clear that "the right of the people to keep and bear arms shall not be infringed." This is directed to our lawmakers, our government, first and foremost. The justification given is, of course, the security of a free state, which means, a free people free from oppression, of course. And since the most effective and widespread oppression that can exist in society has always emanated from governments— monarchs, pharaohs, czars, dictatorships of individual people (Hitler), or groups (the Communist Party)—the contention that the right of people to own firearms, if for no other reason than to be prepared to protect themselves from their government, is perfectly justified.

The intentions of the government to control and even confiscate the people's means of ultimate self-protection must be prevented at all reasonable cost.

It must be emphasized that it is not necessary for people to know that what they aim for is not, in fact, what their actions will accomplish, in order for them to be moving toward accomplishing something not specifically intended. Our government in its drive for gun control and confiscation may have good intentions. These intentions, however, will, in this instance—as in many previous instances—result in grave injustice and possible tragedy to our people and society, if successfully executed. For this reason, every person who respects a free society concept, and its actual approximations as manifest in the United States—imperfectly as that may be—must work for the prevention of the laws now being urged for our nation.

Because criminals and ex-convicts have, by their own actions, forfeited some of their rights in a free society, their status with respect to gun ownership must be viewed differently from that of the law-abiding citizen. For this reason there are grounds for asking people to demonstrate their legal situations when they purchase weapons. My reasoning does not fail, therefore, on account of the fact that some gun laws are perfectly proper in a free society. Thus, the NRA and various other bodies, which oppose the present drive for federal laws pertaining to guns, take a stand firmly grounded on both moral and legal principles consonant with the life of a free people in society. Charges that profit is the only motive for the NRA's stand must be rejected by all thinking persons.

When Nazis and communists are defended in our society for citing our laws in their own legal defense—laws with which they morally disagree—it is despicable that organizations such as the NRA are smeared by references to the possible advantages they might gain by succeeding in their legal arguments against the federal government. One wonders what kind of people we are dealing with in our government when the motive of self-interest is condemned more than the motive of destructionism, as exhibited by Nazis and Communists, who rarely get even a slap on the wrist these days. This situation itself should move us to attend carefully to the present situation.

As one who is not personally interested in the use of weapons—for hunting, collecting, or sharpshooting—I am doing everything possible, as a layperson, to defend my right to protect myself with weapons, if need be, and against the state, if it comes to that.

THE MOST DANGEROUS DRUG IS POWER*

Where is the American Civil Liberties Union when we really need it? Where are all those who criticized Reagan nominee Robert Bork for failing to admit a general constitution prnciple of the right to privacy?

In other words, why are we not asking the question of principle about the matter of hard drug abuse? Should there be any kind of prohibition of drug use and trade in a free society? Let me propose that there shouldn't unless the coercion of minors is involved. Let me also suggest that it is in such hard cases—where popular sentiment is ready to cave in—that the principles of the free society deserve their most vigilant support!

The current debate on legalization of hard drugs is misdirected. Prohibition of alcohol, e.g., wasn't only unworkable, inefficient, or costly. It didn't just manage to foster crime by driving a business underground and making trade in a peaceful industry inaccessible to legal governance. And it wasn't merely discriminatory against the primarily German-born brewers and distillers.

Prohibition was coercive. So is the political war on drug abuse. Coercive policies. violently intrude on innocent people, ones who have forced no one to do anything; people who have murdered, kidnapped, or assaulted nobody, whatever else pernicious they may have done. And the laws of a free people have as their prime purpose to enable one to live with others without such intrusion. Prohibition was morally wrong because of its assault on human rights.

Adult men and women must be free to cope with the temptations in life. Some are simple to resist, some difficult, some almost impossible. For example,, certain initially stimulating drugs, such as cocaine and heroin, are strongly addictive and deadly at that. Even nicotine is addictive, as is alcohol, for many people. And numerous other activities can become addictive and can also be hazardous to some.

Some—e.g., the Rev. Jesse Jackson—argue that legalizing bad behavior shows that the government approves of such behavior. Poppycock.

As a clear refutation, just consider that the First Amendment to the U.S. Constitution fully legalizes the worship of false gods, the publication of vile writing and yellow journalism. The U.S. government is behind the First Amendment proudly and relentlessly. Yet it by no means morally sanctions these detestable actions by those who enjoy its protection. The issue is not government giving moral approval to this or that. The issue is government recognizing that adults must take care of their problems—even the problem of drug abuse and addiction.

Free people ought to know that when the state comes in to protect us from our own possible willingness to yield to temptation, the main accomplishment is that the state gets more power. We are also given a fraudulent sense of security, and our self-esteem gets eroded.

The government should not try to solve the drug abuse problem. In doing so, it is of course wasting millions of dollars that could be spent on preventing

*Originally published in the *Los Angeles Daily Journal* (March 4, 1989).

violent crime. It is siphoning off social energy that could be wisely spent. But most of all it is treating its citizens not as sovereign adults but as wards of the state.

Certainly drug abusers are probably more likely to commit crimes than those who rely on a sound, uncluttered mind to guide themselves in life. Certainly such people are often no good to themselves or to those near and dear to them.

But only when drug abusers violate just laws—e.g., they rob, assault, murder, or kidnap innocent peoole—is it time to go after them. Penalizing them beforehand is a clear case of prior restraint, something that is alien to our very honorable and sound legal tradition.

Drug abuse as such is not the proper concern of the government of a free society. Our system is built on the principle that prior restraint is wrong. We only punish those who have committed crimes, not those who might.

Drug abuse is the business of society—of parents, teachers, doctors, corporate executives, friends, employers, labor leaders, therapists, and others. It is a problem of society, but only few of the problems of society are bona fide government problems. Just as bad literature, theater, science, and many other types of human misconduct are problems of society but not of government, so drug abuse should be handled by competent individuals and groups outside the purview of the state.

Some claim that drug abuse is not a victimless act—family and friends, colleagues, and those close to the abuser are the victims. But this is to stretch a metaphor beyond usefulness and logic. A victim is one who cannot escape another's intrusive actions except at very great and undeserved cost. One's family (especially one's mate), friends, and colleagues are voluntary partners. They could walk away from one who sells or uses drugs, even if we acknowledge that this would be difficult. If we do not accept that some things are a person's private business, however much they might bear on his or her relationship to others, while other things are everyone's business, we lose sight of the basic premise of a free society—of the distinction between the public and the private (including social) realm. No adult is forced into drug addiction. No adult has to start, and almost every adult can begin to take steps needed to stop as well.

There are innumerable private practices that are unwise and even deleterious. High cholesterol intake, heavy drinking, lack of exercise, driving in a state of fatigue, obesity, reckless romantic adventures, and on and on. If drug abuse may be treated politically, all these other activities can be as well, and soon the society will become totalitarian, not libertarian as the founders had designed it and as it has been proven best for the bulk of its citizens.

In a free country, government is limited in its powers—even when this means that it cannot do some wonderful things—e.g., make sure we all read only the best literature, watch only the best newscasts, see only the best drama. This point applies also to government's attempt to cope with drug abuse.

But today in our country—as well as others, unfortunately—there is too much confidence in the wisdom of government and too little fostering of and respect for individual rights and personal responsibility. When the surgeon general of a major free-world superpower can declare, without blinking an eye, that "I want a smoke free America by 1990," one must wonder where the ideal of individual liberty has gone. What if there will be some people who will wish to smoke in 1990? Will the general order them shot? If some people are prone to addiction, then certainly those governing us are prone—aside from all the regular addictions—to the addiction for power. We should worry about that a lot more than we do.

4

Foreign Affairs

INDIVIDUALISM, PATRIOTISM, AND GLOBAL REDISTRIBUTION

Should one support the security and prosperity of one's own country? Some say that doing so is selfish and unfair. In light of the severe misery evident throughout the globe, are those who insist on the growth of their own standard of living and who would oppose programs of wealth redistribution being immoral? Do they lack humanitarian feelings? The debate about the relationship of Northern and Southern hemisphere countries, between developed and developing nations, appears to be motivated in part by the contention that for the North to insist on merely trading with the South—whereby it will help the South only if it gains an advantage in the process—is unjust. The history of colonialism, of previous economic exploitation, simply does not justify this sort of "free trade" attitude but requires greater generosity, even charity, from the North—meaning the United States, mostly.

So it is clear that the answer to our question is not self-evident. When in official and unofficial international forums we hear demands placed at the feet of the prosperous nations by those purporting to speak for developing nations, we must be ready to consider the justice of such demands. For example, should the people of the United States provide goods and services to Third World countries? Should they be forced to do so by their own government or by the United Nations?

Underlying this issue we find very deep philosophical problems. And while current policy decision makers may not be able to wait for solutions, neither can they continue to ignore them. If policy is to be formulated, put to scrutiny, defended or adjusted, some standards are needed. If international relations are to make sense, then we must consider what the standards of good sense must be, however much this may leave the current crop of decision makers unimpressed, given the immediate range of choices that they face. It is better late than never with sound policy.

71

The legal system of the United States rests on the doctrine of individualism and natural rights. That doctrine draws its philosophical support from a variety of sources. While many think that the main source is the view that everyone is ultimately an economic agent—a utility maximizer—that is only one of several ideas that has influenced our system of politics. There is also the view that each person is, by nature, free and equal and responsible to grasp certain ethical truths, laws of nature, which should guide human conduct. And the ethical truths that we should each grasp and live by include that everyone should pursue happiness in life.

This happiness, however, has both a narrow and broad interpretation. It can be understood simply as pleasure, power, or wealth. It can also be understood as personal human excellence in life, flourishing as human beings. The former interpretation is usually given by those who dislike individualism and regard it as at best a temporary myth that helps prepare a country economically eventually to turn into a collectivist society—socialism. The latter interpretation is rarer but, judging by the founding fathers' reputation as readers of the classical as well as modern political philosophers, more reasonable.

Individualism also proclaims that each individual has a fundamental right to life, liberty, and the pursuit of happiness. Simply put, this means that each person ought to be left unimpeded in his or her efforts to live, act, and prosper. Murdering, assaulting, kidnapping, and stealing from people is prohibited. Some argue that this again is just a temporary economic social device that serves to encourage productivity, technological innovation, and the free flow of commerce, only so long as this prepares a nation for a change for the better, toward a more humane society. But in fact these individualistic principles have a very different function.

The reason people should respect everyone's rights to life, liberty, and the pursuit of happiness is that doing so is what secures a genuine equal standing for all as morally responsible agents in a community. If one is subject to the coercive intrusion of a king or even a democratic assembly, not to mention a dictator or politburo, one is not able to be morally conscientious. One is then treated as a child, not as an adult. The rise of individualism, whatever else it did, aimed at destroying the politically dependent status of the bulk of human beings throughout the world.

Marx observed that "the right of man to property is the right to enjoy his possessions and dispose of the same arbitrarily, without regard for other men, independently from society, the right of selfishness." But does this right make possible only the arbitrary disposition of one's earnings and other property? Does it merely allow one to act "without regard for other men"? Not at all. Marx misplaced the emphasis. He focused only on the cynical side of it, imagining that human beings are inherently antisocial and antagonistic toward each other. Marx had a rather pessimistic view of human nature, rather like the view many who endorse the homo economicus idea, namely, that we pursue only the satisfaction of our own preferences, even when we seek to help others. This view, inherited from Thomas Hobbes, is not what has to lie in back of the doctrine of private property rights. The right to private property has another role, again identified by Karl Marx: "The practical application of the rights of man to freedom is the right of man to private property."

But, of course, Marx had little respect for the sort of freedom that is given concrete expression in the right to private property. This is the freedom we have when we are spared other people's brutality, intrusiveness, coercion, intervention, assault, murder, and theft. If one has a view of human nature that regards all people as passive, helpless, the victims of forces of nature, and incapable of flourishing without the leadership of wise gurus, then such freedom is going to harm most of us. We will remain at the mercy of the cruelties of life, unable to extricate ourselves from it. This freedom means that we are doomed and need to be liberated from doom by those who would cast aside our "freedom" in behalf of a "higher" freedom, namely, the freedom to grow as we must, as some of us have determined we ought to. When we hear about all the "liberation" movements led by Marxists, this is the kind of liberation we should be thinking of. It is drastically different from the sort of liberation associated with the liberation of France during World War II by the American forces. When this latter is at issue, we are talking about helping people to get free of oppressors, of intruders, and conquerors. When the Marxist sense of the term is used, it means bringing people in line with what they need and should do, whether they know this or not.

In any case, the individualist insistence on the rights to life, liberty, and the pursuit of happiness (including the right to private property), testifies to a view of human nature that is not shared by many intellectuals who are critical of American political ideals. And that explains a great deal about why America is being urged to give up what its people have produced, why the prosperity of the North is seen as resulting from exploitation, and why justice is seen as requiring extensive redistribution of wealth.

It also explains why so many Americans are reluctant to embrace patriotism. They may feel pleased about being Americans but they are also a bit ashamed for living in a prosperous country while throughout the world people are miserable. They feel that it is in their power to help and that they perhaps ought to help rather than take advantage of their own well-being so as to flourish even more. They feel they are cruel, not helpful. But this is a demeaning outlook.

Once again the motivation involves a misconception of how other people may be helped. What helps someone depends on what that person wants and needs. We may assume that people in the poor countries throughout the world want well-being, health, prosperity, education, recreation, and so forth. This is evident enough from what the North is being asked to do, namely, share its wealth, etc. But what is needed so as to attain these goals? That is the vital issue.

Oddly enough, the very person in whose name much of the redistribution talk is conducted, Karl Marx, understood better than most the importance of private property rights for the creation of wealth. In this Marx agreed with Adam Smith. The difference is that Marx regarded the social conditions of capitalism extremely harsh and in need of eventual transformation. Smith, on the other hand, agreed that only in a society that protects natural liberty can we expect the generation of prosperity as well as good will and peace.

And for individualists there is no reason to believe that such a society is inherently harsh, even if at one time adjustment to it did cause some people hardship, mainly because of the leftover injuries from the earlier system of feudalism. The right to property had never been fully implemented, which left a lot of property in the hands not of its rightful owners but in the hands of feudal barons and their offspring. That this resulted in widespread injustice is not the fault of the system that took the first steps to help matters.

From these considerations we can learn that what the people of developing nations need to make headway toward prosperity is not charity but political conditions that encourage productivity. They need capitalism. They need to learn that stifling capitalist development is tantamount to crushing human progress—the only kind that we can really expect in life, namely, the progress of individuals who rest on the achievements of those who have gone before them and left them with a better understanding of economic, political, technological, and other vital areas of concern.

When, in turn, Americans refuse to submit to international extortion, when they wish to keep up the health and welfare of their own country rather than pour it all into the international pool, they have every right to this. They can rest assured that they are loyal not just to a homeland, a familiar setting, traditions and customs, but to objectively sound political-economic values. They can feel comfortable, provided they understand this, that what they cherish about their country is not simply an arbitrary attribute, something that they are simply used to and feel comfortable about. Rather they cherish a community arrangement that is better for human beings—and can be improved a great deal to that end by making it even a purer version than now enjoyed—than any other tried throughout the world.

The moral support for all this is not arbitrary either. Whether one identifies capitalism with Hobbes, Locke, or someone else, the fact is that from a moral point of view it is far more defensible than other systems. Capitalism respects individual moral responsibility. It sees human beings as adults, capable of striving for a successful, excellent human life. It sees that when people associate with each other freely, rather than by way of caste systems and other conditions of inherited status, they are happier and more creative as social agents than if they live in the static conditions of social stratification. All in all, capitalism, growing out, as it does, from a consideration of the political requirements of human social life—the doctrine of natural human rights to life, liberty, and property—is really a most admirable socio-political arrangement.

Needless to say, capitalism is not all of human life. Commerce is only part of what adult human beings need to do to flourish. There are other aspects to our lives that are only enhanced, not secured, through capitalism. But it is safe to say that in capitalism these other aspects have a far greater chance to flourish, as well, than in any other system. Art, science, love, education, community, spiritual development, etc., are all advanced in a free society, one that is presupposed by capitalism.

In all this one must also recall that such a society does not guarantee against failure. Nor can it guarantee against catastrophe. The Soviet propagandists against capitalism are fond of pointing out that in New York City and elsewhere, there are men and women who live out of trash cans, that there is poverty in the midst of plenty, that we are not a perfect community where everyone is protected against hardship. They also note that a minimal well-being is secured for people in socialist systems, albeit so minimal as to embarrass them whenever someone looks close enough. These kinds of safety net guarantees are, no doubt, impressive to some people, and in certain circumstances one may even be tempted to ask for them, even at the risk of losing all else. But in fact, socialist countries manage to insure against utter poverty only when they receive extensive aid from near-capitalist countries. And even then they pay a very heavy price: the liberty and prosperity of the rest of the people.

Perhaps some people would rather have all of us barely carving out a living than risk having anyone hit bottom. But if we recall that the bare existence could turn to disaster in socialist systems, were it not for capitalist imports, creativity, innovation, risk taking and, indeed, occasional economic disaster, such a system should lose all rational appeal and remain attractive only to those who like to cling to impossible dreams.

Americans may not know this, but they have a good reason to be nationalistic. This does not mean bellicose or arrogant, just comfortably self-satisfied and confident in the propriety of living in a country that is largely free and sees the need of greater freedom rather than less. They should be willing to defend it against both philosophical and other attacks. They should be proudly nationalistic because what their country stands for, most of all and uniquely, is a morally admirable social system.

FIGHTING ISOLATIONISM: FOREIGN POLICY IN AN IMPERFECT WORLD?*

From the beginning, the topic of foreign policy has been somewhat of a puzzle for the United States. Initially, America's great statesmen advocated a form of isolationism. "Tis our true policy to steer clear of permanent alliances," said George Washington in his farewell address at the end of his presidency. "Taking care to keep ourselves . . . on a respectable defensive posture, we may safely trust to temporary alliances for extraordinary emergencies."

But it is far from clear that such isolationism was to be a permanent feature of U.S. foreign policy. Washington's reflections on the topic are often quoted by those who blame many of America's troubles on foreign entanglements. At times the same people who are scornful of "eighteenth-century economics" (the near laissez-faire capitalism of Adam Smith) are unabashedly wedded to the early isolationism. The United States should not have been involved in a civil war in Vietnam, should not have intervened in Chile, should not have meddled in Angola, should leave Central America alone, should keep its missiles out of Europe, and so on.

---

*Originally published in *Reason* magazine (February 1984).

It is not similarly incongruous to find isolationism embraced by advocates of a strictly laissez-faire version of America's political tradition of economic and civil liberalism, the political doctrine on which the country was founded. Even here, though, if we scratch beneath the surface, we find incongruities.

On the one hand, individual liberty implies the doctrine of government by the consent of the governed. If a government rules without being chosen for that function, it is a tyranny. And clearly, to extend the U.S. government into other realms, even for benign purposes, is to breach the principle of the consent of the governed. Government officials must confine themselves, if they object to what is happening in another country, to explicit or tacit criticism—for example, a "human rights foreign policy" that is long on enunciating the principles of liberty but devoid of interventionist actions to implement them around the globe.

Moreover, the government of a free society has its complicated job carved out already, without taking up the affairs of other governments or peoples. It is as if the physician who is attending to one patient were simply to abandon the operation and turn to saving another doctor's patient. It may indeed be distressing that such help is not forthcoming when it would be helpful, but it can also be seen that governments violate their sacred trust as servants of their own citizens when they take on serving others.

Yet it is not at all clear that these considerations imply a strict isolationism whereby the government of a free society can legitimately engage only in defending its borders against foreign aggressors. For example, is it not plausible that such a government could do its job better at times by forming alliances with other governments? Surely mutual advantage might be served in such a relationship, just as firefighting services benefit from mutual aid agreements. To draw up a treaty between two proper governments would seem to offer hope at times against aggressive regimes across the globe.

There is certainly nothing wrong in principle with this strategy. There need be no violation of the duty of the government to protect its own citizens, since the treaty at issue could well be a purely defensive project. Canada and the United States, for example, might each be better defended by the cooperative military and diplomatic efforts of the Canadian and U.S. governments. If one country's government, in the process of providing effective defense of its people, also provides effective defense of another people for some value in return, no sacrifice has been required. No one need be cheated out of proper services.

In a complicated world, with sophisticated military means of aggression available to tyrannical regimes, it would be irresponsible for a government to take an isolationist stance. Such circumstances warrant defensive alliances of considerable complexity, even for a government that adhered perfectly to the principles of individual rights and government by the consent of the governed.

In the world we live in, of course, our own government does not adhere very well at all to the principles of liberty that underlie our political tradition. Yet those who advocate a fully free system nevertheless have to make intelligent judgments about foreign-policy alternatives facing the impure regime. And the application of the principles of liberty is again not entirely obvious.

While the United States and Canada are far from free countries, it is true that far less free countries could pose a threat to them. Insofar as individual liberty is breached in the United States and Canada on many fronts, we clearly have a system that is unjust. Yet even such a system should carry out its business of defending the country against aggressors. So however flawed the political systems that have evolved in Canada and America, it may well be that the governments of these countries should, all things considered, embark on mutual defense efforts if this is militarily advisable. And the potential for mutually advantageous military alliances with other countries exists as well.

Yet as entanglements grow, so does the potential for abuse and corruption of principles. Some alliances may turn out to be far from mutually beneficial. Some may turn out to help regimes that are so far from being worthy of alliances that the alliances could be taken to constitute aiding and abetting a potential aggressor.

It is therefore very complicated to discover just what those who advocate a fully free system should support when it comes to the foreign policy of the United States today. Circumstances can change, so that a country that had not been a good candidate for alliance becomes one suddenly, or vice versa. It is difficult for citizens to be aware of developments that would warrant adjusting their government's foreign relations. Detailed knowledge of foreign governments' military capabilities and intentions are needed in order to formulate appropriate foreign policy and military strategy.

Most of us are not foreign policy experts, have no academic or practical contact with the nitty-gritty of foreign relations and military strategy, and possess little knowledge of intricate developments on the international front bearing on the "oughts" and "ought nots" of foreign affairs. Yet if we deem a free society best suited to the flourishing of human beings, we will be concerned with laying out general guidelines for a rational foreign policy for such a free society. But we will also be concerned with the actual possibilities faced by the country we inhabit, the closest to a free society now in existence.

When considering second- or third-best circumstances in political matters, it is useful to consider such cases in morality. People are unable always to keep only the best of relations in their personal lives. At times, a person can play tennis only if he is willing to play with someone who is in some respect morally condemnable. A feminist may buy food from a male chauvinist if there is no alternative in the neighborhood. Morally mediocre circumstances have to be dealt with all the time, and one can handle them better or worse. An artificial stance of purity—"I shall never have anything to do with that louse"—can spell suicide. Stagnation on all fronts may arise if people fail to work for their own well-being because the circumstances are morally tainted.

In judging America's current foreign-policy situation, it is not a wise idea to insist on some rigid stance in the name of being principled. If the security of Europe, for example, is of some significance to the security of the United States, but it is wrong to be forcing U.S. taxpayers to bear the bulk of the cost of defending Europe, it is nevertheless unwise to demand the immediate withdrawal of U.S. troops from Europe unless there is good reason to think that the slack will be taken up by competent military units. The same considerations apply to U.S.-Japanese defense commitments. And in general there may not be any great wisdom in trying to disengage from all foreign involvements. The matter does not yield to apriori analysis.

Yet that kind of approach to foreign affairs—or any other practical, day-to-day concern of government—is tempting, for those who align themselves with principles seriously are better exhibited by integrating the actual world and its more-or-less controllable variables with these principles. For individuals who care for liberty as the highest social good, as the most important ingredient of a good human community, it is imperative to ask how, personally, they can fully adhere to the principles involved. They must abstain from aggression and its promotion. But at the same time they must consider very seriously the consequences of living with millions of others to whom these principles mean very little.

These people may use aggression any time they believe that by doing so they can get their way. And in the face of entire regimes of such people with adequate power to carry out their designs, the precise moves to be made in foreign affairs are far more difficult to identify than is indicated by any simple statement about the evils of government expansion. Think of how complicated it can be to determine whether someone's use of force constituted aggression in a simple altercation on some street corner. How much more complicated this is at the national and international levels! It is usually a veritable case of shades of gray mingling with shades of gray.

Some societies are more free than others, and it is worth preserving such freedom and the opportunity to expand it. We should not neglect such a task by insisting on treating the world as if it already conformed to standards of liberty we hold dear.

WHY DEFENSE SPENDING CAN'T BE COMPARED WITH SOCIAL WELFARE SPENDING*

For all the years Ronald Reagan has been a national figure, the public has listened to a debate about whether to spend more money on national defense while also aiming to reduce government spending. Washington bustles with the controversy now, when Reagan is asking to increase defense spending and reduce so-called social spending. The question now goes: Should we raise more money for the military while cutting (or reducing the increase) for other areas of government spending?

I am no expert on how much money the military requires to provide an adequate defense of the United States. I do know one thing: Defense is the federal government's primary obligation. It is to secure our rights that government is established, not to provide us with welfare.

---

*Originally published in the *Orange County Register* (April 23, 1985).

When we compare military spending with social spending, we compare apples and oranges—no, apples and volcanoes. The business of government is equipping itself to fight domestic and foreign criminals—those who would murder, assault, and steal from its citizens. That is the reason for government's existence. The rest is luxury.

Even if we do not dispute the moral authority of governments to take from Peter to give to Paul, to try to help science, education, medicine, farming, the indigent, to buy votes, to do good, whatever—we must see one matter clearly enough. Government's military mission is different from the rest. It uses force as its job—the cops and the soldiers are trained to fight, and the rest of government is trained to tell them whom to fight.

The citizens teach, design computers, publish books, write columns, dig ditches, perform operations, clean hallways, and in innumerable other ways try to achieve the general welfare. The welfare state, then, is a reinforcement of what we are already doing—some argue, quite well—and would do even better without government's help.

The general welfare—what government social spending is supposed to advance—is something citizens can promote without government. National defense is not like that. So whether we should cut social spending is a different kind of question from whether we should cut defense spending. It is roughly like the question of whether a city should give up its police or its public parks.

I am not saying that defense spending is too low or too high. I am unqualified to say. I know of all the charges about the wastefulness of government by the Grace Commission. I also suspect the Pentagon could be better managed.

Be that as it may, defense spending is different from social spending. Those who say, "If social spending must come down, so must defense spending," misconceive the situation. Social spending is an extra. It involves taking money from some people and spending it on other people who are supposedly in greater need or who do "more important" things.

Social spending is always some kind of subsidy. Defense spending, whether well- or ill-advised, is for the entire country, all citizens, and does not in principle have to subsidize any industry. Defense requires the production of various goods and services and, when done right, involves paying for work the country needs done in a world that has not wiped out either domestic or foreign crime.

The discussion about government spending, the budget, and deficits should be divided into two parts. One should deal with spending for subsidies, the other with spending on defense. Then the attitude of politicians and commentators could be better evaluated.

When they talk of cutting defense, this will have a certain meaning; when they want to cut the subsidies, that will mean something else. Then the debate would make more sense.

MARXISM AND GLASNOST*

Most people today are proclaiming the victory of capitalism. Robert Heilbroner, for example, wrote in the *New Yorker* magazine that "the contest between capitalism and socialism is over: capitalism has won." He defends this view by claiming that "The Soviet Union, China, and Eastern Europe have given us the clearest possible proof that capitalism organizes the material affairs of humankind more satisfactorily than socialism. . . . The great question now seems how rapid will be the transformation of socialism into capitalism and not the other way around."

Well, wouldn't it be wonderful if it were only that simple. But alas, it isn't.

To understand the situation it is necessary to consult Karl Marx. The old philosopher of scientific socialism argued that before one can successfully organize an economy according to socialist principles—"from each according to his ability, to each according to his needs"—the community must fully experience capitalism in its purest possible form. Marx claimed that capitalism is the most productive economic system. He held that if a community tried to install socialism without having fully weathered capitalism, all that will happen is "the socialization of poverty."

That is exactly what has occurred in the Soviet and Chinese socialist systems. And worse—for even the equality dreamed of has not materialized. Instead these systems are modern mercantile feudal states, with powerful elites ruling the rest of the population. What explains the fact that Marxists would let this happen?

Marx was asked by some Russian revolutionaries whether socialism could be started in Russia, and his reply was that it could, "If the Russian Revolution becomes the signal for a proletarian revolution in the West, so that both complement each other. . . ." Only then can "the present Russian common ownership of land . . . serve as the starting-point for a communist development" (Preface to the Russian edition to *The Communist Manifesto*). This means, in plain terms, that if the Soviet Union succeeds in engulfing the capitalist West, the revolution can succeed. If the Soviet Union can internationalize socialism—export it and thus bring within its orbit those societies that have undergone capitalism—then it will not need to experience capitalism itself.

Now what does this say about current trends in the Soviet/Chinese camp? It suggests, at least, that it is incautious to jump for joy about the victory of capitalism as a political economy in the eyes of those who follow Marx. True, the Soviets and Chinese might have abandoned Marx completely by now. In that case we have a different situation, although it still does not mean that capitalism is their preferred alternative. They could still merely turn to a bit of help from private enterprise, in a desperate economic situation, only to revert to fascism or some other form of statism when the treasury is doing better.

But if the Soviet and Chinese leadership is still Marxist—and this is clearly likely with at least Gorbachev—then what we might be witnessing is a kind of regrouping of energies. It may then be that the Soviet Union and its allies are

---

*Originally published in the *Monterey Advertiser* (July 1989).

going to have a limited dosage of capitalism—maybe even a large dosage—with the clear expectation that once the capitalist experiment has been concluded, socialism can regain and even increase its momentum.

Of course, I don't for a moment believe that socialism can work even after a society has experienced capitalism—although I do think that for a while there can be a pretense at its workability, since the wealth of capitalism can serve the purpose of keeping the socialist system temporarily solvent. But the issue is not what a libertarian thinks about this but what leaders of the Soviet and Chinese states do. Is it likely, as Heilbroner—and, incidentally, Professor Murray N. Rothbard, leader of the American faction of the libertarian Austrian school of economics—think, that the socialist dream has been abandoned?

Clearly most American Marxists haven't converted. One need only read the February 20, 1989, issue of the *Nation,* where Alexander Cockburn valiantly sticks by his socialist guns against Professor Heilbroner. And even if they think that full-blown centrally planned socialism won't do, they still hold out for a very heavily regimented "market socialism." They think big business is the villain and would never risk letting big business be—no laissez-faire, laissez-passe for these faithful.

Even the pragmatists in America hold out for statism, despite the evidence of its demise from around the globe. They favor calling upon the "thousand points of light" but only to boost the economy and there through to boost tax revenues. Then they will be ready to continue with extensive redistribution and invite all the trouble all over again. Why? Because the last thing these folks believe in is that individuals have the right to live for themselves, to work and prosper without paying dues to them in the name of all the poor in the world.

As long as there is one poor person left—and there will always be millions of them in our non-utopian universe—the statists will invoke them as the excuse for ruining everyone else's life a little or a lot.

So let us not rejoice at capitalism's success. Only if people come to realize that it is perfectly right for people to flourish even when some others don't and that no one may prevent such flourishing, however, well intentioned they may be in trying to do that, will capitalism have won. And that time is a long way off.

WHY WE WARM UP TO THE SOVIETS

In a recent issue of *Insight*—a well edited, conservative weekly newsmagazine—which in many ways is a relief from the welfare statist bias and ambiguous mush of *Newsweek* and *Time,* respectively—columnist Woody West asks "Why would the West even contemplate trade, technological cooperation, and financial support with a state so practiced at savage repression [as the USSR]?" This is just the sort of question that will lead knee-jerk liberals to brand someone an ultra right-winger. Never mind that the liberals' own intransigent stance on South Africa is usually paraded as a sign of moral integrity. (We all know that those of us who hate the Soviet government are supposed to wear ideological blinders, while those who hate South Africa's apartheid system are morally principled, uncompromising persons of integrity. But then this kind of hypocrisy is rampant in our culture.)

Despite the sneers of the liberal statist, there is good reason to question the accommodating policies of Washington toward the Soviet Union. Admittedly, the Soviets are a greater military power in the world than South Africa, and this alone would warrant somewhat different diplomatic attitudes toward the two detestable systems. But there is a more basis reason behind the attitude Mr. West has identified.

The main reason that leaders of Western nations are not firmly and in a principled fashion opposed to the Soviet system—the reason most of them love to see some sign of softening and even without it would like to reach some accommodation with the USSR—is that most Western "liberal" democracies are not committed to a political philosophy that categorically rejects the savage repression that is clearly evident in that society.

The West is composed largely of welfare states, not free societies. Welfare states are founded on the political idea that, within some rather vague limits, governments may coerce their citizens to do service to various causes they do not voluntarily choose. As we know, especially during a presidential election period, our politicians in this supposedly free country are vying for support, our leaders are now entirely unapologetic about promising to various factions of the citizenry benefits that government can only secure by robbing the taxpayer blind.

This shows that modern welfare states are only in degree different from the Soviet system, not in principle. Sure the degree of brutality used to extract the wealth and services—in other words, the life-blood—of the citizenry in welfare states has not reached that of a dictatorial system such as the Soviet Union. In that system one does not even need a pretense of democratic support for public policy. All that is necessary is some congruence with official ideology. And there is always that, since under Marxism-Leninism if one does not follow the state, one is either mentally sick or a traitor. The Soviet system sees society as a naturally created team and if someone objects to the captain's instruction, he or she is like a quarterback who throws the ball to the opposition's players.

But that is not all that far from how we view citizenship in the United States of America, where individual liberty is supposed to reign supreme. Here, too, if one opposes the government's redistribution of wealth—its managing of the collective resources of the society—according to some utopian vision (viz., all homeless must be provided with homes, America must be made into a smoke-free society, the war on drugs must gain universal support), one is deemed at least a bad or antisocial person. Jesse Jackson recently condemned even the Reagan administration's feeble efforts at privatization—getting the government back to dealing with those issues that are properly its concern—e.g., criminal justice, defense. Such aims are deemed to be a sign of lack of concern with public service, rather than a drawing away from the totalitarian mentality whereby every concern of humanity must come under state supervision. And Jesse Jackson has huge support in these sentiments.

So we in the West must realize that our official condemnation of the Soviet

Union is ultimately groundless unless we also grant full protection of individual human rights to our citizens. It isn't sufficient just to extol the right to free speech and press. Private property rights, freedom of contract, the right to privacy, etc., which are the true bulwark against statism, also must be fully respected.

Once this has occurred, maybe we could perceive more clearly just how rotten the Soviet system is. Unfortunately, most leaders of the West like political power almost as much as the leaders of the USSR. And the intellectuals seem to sit by advocating ideas that would increase that power. So why wonder that the business, artistic, scientific, and other communities also wish to cash in on this lack of opposition to tyranny?

WHY TRUST GORBACHEV'S NATION?*

It seems that the leadership of Mikhail Gorbachev in the Soviet Union poses for us a question that is worth asking over and over again. It has to do with whether the Soviet Union should be trusted by us.

There is little doubt that some governments should not be trusted. In our time this applies to South Africa, for example. A half a century ago Adolf Hitler's regime deserved no trust from any decent person or government. Other examples abound, but these make my point.

At one time many people wanted to trust the Soviet government but they learned from their mistake and became more prudent. There was some confusion on this score during World War II, when Stalin was an ally. But soon thereafter he showed his true colors again, as he did with the Nazi-Soviet pact, and most decent folks refused to trust the Soviet government. A massive policy of human liquidation simply makes this impossible.

Today there seems to be one area where the Soviet government ought to be dealt with. This is in the effort to avoid war, especially nuclear confrontation, without having to sell out one's independence and liberty. This is no compromise but good sense. (The police frequently deal with criminals for far lower stakes.)

In our own time many sophisticated people will claim that any continued suspicion of the Soviets has to be a sign of dogmatism, stubbornness on a large scale. Why distrust a regime that is led by Gorbachev, whom Gore Vidal regards a great statesman? But they are wrong.

The significant fact to keep in mind is that the Soviet Union has a government that is officially and essentially committed to a fulfillment of the ideals of Karl Marx and V. I. Lenin. Between these two giants of communist ideology a fantasy took shape whereby the Soviet government became settled into a role of leading a historical crusade against capitalism and for the collectivization of the entire world!

The main image that communism holds out to mankind is that of an intelligent ant colony, a world populated by human beings who demand nothing for themselves

---

*Originally published in the *Panama City New Herald* (September 6, 1987).

and live only for the whole of humanity. Love no one more than another! Devote yourself to service to humanity, and completely reject your own identity as a person, as an individual!

This is not an entirely unfamilar idea but only Marxism-Leninism has proclaimed it to be a political imperative, something that must be brought about by the leadership of the state—namely, the Soviet state. Every Soviet leader since Lenin has reaffirmed this vision. As such every Soviet leader has committed himself to the abolition of the political ideal that has always—and rightfully—animated the United States, namely individualism. This is not so much an economic but a cultural ideal that stands in the way of communism by its view of human beings as essentially individuals, not members of a collective.

With this basic contrast between the Soviet Union and the United States, it makes absolutely good sense not to trust the Soviet Union. We do well to regard it not as our friend but as deep down our enemy. That does not mean that all the Soviets, let alone Russian people, are mean, vicious liars, gleefully awaiting our demise, plotting our destruction. No, the story is much more complicated.

The Soviet Union is one of the two most powerful countries in the world and is set on a course of world domination. To some extent, its focus is similar to Iran's. The difference is that Iran has a religious mission, while the Soviets pursue a secular destiny. And that, of course, the USSR is far more powerful than Iran.

Iran, too, has pledged to rule the world—but for Iran this is simply a dream, without the means to realize it. The Soviet Union has no such impediments on itself. It is capable of making many moves toward attaining its desired goal, what it takes to be its historical mission. These moves need not all be violent, mean-minded—the Soviets who still believe in Marxism-Leninism are sincere and believe they are doing the right thing. They are puzzled why others disagree with them. They are sad about it. They can talk to us on American television and be completely honest when they say that they mean well and find it terrible that Americans make movies that paint them as bad guys.

But all this is irrelevant. The Mafia is sincere and yet a grave threat to many people. The Soviet government is committed to Marxism-Leninism, even while some no longer may be under the spell of that ideology. This is similar to how the United States government is legally committed to many of the principles of the U.S. Constitution even while some officials pay little attention to this document and the philosophy behind it.

There is every reason to remain suspicious of the USSR, Gorbachev or no Gorbachev. It may be wise to be suspicious, furthermore, of anyone who refuses to see this point!

THE MEANINGS OF FREEDOM IN THE DEBATE OVER NICARAGUA*

In recent debate concerning aid to the Nicaraguan contras, some prominent opponents of the aid argued that it is unfair to suggest that President Reagan's critics do not take freedom to heart. It may be granted that many congressional opponents of Contra aid nonetheless agree that the Sandinistas are a group of thugs, trying to impose their totalitarian ideology on a people who have had enough misfortune in their lives. Unfortunately, there are also many outright supporters of the Sandinistas who see themselves as taking freedom to heart. Some of these are also members of the U.S. government, others prominent journalists and columnists.

Judging by their explicit claims, Sandinista sympathizers tend to believe that these Marxist leaders strive for the freedom and liberation of the Nicaraguan people, by which they mean that they are a progressive force for the economic development and emancipation of the majority of Nicaraguans. Now these opponents of Reagan's stance are arguably taking a kind of freedom to heart, what has come to be called in political theory "positive freedom," one associated with the political thought of totalitarian left-wing or progressive movements, as well as with rightist authoritarian theories.

The kind of freedom that Reagan seems to have in mind is the sort that has come to be designated as "negative freedom." It is one that we enjoy when no government (or, indeed, anyone or any other institution) intrudes upon people and engages in social regimentation and engineering. This is the kind of liberty or freedom that is associated with the American or classical liberal political tradition.

When totalitarian philosophies defend extensive government planning, regimentation, and suppression of dissent, they know better than to do this with outright attacks upon human freedom. But these philosophies have managed also to forge a different idea of freedom, one they are perfectly willing to defend.

This kind of Newspeak is not really as insidious as Orwell himself argued. Rather it reflects the normal complexity of our language in which "freedom" is used in several senses. For example, one can complain of not being free because of some hardship or obstacle. The famous nineteenth-century English political theorist T. H. Green explained that "when we speak of freedom we do not mean merely freedom from restraint or compulsion but a positive power or capacity of doing or enjoying something worth doing." And Karl Marx insisted that "freedom can only consist in socialized men rationally regulating their interchange with Nature, bringing it under common control."

In contrast, of course, we have the similarly familiar idea of freedom by which we mean that we are free when others are not intruding on us, when we are left to our own resources to do things and others are not dictating to us. This idea is identified by F. A. Hayek, the noted classical liberal economist and political theorist, as "always the possibility of a person's acting according to his own decisions and plans, in contrast to the position of ones irrevocably subject to the will of another." This idea is closer to what has distinguished the

---

*Originally published in the *Orange County Register* (October 15, 1986).

American political order from others because it is connected with the doctrine of the human right to liberty, the free economic system, the absence of governmental direction of the press or the arts.

It is wrong to think that only one sense of this word is part of normal human language or thought. One can thus agree that both Reagan as well as his adversaries "take freedom to heart." But the two mean something different by "freedom."

IRAN-CONTRA AND LEFT VERSUS RIGHT*

The Iran-Contra hearings were a kind of moral-political laboratory in which the moral integrity of our political representatives and appointees could be observed and analyzed. Initially, for those of us who have been through the Watergate affair and subsequent hearings, this event was part *déjà vu*. I caught as much of both of the hearings as I could. While the Iran-Contra affair was more complicated, the witnesses were clearly less morally sleazy.

What came through most forcefully in the end, however, is that members of Congress, and their hired inquisitors—e.g., Arthur Liman (Chief Senate Counsel), John Nields (Chief House Counsel), and Mark Belnick (Liman's executive assistant)—were trying desperately to indict, convict, and, most of all, to scold, rather than explore just what went on and why. The central question was rarely discussed: Why would Admiral John Poindexter, Lieutenant Colonel North, and others try to skirt the Boland Amendment (requiring congressional approval for aid to the Contras) and engineer a windfall from a moderate Iran connection so as to be able to continue some steady support for the Contras fighting the Sandinista Marxist-Leninists? Senator Orrin Hatch and Representative Henry Hyde now and then managed to allude to that issue, as did some of the witnesses such as Oliver North, Robert McFarlane, John Poindexter, General Richard Secord, and Fawn Hall, North's secretary. But some high-ranking Reagan administration officials, including secretaries Schultz and Weinberger, tried desperately to divorce themselves from "zealots" in an effort to seem pragmatic and, thus, reasonable in terms of their critics' standards. (Consider their idea that there are no moderate Iranians. This is almost bigotry, and highly implausible, at that, considering that prior to the present Iranian regime the United States had reasonably friendly relations with Iran.) Clearly, most members of the Select Committee successfully dodged the main issue.

As for the "revelations" of the hearings, is it really all that startling when one hears about government officials who are often eager beavers and will use all sorts of technicalities to accomplish ends for which they have no clear and immediate mandate? Representative Hyde showed the hypocrisy of this, as well as how the various pompous members of Congress had no business parading around as if they were paragons of civic virtue. (Did anyone notice, incidentally, how the Select Committee had no women on it—not one! And do we not get all our

---

*Originally published in *Reason* magazine (1987).

affirmative action directives from these socially conscious politicians?) Is it, furthermore, all that strange that Congress's will was being thwarted or at least diverted on behalf of the democratic resistance forces in Nicaragua? The Boland Amendment was a sorry piece of compromise legislation, which was tied to an appropriations bill and was both preceded and followed by congressional edicts that went the opposite way. It is more likely that instead of genuine outrage about lawlessness in the White House, the righteousness on the Hill stemmed from having their will rebuffed, for the Reagan gang not bending to their political agenda!

In the last analysis, the main lesson from the Iran-Contra hearings is that too many of our Capitol Hill representatives have shown themselves to be unbelievably and blatantly hypocritical. They have pretended to be devotees of law and order, something that most of them used to debunk just a couple of decades ago (when antiwar demonstrators, drug law violators, and draft dodgers were regarded by many of them as heroes). I would bet that they will readily debunk the law and order viewpoint again when next their own agenda is served not by the written but by their handy "higher law."

In the early and late 1960s, two main topics occupied the attention of our politically concerned citizenry: civil rights and the Vietnam War. In both cases thousands of people went about violating laws they believed were unjust, some openly inviting prosecution so as to challenge these laws (which is what civil diobedience is about); others simply violating them, at times with all the force they were capable of mustering to that effect. At the time, this attitude was hailed by many at the highest levels of government—including such members of Congress as William Fulbright, George McGovern, and Andrew Young, as well as Attorney General Ramsey Clark. The law was to them anything but sacrosanct. It was man-made and had to answer to the higher law of conscience, which came from a higher source such as Nature or God. In a country born of revolution, in the name of self-evident truths, against fallible human authority, the reference to such higher laws made initial sense.

But it appears that such references are given their due respect by certain members of our highest legislative bodies only when their own agenda happens to be at stake. It was at this point that the Iran-Contra hearings became a pathetic demonstration of hypocrisy.

Why is it that those on the Left of the American political spectrum—including most of those who carried on the inquisition during the recent hearings—find Lieutenant Colonel Oliver North's goals of an anti-Soviet strategic move toward Iran and support for the Contras such anathema? Why is it that they see nothing noble or decent in their crusade, while when fascistic practices or inclinations are being combatted domestically or abroad they are so ready to rise to the defense of law-breakers in the name of the higher duty to fight for what is right? I believe we can get an answer to this when we look at some of the opinions of those who speak openly about why they like the Left far more than the Right, however extreme the ways may be to which the two resort to produce results.

Some time ago, on a segment of William F. Buckley, Jr.'s program "Firing Line" Murray Kempton, the Pulitzer prize-winning columnist, made a remarkable but not very surprising point. He disagreed with those intellectuals—e.g., Susan Sontag, another famous Left-wing New York intellectual—who regard fascism (including Nazism) and communism as equal political evils. Kempton noted that *as a Democrat* he has found communist aims far more admirable than those of the Nazis. This for him gives communism some measure of credit, however evil the methods that are used to achieve those noble aims.

Mr. Kempton's point was made by Victor Navasky, editor of the prominent and widely respected Left-wing magazine the *Nation,* in his famous book *Naming Names,* about the congressional investigation of Hollywood notables concerning their connection with communist organizations. Navasky wrote: "[There is] the profound difference between Marxists, who identified with the weak and spoke the language of social justice, and fascists, who identified with an elite and spoke the language of racism and violence" (*Naming Names,* p. 411). The idea is that not only the means but also the ends of the Nazis were morally evil. They did it all maliciously, while the communists at least had noble aims; they meant well.

I believe that these remarks by two leading Left-wing intellectuals in America help explain some of the ferment surrounding recent controversies, such as how the United States should respond to South Africa's apartheid policies and the protests of American involvement in the Contras' fight against the Sandinistas.

It seems clear that few influential people on the Left agree with Ms. Sontag. They definitely do not see the Soviet Communists and the Nazis as equally evil. Rather, they have learned to look with forgiveness toward the USSR's past brutality against millions, most of whom were "only" profiteering farmers. Making peace with Soviets is a constant theme of the intellectuals in our society. Every word Gorbachev utters these days is scrutinized for hopeful signs, never mind that like every Soviet dictator he has reaffirmed the revolutionary socialist commitment of his government. *Glasnost* is yet another hope that the "Evil Empire" is really a pussycat at heart, mislead in the past by such madmen as Stalin and Brezhnev. (A very sober yet surprising dissent to this is available, however, from Paul Kennedy, in his "What Gorbachev Is Up Against" [*The Atlantic,* June 1987]. See, also David Satter, "Why Glasnost Can't Work," *The New Republic* [June 13, 1988].)

The American left-of-center press and political leadership has always urged that we trust the Soviets, draw up arms agreements with them, talk with them, invite them on space trips, swap scientists and artists with them, etc. Even though the present Soviet regime is actually no more devoted to human liberty than Hitler's would be now, after its initial blatant brutality cleared the scene of serious resistance, gestures of good will toward them are always being urged on our policy makers by the Left wing in our culture. Yet, the Nazis actually murdered fewer persons than the Soviets even during the time they both ruled within their realm.

It is also notable that the millions the Soviets murdered did not generally form a cohesive group: They were mostly just all those who opposed the state. Their identities have become obscure: Most of them, in the end, were merely disparate individuals with some artificial common traits such as being kulaks or profiteers. Thus whereas the charge of genocide makes the Hitlerian Holocaust a tragedy more in line with collectivist thinking, the Holocaust perpetrated by the Soviets, against mere individuals with no pronounced common denominator among them, does not accommodate current collectivist sentiments. Then, of course, the Soviets also turned out to be winners, and nothing succeeds like success.

The efforts of the Sandanistas to sovietize their country and to internationalize socialism, which Marx (in his preface to the Russian edition of *The Communist Manifesto*) declared to be a vital task for Soviet policy, has not yet passed through a capitalist phase of development, but for our left-of-center intellectuals and politicians it really amounts to no more than attempts to bring about justice! They believe this, otherwise they would treat the Nicaraguan government with the same contempt they treat South Africa's, Chile's, and the memory of the Third Reich.

In part this is explainable by the fact that in South Africa, again, we are talking about a problem of a collective group, namely blacks. Apartheid is similar to genocide in that both single out special groups as victims, not individuals. It is today easier to focus one's moral outrage when victims belong to some definite category—blacks, coloreds, women, Jews, etc.—than if they are human individuals who have little else in common other than being opposed to their government's injustices against them. In an age when intellectuals tend to be statists—favoring approaches to solving social problems via the institution of government—there is a kind of acceptance of the fate that befalls those who oppose the state, even if it should be a dictatorial one. Nicaragua's regime is not hated nearly so much as South Africa's or Chile's—nor is Poland's, East Germany's, or the Soviet Union's. *In these states any individual may be victimized, never mind membership in some group.*

This betrays the ideological predilection of the bulk of opinion makers. Any government that has it in for a group is far worse than one that tyrannizes only individuals without any particular group identity. (That most Soviet victims were kulaks, of course, counts against them in another way: They were entrepreneurs whose death may be too harsh a punishment, but who clearly don't deserve much sympathy from properly sensitive persons! The motive of personal profit simply has not gained the respect it deserves, even from the people who like free enterprise!)

What about this preference for communism over Nazism? Why won't even the Left-wing of the U.S. Congress be as sympathetic to those eager to stem communist progress as they are to those who would thwart fascism and racism? Are Kempton and Navasky right? Did the Nazis do it from obviously far more evil motives, obviously more evil purposes? For that is what seems to make the difference.

George Watson recently explained, in the British magazine *Encounter,* that Adolf Hitler was familiar with Marx's works and there is reason to believe that he wanted to do what Stalin aimed for but in a different way. Goebbels, Hitler's ideological guru, wrote in 1920 *(The Second Revolution),* that the good Nazi "looks towards Russia, because Russia is that country most likely to take the road to socialism with us; because Russia is an ally nature has given us against the devilish temptations and corruptions of the West" (p. 147). Hitler himself said once that "There is more that binds us to Bolshevism than separates us from it. . . ." (*Hitler Speaks,* p. 134).

But there is more to the similarity between Nazism and communism than

Hitler's or Goebbels's testimony or the plain fact that fascists are often military dictators no less than communists—e.g., Poland and Chile! One might, after all, discount all that as mere strategy. And even if we disregard Marx's explicit hatred of Jews—he regarded them as the paradigm captialists—and his overt racism— in which he followed that primitive materialist biology of the Frenchman Pierre Tremaux, who regarded Slavs and Negroes "a degeneration of a much higher" type of human being (*The Letters of Karl Marx,* p. 215)—there are still vital philosophical similarities between Nazism and communism.

What Kempton and Navasky do not appear to consider is that there is a version of Nazism that can be made to sound just as appealing as the version of communism they think of when giving their reasons for their small sympathies with the Soviets. That is what explains, in part, why some very prominent people, such as Ezra Pound, found the fascist idea quite appealing. The idea harks back to Sparta and the general notion that humanity needs to be both physically and spiritually perfected.

Consider that one of the central motivations behind Nazism—as well as Mussolini's and the facism of others—was the unity of all of German culture, the creation out of its disarray of a *whole* community. Many Germans turned away from communism, which, at the time Nazism began to grow, had been a live option in Germany, because communists preached class warfare or divisiveness. Germans found it violent and preferred, instead, Hitler's call for unity, *Einheit.* To many Germans Nazism was the proverbial lesser of two evils, yet with a tinge of nobility attached to its ideals.

Even when we consider Nazism's unabashed racism, could we not see it in a light that gives it some attraction comparable to what communism held out for most people? We could, if we consider that many people have an idealistic preference for healthy specimans of humans and detest the slovenly kind among us—e.g., the fanatics about health food, antismoking, physical fitness, etc.

As for communism, it holds out the promise of total human harmony for sometime in the future. It is supposed to eliminate extravagant wastefulness in the presence of great need throughout the world. It champions the laboring masses; it calls upon charitable feelings and altruism, to which most people can respond. What can Nazism show for itself that is comparable?

It envisions, by way of its Aryan ideology, a human race that has been bred into nobility and thus freed of folly, plain and simple. The purity of the race is a means to an end that many can appreciate and have regarded as highly desirable.

In general, the vision of human community life that prefers the dominance of healthy people—good human specimens—is not unpalatable. The Aryans offered no more than that to many people as a vision to consider for the future of humankind. As an afterthought, they regarded the Jews, the Slavs, the Gypsies, and the rest as defiling elements, just as Karl Marx did! They wanted their environment to be free of such pollution, not unlike the communists who also painted an appealing picture and invited us all to pursue it diligently. It is not at all evident that these motives are so drastically dissimilar as some would like us to believe. All of this is vile stuff, when soberly considered, but it is also the stuff of which many communes, religious orders, political crusades, and other human experiences are forged—enthusiastically and without any moral apology.

If one wishes to be generous, one can be generous with both the communists and the Nazis. The communists and the fascists both want a trouble-free world. They count upon our willingness to fantasize such a world. And then when we have mesmerized ourselves into thinking that it is really a possibility, provided we are dedicated and determined enough, then they both ask us to perform the mass murders, genocides, exterminations, and liquidations that turn out to be *necessary* for ushering in such a preferred utopian ideal.

In the end, of course, neither communism nor Nazism presents a genuinely morally appealing ideal to any thoughtful human being. Such contrived and purified versions of society are necessarily totalitarian and cut deep into the most significant feature of human life, namely, the individual distinctiveness of every person, everyone's sovereignty as a moral being. In contrast to this vision, which has largely animated Western liberalism for the last two centuries, fascists and communists impose on us a model of human community life that liquidates the human individual!

Marx viewed humankind an "organic body." Lenin and Stalin tried to implement this notion by the only method it has a chance of being implemented, massive force and the liquidation of all opposition and dissent. The Soviets are still following their footsteps, even if in a more sophisticated fashion now. Hitler's philosophical leaders envisioned *Das Volk* or the united people as their ideal. Both camps aimed at a grand reduction of human diversity to uniformity. And it is clear that such a dream would really be a nightmare, since it would rob us of one of the most inspiring and edifying characteristics, namely, our infinitely diverse individuality.

Murray Kempton, Victor Navasky, and their ideological fellows are wrong. Susan Sontag, however, was right when she explained that "Communism is successful fascism." The only relevant difference between the two systems is that the former was temporarily defeated, while the latter still flourishes, unfortunately with the aid of some contemporary American intellectuals. The Iran-Contra hearings were in part a demonstration of the evasion of this fact, even in a country that offers the only reasonable and moral alternative today to totalitarianism, the United States of America.

GORBACHEV, PINOCHET, AND AMERICAN INTELLECTUALS*

Some would claim that as a naturalized American who escaped from Socialist Hungary back in 1953, I am prejudiced. That is why I find it curious how Western intellectuals, including academicians and members of the media, react differently

---

*Originally published in the *Orange County Register*.

to developments in the Soviet Union than to those in Chile. The short of it is that they are very easy on the Soviet ruler and very hard on the Chilean ruler.

I don't think I am prejudiced. One need only read the daily press, watch network and public television news, and read some magazines such as the *New Republic* and the *New York Review of Books* to notice that I am right.

General Secretary (and now also President) Gorbachev's policies are thought of in these circles as major breakthroughs, departures from the previous (Brezhnev) era. They are deemed to hold out great promise for the people of the Soviet Union, if only they can succeed. Glasnost (openness) and perestroika (reconstruction) are widely hailed by commentators and pundits as major moves to advance the Soviet Union toward a better society. There are some skeptics, of course. David Satter (in the *New Republic*) doubts that glasnost can work. But on the whole, writers in the *Nation,* the *New Yorker,* and in other prominent publications that are taken seriously in intellectual and academic circles express basic respect for Mikhail Gorbachev's intentions and efforts.

In contrast, there is no one who likes General Agosto Pinochet. What has he done? While he has been a ruthless opponent of political freedom in Chile for almost as long as he has been in power, in 1980 he helped forge a new constitution for that country, one that paves the way to full-scale political democracy. We have just witnessed one major result of this constitutional reform—an initial election in Chile deciding whether Pinochet may serve for another full term or whether he has to step down within a year after his term expires. It looks like the general intends to abide by the latter outcome. In March 1990, elections will be held to decide who will govern Chile. Pinochet has also established the kind of economy in Chile that has led to greater prosperity than in any other Central and Latin American country. (Even if one merely looks at the recently televised pictures of those first demonstrating and later celebrating, one notices how prosperous the people are—the very people who oppose Pinochet's rule!) While Chile, as all nations with a relatively free market, has pockets of poverty, all in all the country has had lower inflation and higher employment than all its neighbors south of our borders.

We clearly do not know what Pinochet will do. He still has the power, and the constitution that gives it to him is far from expressing the will of even the majority of the people and protecting the rights of the minority. Pinochet is a military dictator, there is no doubt about that.

What do we know about Gorbachev? He has certainly proposed no change in the Soviet constitution. This document explicitly prohibits anyone in the Soviet Union from criticizing the Soviet government. Has Gorbachev advocated changing the nature of Soviet society? He simply regards some earlier policies as following from "distortions of socialism." He has no desire, judging by his words, to abandon Lenin's "genuine socialism." What this means is that the means of production in the Soviet Union will continue to be collectively owned and thus exposed to government regimentation. Perestroika may lead the state to relax its regime but certainly not to abdicate its role as ultimate sovereign. (If one recalls that in Marxist socialist theory the major means of production is human labor, Gorbachev is unambiguously committed to treating Soviet citizens as mere cells in the body of the whole, the Soviet Union.) Nor should it be lost sight of that Gorbachev was an enthusiastic follower of Brezhnev. His role in the KGB cannot be ignored either as we appraise him in comparison to other rulers of unfree societies.

Of course, Pinochet's partial embracing of capitalism—via his Chicago University trained finance minister, Hernan Buchi—does not mean that Chile enjoys a free marketplace with everyone's private property rights fully acknowledged and respected. Yet at least Pinochet seems to be bent on heading toward that kind of a system, one that sees the individual, not the state, as sovereign.

Why then are American intellectuals so contemptuous toward Pinochet but not at all very critical, indeed quite welcoming, of Gorbachev? Why would a Gore Vidal, for example, praise the Soviet leader so highly, calling one of his speeches the most profound political talk he has ever encountered (and Vidal is the author of the novel *Lincoln*!)?

I submit that many American intellectuals have been hoodwinked into thinking that regimenting society in the socialist way is a fine thing. Doing so by way of an authoritarian, right-wing military dictatorship is inexcusable. This is even so when the people who live in the latter system are happier and freer!

And I think this is a tragic mistake, one that is leading this country toward policies that will eventually culminate in economic disasters of the sort Soviet bloc and other Marxist-leaning countries are experiencing. The comparison between our attitudes toward Pinochet and Gorbachev can alert us to this folly and might even help to guide us to remedy matters, by reconsidering the merits of the socialist alternative. Gorbachev's rule of the Soviet Union deserves as much disdain as Pinochet's rule over Chile. And since Pinochet looks like he is actually willing to relent, he should be applauded much more vigorously than Gorbachev. That would be a gesture of justice, if gestures are to be made at all.

OUR SOUTH AMERICAN POLICY EXPOSES DOUBLE STANDARD IN TREATMENT OF TYRANNIES*

Need one say it again? South Africa's apartheid policy is immoral and practically renders that political system illegitimate. This point is supposed to be clear-cut enough for any U.S. citizen. A country that declared that each individual is created equal and endowed with unalienable rights to life, liberty, and the pursuit of happiness surely need not be told over and over again how wrong it is to treat some people in a society as if they were the natural servants of the rest.

However, what does seem to require constant reiteration to Americans is that South Africa's apartheid policy is actually just one of many forms of political violence suffered by people across the globe. Still it is singled out for special attention by America's liberal intellectuals and politicians. The fact is that not only do we find gross abuses of individual human rights in China, the USSR,

*Originally published in the *Orange County Register* (August 11, 1988).

Romania, Angola, Cuba, Chile, etc., but also in black African countries—e.g., Burundi or Zaire—when members of certain tribes who have attained political power are subjugating the members of other tribes out of power (often the majority of the country). Clearly blacks are tyrannizing blacks but our liberal moralizers take no notice at all.

Instead, South Africa is described by some members of the U.S. Congress as "the worst terrorist state in the world." These mostly black political leaders wish to discredit even Jonas Savimbi's opposition to Angola's brutal Marxist government because South Africa supports the organization led by Savimbi, UNITA. In trade and other cultural connections these persons and their liberal intellectual apologists scream for restrictions against South Africa. Never mind that even some black refugees—e.g., middle distance runner Sydney Maree—from that racist state recognize that certain forms of ostracism are useless, even harmful to the cause of racial justice. As Maree reportedly noted, "If white South Africans were exposed internationally, they would better see how people respect each other and interact with different races."

But there is great opposition to so handling South Africans, including their athletes. The London-based South African Non-Racial Olympic Committee (Sanroc) campaigned vigilantly to bar the young runner, Zola Budd, from any competition. Sanroc is critical of Maree for his returning to South African and running clinics for mixed racial groups. But as Maree has perceptively noted, "If we can play with the Soviet Union, we can play with South Africa, and still isolate where necessary." Yet that is just the sort of idea that American liberal intellectuals despise.

What lies at the heart of their opposition to treating the dictatorial Soviet Union the same way as they want to have racist South Africa treated? Why do they support the extension of cultural exchange, commerce, etc., in the one case but not the other?

My hypothesis is that these people are motivated by a combination of factors. For one, they think any further involvement of America with racism threatens to call into question our firm resolve against it in our own historically tainted society. Then they also find it easier to moralize about injustice against some distinct group of persons—blacks, Jews, Mexican-Americans, gays—than about injustice against "mere" individuals, however many of these there are (e.g., in the Soviet Union). American liberal intellectuals are collectivists and not individualists. They even skirt racism in these matters. If mere individuals experience injustice, that is not so bad as injustice experienced by some distinct group.

Finally, there is also the fact that many American liberals and their intellectual leaders sympathize with the objectives spouted by the Soviets and other leftist tyrannies. They merely disapprove of some of the methods employed to reach them.

As we saw before, one famous American liberal, Victor Navasky, the editor of the *Nation,* has said that "[There is] the profound difference between Marxists, who identified with the weak and spoke the language of social justice, and fascists, who identified with an elite and spoke the language of racism and violence" [*Naming Names,* p. 411]. Most liberals share this view and so are much more tolerant of Marxist-oriented, leftist tyrannies than of those regimes that use some other ideology to rationalize their brutality toward people.

Yet, this is a wholly misplaced alliance. Marxist-Leninists are no kinder to people than are fascists, racists, theocratic dictators, or any other version of tyrants. True, one can portray any viewpoint in a relative benign light. There are apologists for apartheid who speak as if all they had in mind is the best interest of blacks! And the defenders of Chilean military dictator Pinochet point to all kinds of fine results that that dictator's economic policies have produced.

The plain fact, however, is that tyrannies are inexcusable by any ideology, leftist or rightist. The question as to how to treat them should be divorced entirely from whether certain of the goals they promote have merit.

South Africa should be treated as any other morally and politically repugnant state—justly, as the system and its leaders deserve. And if some policy— e.g., cultural, sports, or scientific exchange—is appropriate in one case, it should be deemed just as appropriate in another where the moral and political transgressions are of equal weight. It is sheer hypocrisy to proceed in any other way and indeed, doing so jeopardizes the credibility of one's moral outrage at the unjust system. It makes it appear, rather, as an expression of some kind of psychological need, not an objective judgment of disapproval.

DON'T CLOSE THE DOOR*

Amid all the debate about illegal aliens and how to punish those who hire them, we have failed to develop a principled approach to immigration in general, based on the idea of a free society. This approach should be based on the idea that, outside of matters of national security, no limit should be placed on immigration for those wishing to make a new life here.

One could think me biased, since I am a refugee from Communist Hungary, perhaps just clearing my own conscience for "invading" these shores. But there are very good reasons, consistent with the American political tradition, for not barring people from making their living in a free society if they so choose. And there are very good reasons for pardoning all those who entered "illegally"— that is, in violation of an unjust law barring them from entering a supposedly free country—and for abandoning the revolting idea of punishing the American employers who make a living possible for such immigrants. It is wholly unbecoming of a society whose gateway is the Statue of Liberty to follow anything other than an open-door policy.

The major objections to such a policy have been forcefully stated. Foreign workers will displace native workers, add to an already overburdened welfare state, exhaust the patience of our taxpayers and accelerate the degradation of the environment. Finally, it is argued, it would be morally wrong to pardon illegal

---

*Originally published in the *New York Times* (August 2, 1984).

immigrants when legal immigrants were subject to severe restriction and told to wait their turn.

These arguments carry great appeal across the country, but they aren't good enough to support abandoning one of America's most important historical missions and the fundamental principle of liberty. Government was established not to secure our right to a certain standard of living, but to secure our right to liberty.

Recent studies have challenged the assumption that immigrants threaten American living standards. But even if the "threat" to American employment exists, it should not be repelled at the expense of liberty. In a free, competitive society one has no more right to one's job or level of income that an athlete has to keeping "his" world record. And isn't there something obscene about complaining about a temporary setback in one's standard of living when those who would compete with (not rob) us are fighting for bare subsistence?

As to immigrants going on welfare, many who come to this country are probably in need and would turn for help to our many government and public service institutions. But here, too, the matter does not end with the figures alone. If it is indeed morally proper to accommodate the needy, shouldn't all persons benefit from such moral convictions? Restricting humanitarianism to Americans is certainly a phony moralism.

As to the overpopulation issue, the morally acceptable way to cope with it is to seek out new frontiers, including new solutions to old problems—yes, even outer space. For that, no greater resource exists than the talents of the most eager people of the world, those who want to make a real change in their lives. No other groups fit that description so well as immigrants, who by definition are people who are willing to assume risks so as to bring about a brighter future.

Finally, the matter of pardoning illegal aliens should be thought of as righting a mistaken policy. It should not be difficult to understand once we appreciate the principles at stake here. We complain about other nations—the Soviet Union, for example—closing their doors to those who wish to leave. But this is a hollow complaint if we, in turn, close our doors to those who wish to enter with good will and the determination to do well in life. How could they help but be an asset to our society?

5

Politics

TO REDUCE STATE POWER, TAKE AWAY ITS PROPERTY

America's distinction has been its official declaration that a society of free individuals is preferable to other kinds. Individualism has meant just that. Capitalism is a side effect, and so is the tremendous progress in science, technology, the arts, and education.

Other societies have clung to statism and have even influenced American culture to return to many statist ways. But, although America betrayed its libertarian ideals with slavery and other public policies—e.g. military conscription, taxation, local and federal controls on personal and professional conduct—it has been far and away the most libertarian society in this world. This distinction is in danger of being abandoned.

For about fifty years Americans have gradually expanded the scope of the state. Democrats have turned to government to improve people's welfare and created the massive economic welfare state. Republicans turned to government to improve people's souls, creating a massive spiritual welfare state.

What is happening is almost inevitable. People want medical aid, Social Security, farm subsidies, professional licensing, public parks, public education, federal insurance of their savings, safety and health regulation, drug-abuse prevention, control of prostitution and pornography and pollution. They vote for politicians who promise legislation. Laws are enacted and government's power grows.

Recently the state has increased its concern about drivers' safety, and some states have enacted mandatory seatbelt laws. Of course, there is a point. Buckling up is safer for most of us.

But the roads are run by governments, so how can one protest this move toward even greater police supervision? Spot checks will be instituted and police

---

*Originally published in the *Orange County Register* (May 31, 1985).

97

will be empowered to check us out in our cars. Safety has been determined to be very important, so individual liberty is squashed.

One might respond that the state must regulate our conduct on government property. So of course the state should make rules for the road. But the scope of where government runs things is increasing by leaps and bounds.

Several municipalities have enacted ordinances requiring restaurants to set aside sections for nonsmokers. Smoking is a nuisance and often a health hazard, but why not leave this to the discretion of restaurant owners and customers? One argument is that since restaurants use public streets, they are not really private. And this is partly right.

Yet everything we do is tied in some way to public areas. Newspapers and magazines are usually sold on the street, delivered on roads, mailed through the Postal Service. Does that mean public officials should have power to determine what they contain, to assure that there are no journalistic indiscretions?

It is time to roll back the state. We need to privatize as much of society as possible. We need to begin to retake the property that government has acquired, expropriated, arrogated to itself. Since government ownership confers government authority, it is necessary to reduce it.

Whenever possible, parks, buildings, lakes, rivers, highways, organizations, libraries, and museums should be taken from government and placed in the hands of private citizens and groups. If we divest government of its property, we will have divested it of much power—and restored, little by little, the liberty and responsibility of individuals.

This won't mean that everything will be solved, but the promise that governmental expansion will solve our problems has been a lie all along. Where they have tried it, in the Soviet Union and China, it has failed.

The Eastern European countries are now flirting again with the idea of a free market. Dictatorships in Africa, Southeast Asia, and Latin America do not work. Freedom is not only morally appropriate, but more practical and efficient for the attainment of what human beings want in life.

TOWARD TRUE RADICALISM*

It is a widespread belief in America that the free enterprise system of economics is a relic from the past, an old-fashioned idea that might have worked in the real world at one time, for a little while, but must now be considered ancient history. This view is not only believed but taught in high schools and colleges across the country. Especially obvious is the popularity of the position when we hear or read discussions about the economic systems of developing countries in Africa, for example.

Actually, free enterprise is still the most novel and radical economic theory humans have developed and offered one another. All other economic systems,

*Originally published in the *Orange County Register* (circa 1969).

including socialism, communism, the welfare state of mixed economics (Keynesianism), and others have been with us for much longer than laissez-faire economics. Adam Smith, despite all his mistakes (e.g., his labor theory of value), is still the most radical economic thinker in history; even later free-enterprise economists, like members of the famous Austrian school, have merely modified and improved on Smith's views.

Smith's central contention was that if we leave men free to produce and exchange goods and services, society will enjoy optimal economic conditions. In other words, remove central planning from the marketplace, leave business alone, and you will have the optimum production, distribution, and consumption. No other economic theorist has yet proposed a more rational and more radical solution to the problem of how to produce, exchange, and distribute goods in the most efficient and just manner among human beings.

Yet today this view is considered old-fashioned, while far more archaic views, like those of Marx and Keynes, are thought to be major breakthroughs in economic theory. Actually, mercantilism, feudalism, and all forms of centralized planning, which were the essence of economics prior to American and British capitalism, are just varieties of socialism and Keynesianism. They all endorse the governing of some people's productive and trading activities by others—rulers of one kind or another. Kings and their helpers, feudal lords and pharaohs have always ruled over the economic activities of their underlings. The use of duties and tariffs is far more ancient than free trade among different peoples.

The important thing to learn from this delusion concerning the novelty of various economic theories is that radicalism is far more subtle than we think. Varieties of ancient rituals and practices often appear to be new and radically different, yet, in fact, are older than what they supersede at the moment. So when various solutions in contemporary society are proposed, solutions that are close to ideas popular since the eighteenth or nineteenth centuries, we must not jump to the conclusion that these proposals are either outmoded or bad. Our prejudice in favor of that which appears to be modern should not deceive us into accepting a mere new polish on ancient dogma for the radical new theory its proponents claim it to be.

Socialism is rule by force of arms applied to people's economic activities, nothing else. Modern welfare-state economics is a feeble attempt to have it both ways: a bit of force and a bit of freedom, mixed well so that we can't tell when we are being forced to act in certain ways and when what we do has been freely chosen. Even today freedom is still the only truly radical idea.

LIBERTY STEP BY STEP*

Libertarianism is, among other things, a life-supporting political theory. Its aim is to help advance life, not to defeat it. It is thus genuinely progressive, unlike

---

*Originally published in the *Libertarian Party News* (Autumn 1986).

communism, which talks of the impossible progress of the collective whole of humanity, all at once.

Progress requires taking steps to bring about a better state of affairs, to improve the existing conditions of life. It requires, in short, incremental steps, going from condition A to condition B, and the rest, until one gets to whatever is the most clearly conceived and best alternative.

The temptation here is to say, "Well, this is right but it implies for libertarians that we must do nothing other than try to convince others of the correctness of our view." This idea reminds me of the view that there can be no cure of an illness other than one that instantaneously leads the patient from illness to full-blown health. Unless the doctor's measures accomplishes this result, it betrays the profession of medicine.

Similarly, to move from ignorance to the state of "learnedness" requires taking steps, but these steps do not achieve the end result in one instance. Rather, from ignorance one moves to various stages of partial education, until one reaches the optimum stage. To some, however, libertarian gradualism is acceptable only if it is not tinged with the evil of statism, a position that would rule out such things as educational vouchers. What is permissible, in this view, is only to try to persuade people, which admittedly must take time and go through stages of relative success. But any actual acceptance of partial measures is said to involve betrayal. Let us move on to some hard cases.

When Ed Clark ran (in 1980) as the Libertarian Party candidate for president of the United States, he proposed certain tax reforms. Libertarianism regards taxation of any kind as morally and politically impermissible. (I assume there is no debate about this!) Was, then, Ed Clark betraying libertarianism?

Consider the doctor who knows that his patient would be optimally healthy only if the patient stopped his addiction to heroin cold turkey. But the doctor is also aware that his patient is hooked and is psychologically unable to kick his habit fully. If, however, he first undergoes a methadone program, the chap can advance to a stage from which the further advance toward kicking his drug dependency is more likely, albeit not guaranteed. Would the doctor betray his profession by recommending this course of conduct? It is clear that he is not at this moment recommending the full attainment of an idea of optimal state, but it is also clear that he is doing the right thing. So may indeed have Ed Clark in proposing tax reform!

The basic reason for this is that morality is always constrained by the principle that "ought implies can." Whenever one says that "A should do X," this could only be true if A can do X. Recommending a partial measure that is the optimal means for reaching closer to the fullest realization of one's standards or principles is itself fully justified by those same standards or principles.

Consider another, perhaps more apt analogy. A police officer is fighting crimes perpetrated upon real victims. Our officer is conscientiously striving to do her duty but it turns out that in order to catch a tax collector gone bad, she must cooperate with a pickpocket who, though himself a thief, is in fact far less menacing than our private tax collector. Without this measure, the defender of private property will only be able to remove the pickpocket from our midst, but by cooperating she can catch the more menacing criminal, without necessarily condoning the pickpocket but merely postponing her efforts to deal with him. Are we to say that our peace officer is betraying her principles? I don't think so.

Here emerges an important principle of libertarian revolutionary ethics. It is clear that such ethics must be consistent with a central ingredient of libertarianism itself, namely, that it is essentially a life-supporting political theory. Self-sacrifice cannot be required in such a political theory, nor can practical policy proposals include self-sacrificial measures. The libertarian ethic of political change, including its revolutionary ethics, preclude those measures that are self-sacrificial.

Let me emphasize that none of the above condones the policy of betraying principles to advance narrow self- or vested interests. If a libertarian cooperates with the statist for purposes of gaining a better salary or obtaining a position in a better climate—to give some clear cases of narrow self-interest—or merely to advance his standing in the organization—a case of promoting vested interest—then he is clearly betraying principles. Let me offer a case in point.

Governments distribute a lot of money these days, and it is very tempting to go along with the game and dip into the coffers just because there is nothing much one can do to combat the policy. After all, when governments distribute wealth, some of that wealth belongs to the people to whom it may well be distributed, so it might be argued that it is just getting even to get some of it from the state.

If there is a gang of burglars in a community, and the citizens have no legal authority to retaliate against it, the gang occasionally may well give some of its loot away; but though it might be sufficient to know that the goods do not belong to the gang in the first place and some of it belongs to the citizens, in order to justify those in the community standing in line with their hands out, there is the added dimension that these citizens have an obligation to fight the gang. Unless the community uses this measure for combatting the gang, taking the loot may well be a betrayal of its belief in property rights because it contributes to the legitimation of the process in which the gang is engaging.

Similarly, if someone takes a handout from the state but uses it to help destroy the very process that makes giving handouts possible, there is nothing necessarily wrong with what the person is doing. But if it merely serves to enhance some other goal, including his narrow self or vested interest, then, in light of his obligation to promote justice, what he is doing is wrong.

Now, finally, if it is believed that I have not managed to come up with a very precise criterion for distinguishing justified from unjustified cooperation with the state, let me plead guilty. The simple fact is that when one must carry forth with dignity and decency in highly complex, morally muddied situation, then discretion is indispensable and no reliance on firm, stable rules is possible. No libertarian can escape from the requirement of clear thinking, which involves invoking very general principles to highly diverse, unanticipated concrete contexts. In short, no codebook of revolutionary conduct can be written. But neither is it the case that anything goes.

One need not become a Leninist and abandon moral considerations in fighting the good fight. But the good fight cannot be fought if we insist on living by arid rules, the implementation of which already presupposes that the freedom revolution has been successfully won.

SEEING LIBERTY'S BENEVOLENCE*

I recently spoke with one of England's widely respected philosophers. We discussed, as might be expected, political philosophy. Learning of my views, this distinguished thinker pressed me on just how far I would take my position that in the general community the principles of voluntary association, respect for private property, and prohibition of forced labor should all be upheld. "Surely," I was asked, "you wouldn't go so far as to condemn the British National Health Service? Surely you would admit that regarding essential medical services there is no room for a free market—which is to say, for leaving everyone, rich and poor alike, to fend for himself?"

I am not some knee-jerk altruist, nor do I find it psychologically troublesome to stand in opposition to what prominent members of my profession believe, yet I didn't simply say, "Of course, I favor the free market in any productive endeavor, even if the service involved is medicine." For one, the individual I spoke with really wasn't familiar with such a radical viewpoint, and considered it to be callous and cruel, almost a feeble wish to turn back the clock to, say, slavery or serfdom. When facing such an individual, and when I know exactly how I will be understood, I shy from reckless bluntness. The free market suffers from a very bad reputation because it is often presented out of context, with little explanation. People cannot be expected these days to know its nuances and intricacies. I got out of the discussion somehow, without having to breach my integrity, yet without making it appear that those who prize freedom suffer from congenital callousness. In retrospect I figured out what I should have said.

Without question, some socialist programs produce desirable consequences. That's the first thing to admit. To cling to the silly idea that all of one adversary's ideas are mistaken would be stubborn and dogmatic, not to mention erroneous. But it is surely absurd to believe that nothing good could come from generally bad policies. Who could deny that sometimes doctors serving with the National Health Service do help out some of their patients? Even the U.S. Postal Service gets the mail around reliably enough most of the time. When looked at on a case-by-case basis, government-supplied goods and services can benefit quite a few people, and I don't just mean by way of giving jobs to ambitious bureaucrats. In the absence of any better alternative, it can look positively horrid to insist that these services should be abolished. And in the absence of ideas showing clearly that such alternatives and better systems are possible without sacrificing liberty, it is no wonder that abolitionists are viewed with moral suspicion.

Even in the case of slavery, abolition may be somewhat sudden. Slaves, being

---

*Originally published in *Individual Liberty* (May 1982).

human beings, would readily fend for themselves when set free. Yet even here there can be exceptions. (Some may have been made so inept in slavery that being set free may at first be disruptive.) In the case of specialized service such as mail or medicine, the situation begs for some explanation. Abolishing the government-run mail service, which appears to rely on taxation and legal power to reach numerous parts of the country, will do a great deal of damage unless an efficient substitution is found. Similarly, in a country where millions of people depend entirely on government-supplied health care, abolition of the service without clear ideas as to what will take its place is irresponsible. The point is that unless one theoretical foundation is supplied and promulgated for the view that in freedom human beings can and indeed will do much better than they can and will in totalitarian or even welfare systems, advocacy of abolition is irresponsible.

Of course without the welfare system innumerable alternatives would arise to substitute for the services now supplied by the government. Health insurance systems, loan services for medical expenses, even voluntary charities to take care of the destitute, can all make their way into a free society once we crush the illusion that government has found some infallible, costless, harmless means by which to render the services.

The real question is never whether something should be done by tomorrow morning at 9 A.M. When something is impossible to do in a certain way, to suppose that doing it that way would be the ideal is plainly silly and destructive; it misdirects attention from real to silly concerns. The real question is whether social policy, law, and popular opinion should be directed toward enhancing the free society as opposed to thwarting it. And on that issue the answer should be clear.

Some months ago I visited a childhood pal who now lives in Montreal. I hadn't seen him for thirty years but learned he had left Hungary and moved to Canada. I kept checking the phone books whenever I visited Canadian cities, and one time I found him. After a joyful reunion, I met his two children: One was a young girl of eleven, then in elementary school and doing rather poorly, I was told. Having learned of my profession as a college teacher, my old friend asked what I had to suggest about the girl's poor performance. I said I had no such expertise but perhaps asking her would give some clues. I asked the daughter why she didn't study and she said that she wasn't interested. I asked whether she had any concern about finding something of interest, so later on she could be prepared to live reasonably well. And then the entirely unexpected answer popped out of this child. "But why should I worry about this? The government will take care of me."

When a society has geared itself to live on welfare, when institution after institution has been linked to the government, even the most mediocre performance on the part of the state can appear to be indispensable, in the absence of clear ideas on how to abolish it and to provide a better substitute. The free society often appears to its critics as a negative idea. It does so because it stresses the value of leaving people free, removing obstacles, and offering protection against intrusions. But this is only the political portion of the free society. One needs to pay close attention to the enormous creative energy that removing the shackles of government will release.

THE SLEEZE FACTOR IS INHERENT IN THE WELFARE STATE*

When I hear about the "sleeze factor" I choose to become deaf; it is such a phony issue. It is not that government officials are all upstanding people or that every government worker upholds the several virtues we know characterize a decent human being. It is rare that ordinary people should do this: Most of us tend to get caught in dishonesty, disloyalty, cowardice, intemperance, injustice, and other vices now and then. But when it comes to talking about ethics in government, we have to ask ourselves whether the structure of government is conducive to ethics in the first place. And the answer here is clearly no.

How could a government be conducive to ethical conduct when its main business is stealing from some people to support the projects of others? How could a government be just when it treats one class of people, those in religion and publishing, as free to govern themselves—to follow or not to follow its own professional standards—but other classes such as doctors, business people, and financial advisers as in need of extensive supervision and regimentation? How could a government be ethical when it sets one set of standards for bureaucrats (appointed officials) and another for politicians (elected officials)?

But the main farce about ethics in government is that those in it wish to have it both ways: They want to impose ethics on everyone but run the government by explicitly unethical standards.

The welfare state is explicitly committed to robbing Peter to help Paul in getting what Paul wants, thus preventing Peter from doing what he wants to do. If people are forced to pay for projects they don't want, this is usually called "extortion"—except where government finance is concerned. If I financed my own restaurant with such methods, I would soon end up in jail. But every year the thousands of levels and bodies of government engage in just such extortion. They levy taxes on gasoline, cigarettes, food, furniture, and other commodities and services to consumers, to finance projects they deem worthy. They pay no attention to the idea that private property may be taken from people for "public" purposes. They have managed to obscure the idea of "public purpose" by translating it as "whatever anyone who is a member of the public wants and can get politicians to enact as law!" That is not a public project but a private project masquerading as "public purpose." And billions of dollars are spent by politicians on just such private projects—with monies stolen from private individuals.

Now how could any of this go on in a climate of ethical purity? All these "Mickey Mouse laws," as Lyn Nofziger so aptly called them, make no sense at all. After leaving service an appointed official may not return to government for a year to help secure some goody the government is dishing out to the people as a way to keep everyone on the dole and make the system work! (Never mind that Congress is not bound by such laws. How could it be? How could such a law be enforceable? And how could law enforcement remain clean if the detec-

---

*Originally published in the *Orange County Register* (September 11, 1988).

tion of such "crimes" must involve a multitude of undercover operations, betrayals, and the like?)

The welfare state is the cause of the "sleeze factor." It is only a question of how clever one can be: working with the system or going astray of its many phony rules that aim at creating a facade of decency. The bulk of our laws are clearly immoral, unethical; they have created a leviathan, a behemoth of an extortion gang.

If there is any place left for ethics in government, it could only be among thieves and other criminals: the ethics of fairness, the ethics whereby the tyrants make sure that all of those doing the extorting are equally well rewarded and no one gets an extra advantage. This is what all the sleeze factor is about, nothing more.

Since the Democrats love the welfare state far more than the Republicans, it is no surprise they are cleverer at manipulating its rules. It is no wonder that they can navigate its laws, making it possible for them to pretend that they are decent, while engaging in actions for which ordinary men and women would have to spend decades in jail if they were caught.

Only if the government is put in its place—if it is willing to reduce the public sector to that of defending individual rights, nothing more—will there ever be bona fide ethics in government. Until that time we will be witness to varieties of smoothness and roughness exhibited by members of our various governmental bodies as they skirt, maneuver, and often trip up on all the rules they have made up to hide their basically immoral (and what should be criminal) activities associated with the distributive welfare state.

ADIEU REAGANISM
Consensus-minded President Bush Abandons Principle of Politics*

Ronald Reagan's main appeal to me was his constant use of ideological language—just what so many in Washington, including members of his party, found so annoying about him. Although Reagan didn't follow through on much of his rhetoric and often betrayed it—e.g., when he accepted the distinctly anti-libertarian agenda of social conservatism—at least he kept the terms of individual liberty, limited government, anti-totalitarianism, free trade, and privatization within the vocabulary of contemporary public policy.

I am afraid that President George Bush will fall far short of Reagan's modest accomplishment.

We heard only a peep during Bush's presidential campaign that could remind us of the Reagan rhetoric of individual freedom. That was the famous "thousand points of light." Even this was but a metaphor, betraying considerable shyness about the substance that undergirds it, namely, the doctrine of limited

---

*Originally published in the *Orange County Register* (April 9, 1989)

government and the responsibility of the private sector to solve the bulk of society's problems. (And there again, why not 200 million points of light?)

By the time Bush reached Washington and went public on Capitol Hill with his first major speech as president, all the legacy of the Reagan rhetoric was gone. The departure was duly noted by all commentators when Bush announced that except for the problem we face with the deficit—i.e., except for our financial crunch—he'd gladly spend more government funds. "There are many areas," Bush said, "in which we would like to spend more than I propose, but we cannot until we get our financial house in order."

Of course, the reason the financial house is not in order is that a great deal has already been spent on myriad projects our government ought not have anything to do with. There would be no financial crunch if spending had been confined to what government ought to be doing in a free society—defend against foreign and domestic aggressors, keep the laws developed consistent with the principles of the Constitution, and enforce these laws in the most cost-effective and just manner possible.

Reagan at least spoke in a way that rekindled these ideas in the minds of some Americans. But Bush appears to be heading in the direction where they will vanish from the public consciousness. Most recently, he caved in on tuition tax credits, thus selling out further the principle of privatization in a vital area of culture, one that government has monopolized and mismanaged for too long. His refusal to prevent double-billing of parents for the education they provide their children is both a blow against individual liberty and quality education in our society.

Obviously, this is welcomed by those in our country who want to forget all about individual liberty, property rights, free trade, and personal initiative. The left wing of the Democrat-controlled Congress will make sure that from now on Bush and his team are pressured toward thinking more and more along lines conducive to favoring the terms of the welfare state, if not outright socialism. Even though the rest of the world—even the Soviet bloc—is demonstrating the poverty of that view, our modern liberals are still enamored of it.

But now, it is no longer possible to pretend that they think of such statist ideals as really good for the country—that has been discredited worldwide. Not even the claim that socialism, at least, prevents dire poverty is credible, what with reports by a more open press in the countries of the Soviet bloc discovering massive destitution in the midst of supposedly egalitarian socialism.

Now, the only sensible explanation is either utter stupidity or sheer hunger for power. These folks are either utterly ignorant of economic—not to mention political—realities in statist societies or they just want to dictate where all of our funds will be spent, never mind the certainty that from such redistributionism comes nothing of lasting and general value, but a lot of agony and violence.

Bush, by trying to be such a nice man, by trying not to antagonize the largely statist Congress, is setting the terms of an agenda fully accommodating to the influence-peddling mind-set of those in Washington most threatened by the ideals (and even the words) of individual liberty, property rights, limited government, etc.

It was a sad spectacle that Ronald Reagan barely managed to get beyond his rhetoric. Yet there may soon be a time when all those who cherish liberty will be wishing that the great communicator was back again to help make all the statists squirm with pain from all the good talk about individualism and giving back power to the people by taking it from Washington, D.C. Some day, indeed, the country may remember Reagan, whose words started something we ought to have cemented into our public policy.

MIND-BOGGLING GOVERNMENT*

It's November, the season of voting. For many months we will be urged to go out and vote, never mind for whom or what. Voting will be praised from east to west and north to south.

When elections have passed, we will be told how shameful it is that only 40 or 30 or 50 percent of us voted. We will be called the most apathetic country in the world. We will be told that in Germany, France, Italy, Korea, Japan, and the other near-democratic countries a much higher percentage of the population chooses to vote. We will be told how spoiled, irresponsible, and lazy we are and how we do not deserve our wonderful lot.

There never seems to be an end to people who love wagging their fingers at us. Election years are another opportunity for them to indulge in this vigorous exercise. But are they right? Should we really feel so badly if we do not vote? Is it such a crime? Is it so irresponsible to stay home or go fishing on election days?

Let me answer this somewhat personally. As a naturalized citizen I always vote. Even when I spent a couple of Novembers working in Europe, I wrote for ballots and made sure they got back in time to count. I am a dutiful voter.

But it takes its toll. For me to have any confidence in my repeated political acts, I have had to become a virtual full-time political student.

In my life politics is virtually everything. I am certainly a man without hobbies. I barely have time for my family, and I am only able to keep up with my profession because it largely revolves around studying politics.

For someone to have any reasonable confidence in being a good voter— to perform his civic duty in good conscience—one has to go about preparing for voting in a relentless, demanding fashion. In my case this meant searching out the best political principles one can identify and then voting in the way that most effectively supported them. This requires extensive study: not just reading the paper, following the record of the candidates, reading the various measures up for decision by referenda, knowing the persons likely to accompany the candidate to his or her political post, and so on. Most important it requires keeping one's mind on some very big questions, such as "What is justice?" "Is freedom more important than security?" "What is best for a human community?" "How far should democracy go in a country?"

---

*Originally published in the *Freeman* (October 1988).

Indeed, this last question is what prompted me to write these words. Can you imagine anyone being a competent, conscientious voter who is not somewhat in tune with these issues? I cannot. This being the case, very few people really have good reason for voting. They may have motives to vote, but that is different. One may try to influence someone in Washington or in their respective state capitals so that some project will get attention or some bill will garner support, but that is not the heart of politics and democratic participation. What counts is whether one is furthering the public good, promoting the general welfare, insuring domestic tranquillity, securing the blessing of liberty, establishing justice—all those points listed in the Preamble to the our Constitution whereby our founding fathers and framers sought to fulfill their political responsibilities.

But there is more to our problems. The task of voting in a bloated welfare state is an unbelievably demanding one. It is very doubtful that one percent of those who go out to vote actually make a contribution to fulfilling it. And how could they? It is certainly not their fault that in order to be politically savvy one needs to be omniscient if not omnipotent and all wise as well. Aside from the big issues in which politics are involved, there are the many more or less big issues in which politics do not play a part.

The people we send to our various political power centers are embarking on missions that would baffle the Almighty. Most of them have to decide on issues ranging from what fish need to be preserved to where to build the next interstate highway, from how best to fight AIDS to whether surrogate motherhood for pay should be legalized, from whether a judge is suited to sit on the Supreme Court to how much this year's tobacco subsidy ought to be, from how many helicopters Angolan freedom fighters should receive to how best to tame the greed of traders on the New York Stock Exchange. And this only at the federal level!

In short, the political wisdom our representatives need is inestimable. No normal or rational person could possibly tell who is best qualified to serve in such elective offices. We are certainly not clear on what character traits ought to be possessed, let alone which will ensure that they will do what is best for the nation.

Indeed, the very idea of politics as a profession or calling makes little sense in light of the multifaceted tasks politicians face. Each single politician must be a multinational conglomerate as far as talents, skills, understanding, and attention span are concerned. There is no job description that fits these people; they are perhaps best described as human engineers. Could anyone feel confident about selecting one over the other to do his or her tasks well? I am certain that this is impossible.

One reason I suspect the founding fathers and framers tried to build a society with a limited government wasn't that they worried about the size of government. It is the scope of governments that matters. They meant for all the people to participate in the affairs of government, so they wanted those affairs to be relatively specific. This is one clear reason to limit the power of government. In the market we can judge the baker, the restauranteur, the dentist, the carpet cleaner, the banker individually, and if we deem their work inferior, we fire them and go somewhere else. In government, however, we have to cast a vote for people whom we cannot judge since we have no idea exactly what they will do, and even if we have some inkling, we have no skills to judge them at the tasks.

So if you stay home on election day, don't feel guilty. The guilty ones are those who have made our governments into bloated conglomerates, institutions that have acquired tasks and powers no one can keep an eye or mind on, let alone evaluate and make decisions about.

Unlimited government is incompatible with democracy.

SCANDAL AT THE WELFARE STATE*

There is today much talk about government corruption. Scandals abound and usually involve various special benefits obtained by organizations from certain branches of the federal and state governments. Government officials are accused of playing favorites as they carry out their duties. They are charged with accepting gifts or campaign contributions in return for special treatment of those who support them.

But there is reason to believe that all the more obvious improprieties are merely routine behaviors carried out somewhat ineptly. In other words, it is very doubtful that in our society politics involves anything more noble than playing favorites, serving certain special interests, and entirely neglecting what could reasonably be construed as the public interest.

Although the distinction between the public and the private interest is quite meaningful, the democratic welfare state totally obscures it. Such a system favors majority rule regarding any concern that some member of the public happens to have (if it can be brought to public attention). It treats each project, whatever it might be, as a candidate for public support. And, of course, most every person and group has its own special objectives. Thus, so long as these objectives can be advanced by political means, they can gain the honorific status of "the public interest."

It is noteworthy that just this may be the result of advocating what Professor Benjamin Barber of Rutgers University has called a "strong democracy," i.e., a political system that subjects all public issues of concern to a referendum. This approximation of strong democracy—where just wanting to add a porch to one's home must be cleared with the representatives of the electorate—has produced our enormous "welfare" state. Yet it was just this prospect that the framers of the Constitution wanted to avoid. That in part accounted for their insistence on the Bill of Rights, namely, on denying to government—whether democratic, monarchical, or otherwise—the kind of powers that strong democracy entails.

To see how confusing things have become in this kind of strong democracy/ welfare state, consider a few current topics of "public concern." Take, for example, wilderness preservation, an issue that certainly appeals to many and cannot be considered a bad example. Those who favor the welfare state certainly believe that this public policy is in the public interest.

---

*Originally published in the *Freeman* (February 1989).

Yet is it not obvious that some people have a far greater concern even with this cause than do others? It is not unreasonable to suppose that bowlers, race car drivers, amusement park builders and operators, computer wizards, and other technophiles do not have the wilderness as their priority? Sure, they might like and even benefit from some of it. In the main it is probable that they prefer having the wilderness given up in favor of lots of technological artifacts that suit their purposes and may even be better for them.

Or take all those consumer advocates for absolutely safe automobiles, risk-free medical research, and the banning of biological experimentation, to name just a few. Surely these paragons of the so-called public-minded citizen are without a self-interested bone in their bodies. Whatever their motives, it is a fact that their concerns are quite legitimately not shared by many citizens. For example, one such group of dissenters would be those who prefer more powerful, maneuverable automobiles that are not so encumbered with safety features but are able to get out of tight spots.

These individuals might well lead a much better life without all this worry about safety; they might be better drivers and for them all this concern is superfluous. Jeremy Rifkin, a Nader-type who would ban all genetic experimentation, is another who considers himself a public-interest type, presumably without a tinge of self- or vested interest. In fact, such persons are serving quite particular interests. These and like-minded individuals clearly do not favor the public. Instead, they favor some members of it.

The point is that when government does so much on behalf of virtually anyone who can gain political power or savvy, it is impossible to tell when it is serving the true public interest. Everyone is pushing some agenda on the government in support of some special group of citizens. Under such a system, there is hardly any bona fide public service at all. The various laws of the society often serve a private or special purpose—e.g., bans on smoking, prohibiting gambling, mandatory school attendance, business regulations that serve the goals of some but not others. Such a bloated conception of the "public" realm even undermines the integrity of our judicial system. Courts that adjudicate infractions of such special interest laws become agents of a private crusade, not servants of the public.

One consequence of this is that confidence in the honesty and integrity of government officials at every level, even those essential to the function of government, will erode. The defense and judicial functions are suffering because government is so unlimited.

One of the unexpected results of is that under such circumstances "scandals" in these various areas may be expected as the norm. They certainly cannot be taken as surprising. They merely represent the less than clever, the more obviously inept ways of trying to get the government to do our private bidding.

It is all just a matter of each individual getting his part of the pie from Washington—whether it be child care, a monument to some favored historical figure, scholarships for students taking some favored course of study, help to unwed mothers, support for Chrysler-type faltering corporations, or protection of the textile industry from foreign competition. Everyone wants to get the government's weapons on its side. Some people do this in ways that make it all appear on the up and up. They hire all the necessary legal help to learn how to navigate the complicated catacombs of the welfare state.

In such a climate it is actually quite surprising that not more scandals erupt. Probably this is due to even more corruption—in this case cover-ups.

With government doing something more nearly within its expertise, namely, protecting individual rights from domestic and foreign threats, some measure of ethical normalcy could be expected from it. But when despite all the failures and mismanagement of government, people continue to go to it to ask for bailouts, for the solution to their problems, why be surprised when some do it more directly, without finesse? And why wonder at their claim, when caught seeking favors openly and blatantly, that they are innocent? Any surprise at such scandals has to be the result of colossal stupidity or naiveté.

With all that, an old adage gains renewed support: The majority of people do apparently get just the kind of government they deserve. It is they who carry on with all the clamoring for state favors by dishonestly calling their objective the *public* interest. Just notice how many look to our prospective legislators for future favors, how many support this or that politician because they expect a quid pro quo once the state office has been gained. Unfortunately, many of us who do not choose to play that game have the results imposed on us despite everything we do to resist the strong democracy and phony welfare statism.

It may be surprising, after all this, that there are certain matters that are of genuine public interest—the founding fathers had a clear enough idea, as did most classical liberals in history. The public interest amounts to what is in everyone's best interest *as a member of the community:* the defense of individual rights from domestic and foreign aggression. Here is where our individual human rights unite us into a cohesive public with a common interest. We are justified in establishing a government, with its massive physical powers, only if our goal is to protect and maintain the public interest so understood.

Once we expand the scope of the public—in effect making the concept "public" quite meaningless—the powers of the state get involved in tasks that serve only some of the people, and often at the expense of others. And that simply breeds bad government, whether hidden by phony legislation and regulation or by means of out-and-out corruption and subsequent scandal.

It is not surprising therefore that government is so susceptible to misconduct. Nor is it surprising that our society with its free press gets to know about it so often. The lesson we ought to take away from all this is that the scope of our government ought to be reduced to proper proportions, namely, the defense of individual rights.

HONESTY ON TAXES*

It is no great wonder that President Ronald Reagan and his team found it virtually impossible to sell their economic philosophy to the public, let alone to the intellectual community. In the last analysis they have failed to show the moral courage required to do it in a way that holds out some promise of success.

The ultimate foundation, even if unstated, underlying Reaganomics is that taxation is wrong, at best a necessary evil that should be minimized. By this doctrine, taxing rich and poor alike is wrong. In fact, taxation is a remnant of the feudal age, not becoming a system of government that stands in service to the citizenry rather than as the patriarchal guide to its subjects.

The fact that taxation is achieved via some measure of democracy makes it no finer a thing than lynching with majority support. That our representatives vote for taxation does not escape the fact that it is legalized theft or, as the philosopher Robert Nozick has called it, "forced labor."

Of course, members of Reagan's team will not say such things, although the president has hinted at similar points: for example, when he called the corporate tax "unjust." Most are committed to approving of theft when some lofty purpose is at stake. In this they differ not one iota from John Kenneth Galbraith. Their advocacy of trickle-down economics still rests on some promise of altruistic results instead of the rights of taxpayers.

But let us face things squarely for once. Perhaps, eventually, taking welfare payments away from those who now receive them and letting those who earn these funds keep them for their own purposes will be incentive to induce some people to go to work. What is plain is that it might not do this in many cases.

In short, some people will have a very bad time of it without welfare payments. It is no use pretending that no one will be hurt or that being hurt is good for you. The plain fact is that Reaganomics (and any other variant that gives money back to those who actually own it) does deprive some people.

But perhaps, it will be argued, only the undeserving poor will find themselves in such straits, and they have it coming to them. But this is bunk. In point of fact the children of the undeserving poor—accepting for a moment this fantasy of perfect control in the distribution of welfare funds—are never deserving of the hardship they have had foisted on them by irresponsible parents.

These parents are often able to feed their children, cloth them, provide for their other needs only because they receive money taken from others via taxation. Without such support the children, or at least some of them, will suffer even if others could obtain help from private charities.

So what is Reaganomics going to do in light of this plain truth? It will scramble, run for cover, equivocate, and pretend the motivation behind supply-side/trickle-down economics is altruistic, all of which is as phony as a three-dollar bill.

The dispute between the liberals and the conservatives is still only a matter of degrees. Conservatives don't grasp the ultimate meaning of the Declaration

---

*Originally published in the *Orange County Register* (May 20, 1983).

of Independence even though they pretend to defend its political philosophy. But they do not believe, as the Declaration states, that every individual has an inalienable right to do, with his or her life and estate, what he or she judges right, so long as others' rights are not trampled.

The Declaration does not speak of such obscure and invented "rights" as the right to welfare, the right to education, the right to a decent wage, and the right to a vacation. It speaks of the basic natural rights (life, liberty, and the pursuit of happiness), which clearly imply the right to one's labor and its fruits.

At this point someone will mention national defense, even though it is not true that such defense requires taxation per se. An extensive contract fee system—whereby government charges those engaged in contractual transactions for defending the integrity of contracts and the system of justice such defense makes necessary—may well handle the expense of legitimate government. And national defense aims precisely at protecting the rights mentioned in the Declaration, the background to the kind of civilized society that respects the sanctity of contract.

Given the fact that the Declaration is the central philosophical document of the American political tradition, conservatives might be thought to have the courage to defend it fully, consistently, without compromise. Instead they smuggle a few bits of the tradition into their current political agenda.

However, liberals are no fools. When they say Reaganomics is greedy and mean, they are hinting at an important truth: The main principle on which America was founded is not altruism—as George Gilder, the author of the "bible" of supply siders, *Wealth and Poverty,* desperately maintains—but individualism, the belief that it is right for everyone to seek his or her happiness in life.

The political side of this truth is that no one may intrude on the judgment of individual citizens in a free society. That is what attracted millions to America, people who came to its shores to escape the feudal systems of the old world.

So instead of hiding the facts, Mr. Reagan and his team would do well to proclaim, forthrightly, that his economic ideas are indeed focused mainly on justice—the justice of people having a basic right to that which they have honestly earned—not on charity and Robin-Hoodism. With such honesty, the people of the United States might not only come to have some respect for Mr. Reagan but may be reminded of what made the country of which they are citizens the best in the world.

TAXATION AND HUMANITY*

Some time ago I characterized taxation to a friend of mine as legalized theft. I told him that taxation was the expropriation of property (money) from a person without legal means of recrimination.

At one point in our conversation, I said that in the societal circumstances most proper to my way of thinking, it is possible that some people may not

*Originally published in the *Goleta Advisor* (circa 1969).

be as well off as others and yet the government won't be allowed to do anything about it. I admitted that I did not believe in government financing of welfare programs, education, and the like. In response, my friend called me "inhumane": He characterized my political philosophy as lacking in humanity.

As most people know, it is not always possible to explain one's political outlook in full during a casual conversation. Neither side has the time and presence of mind to defend all of its claims. I will now make clear why I think my political views are not at all inhumane, especially when contrasted with the present welfare-state political structure.

I hold that if you know someone who is in need of help, and they are not obviously undeserving, you ought to help him out if you have the time and ability to do so. I do not believe that a person must receive help regardless of his circumstances. My own life and the lives of those I love come first. I am convinced that this would hold in any society, in the final analysis. The question now becomes: In what kind of society will others be able to receive the help they deserve and need?

I think that a free society, without any kind of government regulation of the economy, will be best able to supply that kind of help. Is it, then, less humane to expect help from people voluntarily than to expect that help through coercive government measures? Surely, it is far more humane to trust that human beings will help each other voluntarily when in need, than to force them.

Clearly, the attitude that leads some to force their ideas about helping people on others is far more inhumane than not helping at all. If you believe that you have the right to force others to follow your views about assisting those in need, then you believe that you have rights (to follow through with your edicts despite the wants of others) that supersede the rights of others to conduct their lives as they judge best.

If you do not respect the right of individual human beings to lead their lives as they see fit, you certainly cannot call yourself humane. You are like a dictator who believes that his concept of "the good" must prevail before anyone else's.

I believe that free people can bring about a better society than those who are forced to do the good others conceive for them. And since taxation always contributes to the good that another person or group has thought up, I believe that taxation can never advance the welfare of humanity. At best it can advance the welfare of a few at the expense of others.

THE CONSERVATION OF FREEDOM*

For centuries human freedom has been under attack from various sources. Only rarely did the attack emanate from malice: Instead, the cause has been the willingness of some to sacrifice the lives and freedom of others in behalf of so-called nobler aims. From the pyramids of the pharaohs to the orbiting space shuttles

---

*Originally published in the *Orange County Register* (circa 1968).

of today, human freedom has fallen victim to the "noble" aims of majorities or those of strong rulers.

A recent argument in defense of depriving people of their right to be free focuses on the issue commonly called "conservation," which is the activity of preserving the natural resources of today for future use. In our country various private and governmental groups are supposed to be concerned with conservation. The Sierra Club is the most active private organization concerned with the matter; it promotes the cause of conservation not only among private individuals but through political activism, urging various kinds of legal measures to insure the satisfaction of its goals. The Department of the Interior is the center of activism in this area.

The arguments in support of greater limitation on human freedom in order to induce conservation are based on theories about the future of mankind on earth. Based on certain data of the past and present within the fields of land, wildlife, water, and plant use, those who urge government action for purposes of conservation contend that we are in dire need for greater restriction on the use of these natural resources. To this end, land is purchased, restrictions on hunting and fishing are instituted, regulation of the use of pesticides increases, and various industries are forced to produce goods in such a way that they do not contribute to air and water pollution.

Presumably without these regulations, purchases, restrictions, and similar measures the predictions for continued human life on earth are bleak. So, since freedom is worthless if life is impossible, it is said to be justified that government deprive us of our freedom in order to prevent the predicted destruction of human life.

One example conservationists offer to support government action is water pollution and its resulting effects on food production. It is held that at the rate at which water is polluted in the United States, the effect on food production would be so severe as to require artificial foods to replace inedible natural foods. The crop and livestock from which the varieties of foods are produced would vanish and humans would be left with nothing but vitamins and similar nourishments to keep them alive.

Implicit in this prediction is a crucial assumption about human nature— actually, not one assumption but many related ones. It is assumed first of all, that future technology will make no advance toward coping with this problem. The conversion of saltwater to fresh, for example, is a process the perfection of which is well under way. The neutralization of polluting materials may well be the next antidote to pollution. Similar techniques could develop within the area of the air pollution. That free people have managed to cope with the problems nature has posed for them is a well-documented thesis. That they have been limited in their advance by the actions of other human beings whose intention was to protect everyone, is equally well known; a brief look at the bureaucratic red tape that characterizes all governmental activity should provide just one important example of the evidence. The pessimism about human nature and its capacity to cope with the problems of the future without limiting freedom is clearly unwarranted.

Another factor that contributes to the often hysterical approach to the conservation issue is the failure of conservationists to realize that the future may have in store for us an increase not only in technological capabilities but changes in human tastes and preferences. While today the redwoods may be the most valued plants for humans to enjoy, the values of the redwoods cannot be guaranteed to be permanent. It is not unlikely that the kind of life humans advance toward will bring with it a new set of highly preferred activities and objects. Instead of mass visits to the woods, people might frequent the depths of the oceans with the newly developed equipment that will be available to them. Humankind's past indicates that its tastes and pleasures change, even if its moral principles do not. Those who demand that we sacrifice human freedom in order to cling to a past that may soon become defunct—not only as a utility but a means to enjoyment—are forgetting about realities that stare us in the face. To project our desires and pleasures upon a future generation is illogical; to compel us to provide that future generation with what we value most highly is to coerce not only some of us but also all of those who will follow us.

The notion that businesses, if left alone, would "exploit" natural resources unreasonably is equally unfounded. If we remember that business is interested not only in immediate profits but also in investment, then we will realize that reasonable conservation is to the greatest advantage of those who are earning their livelihood from providing us with the values to be gained from the use of natural resources. Those who furnish us with the product of raw oil and gas have as much interest in economizing and rationing the output of their natural supplies as any conservationist does—and then some. In fact, it is very often the government, which claims to be interested in preserving natural resources, that contributes to its reckless use. Subsidized farming contributes to overproduction and the unnecessary use of land. The market, after all, does not demand this kind of use and waste. A discontinuation of such subsidies would, most likely, induce a good portion of the farming population to seek other means of earning a living.

Professor Scott Gordon put it very succinctly when he wrote: "Like many aberrant mental processes, those of the radical conservationists are logical enough within their own frame. The difficulty lies mainly in the fact that the framework is far too narrow to permit the making of satisfactory judgments on the large subject of the permanence of economic progress" ("Economics and the Conservation Question," *The Journal of Law & Economics* 1 [October 1958]: p. 112).

The predictions of conservationists who would limit our freedom are like those of a bad science fiction writer: He often advances the earth's history a thousand years in most respects, only to impose total stagnation upon some part of human life to provide him with an interesting plot. But in the case of conservationists, the omission does not merely make for bad fiction; it leads to the tragedy of the loss of human liberty.

WHY I VOTE LIBERTARIAN*

The 1988 presidential election was one of the vital political contests in recent history. As one of my Marxist colleagues said some years back, Ronald Reagan is like the last blast of bright light in a burnt-out bulb. The United States is surely moving to embrace the alien politics of collectivism. And the Democrats are closer to that stance than the Republicans. So anyone who cherishes human liberty and the free society would have had to vote for George Bush. Is that right?

In fact, while the rhetoric of the Republicans differs from their Democratic opponents, the actual policies recommended by the two parties are not very different. Sure, Reagan and now Bush talk of individual responsibility and restricting the power of government. Yet both parties cave in to calls for the expansion of state power. Usually the (liberal) Democrats use the excuse that economic hardship justifies it: We need higher minimum wages, import quotas, plant-closing laws, a return to airline regulation, closer ties between government and business, and on and on. These Democrats, who now lead the party, treat government as if it were the savior of the poor, the farmers, the sick, the uneducated, the artistically impoverished, and a whole host of other groups.

But Republicans are no better. They trust in government to save our souls, force people to think right, to believe in God and pray, to live more virtuously as far as their sexual behavior is concerned, and the like. Even in economics, Republicans tend merely to respond to their opponents with less drastic measures and a bit later. Ronald Reagan betrays his rhetoric of international free trade. And Dukakis rightly noted, during the first debate with Bush, that while the latter once (rightly) called Medicaid "socialized medicine," he then embraced it fully.

Republicans embrace government welfare for many segments of the society, especially for faltering corporations and banks, the homeless, people in need of child care, and others. Both parties are irrational when it comes to dealing with the problems of drug abuse: They trust the might of government to solve what is clearly not a judicial but a moral problem—the self-destructive actions of many Americans. They want to throw away the Constitution when it comes to "fighting drug abuse."

So what could a voter do who is loyal to the American political tradition and does not wish to turn the clock back to feudalism, national and international socialism, and mercantilism? What could such a voter do besides making a mere symbolic gesture, as did Bush, with vague self-righteous chants about the Pledge of Allegiance and the flag?

Such a voter could have cast a protest vote by supporting the Libertarian Party candidate, Dr. Ron Paul. I don't agree with everything Dr. Paul stood for but I still find Libertarians to be better for America than are the other parties today. The Libertarians are the most consistent upholders of the principle of our individual human right to life, liberty, and the pursuit of happiness. Libertarians

---

*Originally published in the *Franklin Gazette* (1989).

believe that government has as its proper function to protect these rights and not to pretend to offer cure-alls for our troubles. The Libertarians view America as the only country where the principles of individual liberty, limited government, and cultural, religious, and philosophical pluralism can still be implemented—although they admit that matters are getting so out of hand that it will take constant vigilance to rejuvenate the most important revolution in human history, the revolution that established the sovereignty and ultimate worth of every person.

I personally have a major stake in fighting this battle. In contrast to Governor Dukakis, I am a first-generation refugee in the United States. I came from behind the Iron Curtain and like millions of others, I did not come to here to live off the efforts of my neighbors, to have the collective wealth redistributed, or my soul saved by the government. I came here because the principles this country embodies promised individual liberty and a chance to make a life for myself in peaceful cooperation with others who are similarly inclined.

Individual liberty, not welfare statism—economic or spiritual—lies at the center of the United States. Neither the Democrats nor the Republicans understand this fact any longer—or if they do, they have decided not to remain loyal to America's unique political tradition.

By voting for the Libertarian Party candidate, one could still declare loyalty to the American ideal of a society of free and responsible human beings. They trust government only to do what is its proper business, namely, protect our individual rights from domestic and foreign aggressors, but withhold the powers to govern their own lives in all other respects. That way a society has a better chance of solving all the problems that politicians whether from the Left or the Right want to trust to the wisdom of the State. By voting for the Libertarians, one could at least send an admittedly faint but still vital message: Keep liberty alive, and, above everything else, use government to protect it.

6

Economics

UNDERSTANDING THE FREE-MARKET SYSTEM*

One of the greatest benefits many Western political systems bestow upon their citizens is a substantially free market economy. In this system individuals are not legally prevented from seeking their economic advantage in the company of others who may be counted on to do the same thing. While there is no purely free economic system anywhere, surely the main difference between other political systems and Western liberal democracy is the presence of the economic opportunity afforded by a relatively free market.

There are those who dispute this but they usually do not deny the presence of greater economic opportunity in the West; instead, they frown on the value of this opportunity. Critics from the Left and the Right have alleged the corrupting influence of a political system that makes commercial prosperity more likely than other systems do. These critics tend to see the free market as one that caters to base human inclinations—self-interest, greed, lust, etc. When one is rarely hindered, let alone prevented, from pursuing wealth, one will (so the critics say) focus all of one's attentions on this pursuit. Thus, we are told, free market systems give us the commercialization of everything from religion to art. Doctors do not worry so much about medicine as about prospering economically. Lawyers, evangelists, educators, scientists, artists, politicians—members of all vocations and professions with talent and skill—concentrate predominantly on the bottom line.

Now there is something to this charge, if we only look at the evidence before us in most Western societies. But it is unfair to judge the matter from a narrow empirical framework. For example, it needs to be stressed that economic liberty is a recent phenomenon, following centuries of repression and oppression during which prosperity was out of the question for the bulk of the people in the world. It is therefore not surprising that for a few centuries people would focus their

---

*Originally published in the *Freeman* (1988).

attention on attaining reasonable material prosperity, in addition to a number of other important goals.

In any case, my concern here is not so much to defend the free market system but to discuss one of the prominent ways in which it is defended against a persistent indictment. Professor Paul Samuelson, a critic of the free market system, has made the following serious charge: "The Invisible Hand will only maximize total social utility *provided the state intervenes so as to make the initial distribution of dollar votes ethically proper"* (*Collected Scientific Papers* [(emphasis in original]). In other words, the justice of such a system is predicated on the presence of a strong government that first distributes wealth equitably. If we start out with some people having much more than others, with no moral justification, then the results of market processes will be contaminated with this initial defect of unjust distribution. From this indictment follow almost all the other indictments levelled at the free market: The rich get richer, while the poor get poorer; the important professions lack support while trivial pursuits are well rewarded; and so on.

Hardly anyone can claim not to be concerned about these criticisms, coming from Left and from Right, with only the minor difference that the Left's criterion is "need," while the Right's is "spiritual salvation" or "superiority."

Defenders of the market offer different replies, but one of them is very prominent, coming from the best-placed group of such defenders, namely, economists. Professor Murray N. Rothbard summarized this defense most aptly when he wrote, "There is no distributional process apart from the production and exchange processes of the market; hence the very concept of 'distribution' becomes meaningless on the free market. Since 'distribution' is simply the result of the free exchange process, and since this process benefits all participants on the market and increases social utility, it follows directly that the 'distributional' results of the free market also increase social utility" ("Toward a Reconstruction of Utility and Welfare Economics," in Mary Sennholz, ed., *On Freedom and Free Enterprise* [New York: 1965], p. 251).

The crux of this defense is that, apart from what people actually choose to do in a free market, there is no other measure of what is good for them. Putting it more generally, this is the subjective value theory defense: How could we dispute the free judgments of market agents as to what is the best decision for them to make apart from what they actually do make as they carry out their commercial transactions? And if there is no way to criticize those decisions, how could anyone propose that the overall results of market transactions are defective and require state intervention? There is, in short, no justification for state intervention, because there is no other standard of value other than what people in fact individually and freely invoke in free market systems.

But there is a serious implausibility about this defense. People may often be subjectivists in their general outlook, but in particular matters they are not. They may say, everything is relative as far as value judgments are concerned— e.g., like beauty, goodness is merely in the eyes of the beholder. But when they see someone indulging in reckless purchases such as accumulating eight Rolls

Royces, as did the late Liberace, or obtaining cocaine or pornographic books, they are perfectly willing to say that, contrary to the economist's theory, these people do not really benefit themselves in trade but are guilty of fadism, fetishism, excesses, immoderation, and the like.

These people will conclude, if they are without a contrary theory that accepts the legitimacy of ethical criticism of market behavior, that any society in which people are permitted to be indulgent—in ways people evidently are in systems with substantially free markets—must be ethically flawed. People often enough and quite reasonably dispute that "[the exchange] process benefits all participants in the market and increases social utility," at least as they observe the market in their particular situations. They then go on to share the view of social critic John Kenneth Galbraith that the market produces many failures of distribution— people often fail to benefit themselves and their society when they produce and sell in the free market. Would it not be better that the money spent on pornography or heroin or even Michael Jackson gloves would go to medical research, the arts, or economic education? Perhaps they won't know how to give a thorough philosophical defense of this conviction, but they will nevertheless hold it.

And they are right to do so. Free men and women can indeed make very bad, even evil judgments: There is no guarantee that when people enjoy freedom from the dictation of others, even in markets, they will always choose to do the right thing. Anyone who proposes this view, as some economists do, will fly in the face of unshakable convictions and common sense. The very idea of freedom implies that one can do both good and evil, even while carrying on as a market agent. The details could only be known from close up, but they are no mystery—self-indulgent people are a dime a dozen. Misallocation of resources, therefore, is easy to conceive in free markets.

But does this not concede the case to those who would wish to intervene in the market? Not by a long shot. First of all, just as market agents can make bad judgments, so can those who would interfere with their behavior. And there are fewer pressures on the latter than on the former, since they enjoy "sovereign immunity" (e.g., government regulators cannot be sued when a mishap occurs in an industry they regulate, as is clear from the recent industrial accidents in airline transportation, chemical manufacturing, etc.). But even more important, it is meaningless to even talk of good human conduct without freedom. Persons who are fully or even only partially enslaved—dictated and forced to behave by others—simply cannot be given credit for good or evil conduct. They are in effect reduced to the status of robots.

Thus, to the extent that it lacks freedom, an unfree system is a dehumanized system. What needs to be recognized is that the utopian dream of making people perfect through limiting or regulating voluntary, self-regarding conduct is a dangerous dream, not some beautiful ideal as many suppose. So the free market must be seen as the best that we can do. Whatever failures it is exposed to can only be resisted by education, exhortation, and example—not by coercion. Nor will it do to deny that the free market is open to failure (as economists sometimes do), or to try to eliminate the failure by way of state intervention. This struggle

and its intensity should not be surprising, since the quintessential human characteristic is, after all, our capacity for good or evil. Why should we expect anything
different from such a perfectly human enterprise as the pursuit of economic welfare?

IN THE MARKET FOR ECONOMIC SENSE*

When during the 1984 presidential campaign the ranking member of President
Reagan's Council of Economic Advisers called comparable worth a "medieval
concept" and compared it with the doctrine of just price and just wage, he invited
much scorn. Democratic candidate Walter Mondale shook his head contemptuously,
saying that these Republicans just don't understand women's issues at all.

It is not tactful to dismiss the idea of comparable worth these days. But
we need to try to understand why the nation's top economist so confidently rejects
the idea. He does, after all, represent the thinking of most academic economists
in this country, who hold that economics does not deal with such notions as
right and wrong, good and bad. Prices are never right or wrong. Wages are
never too low or too high. Such talk, they hold, betrays a misunderstanding
of how prices and wages work.

Economists hold that in a relatively free, unplanned economic system, wages
come about by the interaction of the demand for and the supply of some type
of skill. When some kinds of work get such and such a wage, that is really determined
by massive, complicated forces and cannot be adjusted by individuals who may
wish to have the wage higher or lower. Nor can it be changed by bureaucrats
who think the demand may be decent or thoughtless, hasty or well considered,
benign or mean, greedy or benevolent; or the skill involved complicated or simple,
packaged or unadorned, competent or sloppy, noble or base, performed by women
or men.

When an economist talks of demand, he means what people in the market
want and are willing to pay for. When he talks of supply, he means the level
of availability of what is demanded. Accordingly, when women get lower wages
than men for some types of work, the reason is simple: They are not wanted
as intensely in the marketplace. Or putting it somewhat differently, people don't
want to pay women what they want to pay men.

People do get shafted and ripped off in the marketplace. Economists don't
care. They have concluded that explaining, describing, and predicting the way
markets will perform is more important than dealing with whether people in markets
behave decently, justly, or considerately toward one another.

The problem is that some economists go into government to give politicians
advice about how markets should be dealt with: left alone, manipulated, regulated,
or planned. When they get embroiled in policy formation, it becomes difficult
if not impossible to avoid making value judgments.

What the president's economic adviser should have said is not that comparable

---

*Originally published in the *Orange County Register* (March 8, 1985).

worth is a medieval concept. What is crucial to say is that as an economist, one is not in the business of evaluating people's behavior. And a Reaganite economist does not believe in setting prices and wages by some outside, nonmarket force such as government.

Remedying the problems of the marketplace is wrong because it makes government a petty tyrant with parental authority over the citizenry. This is not only unsuited to a community of human beings, but it implies the ethics of a nursery.

Comparable worth is a notion being used to get government to "fix" what happens in the marketplace. That is what is objectionable. What is wrong is the nature of the policy being recommended to cope with a problem that all can recognize. The issue is whether bureaucratic intervention ought to be deployed.

THE DEBATE ON PLANNING*

The battle lines of ideological wars are drawn on many fronts, not the least of which is the domain of popular political debate. What happens in Washington and other citadels of power may be influenced by special-interest lobbying, stupidity, and the desire for political authority, but in the end there must be a rationale that lends policy an air of legitimacy.

For some years economists and legal theorists from the University of Chicago have been in the vanguard of the war against government regulation of the economy. Their research consists mainly of empirical investigations into the consequences of regulation and assessments of whether the costs exceed the benefits. For example, Sam Peltzman (of the University of Chicago) has studied the results of the 1962 Kafauver Act, which came on the heels of the thalidomide scare and was intended to ensure greater safety in drug use. Peltzman shows that the costs of such safety—i.e., severe reduction in the development and marketing of new drugs that could have saved lives—have outweighed the benefits of keeping unsafe drugs off the market. Many similar studies (by the Food and Drug Administration [FDA], the Federal Communications Commission [FCC], and the Federal Trade Comission [FTC], for example) also suggest that regulation is more harmful and costly than not.

While little policy change has resulted from these studies, the rhetoric against the regulatory system is gaining momentum. The work of the Chicago theorists, which was once published in scholarly outlets such as the *Journal of Law and Economics,* the *Journal of Political Economy,* and the *Journal of Legal Studies,* is now being aired in general-readership magazines such as the *American Spectator, Barron's, Harper's, National Review,* and *Reason.* President Ford has become the first chief executive to introduce the issue of regulation to the general public. And within the regulatory structure itself, officials are sheepishly owning up to the faults of the system that supports them.

But it would be premature to begin celebrating the rejuvenation of the free

*Originally published in the *National Review* (June 11, 1976).

market. There is a very large wrinkle in this trend, one that could well lead to worse things than regulation.

Consider two recent moves by foes of the efforts to restore the free economy. One is the Javits-Humphrey bill, which proposes the creation of an Economic Planning Board. The Economic Planning Act of 1975 is picking up spirited support from such notable Americans for Democratic Action-New Deal types as Arthur Schlesinger, Jr., Leonard Woodcock, and (naturally) John Kenneth Galbraith. (It should be noted that many businessmen are behind such plans, which gives the lie to the Marxist idea of class consciousness and proves that many businessmen haven't the foggiest idea what is in their own interest in the long run.)

Watchdogs' Watchdog

Schlesinger may be regarded as the popular spokesman for the planning idea. His essay "Laissez-faire, Planning, and Reality" (*Wall Street Journal,* July 30, 1975) tries valiantly to debunk all attempts at decentralization. The very idea of the author of *The Imperial Presidency* supporting a bill that "would create an Economic Planning Board (EPB) in the executive branch" calls to mind *Alice in Wonderland.* Then this desperate but determined piece quotes F. A. Hayek totally out of context to make it seem that even he admits the free market cannot prevent unemployment. (Of course, what Hayek meant was that after decades of governmental tinkering and inflationary Keynesianism, we may not be able to do anything about unemployment.) Schlesinger rarely relies on hard evidence to make his case; he merely cites such authorities as Joseph P. Kennedy and J. P. Morgan. He calmly announces that, for the EPB, "There would be no enforcement authority, no interference with the making of private decisions, no revision of the pattern of ownership, no action except"—are you ready?—"on the basis of legislation." How useless, after all, would be the "gathering of information, the estimation of natural resources and requirements, and the coordination of national policies" without legislation to back up the jaw-boning! Schlesinger's piece is a prime example of how the centralizers have the upper hand in the arguments about regulation.

Consider a second backlash measure: the effort to establish a super-agency, a watchdog over the rest of the inefficient and wasteful watchdogs, the Federal Consumer Protection Agency (FCPA). This is the product of Ralph Nader. He too admits that regulation has not worked. Now that the University of Chicago economists and their students have spelled it out, he also sees that regulatory agencies tend to work in collusion with the industries being regulated. After all, where would the Federal Aviation Administration get its experts but from the airline industry? Where would the FDA get its experts, but from the firms that produce drugs, food, and chemicals? Mr. Nader, however, does not draw the same conclusions as the Chicago economists, namely, that decentralization and a closer approximation to the free market are the key to improving our economy. Instead, he wants to give regulation another try. If the FCC, FAA, FDA, FTC, International Trade Commission (ITC), Civil Aeronautics Board (CAB), and the rest haven't done well, maybe the new FCPA will. And what can the Chicago group, the empirical students of regulation, offer in objection to this persistence?

Wait Till Next Time

The shortcoming in their case for the free market is that empiricism provides no foundation for the establishment of economic principles, let alone principles of political authority. Empirical objections to a particular proposal for regulation cannot in themselves invalidate the general course of conduct. So what if studies demonstrate that this particular effort of such and such a regulatory agency has not worked? The next one might. Especially if we change some features of the policy in what appear to be significant ways. From piecemeal regulation we can move toward wholesale planning; from regulation of industries by specialized bureaucracies, we can move to a regulatory super-agency to keep the specialists unwavering in their zeal to protect the public from the evils of businessmen, industrialists, and their own bumbling. Economists, armed with the empirical method, are powerless to discredit such suggestions, for the simple reason that they have not yet been tried in America.

Even when it is demonstrated that empirical studies are really quite theoretical and systematized analyses of the marketplace, the argument against planning starts at a disadvantage. For the planners do not promise a huge success. All they say is that it is worth the inconvenience and cost to aim, at least, for the goals of planning.

The Unasked Question

The chief difficulty is that planning and regulation are never challenged as patent interventions in the voluntary activities of citizens. Only the costs and benefits are weighed. Many actions, however, are—and must be—undertaken largely in disregard of economic benefits or costs, even if economists try at times to reduce all values to economic ones. The effort to save a friend from drowning ought to be made for moral reasons, even if the rescuer is a poor swimmer and is wearing an expensive dinner jacket. The main arguments advanced by Nader and others tend to be moralistic. Indeed, the good that Nader desires for people is more than likely worth having. It is no use, then, to demean the values of proponents of regulation. They are not unaware of the general case against governmental regulation and planning. They simply believe that these are worth the cost, the inefficiency, the sacrifice.

What is missing, then, is not an economic but a moral case against regulation. The economic case is crucial. It can discourage federal planning by showing that, in the main, governments cannot achieve their goals by regulation or massive planning. What it does not show—what mere tools of analysis do not equip the economist to prove—is that regulation and planning ought to stop; that it is morally wrong to regulate people's lives.

In the domain of public debate, the Schlesingers and the Naders can count on a value system, an entrenched moral atmosphere, that sanctions—at least by implication—the practice of seeking generally agreed-upon goals through coercion. Toy producers, airlines, and barbers are forced to conform to the rules at whatever cost in terms of time and money, and the taxpayers are forced to pay for this coercive activity, even though no wrong has been established or guilt proven by due process. This injustice is simply tolerated. The question as to whether people ought to be penalized when nothing more than the possibility of wrongdoing has ever been shown is never raised.

Many people who support the free society because they consider liberty a great human value have used the findings of the economists to attack the regulatory bodies. But in their efforts to remain empirical or scientific, they have based their arguments against planning only on its inefficiency, high cost, and meager benefits. In so doing, they have tacitly conceded to the regulators a crucial point: that their moral concern for liberty is little more than a "value free" preference.

The Greater Argument

Now if the morality supported by public spokesmen is of the Nader variety—i.e., the absolute priority of public safety, of the consumer's protection from even the chance of carelessness by producers—then the morality in which human liberty has priority can fall by the wayside. If liberty is never mentioned, for fear that such a reference will make the case against some governmental policy less than scientific, then the defenders of the regulatory system win by default. People like Nader and Schlesinger do not hesitate to claim that it is everybody's moral and political duty to support their goals, like them or not. They understand one thing that supporters of the free society have never quite grasped, namely, the priority of moral considerations in the debate over political policy. They see what many of those who are freedom's friends (positive economists) have been blind to for so long: that one must deal with questions of human action in moral terms in order to win the intellectual victory. Win the greater argument and you've won the lesser.

The late Leo Strauss made the point well: "Political freedom, and especially that political freedom that justifies itself by the pursuit of human excellence, is not a gift of heaven; it becomes actual only through the efforts of many generations, and its preservation always requires the highest degree for vigilance." One should add that this vigilance must be exerted in the area of popular debate. In that debate, the best case is to be made in behalf of political freedom, which "justifies itself by the pursuit of human excellence."

PUBLIC SERVICE UNIONISM*

At a time when much is being said about shared burdens and belt-tightening, not much is being said about strikes. In a way this is understandable. If there

---

*Originally published in the *Orange County Register* (August 20, 1981).

is something on which liberals and conservatives agree concerning the merits of a relatively capitalistic society, it is that in no other country can workers feel so secure in the protection of their right to strike. In a socialist society, after all, the means of production are owned by all and rationalized by government; labor surely is the ultimate means of production. Marx certainly believed this, as does one of America's most respected Marxist economists, Robert Heilbroner. Socialism, Heilbroner says, "requires the curtailment of the central economic freedom of bourgeois society, namely the right of individuals to own, and therefore to withhold if they wish, the means of production, including their own labor."

Yet something quite odd occurs when all this is applied to an understanding of public service unions such as the postal workers or air traffic controllers or, on the local level, to hospital workers or members of the police force. When these people walk off their jobs, it does not feel like a simple matter of the exercise of the right to strike.

No wonder. One reason that certain services are taken over by the government and not left to private industry is that these services are supposed to be essential to the public welfare. It is usually argued that when such vital forms of production as providing health care or delivering the mail are at stake, the private market should not be relied upon to provide the people with what they need. Nor should people be counted on to pay for these services or goods willingly, so they must be taxed to obtain the funding of these public goods and services. Taxation is not an economic means for securing the funding of production but a political approach to the problem of finance. People are threatened with fines or jail and, even if many would pay willingly, there is always this final recourse against those who would not. Virtually all public service employees are paid out of funds collected by means of taxation.

In turn, ordinarily the Internal Revenue Service, as well as all the other taxing authorities, look askance at those who would take it upon themselves to refuse to pay their taxes because they do not like the services they receive. Tax strikes are a serious affront to the system of public finance, and the various tax courts have moved swiftly against anyone who might initiate such measures. The recent attempt in Flint, Michigan, to carry out a tax strike met with unhesitating government rebuke. Officers of the IRS made clear in no uncertain terms that they regard tax strikes as a felony and will prosecute without mercy.

In short, we do not have the same relation toward the productive and service endeavors of governments as do we toward these things when done by private enterprise. If the workers at Ford Motor Company or Alpha Beta Markets go on strike, we can go elsewhere or even start our own grocery stores. We are free to withdraw our trade from most private firms (excepting the utility companies, most of which are government established and protected monopolies). The funding of the production process at private firms comes about by way of providing a good deal to the consumer, not by way of threatening him or her with fines or imprisonments.

But then what about those who work for such productive enterprises that do not wait for customers to appear willingly at their sales offices? Why, if the thing is so crucial to public welfare or other elements of the public interest, is it permitted that those who provide these goods and services are simply free to walk away? Why are the rights of the workers to strike given such solid protection and defense while the rights of the people who are made to fund their work to keep their income and spend it as they see fit is infringed as a matter of course?

There is clearly an inconsistency here and it is going to have serious consequences in this country soon enough. In the last analysis, something along the lines that has emerged in England will probably occur here. Public service unions will acquire enormous power and will be able to shut down the entire country at will, setting up a persistent antagonism between themselves and the rest of the citizenry. Alternatively, not far off in the future the idea will no longer be tolerated that workers are free to walk off their jobs when they find no satisfaction with their employment (for whatever reason). Neither of these is a satisfactory resolution, however.

Much more preferable would be to admit that many of the goods and services now regarded essential to the public interest are in fact merely widely expected and strongly desired, nothing more. And they should be returned to the private market, without any threat to the right to strike or the right of consumers to stop purchasing.

FRIEDMAN'S VALUE-FREE VALUE: HUMAN LIBERTY*

In his exciting book *The Machinery of Freedom,* which deserves thorough study from those interested in how well a market system can solve problems that most of us acknowledge require solution, David Friedman makes some by now familiar disclaimers about the usefulness of morality in political discourse and action. He tells us that "I have said almost nothing about rights, ethics, good and bad, right and wrong, although these are matters central to the ideas of most libertarians." He goes on to explain that he has "couched (the) argument throughout in terms of practicality."

Friedman expands on the decision to avoid moral questions by telling us that "I have found that it is much easier to persuade people with practical arguments than with ethical arguments." And he ends the section containing these disclaimers— a single page, entitled "Postscript for perfectionists"—with the observation: "I have never met a socialist who wanted the kind of society that I think socialism would produce" (p. 223).

For succinctness David Friedman must especially be commended. Of all the "value-free" defenses of human liberty—an odd notion right off—Friedman's is the least cumbersome as well as the most revealing. I will not attend to anything but these remarks of his, mainly because they pertain most directly to the kind of work I consider valuable in the protection and preservation of liberty. Indeed the sorts of matters Friedman would consider less likely to succeed in efforts

*Originally published in the *Libertarian Forum* (circa 1976).

to establish greater liberty are considered by me "central," possibly due to my personal experiences that have been very different from Friedman's. I venture to say there are socialists who want the kind of society socialism produces. I lived in such a society and indeed many around me wanted it badly enough to wipe out those who preferred otherwise. But these matters may be the result of Friedman's not having met enough socialists.

To turn to this discussion by Friedman, let me say first that he does indeed say a lot about rights: He speaks of property rights throughout the book. And he says a great deal about good and bad, right and wrong, as when he tells us that "I have described what should be done, but not who should organize and control it" (p. 220). The "should" is here surely something like the "should" of morality: Friedman then is describing the right sort of actions to be taken by us. What he does not tell us is, indeed—and to some deficiency of his thesis— why these are the right things to do. Perhaps he would answer: Because they will produce liberty. But it still needs to be learned why that is good. And here Friedman says he has only "practical arguments" to offer. Such arguments usually take the form of "If one's purpose or goal is X, then, by reason of our familiarity with the better and worse ways to achieve X, one should do such and such." Thus to become free, we should give up government or the state. Since the argument is conditional, one who does not have as his purpose to become free has the logical right to reject the advice offered.

Friedman may be right to think that most people want to be free but just don't know how to do it. So not a political treatise but a manual for liberty will achieve enough to establish the required case. But then the case serves only those who already want freedom. The case for freedom is assumed; the audience is taken to have bought it prior to coming to Friedman's advisory bureau.

That is why Friedman must spend some time persuading the reader that there are no socialists who really (deep in their hearts) want what socialism amounts to, i.e., lack of freedom, or slavery. But his efforts here are indeed meager to the task. They seem, although perhaps only facetiously, to rest on Friedman's having met a select class of socialists—those who don't want socialism.

But this may not be fair. Don't all people want freedom? In a sense most, at least, do—for themselves (although you will find hosts of them defending taxation and laws prohibiting hundreds of sorts of activities on their part). Taking it that most people want freedom, this usually amounts to wanting others off one's back in areas or activities one wants to perform. But not in those one cares little about. So most people want a type of freedom that does not quite amount to the political liberty Friedman and other libertarians want: the freedom to do what they consider the right things, the freedom to act as one should act. But not the freedom to do what one should not do—never mind that these doings may have nothing to do with hurting others, enslaving them, or the like. The kind of liberty, then, that most people want (implicitly—for few of them expound on it fully rationally) is what Professor John O. Nelson has called the "continental conception" (Hegelian or neo-Hegelian/Marxist type) of freedom. (Two sources should suffice to get one clear on this matter: Nelson's own essay in my anthology *The Libertarian*

Alternative [1974], and Andrew McLaughlin's essay "Freedom versus Capitalism" in my *The Main Debate* [1987]) Its basic feature is that freedom is the power to do the right thing, while slavery is the weakness or impotence that leads to doing wrong.

Surely Friedman does not have this sort of liberty in mind. Yet this is what most people want, judging by their actions and acquiescence concerning political and legal practices today. The unproven but assumed premise Friedman's practical arguments require is not the one Friedman has succeeded in finding even among those socialists he has met. Their meaning of the concept "freedom" is totally alien to what I take to be Friedman's.

None of this shows that the practical arguments have no value, only that they do not do the work Friedman asks of them, i.e., to show how we should get where "almost everyone" wants to get, to a free society. Nor does Friedman fail to give support to liberty with his able delineation of how its absence has produced all sorts of misery for people. What he hasn't shown is why it is wrong to produce such misery. And do not say, well, that is obvious. The lover of freedom is not hostile to the misery of those who would obstruct it. After all, thieves and murderers should be miserable in consequence of what they have done. A clear identification of why misery, through the absence of liberty in the lives of those who have not murdered and stolen, should not obtain is, then, not provided by Friedman.

Let me now touch on a very practical problem that arises by "couching arguments in terms of practicality." Ralph Nader and David Friedman both agree that the federal government's regulatory agents have done more harm than good for us all. But Nader advises that therefore we should make them more efficient, install better people, expand the powers of these people, etc., while David Friedman—as well as Milton Friedman and the entire Chicago crew—counsels that therefore we should get rid of these people, fire them, and leave people free to run their business in voluntary cooperation.

The source of the discrepancy in the face of such clear agreement should interest the value-free folks. Ralph Nader has values! Oh, he may be unable to demonstrate their validity, to justify them. But we might say that "these values are widely held by people." They include a safe toy, harmless drug, lack of soot in the air, low prices, protection from nasty businessmen, the reduction of racial prejudice, and so on. These are the values Nader has in mind to secure by way of improving the quality of regulation, by electing and appointing virtuous statists. These are the goods that he accepts, the ethical purposes for which he asks for the statist measures we all know well.

Without benefit of ethics Friedman can respond to Nader only by citing cost/efficiency data. But Nader says: Wait until I get the right folks in the driver's seat, see if we cannot have the service for the cost and the efficiency of the performance to attain our goals. But, says Friedman, history speaks against that. Nader can then say: History hasn't heard of me—and anyway, is there nothing new under the sun? Might it not happen this time? As a good empiricist, Friedman cannot resort to his kind of logic here. For indeed, as the high priest of empiricism, Hume, has told us, anything might happen so far as reason is concerned.

Yet this again might sound unfair. Let us grant that strict deductive logic does not prove the impossibility of Nader's success. Surely good common sense militates against it, and that should be enough.

Unfortunately here Friedmanesque arguments cannot match the ethical ones. The plain fact is that where moral matters are involved we often do and should ignore cost and efficiency. Bad swimmers in expensive suits will jump to save drowning friends: The goal is so important that risk of failure and ultimate injury to self simply have no significance. Nader, then, would simply admit that, granted it isn't likely that the federal government will do much to solve our problems, to achieve our values, our morally respectable—even commendable—goals, these are too important to give up in the face of minor matters such as cost and impending failure. So the drowning person may not be saved: It looks very unlikely from here that we can do much for the chap. But trying is itself better than nothing, even at great risks.

In short, in the face of values that have even the appearance of moral validity, efficiency, practicality, and the host of so-called value-free considerations are impotent. Yes, in the practical task of persuading people, just what Friedman is after!

To fight the argument that Nader offers, one has to produce a moral argument that shows that doing what the government does—even cheaply and efficiently, not as it has been done thus far—is wrong. We need not even bother to show that what Nader wants to achieve is itself wrong; quite the contrary, we may have to accept that unsafe toys are bad, that dangerous drugs and vicious businessmen are all bad. The issue is whether it is good to deprive others of their liberty to prevent the occurrence of these bad things; not whether we at times—even most of the time—fail to achieve the goals Nader has in mind without incredible cost and inefficiency. That is to be expected when great things are at stake. No, we are concerned with whether Nader's suggested cures, even when perfectly administered, at low cost, are not in fact worse for us than what he aims to avert with them.

Thus, imprisoning people because they *might* engage in "monopolistic" practices is a violation of their human rights; does it not violate the principle "innocent until proven guilty" (not proven merely capable of guilt)? Does forcing toymakers to produce this instead of that kind of toy because the latter *might* harm some child presume guilt before proof? Should people be deprived of honest earnings and acquisitions just so the safety and pleasure of others can be achieved? In short, should force be used to achieve some admittedly admirable goals? And unless a moral argument can be produced, one that can stand the test of scrutiny, the Naders of our land have the better side of the argument—morality versus value-free liberty. (Just consider, valued purposes and goals versus value-free purposes and goals—how can they miss?)

But enough. Friedman's moral advice against offering moral advice lacks what much of his competent book lacks—moral justification. Yet the machinery of freedom needs just that.

SOME SORE POINTS OF CAPITALISM*

If there is an Achilles heel of capitalism, certainly most people believe it is the labor market. Periodic unemployment seems unavoidable. Does not a free society do badly—callously, inhumanely, ruthlessly, without compassion—when it comes to dealing with workers who lose their jobs due to changing market conditions, competition with foreigners, or plant relocation?

When people change their preferences—from small to big cars, from typewriters to computers, from pet rocks to Michael Jackson gloves—or innovators create new ways of producing food, shelter, transportation, entertainment, and the lot in different, more efficient ways in a free market, adjustments may well need to be made by those involved in the commerce of the past. Consumers, inventors, and the rest are not commanded to act as some planners decide. That poses various challenges and problems. In a command economy full employment is promised. What about this?

A free market is dynamic, not static. When the automobile was invented, the horse and buggy had to go; when video tapes were introduced, home movie equipment took a beating on the market; when the prefabricated home came on the market, construction firms probably felt the pinch. When Japan made the economy car, Detroit no longer could take its gas guzzlers for granted.

Of course, sometimes change is brought about in ways that people regard, at times rightly, as quite unfair. Thus some governments abroad subsidize steel production that lowers the price of the goods of the country's steel manufacturers. This makes it more attractive to buy foreign steel rather than what is produced in a relatively free and unsubsidized market. Textiles, footwear, and microchips have all experienced the phenomenon of "unfair foreign competition."

Those who own businesses, including corporate executives and the stock-holders, are seen as either wealthy enough to last out transition periods or they haven't a great proportion of their wealth dependent upon some one firm or industry's economic welfare. However, workers in automobile or steel plants seem to depend fully on the solvency of their company. If steel plants are closed, the shareholders may take a small loss, relative to their total income or pension funds, but they seem diversified enough to survive quite comfortably. But the workers appear to depend on the plant for their very livelihood. So its closing is a devastating event for them.

Karl Marx, the most severe critic of capitalism, prophesied that such un-avoidable, inevitable upheavals in the labor market would spell doom for the system. The growing number of unsettled workers would become fed up with capitalism and would vote for more and more government intervention, so that eventually the system would change from capitalist to socialist.

And there is reason to think that something of a revolution is under way, what with all the legislation making it more and more difficult for business to carry on profitably. And many people can sympathize with this result. Only a

---

*Excerpted from the *Florida Policy Review* (1988).

few actually see the danger of such protectionist, anti-free-trade sentiments. They argue that the fault lies mainly with interventionism, not free trade.

Marx believed, along with some non-Marxist economists, that capitalism depends on wage labor. Marx had to see it this way since he believed that capital accumulation occurred as a result of worker exploitation. But he was wrong on this last point. And he was also wrong about wage labor, namely, that it is a necessary condition for the existence of capitalism.

Capitalism has been misrepresented by intellectuals, and by the activists who listened to them. They promulgated a viewpoint that made workers seem only as victims. The capitalist, in turn, was seen as the enemy, a different species of human being entirely, one who just looked to exploit the workers, never mind what happens to them in the process. From this antagonistic coexistence in the marketplace, workers had very little to gain. A few could extricate themselves and become small capitalists. But the bulk remained in the work force. Even partial escape from total victimization seemed to require to most the formation of massive labor organizations protected from competition and market forces by the government. By pooling their political strength, labor set out to strike some better bargains.

Yet this really did not do a great deal of good, because as soon as wages rise collectively, independent of higher demand or more efficient productivity, the ripple effect is that prices, on the average, will also rise. The workers who organize may receive, as a result of organization, a bit of artificial job security, but not a significantly more abundant life.

What was substantially suppressed is that this is not the only alternative to the working person's situation. It is easy to think of a far more profitable approach, namely, the forming of labor corporations, partnerships, firms, etc., and the utilization of private insurance to cover the contingency of unemployment on those rare occasions when it cannot be avoided.

Many workers could establish their own business, even if others—for instance, younger people—would prefer the wage earning arrangement and thus run the risk of periodic dislocation. Certainly, the incorporation of labor is familiar in such areas as lawyering, doctoring, banking, education, etc.

Basically all that is necessary is raising and/or borrowing some capital—just as in any other business—and the management of the service, labor, in line with its demand on the market. Of course there are risks, and to those who wish for a risk-free economic world there really is no way out. But at least in this set-up the worker is no longer so much at the mercy of others, namely, employers. Rather, workers can manage their own labor corporations, go out on jobs, sign up on retainer, have pension programs within their own firms, reinvest, set up retraining centers that keep an eye on the ever-changing marketplace, etc.

Nevertheless, in a free society anyone would be free to offer his or her services for wages, in the now familiar fashion, and many may do this as their most preferred arrangement. Not everyone likes to bother with business: Some want to put in their hours on weekdays and then do something else the rest of the time. But this kind of life carries its own risks: e.g., periodic unemployment, should the business one works for discontinue. But here again the issue is that no risk-free world is possible, and demanding it and trying to adjust the legal structure to do so will backfire.

THERE'S NO MYSTERY TO THE "THOUSAND LIGHTS*

I am no George Bush fan but I must defend him about this: Ever since the debates, Bush has been getting it from all sides for his use of the "thousand points of light" metaphor. He used it to indicate how he believes the problem of the homeless should be solved.

Afterward Mike Dukakis claimed he does not understand what Bush is talking about. Then all of Mike's helpers descended on the news media making the same claim—they just totally miss Bush's point, sorry.

Well, I for one don't buy it. Dukakis and Co. aren't that stupid. They must have known that Bush meant simply that instead of having the central federal government take care of the homeless problem, let all the various agencies and charitable groups—churches, philanthropic organizations, and municipal, county, state, and related social services at the local levels of government—get a handle on the problem and solve it.

You might not like this approach—I am sure by now many Americans have lost confidence in anything but Big Uncle Sam to do anything in our society that needs doing. Especially if it involves helping people. Never mind that the feds' innumerable programs since the New Deal, Fair Deal, New Frontier, and Great Society have not managed to alleviate poverty and remedy everything without, at least, a very firm regimen from the government. Sure, you can make the trains run on time if you promise to shoot everyone who won't help. But sooner or later you'll have someone with other priorities come after you. Or you get a country of patsies.

In any case, Harvard University (J.F.K. School of Government) Professor Michael S. Dukakis surely must have heard a similar world famous metaphor—Mao Tse-tung's "let a hundred flowers bloom"! Mao, that famous saver of humanity and social reformer, who may have inspired many people who are constantly craving strong leadership from the central government, meant that the communist revolution must be conducted in many different ways, not just one. This alone ought to have helped the Dukakis gang to understand George Bush, that counter-revolutionary conservative who wants at least some of society's problems to be solved by means other than getting the federales involved and by throwing a big bunch of federal tax money after it.

There is nothing terribly peculiar in Bush's idea. It is irritating to the likes of me but understandable why he keeps using metaphors rather than making the point in a straightforward way. Wouldn't it be wonderful and courageous if a major political candidate could come right out and say, "I believe that the

---

*Originally published in the *Orange County Register* (October 2, 1988).

problems of human beings in a free country should be solved by the human beings themselves, not by some alleged all-knowing elite at the head of state. That method has been tried by our new friends, the Soviets and the Chinese, and by numerous other gangs of dictators, and it has failed miserably. "What I am for—regardless of what I used to be for in the past or what many in the intelligentsia would urge me to be for—is to leave problems to be solved by the people close to the problems. I will let our government worry, instead, about truly public—universal—problems that befall our country—justice, liberty, and defense."

Please forgive me, but one can dream now and then, no? The fact is that in a relatively free society the people, not the political candidates, determine what is politically palatable. And Bush not only cannot say such things until the constituency he is counting on feels similarly but he probably doesn't even believe it fully himself. He may only realize—or some of his aides might—that at least a large segment of our voting population is reasonably committed to individual liberty, privatization, personal and community initiative. And the "thousand points of light" metaphor was probably devised to signal to those people some hope under a Bush regime.

What irks me, however, is that Dukakis and his gang cannot come right out and say, we understand the "thousand points of light" ploy but we disagree with it—we believe in the one bright light theory—let Washington, D.C., handle things because from there we can force everyone to comply with our plans. Leaving it to the thousand points of light does not offer a guarantee, which is what we are after. We want to make absolutely certain—by way of federal legal sanctions— that no one is left homeless, uninsured, out of a job, without his farm, etc.

Had we gotten this kind of response from Dukakis, we might have seen a debate unfold as to whether this kind of promise can be fulfilled. As I noted, I am a convinced skeptic about it—I don't even believe anyone ought to try such schemes. But at least let's talk it over, folks. Then maybe the American voting public could make its mind up in this election based on serious, meaningful discussion, not sniping and name calling and the pretense at mystification.

7

Business

PROFITS WITH HONOR*

Capitalism is largely held in contempt in today's moral climate. A culture's moral climate is the prominent opinion about what sort of conduct is proper and improper. Those who accept and seem to practice it need never explain their conduct. Its rejection in theory and practice, however, calls forth rebuke, censure, and condemnation by the media, politicians, religious leaders, and others who dominate forums of opinion in society.

In earlier eras, too, aspects of capitalism were widely condemned by spokesmen of the times. The system continued to function anyway, mainly because of its undeniable productivity. Today, however, the criticism of capitalism has reached a crescendo, even though what capitalism ever really existed has virtually vanished.

Does capitalism fit into our culture's moral climate? If not, is this climate misguided and unhealthy, or should capitalism be abandoned for some other system? One thing is certain: It is impossible for any social, economic, or political system to flourish in a climte morally opposed to that system.

Two main currents dominate our moral climate. One is altruism—the belief that everyone's primary purpose in life is to serve other people, to promote others' welfare, or at least to provide for those who are in need. The other is pragmatism, which in this arena translates into a belief that morality is a mythical notion and that only a scientific or technological outlook makes sense today.

Altruism is usually contrasted with egoism. The virtues of self-sacrifice, of giving and not taking, of humility instead of ambition, are stressed by those who favor altruism. And egoism, for them, involves callousness toward others, inconsiderateness, crass self-gratification, and no concern for principles and ideals.

More generously understood, though, egoism *is* informed by principle and actually involves a positive goal—the enhancement of one's own human life. This

*Originally published in *Reason* magazine (May 1983).

isn't achieved by simple-minded pleasure seeking or by running roughshod over others, however, but by bettering oneself as a rational being, by fostering mutually beneficial relations with others, and by securing political principles for one's society that protect the rights of everyone.

Altruism is the far more prominent view. This may be obscured by the occasional popularity of doctrines like the *Playboy* philosophy, the hedonism of the "me decade," and the sales of such self-help books as Robert Ringer's *Looking Out for Number 1* and Wayne Dwyer's *Pulling Your Own Strings*. In fact, however, these phenomena are hardly prominent and, when they threaten to become so, they are frowned upon. From pulpits, pundits, and politicians, the prevailing message is altruism, with its call for self-sacrifice, for tightening our belts and reducing our standard of living so the needy and the poor of the world can benefit.

In politics, altruism leads to social-welfare measures, even at the expense of the liberty of many to better their own circumstances. At times, of course, there arises a political sentiment that counters altruism. When Californians passed Proposition 13, which rolled back property taxes and therefore government spending in the state, opponents of the measure found it selfishly motivated. Many insisted that it gave evidence of an abhorrent "me first" mentality.

Yet, defenders of Proposition 13 did not counter by declaring it quite all right to think of one's own prosperity, to assert one's right to a decent life. Instead, they spoke of waste and abuses in government. This testified eloquently to the prominence of altruism. Even when people do act for their self-interest, they deny it in public, searching for explanations that make it appear that this was not their intention.

Ideologically, those who have been called humanitarians or collectivists—who have favored sharing the wealth or redistributing the fruits of work—have tended to be altruists. Those, however, stressing individuals' liberty and the right of anyone to succeed by his or her own effort have tended to favor individualism or egoism as their ethical position. Two examples illustrate the division quite clearly.

Karl Marx in his earliest days, before he had worked out anything like a total system of thought, was an ethical altruist. In an essay entitled "On the Jewish Question," Marx wrote:

> The actual individual man must take the abstract citizen back into himself and, as an individual man in his empirical life, in his individual work and individual relationships, become a species-being; man must recognize his own forces as social forces, organize them and thus no longer separate social forces from himself in the form of political forces. Only when this has been achieved will human emancipation be completed.

People, Marx was arguing, should cast off individuality and organize their lives for the benefit of the whole—which amounts to living and working for the benefit of others.

The point comes through even more clearly in Marx's attack on the doctrine of individual rights, especially property rights:

> The right of man to freedom is not based on the union of man with man, but on the separation of man from man . . . . The right of man to property is the right to enjoy his possessions and dispose of them arbitrarily, without regard for other men, independently of society, the right of selfishness . . . . It leads man to see in other men not the realization but the limitation of his own freedom.

Marx *complained* that the right to freedom and to property makes ample room for individuality, for personal autonomy. He was right on target; these rights do indeed permit a sphere of privacy wherein the individual is not subject to others' claims and demands. But Marx found this unsuited to the goals he recommended for human beings—their collective emancipation, the development of the human species as a whole.

In contrast to the connection between altruism and collectivism, there is the link between egoism and individualism. Ayn Rand, the novelist-philosopher who gave capitalism and the free society much support during the last few decades, was an ethical egoist. In one of her essays, "What Is Capitalism?" she wrote:

> The recognition of individual rights implies the recognition of the fact that the good is . . . a value pertaining to . . . the lives of individual human beings (note the right to the pursuit of happiness). It implies that the good cannot be divorced from beneficiaries, that men are not to be regarded as interchangeable, and that no man or tribe may attempt to achieve the good of some at the price of the immolation of others.

Self-assertion and self-interest are commendable, Rand argued. And the free society, she insisted, with its capitalist economic system, is the best means by which individuals' interests may be pursued. Altruism, with its subordination of the individual to the whole, is explicitly rejected, especially when imposed, as most often urged, by force of law.

With capitalism and altruism so diametrically opposed, it is no small matter whether the case for altruism is sound. The question is not whether helpfulness, considerateness, generosity, and the like are to be counted among the human virtues. The question is whether we have a primary moral duty to devote ourselves to bettering the lot of others.

No philosophical system has successfully defended altruism as an ethical position. No one has demonstrated that we should indeed live for the sake of others. And it is not for neglecting to try.

Why is the doctrine insupportable? Altruism, Nietzsche noted, is the master-slave morality. It demands that humanity split itself into camps, one preaching and reaping the benefits of altruism, the other abiding by the doctrine and assuming the position of servitude. But even if Nietzsche's forthright polemics are rejected, we find that on logical grounds alone altruism collapses. Why on earth should each person live for others' sakes if, as it surely follows in this doctrine, all these others must do the same, ad infinitum? Who is the ultimate beneficiary of this kind of conduct—who deserves, finally, to be honored with a decent life of his or her own? Some abstraction called "humanity" or "the species" or "society" is frequently proposed, but what are all these if not the individual members they comprise? Why, then, should all these individuals be orienting their lives to serve others? Why don't we simply encourage all people to do well in their *own* lives, thereby cutting out the "middleman"?

The most common answer to this line of questioning is that not everyone will fare equally well if individuals are encouraged to pursue their own self-interest and prosperity. And this exposes the real incoherency of altruism: It rejects excellence—that is, excelling as individuals. A decent life for each and every individual is touted as the highest ideal, yet anyone who achieves such a life for himself is castigated as selfish.

Altruism is not prominent because it hangs together as a coherent position. It is prominent because no alternative moral doctrine has been effectively promulgated. From the earliest times of human thought, when most of mankind lived in subjugation, altruism seemed to a few to be a benign morality. To many more, it was a convenient doctrine by which to extract service from others. Because of its incoherence and impracticality, human beings could only implement the doctrine ineffectively, suffering guilt all the while. Yet, since it was not effectively opposed, altruism continued to serve as the standard by which human beings judged themselves and each other.

It is no surprise that many, aware of the hopelessness of a morality of altruism and equating altruism with morality, turned their backs on morality altogether. Thus, supported by the evident success of science and technology and by certain trends in philosophy, we find pragmatism alongside altruism as a main current in today's moral climate.

Scientific knowledge is highly regarded in pragmatism; and since claims about what is good or evil cannot be proven by standard scientific methods, morality tends to be discounted. As reflected in our use of the word *pragmatic,* pragmatism rejects principled conduct and is instead interested in efficiency, usefulness, and practicality.

This is the stance of economists who defend capitalism or the free market. In an effort to give economics scientific standing, economists have tried to rid their study of human social life of any mention of value. This "value-free" approach is well known in many social sciences. It is less well known that the most prominent defenders of the free market embrace this stance.

Those economists who reason along the value-free line argue that moral judgments, convictions, and principles and related aspects of human life really amount to no more than biases or personal preferences. There is, in their view, no meaningful difference between one person's preference for strawberry ice cream and another's preference for honesty. Though some people price honesty more than their favorite ice cream, that some don't is merely a natural phenomenon. Science—which is the only route to *knowledge*—can say nothing about this. All it shows, as Milton Friedman once expressed it, is that "every individual serves his own interest . . . . The great saints of history have served their 'private interest' just as the most money-grubbing miser has served his interest. The private interest is whatever it is that drives an individual."

A naive view of science does appear to support such a view. If all that concerns science is finding the causes of events—which many thinkers believe—then finding what drives an individual will suffice for scientific purposes. This view gives one the satisfaction of having a simple tool by which to explain human affairs. Moreover, progress seems to be on its side. Science and technology have facilitated innumerable advances in human life. They have produced the theories and tools by which we can manipulate the universe quite efficiently. And so the question arises, Why should they not succeed as well when it comes to human affairs?

The economic defense of capitalism—the so-called scientific defense—seems a promising one. Why is capitalism sound? Because it accords with the way we really are; it is the empirical way of things. Given this view, interference with the free market is artificial, disturbing of the natural balance. The theme has been advanced before, on numerous occasions, in support of various systems and policies. It might help capitalism too.

And capitalism has all along been in desperate need of help, with attacks upon it coming from both the political Right and Left. Baudelaire wrote: "Commerce is satanic, because it is the basest and vilest form of egoism." Balzac, in *Melmoth Reconciled,* declared that "when commercial interests are at stake, Moses might appear with his two luminous horns, and his coming would scarcely receive the honors of a pun; the gentlemen whose business it is to write the Market Reports would ignore his existence." And then there were, of course, Marx and Engels, writing in the *Communist Manifesto:*

> The bourgeoise . . . has pitilessly torn asunder the motley feudalities that bound man to his "natural superiors," and has left remaining no other nexus between man and man than naked self-interest, than callous "cash payment." It has drowned the most heavenly ecstasies of religious fervor, of chivalrous enthusiasm . . . in the icy water of egotistical calculation. It has resolved personal worth into exchange value.

How can those schooled in economics reply to such erudite, lofty assaults? They can dismiss it all as motivated by private interest and as unscientific "music," to quote Milton Friedman again. If the scorn of Baudelaire and Balzac, of Marx and Engels, is what morality has to offer, then no wonder people concerned with the actual world turn their backs on morality and claim a more realistic, scientific view of human affairs. Practical people realize that freedom of trade is responsible for prosperity. So if morality condemns freedom of trade and commerce, morality must be something confused—an obstacle to what is useful and workable. Morality, by its wide association with altruism, is thus rejected in favor of pragmatism, of practicality and efficiency.

But this is a mistake; for there is no escape from good and evil in human existence, and failing to think about them simply leaves the sphere for others to conquer. Nor does science require that we deny the place of morality and principles in human life. There is no sound reason to expect human life to be fully explained and understood along lines suited to physics, chemistry, or biology. Persons are beings with physical, chemical, and biological attributes, yes—but that is not all. Attempting to reduce the study of man to the study of other objects in the world doesn't make sense when the object is to understand something that is distinctive about human beings.

Ultimately, the value-free scientific approach to defending capitalism will not work, because human beings do have values. Science does not show that the system is decent; it shows only that if the system is adopted, we can mainly expect widespread economic productivity. Why should this be considered so crucial? Value-free economics does not have an answer.

There is an answer, however—that productivity is indeed morally right for us. We *should* lead lives that are productive. And we should do so because we will benefit from it, because we will live more in accord with our human nature if we produce things, if we strive to earn profits in business, if we seek to achieve our self-interest.

But it won't do to say only this much. The answer must be fleshed out. What is the meaning of *self* in *self-interest?* Is one's *interest* simply whatever one prefers or wishes for? How does the pursuit of one's interest square with the best ways to live in a society?

The idea of self involved here rests on the fact that each person is *human* and is *individual.* Identifying one's self-interest must take account of oneself both as an individual and as an intentionally social being.

There is no conflict between self-interest and the interest of others when all pursue their self-interest—not unless we construe the universe to be absurd from the outset. Why doesn't the basic interest, or good, of an individual clash with that of another? It could only do so if we mistakenly identified all our desires, wishes, and unreflective wants with our basic interest. But what is in our interest is not so simple as that.

A human being's basic interest cannot conflict with his basic human nature. Our basic human nature is characterized by the fact that we are rational living beings; that is, we are animals capable of thinking, reasoning, imagining, and so forth. As rational living beings, we benefit enormously from social interaction. Language, love, education, science, commerce, art, and the other fruits of social intercourse benefit us, because we can both learn from and enjoy them tremendously.

Because we benefit from social interaction, rules of social life that promote decency and consideration are extremely beneficial to each of us. Indeed, such rules are the very *means* for constructive human associations beyond the narrow ties of family or clan. The appropriate principles of law and politics are the rights of individuals—on the order of the Bill of Rights that is part of the Constitution. These principles spell out the basic rules for organized social life that are to the mutual advantage of all members of society. The natural human rights all of us possess are principles by which we can guide ourselves in our relations to others for general, overall mutual benefit. Even if every wish or desire we have cannot be satisfied as we abide by these principles, they are to our general welfare, because they grow out of our human nature and what it requires for social life.

This is the framework within which a capitalist, free-market society is morally defensible. The guiding morality, drawn from a recognition of what it means to be a human individual, is the morality of rational self-interest. Let us consider, then, the consequences of this morality for commerce, the most visible feature of the system. What is the role of productivity—or profit making—within human life and in the social system that suits such life best?

I am referring here to the *virtue* of working for a profit. To strive to improve one's life, to be thrifty and prudent as well as self-fulfilled and joyful—all of this is morally admirable, commendable. To seek profit is right, indeed, for everyone.

Let me dispel a common confusion, however. Making profit cannot properly involve assault, fraud, theft, and other parasitic activities with which profit making is so often identified. The morality of productivity—of *making,* not taking profit—cannot, by its very nature, include stealing the productive results of others' activities. Profit making consists of activity that produces more than there was previously.

Beyond outright theft, embezzlement, or other forms of confiscation of private property—including the fruits of labor and ingenuity—there are less obvious ways of seeking to gain by coercion and interference with freedom. Government regulation, for instance, is a clear intrusion into the lives of citizens who have not been proven to be guilty of any violations of others' rights.

Usually, government regulation of our economic affairs is advocated on grounds that the poor, helpless, uninformed, and easily duped require protection. Regulatory agencies are assumed to express the care and thoughtfulness of politicians and the electorate.

But if we are as helpless and careless as some supporters of regulation may sincerely believe, such care would be futile anyway. For why, if we are so hapless, have bureaucrats escaped this fate? Why, if our local merchants and manufacturers, or those in large corporations, are crooked and malicious, wishing for a buck even if gained at the expense of someone's life or well-being, are politicians and their appointees immune to such temptation? And if they are not immune, is it not clearly unwise to centralize the forces of incompetence and malice instead of leaving them dispersed throughout the population so that individuals and organizations might cope with them more effectively?

Furthermore, government bodies set up to help us help ourselves often are captured by special-interest groups who use them to further their own ends. Licensing bureaus in the health and other professions, for example, do just exactly this. The proffered justification is that licensing locks out competition—from "fly-by-nights" and incompetents, of course—so as to help us. But all this kind of help comes to is a usurpation of our individual authority, our freedom.

It is the doctrine of altruism that supports such government interference with our freedom. In the name of helping others or improving society, our liberty to pursue life by our own judgment is curtailed constantly, even in a political community that was founded on the principle of individual rights. The mere chance that a marketplace exchange might leave the consumer or worker less well off then expected—the mere chance that such will occur justifies, from the altruistic point of view, the limitation of everyone's liberty. After all, according to altruism, what we do for ourselves with our liberty is negligible. So it doesn't matter if, in order to reduce the probability of wrongdoing, the chance of doing well by ourselves is curtailed or even eliminated. It doesn't matter if it will take millions of dollars to install airbags in all new cars—so long as this *might* help some people. Never mind that such policies deprive millions of people of the opportunity to choose whether to spend their funds for that or for something else for themselves or those for whom they care.

All this is crucial not only to the survival of a free and civilized society but to human life itself. That is why the altruistic ethics, which levels such a frontal attack on the idea of profit, must be confronted directly—on moral grounds— instead of pushed aside in favor of considerations of waste, of helping the unemployed, and of other pragmatic defenses of the profit system.

Ironically, it is not only intellectuals and politicians who distrust profit making—so do those who make profits. Most of them shy away from defending it. When confronted by sanctimonious politicians—at congressional hearings into the operations of various industries, for example—business representatives often offer lame excuses for doing well at their business instead of a straight, indeed proud, declaration that they are in the profession of making profits, and when these are big, they have done their work very well.

Many who are all too willing to have government regulate the business profession are eager to keep their own professions free of such regulation. The news media and the publishing industry are prime examples. While quick to resist government interference in their endeavors, they rarely speak out in support of other professionals who are regulated to the hilt. Yet many—perhaps most—books are written irresponsibly; numerous magazine articles contain flasehood and distortion; the news is often biased. Why is none of this seen as terrible enough to control the press? Because people in publishing know well enough that the risk of going wrong— including misinforming people, ruining reputations, and so on—is worth the creativity and progress that is only possible if their field is left free of coercion. They simply will not generalize this to cover other professions as well.

Those in other professions, however, are not favored by an explicit First Amendment in their own behalf. And those in business are not even of one mind about economic freedom. This lack of solidarity in the business community is not, however, very surprising. Ideas about what is right and wrong do not emerge, contrary to Karl Marx's teachings, from one's economic environment. Some of the most entrepreneurial individuals in the world are political socialists, while some of the most fervent advocates of capitalism are plain lazy. There simply is no "class consciousness" that governs people's thoughts on politics and ethics.

The business community's lack of concern with its own best interests is evidenced, for example, by the practices of Mobil Oil, IBM, Xerox, and Texaco when it comes to the investments they make apart from direct enterprise. Such corporations repeatedly support artistic, scientific, educational, and related nonprofit endeavors that are unambiguously hostile to capitalism. Movies, plays, television programs, foundation projects, and universities receive funds from these corporations. Yet, evidence indicates that most of these directly or indirectly attack the very principles that make corporate business possible.

A few years back, to offer an illustration, there was the motion picture *Heaven Can Wait*. The only villain in the story "happened" to be a capitalist who supported free enterprise. The protagonist counted among his virtues his refusal to take the free-enterprise approach seriously. Innumerable television scripts equivocate between wishing to make a profit and criminal motivation. Virtually every major crime, from murder to rape, is treated in television dramas and pulp movies as a necessary consequence of people trying to prosper in life. The implied indictment of human nature itself is staggering. Still, sponsors continue to support such programming. The business community also continues to sanction hundreds of magazines and newspapers whose editorial stance toward the capitalist system is one of hostility. And this is the very system, of course, that keeps sponsors solvent and the press free from government dependence—unlike in socialist societies.

So, Marx was wrong—business folks do not always know or pursue their interests. There is no reason to believe that the so-called bourgeois class takes any better care of itself, of capitalism, of its own alleged base of operation, than others would. This is not surprising, but it *is* a pity.

Capitalism, the commercial life that it fosters, the general freedom that accompanies it, and the prosperity that results—capitalists need apologize for none of this. The moral support for their system is that within it, the pursuit of happiness by human individuals is made possible to a far greater extent than in the other systems under which the peoples of the world have lived and do live. Indeed, capitalism's fundamental humanitarianism, as humanitarianism should be understood, must be stressed.

The point here is not to appear kind and altruistic! It would be dishonest to advocate a political and economic system simply on grounds that it benefits others. No, capitalism needs to be supported unapologetically as a system in which one's own well-being has the best chance to flourish. Unless this hearty support is given more and more, the morality of self-sacrifice, of altruism, of human self-debasement and servility, will triumph; and along with it, all types of statism—the systematic threat to human liberty everywhere.

Turning away from the moral issues isn't an answer, contrary to the claims of some defenders of capitalism throughout the system's history. There is too much evidence of the reality of moral concerns in our day-to-day endeavors. Instead of renouncing morality, defenders of capitalism must show that the basic values and virtues stressed in our moral climate are wrongheaded. Altruism alleges the supremacy of what should be simply one aspect of human concern—

namely, the welfare of others. If this is recognized, the political and economic system that makes supreme the human individual—that is, capitalism—will emerge as demonstrably superior not only in practical but in ethical terms.

An Unexpected Defense of Businessmen's Rights*

Anyone who has watched television or read pulp novels recently will confirm that no character representing the business community ever comes off looking good. Following Karl Marx, modern writers simply "paint the capitalist and landlord in no sense couleur de rose." Quite the contrary. Even the news media tend to take it for granted that those in business must be shady in some way or another. Big oil, the fat cats, the developers, the apartment owners, the condominium converters, and the like stand there in the shadows of vice and callous disregard for public-spiritedness, while advocates of solar energy, adherents of small-is-beautiful, promoters of rent control, defenders of whales, seals, and economic democracy represent virtue and the interests of humanity.

Last Thursday the nation experienced the first observance of "Big Business Day," stressing this and assorted familiar themes, with the august support of such undeniable champions of justice as Ralph Nader, John Kenneth Galbraith, Michael Harrington, Barry Commoner, Ed Asner, and others who stand firmly against greed and avarice. Various spin-off groups and organizations across the nation strove to make their message crystal clear.

Commerce is bad, and to the degree that we must, unfortunately, put up with it (until the revolution can wipe the darned thing off the face of the earth forever), it should be controlled by public-interest-minded groups and individuals, who are as influential as the boards and officers of the large corporations that now operate in the anarchy of dog-eat-dog capitalism. At any rate, what is required now is some government action to make corporations accountable to, well, those who take it upon themselves to represent the public.

Let me be clear about the central point here. The issue isn't that some corporations have behaved badly, even criminally, and should be held culpable. There is no disputing that fact. The issue is whether the institution of corporate commerce is to be regarded as basically legitimate or in need of radical reform, if not abolition.

The corporation in a free society is a voluntary association—not a feudal "creature of the state," as Nader would have us understand it. Except for some defective features of some corporations—most notably certain aspects of corporate limited liability provisions—there is nothing about the corporation that cannot be fully understood as the association of various individuals for purposes of economic prosperity. Shareholders invest and leave it to those well paid for their services to obtain the benefit of dividends and profits in return for good judgment.

The only power that corporations have—as distinct from some political clout

---

*Originally published in the *Los Angeles Times* (April 1980).

they may purchase whenever politicians are willing to sell out—is economic power, and they have no more of this than the degree of their economic success will permit. Certainly this economic power is impressive at times, but for it to be lamentable it would have to be demonstrated that it had been obtained through force and fraud. While there are instances of this—just as teachers can obtain professional success by playing to the fads students happen to have embraced recently—corporate business is made up of human beings making an effort to improve their economic welfare by means of finding some endeavor that is of benefit both to them and to those who comprise the consumers of the products in question.

Of course, this is only a model, and the various claims concerning the failure of the free market, and thus of corporate commerce, need to be fully investigated to examine the model's overall merits, Still, there is far less substance to those stories about the "robber barons" found in ordinary history books, just as there is far less substance to "crime in the suites" than Ralph Nader suggests.

What is disturbing about the widespread hostility against big business is that it is so hypocritical. Rarely does anyone suggest that perhaps the educational community houses extensive abuse and irregularity. Why is it that the media seldom expose the abuses of the newspaper business, or law school education, or the arts, or the profession of academic teaching in the humanities? Why should they be less suspicious of college professors than they are of business executives? The professor has ample opportunity to betray his trust, to fake teaching, to make use of the classroom as a place of indoctrination instead of education. If product quality and corporate liability are our concern, surely those in the business community are far from being the only ones whose work provides them with the opportunity for abuse, corruption, "ripoffs," greed, and similar viciousness.

It will be said that the professions listed above are protected by the U.S. Constitution, that government must not attempt to prevent wrongdoing by religious groups, by the press, by artists and educators, since this would constitute an encroachment of certain vital freedoms.

The Constitution may be negligent in omitting specific mention of the rights of those in the business community. Nevertheless, excluding them from the protection and preservation of their right to freedom of action is sheer discrimination. Those who now agitate for greater control over people in the business community should realize that what they want is to discriminate against members of some professions.

The Fourteenth Amendment applies here quite clearly. Members of other professions may not be harassed by government unless it has been demonstrated in a court of law that they have wronged someone; in the name of due process, even known murderers are allowed freedom. However, members of the business community are regulated simply on the grounds that sometime, somewhere, some crooked members of that community will engage in wrongful conduct. By that process of reasoning we could put everyone in jail, for there is no doubt that someone among us probably will someday act wrongfully.

This is by no means to be taken as special pleading in support of members of the business community. There is every likelihood that the proportion of evil is fairly equally distributed across all professions—educators, artists, politicians, businessmen, journalists, and, yes, even the valiant crusaders for the public interest who in the name of "preventive justice" would wipe out the liberty of some people and stand tall and proud for having done so.

THE IRONY OF THE "GREED" OF THE WRITERS' GUILD*

What the Writers' Guild wanted (in the summer of 1988 when it struck the networks) is more money for writers. This is plain enough, following the five-month-old walkout. But there is an ironic twist to it. The bulk of writers for American network television despise the profit motive. The attitude is aptly expressed in the exaggerated remarks of NBC's David Letterman, who kept referring to the business people in television, the producers, as "money-grubbing scum." This is indeed what the artisitic community behind American television thinks of those who try to gain as much monetary benefit from their work as the market will bear.

Several months ago, the Public Broadcasting System (PBS) ran a program titled "Hollywood's Heavies," which clearly demonstrated that most of those writing television scripts regard moneymaking as the greatest of all evils. For them seeking profit is the source of all the evils in the world. And anyone can check this out.

Whenever anything malicious, murderous, vicious, or otherwise evil happens on a television drama or even on a sitcom, the blame ultimately is laid at the feet of some business executive, corporate head, owner of a cattle ranch, or some other representative of the capitalist and land-owning class. This vulgar antibusiness attitude is so typical that one has to become tolerant of it just to be able to enjoy other values associated with a show.

And, of course, there is no difference between the high dramas of Broadway and the cheap stuff of network television on this score. Consider that the famous Arthur Miller play, *The Death of a Salesman,* came to little more than a dump-on-business tract, never mind some of the imaginative ways this was brought off in the work. And while on-screen technical virtuosity and diversity continue to flourish, most flicks rely on the business-bashing leit-motif for their themes: from the obvious case of *Wall Street* to the less obvious one of *Who Framed Roger Rabbit.*

Will the writers learn from their current experiences? Will they realize that seeking profits—as much as they can manage, based on playing the kind of market hard-ball that can impoverish thousands of actors and other professionals dependent upon the work they perform—is not only legitimate but morally imperative? Will they transfer their own perfectly valid and honorable interest in more money into their work and portray men and women professionally engaged in seeking money as capable of virtue and decency?

Of course this antiprofit, antibusiness attitude is certainly not new and not

---

*Originally published in the *Orange County Register* (February 28, 1988).

confined to Hollywood. For centuries artists and others have been as ambitious as any Wall Street hustler—albeit in a different line of work—yet have snubbed the profiteer as scum. Indeed, so widespread has been this hypocrisy that it is arguable that both the major holocausts of the twentieth century—Hitler's extermination of Jews and Stalin's liquidation of the kulaks—may in part be attributed to it.

Jews had been denied a home in European culture because they were not adverse to business. Then when they flourished in the field, the rest of European society began to resent them to the point of violent hatred. We all know where this led. Stalin, in turn, followed Karl Marx, who despised capitalists and thought that those attached to the task of making private profit must be cast out of the human race. (Marx, incidentally, found Jews as the typical capitalists, sharing at least this much with the Nazi ideology!)

So if you are hoping that their own struggle for extra income—never mind all the hardship this inflicts on members of their industry—will reform Hollywood's writers, forget it. Much more self-understanding and integrity would be needed than is likely to emerge from a mere case of doing exactly as the business folks whom the writers constantly deride, namely, seeking good returns on their investments.

UNDERSTANDING ANTI-BUSINESS*

"Commerce is satanic, because it is the basest and vilest form of egoism."
                                                        —*Charles Baudelaire*

Many Americans, among them vocal and influential ones, abhor corporate commerce. Catastrophies such as those at the Union Carbide plant in Bhopal, India; the insider trading scandals on Wall Street; the corporate involvement with environmental mismanagement; the limits on the liability of nuclear power plants; and many less notorious matters, would all appear to lend support to the anti-corporation mentality. Professionals and institutions in other fields are just as frequently found guilty of vices and crimes. The president of the junior college system in Alabama is found having faked his résumé and publication records, but few pay attention to that. When a scientist fakes evidence, no one would think it smears the entire scientific community. But, from the few cases of misconduct and suspicious legal practices involving corporations, the world of corporate business has gotten bad press indeed.

Despite their obvious beneficial impact, corporations are often despised. But why? Other professions and their institutions, such as medicine and hospitals, composers and orchestras, etc., are admired for the most part. So what makes business and the corporations such targets for abuse?

The most important reason is that they represent a concern for something

---

*Originally published in the *Orange County Register* (1987).

that even in our time very few people comfortably admit. This is profit—in other words, earthly prosperity. Corporations are, from beginning to end, massive efforts to please people. They aim to get rich by reading the market right, which means by satisfying other people's desires for goods and services. The market is where people express their desires for pleasure and well-being most forcefully, through the way they spend their money.

People praise altruism, the joys of spirituality, the nobility of self-sacrifice—but mostly they want a decent, prosperous, enjoyable life. And corporate business is there to do this for them in a very big and efficient way—indeed, while getting rich from the effort. It is all an unabashed mutual effort to make the most of living this life on earth.

It is one thing to seek pleasure and satisfaction, it is another thing to be happy about doing so. We tend to be schizophrenic—we want to live well, seek joys and delights, but we also claim to honor and respect those who care very little for such trivia. We express disdain for people who make a living off of our pursuit of satisfaction, yet we carry on with this pursuit nevertheless. Praise Mother Teresa and then go shopping.

Oddly, corporations more than governments treat us as adults. If we want Michael Jackson gloves, we get them. If we want pornographic books, we get them. If we want Disneyland and Disney World, and pet rocks and Cabbage Patch dolls, and Nehru jackets, and Pac-man software, we get it all, usually at a reasonable price. We are the boss, the corporate executive says.

But whenever some institution or practice is treated with significant disdain, yet also felt to be indispensable, it remains outside the scope of morality. This is well illustrated by the underground economy—for example, in drugs. When a business is driven outside the law, it begins to be conducted in a criminal fashion. During Prohibition, the business of making wine, beer, and other alcoholic beverages became thoroughly demoralized. Those associated with it were placed outside the law and thus no distinction could be made between those who participated in the business and acted decently and those who were crooks. In any underground economy, we find this to be the case. If institutional support for doing business decently is lacking, then the entire industry tends to get corrupted.

A somewhat milder version of this obtains with corporate business and, indeed, business itself. In the eyes of many who discuss moral issues in our society, business is regarded as wholly base or, at best, tolerable because it is necessary. Even those in the business world often reinforce this picture when they talk about the need for realism and the lack of room for naive idealism in business. In short, people in business—managers, executives, and employees of corporations—tend often to accept the view that they see depicted on television, in novels, and by the commentators on our society. They see their profession as amoral, if not virtually immoral.

When this happens, is it surprising that business would not behave very decently? Is it any wonder that everyone is suspicious of corporations? Since they are in fact indispensable yet are held in contempt by those who forge the moral opinions in the land, the very idea that there could be decent corporate conduct, that we should in fact discover the standards of how corporations ought to behave, vanishes.

In the end, corporate commerce does rest, ultimately, on the view that human beings are most often doing the right thing when they concern themselves with their own well-being, with the welfare of those whom they love (more than with the welfare of strangers or even neighbors), and with their own community before the communities of others. If this be morally offensive, capitalism and corporate commerce must plead guilty. In a moral climate dominated by praise for self-sacrifice (though not necessarily by acts of benevolence), it is no wonder that corporations receive a bad press.

SOME PROBLEMS WITH PRIVATIZATION*

Privatization is a current movement in the Western world, as well as in some Third World nations, whereby various functions that government had assumed are gradually returned to the private sector. Sometimes privatization involves no more than government contracting out some of its assumed functions but retaining legal supervision over them. At other times it means inviting private-sector parties to share in the ownership and management of some government managed activities. In general, however, privatization aims at removing from government control those functions that could be performed by private individuals or businesses with no moral damage to anyone and with considerable overall economic benefit.

Many people support the privatization of all functions of government, except those directly related to the maintenance and preservation of social justice: i.e., protection of the basic rights of all individuals to life, liberty, and property. Of course, not all who favor some privatization agree with this ultimate goal. The issue is of concern to some of the major movers and shakers involved in promoting privatization—e.g., the Adam Smith Institute in England, the Institute Economique de Paris in France, and the Reason Foundation in Santa Monica, California—and the consequences of such a proposal are being explored.

There is one issue with which supporters of total privatization have never fully come to grips. This is the problem economists call "uninternalizable negative externalities" or, as those who are concerned with the protection of individual rights might put it, the unavoidable violation of such rights involved in some productive activities, ranging from the manufacture of steel or automobiles to transportation.

Professor Kenneth J. Arrow of Stanford University has noted that the dumping of waste into the atmosphere, which has unavoidable rights-violating consequences, is judicially inefficient. For example, when we pollute the air mass over various populated regions, and some people suffer respiratory injury, the culprit and the victim cannot be linked. The former can't be penalized, the latter can't be compensated.

For the most part, government has instituted substantial regulation of air

---

*Originally published in the Orange County *Register* (1987).

and water quality. Yet this merely rations costs and benefits in line with some arbitrary notion of what constitutes "permissible" victimization.

Total prohibition or quarantine has been resisted by free market advocates because some who would be victimized might in fact welcome this in return for the benefits reaped from the activity that involves rights violation. But this is a dangerous attitude: It could justify any number of crimes on grounds that the culprit might of course bestow some benefits on the victim by way of his criminal conduct. If I kidnap you and take you to a health clinic to check up on your physical condition, you might indeed benefit from this; yet I would still be acting criminally for not having asked you whether you choose to obtain this benefit. If you destroy a cigarette factory, in the last analysis you may have caused far greater overall benefit than harm, yet you would still be wrong to do it because you failed to gain the consent of the owner, the workers, the customers, etc.

Similarly, governmental air-quality control may well succeed in benefiting those who are subject to it but this still does not fulfill the requirement of a morally acceptable policy. Consent of the government must not be hypothetical or wait for retroactive confirmation!

There are cases in which something approximating the quarantine approach— i.e., outright prohibition of pollution, based on some assessment of what constitutes the difference between waste disposal or emission and pollution (*injurious* waste disposal or emission)—is being tried. For example, since 1976 the Environmental Protection Agency's emission control requirements may be met by trading emission reduction credits (ERCs). This is now regularly done. A recent example is Sundance Spas, a Chino, California, company that purchased ERCs from other companies that no longer needed to engage in extensive emission in their own production processes. While this approach was initiated by a regulatory agency, it is not itself a typical government regulation but a form of judicial administration. It is based on what can be regarded as the protection and maintenance of property rights and the adjudication of their violation, should that become necessary in case of dumping or trespassing. Ideally a certain limit would be set by law on how much waste disposal it tolerable. It would be based, in part, on how much natural pollution would exist in a given populated region. Within this limit firms may dispose of waste or trade their disposal rights. The process is now employed in connection with the trading of ERCs, but unfortunately the precise judicial status of such an approach is not recognized as the implementation of a system of property rights.

In many places, however, the problem of waste disposal is still handled through government regulation. This involves setting acceptable levels of pollution, based on cost-benefit analyses, which leads to the sacrifice of individual rights to some politically determined general good! And privatization experts have not yet put forth a consistent theory as to how we can divorce government from the business of rationing levels of waste disposal and at the same time preserve the individual rights of those who may not choose to be victims of pollution (beyond what they would be if human beings would not engage in waste disposal).

It is quite unrealistic—indeed, utopian—to ask for the kind of pristine environmental conditions many zealots demand. But it is not unreasonable to demand that no one be injured by polluters or dumpers beyond the natural pollution of the environment. Until privatization theorists develop a consistent and practical theory dealing with "uninternalizable negative externalities," the privatization movement will not have achieved the success that its ideals deserve.

LOST IN THE SMOG*

The problem of pollution remains essentially intractable. The popular idea still exists that pollution is created mainly by greedy business people and our commercial society. So it is held that if people's attitudes could be changed so that we had a culture less fixated on profit—if more citizens felt like Ralph Nader and fewer like Donald Trump—then the problem could be solved. Barring a change in people's attitudes, the firm hands of government are needed at the helm. Unless government restraints are imposed, business will continue to pollute. (Why bureaucrats are free of immoral temptations is unclear.)

Sophisticated anti-business sentiments are voiced mostly by members of the university community, excepting the occasional economist whose views, because of the discipline's close ties to business, are always suspect. The basic motives of business are assumed to be exclusively mercenary and unchangeable.

Not long ago, in a one-hour NBC-TV special on government regulation, proponents of more regulation came from so-called public interest centers, think tanks, and universities. Opponents came from industry or the Reagan (pro-business) administration. Of course, most viewers would see the show as a battle between objective, compassionate, truthful scholars, and greedy, ambitious, something-to-hide business lobbyists.

Yet pollution is not actually the fault of those who carry out the nation's business. The government has always been the real culprit. To put it briefly, when private business pollutes the property or persons of other private parties, this is open to legal remedy. Such *dumping* is legally actionable. But when private business pours soot into the public sphere—into the air and lakes of our neighborhoods—the legal system has handled the problem differently. Instead of prohibiting such acts, government has chosen to regulate them. What government has done in the past (and is still doing) is to treat some invasions upon people's lives as illegal, and some as in need of regulation.

Regulation, in contrast to prohibition and outright ownership-management, involves accepting some conduct as legitimate but setting enforceable standards for how to engage in them. In Los Angeles, for example, cars, factories, chemical firms, and nuclear facilities all engage in pollution, putting harmful substances into the public domain. But what does the government do about this? It regulates the levels of pollution, leaving polluters to violate some individuals' rights, but this time with government sanction. There is a better, ethically superior, and more

---

*Originally published in the *Orange County Register* (December 7, 1986).

just way of approaching the issue. It might well lead to the abandonment of pure social cost-benefit analysis, which ignores some innocent bystanders.

We can approach the problem by considering public policy toward someone with contagious disease. If such a person wanders about in public he or she will definitely hurt others. Except in mild cases, such an individual would be quarantined, regardless of the many important things he or she might have to do. If one cannot do these things without hurting others, one is not permitted to do them, period. The general idea is that if even the most legitimate, proper activity cannot be done without inflicting undeserved harm on other people, such an activity must be prohibited. The details of the matter can become complicated, but the principle is clear: No one may violate the rights of individuals, not even to further some perfectly worthwhile cause.

But does government treat polluters this way? No. Instead, it engages in the *rationing* of rights violation. This practice really isn't morally different from allowing, say, lepers, who may very well have important and productive tasks to perform in public, free reign of the public realm.

The problem of pollution is complicated by the fact that differences in scale can produce differences in kind, e.g., between mere *emission* and *pollution*. The former consitutes harmless dumping. For example, one car in the Los Angeles basin does not produce enough exhaust fumes to harm *anyone* because the fumes are diluted in what engineers call the "infinite sink" of the atmosphere. It is only when the scale of emission, compared with the carrying capacity of the sink (air, water, etc.), reaches a critical point that adverse health effects (or other forms of harm) can be identified and do actually result. There is a threshold at which point any further emission would constitute pollution, harmful emission; and with our better technology of measurement, there can be some change in what will be identified as actual pollution.

None of this changes the principle of the matter. Once a certain level of emission has been reached, any addition or increase would amount to pollution. And permitting such pollution amounts to accepting the moral and legal appropriateness of some people causing injury to others who have not given their consent and who cannot even be compensated! A just legal system would prepare itself to deal with these complexities, as it does in other spheres where crime is a real possibility. The failure to do so produces our present destructive pollution problems.

One response to this idea may be that the measures implied are too devastating for an industrial society. Yet in principle this does not differ from the response given to the proposal to abolish slavery in the American South; that, too, implied devastating consequences for the economy of the region, at least in the short run. A gradual adjustment to the requirements of justice can avoid the threat of any sudden disruptions in a community that has depended on unjust ways for too long.

So, as damaging as rampant pollution is, it isn't the fault of members of the business community as such! It is not they who are sworn to secure justice. The remedy must come from the courts.

JUSTICE, ETHICS, AND GOVERNMENT REGULATIONS*

Numerous economic studies show that government regulation of business is costly, ineffective, harmful, stifling, and otherwise destructive. Yet past regulatory activities continue, new regulations proliferate, and millions continue to believe in the desirability of more and more government regulation.

Some public figures have even answered the economists' complaints by noting that government regulation was never meant to be cheap, productive, or economically advantageous. What government regulation was and is meant to accomplish is the achievement of noneconomic values—equality, justice, fairness. And these values may require great expense, even sacrifice.

Those who defend the propriety, justice, or similar moral value of government regulation do not, however, really make a case for their position. Ralph Nader, for instance, talks freely about justice, fairness, equity, and all that. But he is simply working with vague concepts that neither he nor anyone else has bothered to examine in detail.

As a result, it may prove constructive to supplement the economists' findings with ethical considerations. It may well be that collectivism—the idea that the welfare of the society or nation should be advanced at any cost—provides the moral support for government regulation. And this collectivist morality, which emphasizes the superior status of the group to that of individual human beings, may just be wrong.

An alternative individualist morality, more in keeping with America's culture and political tradition, does not lend automatic support to government regulation. Indeed, in such areas as treatment of the accused, the legal status of those deemed to be mentally disturbed, and intrusion by governments into people's private affairs, we make implicit use of moral notions that would appear to be equally applicable to deregulatory efforts.

Consider the idea of unjust discrimination. Imposing burdens upon members of a group on grounds that some of those members have acted improperly is generally considered unjust, especially when the practice is made public policy. The basis for this judgment is an individualist morality—the idea that individuals should be treated as individuals rather than as members of a group. Yet regulatory practices discriminate against entire groups of professionals, such as business managers or accountants, on grounds that only some of them have abused their unregulated professional opportunities.

Consider, also, the idea of due process of law. If someone is considered very likely to engage in criminal conduct, the burden of proof rests on those who entertain this idea. The individual is regarded as innocent until proven otherwise. However, when people enter a business in which they might act so as to harm others (for example, in the production or sale of toys or of drugs), they are automatically made to suffer burdens, comparable to penalties, without it having been demonstrated that they have violated anyone's rights.

---

*Originally published in the *New York Times*. Written with Alan Reynolds (July 8, 1978).

The goals of regulation are not necessarily disputed when one invokes these ideas and ideals. Product and occupational safety are desirable goals; no one need dispute that. But if only such goals are admitted as having moral relevance, then mere pragmatic considerations that it costs a lot to attain those goals, or that the effort has not been successful, must fail to be convincing to decent people. But if we recognize that pursuing the usual goals of government regulation is likely to violate accepted principles of justice, then we can consider what means, other than government regulation, might exist to attain those goals.

At this point, the economists' case becomes crucial. Economists have shown that the free market has it own mechanism through which reasonable success is possible in such endeavors as seeking product safety, drug safety, safety at work, equality of opportunity, widespread employment, fair housing, decent wages for those willing to work, and so on. No one could promise perfect results in the attempt to attain these goals. But what the economists are telling us is that in a free market these results can be expected to be more nearly achieved at less expense than with government regulation. We should add that they can also be achieved with less risk of violating accepted principles of justice.

SAM'S YOUR UNCLE, NOT YOUR MOTHER OR FATHER*

Quote highlighted in the *New York Times,* July 28, 1988: "Caveat Emptor is not enough of an ethic where making babies is concerned." The source: Arthur Caplan, director of the Center for Biomedical Ethics in Minneapolis, Minnesota.

As Black's Law Dictionary tells us, "caveat emptor" means "Let the buyer beware (or take care)." The comment from Mr. Caplan is curious, to say the least, since as Judge Richard Posner points out in his *The Economics of Justice* (Harvard, 1981), "the rule of *caveat emptor* in nineteenth-century Anglo-American common law [has] giv[en] way to *caveat venditor.*" That is, instead of the buyer taking care out of an obligation to be prudent, these days it is the seller who is forced to take care so nothing untoward happens to the buyer, not merely where making babies is concerned but in virtually every field of production and trade.

For an executive director of an *ethics* center to pretend that the doctrine of *caveat emptor* is these days in effect throughout the marketplace is disturbing. Ethics should teach one not to distort the truth, not even for good effect. (Indeed, the truth-in-advertising campaign of some years ago addressed just this problem.) Yet it looks as though promoters of what they regard as the public good need not adhere to such trivial matters as truth.

Mr. Caplan's evident willingness to perpetrate a distortion is also quite instructive. It clearly suggests how useless it is to set up supervision of the marketplace. Those who would volunteer for this job tend themselves not to behave all that correctly.

In fact there's hardly any form of trade that is not regulated these days by

---

*Originally published in the *Orange County Register* (October 18, 1988).

some arm of the state. And the phenomenon of government regulation comes about just the way Mr. Caplan seems to desire it.

First, pretend that the marketplace, with its doctrine of *caveat emptor,* is a fine institution for some purposes but then make all sorts of exceptions to it. It's okay to trust buyers and sellers to reach satisfactory terms of trade and results, but then exempt pajamas because they are, after all, worn by little children who should not be victimized by potentially reckless manufacturers. Automobile manufacturers would have to be regulated as well and thus not allowed to produce at their discretion and good judgment, since the ignorant customer cannot be expected to take care of his own needs. Then again, food is too important to be left to the market, so the Food and Drug Administration must be established and trusted with safeguarding our food and drug supply. Keep this up and gradually everything is encumbered with state regulation, with no free market left.

A scenario can be painted involving virtually any kind of free-market activity where some abuse or neglect occurs and where the results are potentially drastic. You could purchase an apple and in it find a worm poisoned with some pesticide. Thus the buying and selling of apples must be government regulated. Or toys. Or recreational equipment—tennis rackets, football helmets, and whatnot. There is always the possibility of some mishap when people are involved. In each case someone like Mr. Caplan turns up—or Ralph Nader or Jeremy Rifkin—shrieking about all the hazards of the marketplace, and a new bureaucracy gets created to make sure that these market failures do not occur. There is some resistance, of course, but certainly not by those urging all this supervision of free trade!

Never mind that the market failures keep occurring anyway—indeed, they are likely to multiply, because now the word is out that we need no longer worry, the regulators have come to the rescue! Never mind that the regulators are never held legally responsible for having failed to regulate well enough—they enjoy *sovereign immunity.*

In addition, the regulators are not superhuman. They are no saints themselves, so there will be trouble surrounding their activities: scandals, political corruption, neglect, and the like. So after setting out to protect us from ourselves, this paternalistic approach to the role of government in our lives increases rather than decreases our problems.

The market is not perfect: Anyone would be foolish to pretend that it is. But the market does assume that individual human beings and their voluntary associations are best equipped to cope with life's many difficulties and challenges. If the law protects individual rights, if the courts adjudicate disputes as to whether some basic right was violated and assesses the damage, this is the best we can do.

In vitro fertilization is just the most recent issue. Newspaper headline writers love to call up the image of market failure, so they will headline a story on the topic: "Pressure to Regulate *in Vitro* Fertilization Grows as Demand Rises," which could have been worded, "Anxiety May Lead to State Regimentation of *in Vitro* Fertilization."

No, there is no reason to trust government bureaucrats, including their friends at the Center for Biomedical Ethics. They give bad ethical advice. It is better to beware and take care, however complex the issue happens to be.

Our founders got rid of King George because he meddled with their lives too much and didn't govern properly. That should still serve as our leit-motif in dealing with government: It has its place, as a referee, but not as a supervisor, inspector, regimentor. Uncle Sam is not Father or Mother Sam!

SAFETY LIES IN COOPERATION, NOT REGULATION*

In recent years, there has been some progress in the direction of the deregulation of American business. But this trend has been confined to what is called "economic regulation," involving setting prices, restricting sales or marketing practices, prohibiting advertising in certain professions, limiting market entry in such areas as commercial transportation, and the like.

The Interstate Commerce Commission, the Civil Aeronautics Board, the Federal Aviation Administration, and similar old-time regulatory bodies have been exposed to much criticism from various sectors in our culture. This does not mean, however, that deregulation has been progressing steadily under the Reagan administration. Quite the contrary. There is little actual movement, as distinct from fervent rhetoric, toward reducing the government's involvement in the business community by way of the alphabet soup agencies.

Those who talk about such things tend to agree that deregulation in economic matters is generally a good thing. Such commentators as Professor Steven Kelman of Harvard University's J.F.K. School of Government, believe that economic regulation no longer makes much sense, if it ever did. It is widely agreed among even the most liberal public policy analysts that deregulation in many areas is a good thing, if only because the consumer benefits from the resulting increase in competition and related developments in the marketplace.

But there is another sphere of regulation that is opposed primarily by businesses. These are the new "social regulations." The two main regulatory bodies dealing with these are the Environmental Protection Agency (EPA) and the Occupational Safety and Health Administration (OSHA). Though not accepted, they are given vigorous support by many interventionists. Professor Kelman, again, has provided us with a good example of current trends. He has been a supporter of OSHA and a critic of the old-time regulatory agencies, even though he himself was a staffer at the Federal Trade Commission (which is an agency that falls between the two).

Now the main appeal of the "social regulations" is that they deal with the protection of workers against safety and health abuses by business. Aside from the cynicism of this view, which makes it appear that those in the business world must somehow be callous (as distinct, we may suppose, from those in journalism, government, the church, and academe), the opinion is shot full of problems, one of which bears closer scrutiny.

---

*Originally published in the *Orange County Register* (April 5, 1987).

There is an assumption, shared by all supporters of safety and health regulation, that the kind of threats to which people in the business world respond can only come from government regulators. This is false. Robert S. Smith, and others who contributed to *Instead of Regulation,* edited by Robert Poole, point out that the common law does provide a way to remedy safety and health problems at the workplace. True, there may be incentive problems about getting workers to take legal action, but here is where an entirely different idea needs to be considered.

Why aren't labor unions doing their best to stand behind the workers when it comes to any harm they may experience from lax safety and health provisions at the workplace? Sure, in some of these cases the workers themselves are at fault and, with government regulatory bias, this is often forgotten.

Workers should ask about safety and health conditions and if they find them intolerable, they should refuse to work in such places. Or if they are misinformed by employers, they should take legal action. If they are not properly informed, then their employment has been based on fraud and they have a case, even without so-called right-to-know laws, which their unions could help them press.

But suppose workers have done their best to keep informed and despite all this they are unjustly harmed on the job. They can be helped by their labor organizations in numerous ways. Unions can spend membership dues on adequate legal insurance so that when a campaign arises, the worker need not rely entirely on his or her earnings to risk very costly litigation. Unions could prepare workers for alternative occupations when they learn that available jobs pose severe enough safety and health hazards. Many of the measures that could be taken by labor organizations in behalf of the worker could pose every bit the threat that "getting inspected" poses.

What is necessary is the realization that government regulation is preemptive "justice," something that a free and decent society should not tolerate. This is not a matter based on the high cost of regulation or any such thing but on the immorality of imposing burdens on people in business prior to their having been shown to have criminally harmed someone. Once this is understood, many ways outside the bounds of government regulation could be found to discourage people in business from mistreating their employees.

It is time that the role of organized labor change from that of a lobbyist for extending the power and scope of government to that of a genuine supporter of the legitimate interests of the workers.

COMPETITION*

One of the most upsetting elements of the free market is competition. Defenders of capitalism emphasize that competition results in better production, finer products, lower prices, diversity, and a good deal more that is judged by them to be of benefit. Critics of the free market talk a great deal about the personal

---

*Originally published in *Reason* magazine (March 1975).

agonies of competition: the element of defeat that goes with it, the emotional concomitants of fear, anxiety, exploitation, estrangement, hostility, etc., which go hand in hand with this ingredient of the free society and market.

Now competition is surely instrumental in bringing about some of what both of these factions talk about. However, note that underlying the manner in which competition is viewed by supporters and critics of capitalism alike is a view of social life that is worth focusing on. In both cases the emphasis is on the social consequences of competition, i.e., those results that accrue to society in general, to the group! If one is concerned with the welfare of the community at large— general welfare, overall wealth, productivity in general—then, indeed, competition can be identified as giving rise to such benefits. If, however, one concentrates on the presence of hardship, agony, defeat, failure, and the accompanying psychological and spiritual experiences, then it is equally correct to point out that a competitive society will experience enough of these factors to command attention.

Both approaches to the situation fail in an important respect. Their focus of attention is society. In judging a society without any consideration of how human conduct ought to ensue, one is easily misled about the significance of competition. Those who are interested only in the successes of society will easily construe competition to be of enormous benefit to the social group. The economic results of competition will be of great importance to them, if for no other reason than because such benefits are measurable. Gross National Product (GNP) and similar concepts seem to fit into the model of what can be quantified, whereas personal agonies or victories are difficult to count up.

Those, on the other hand, who do not give a hoot about quantification but have their pulse on the private outcries of people in a society, who find the presence of personal struggle, agony, defeat, or fear in and of itself a sign of very bad times will consider competition an enemy of a culture. Aside from the poverty that inevitably falls upon some people in any culture—for it is a myth to believe that total equality of wealth is a real possibility in any human community— these people will point to the psychological pain that is found not just in ghettos but in some of the more prosperous (but often desperate) elements of the community.

The consequences of this sort of thinking are interesting but lamentable to observe. Focusing on measurable social indicators can lead to schemes such as those of Keynesians: at whatever cost necessary, simply increase the overall wealth of a nation, never mind the long-range consequences to either persons or human communities. This haste to increase overall social wealth produces deficit spending and a good deal of economic intervention aimed at spurring the economy into action, on the model of taking stimulants. Of course everyone must pay, eventually—except that it is usually those who had no say about the matter who will do the paying!

Focusing on the hardships that result for many from fierce competition (never mind why they suffer, whose fault it is, or any such individualistic issues) is equally misleading. Those concerned with consequences will urge that measures be taken to relieve the troubles of those who have fallen victim to competition. Antitrust laws, welfare programs, social security measures, forced insurance against medical disasters, unemployment compensation, and similar measures aimed at helping the unfortunate become the objects of crusades. While some strive for greater social wealth, others strive for greater social welfare, i.e., security.

Now what is wrong with all this? Well, for a start, competition is actually only a sideshow in a free market. True enough, as with the various events at the Olympics, it appears that people are in it for the contest. Yet what the market makes possible is only incidentally a matter of contest. More accurately it is a matter of excellence. In a free market people can excel at what they do, even if there is no one challenging them. If there are many who want to excel at some craft, profession, or art, then here we find competition. It is true that for some people only a contest will suffice to bring them into the field. But that is not crucial. Freedom allows those who want to work at some task to do their best without punishment; since there are many people around wanting to do similar things, competition results. But, without first wanting to be in the field, the competition would not ensue. Nor would the failures.

The important thing is that the failures result only because those who might not really like to engage in the productive activity get into it anyway. People do not really have to be economic successes in a capitalist world. There is no reason for someone to get involved in the hustle; he or she could stay outside, live for small pleasures, travel little or none at all. The phenomenon of "rising expectations" could be resisted, and thus failure avoided.

For failure is not in taking second or even 300th place in the contest; it is not liking the battle in the first place. And when I say battle, I am speaking somewhat carelessly, for it does not have to be a battle; it does not have to involve wanting another to lose. It is a mistake to look upon the free market as a boxing ring where there are only winners or losers (although even there we find tournaments where people take positions of first, second, third, and so forth on a long continuum between winner and loser). The free market is more like a marathon run: thousands starting, one finishing first, many right behind, some in the middle, then some more following, until we come to the end, with only a few actually dropping out of the race. Yet all of them have the choice to be part of it; because their first love is running, competition comes only as a result of learning that others like to run also.

Competition is a social phenomenon that cannot be understood without first paying attention to what sort of entities take part in it. When one learns that people compete, then a better understanding of competition may be obtained. Unfortunately competition has always had more social significance than what it really deserved. If we looked upon it as a mere consequence of free actions by individuals, neither losing nor winning would have national significance. What should, in fact, be of national significance is that competition is possible, not that it occurs. Paying much attention to national wealth and national despair can only distort one's view of what should be happening—free action. Human beings ought to be free to try their hands at what they want to produce, and if their desire is to produce what no one else wants, then this, too, ought to be something that they have the right to do. Excellence at one's craft, no matter how many others practice it, is what should be the prime object of human beings. Provided one's craft is creative instead of destructive it makes little difference to a person if he wins or loses in a race. His goal is not to defeat others but to conquer a goal, a vision of his own, no matter how many others try to travel the same path.

Viewing competition in this context, a person would not be inclined to make much of it and would refrain from trying to boost it or destroy it. It would no longer become a central issue. Excellence matters, not comparison. And the excellence of human beings, individually (not in collectives thrown together by mere happenstance) is what should matter to a careful observer of the human scene.

But then how many careful observers are left? How much easier it is to play with statistics of growth or misery, and cry for coercion when dissatisfaction with either occurs.

BUSINESS AND ITS DISDAIN OF CAPITALISM*

Periodically I read eloquent pleas to the members of the business community about how it would be wiser if they contributed to organizations favoring the marketplace, capitalism, and the free society instead of giving their support to general funds of colleges and universities, think tanks that favor the Left's agenda, and the like. I have seen this message come from the pen of Professor Irving Kristol and, more recently, from former secretary of the treasury and president of the John M. Olin Foundation, William E. Simon.

Let me admit that I share the desires expressed in these views, not only because I would probably benefit from the course they recommend even more than I already do but because I fear so much for the ideas of freedom in this country and worldwide. I share the concern for the diminished role that the idea of individual freedom plays in American politics and law. I share the worry that capitalism is going to be allowed to vanish from our culture, not just because of attacks from hostile critics, but because of scholarly and intellectual neglect. I am very concerned that more extensive research support goes to people (and organizations) who despise the very framework of production that makes voluntary funding of research possible.

But I have to confess that calling upon the business community to be more mindful of its own interest seems to me to be a futile effort. More than that, it seems to be a measure that follows an idea that is incompatible with the philosophy of the free society. Contrary to Karl Marx's views, people in business do not necessarily do what is in their interest, e.g., back sympathetic scholars and organizations.

Furthermore, I do not like another idea behind issuing a call for support to the business community. Why not a similar call to labor unions and one to scholars and artists? The fact is, contrary to widespread impressions, people in

---

*Originally published in the *Orange County Register* (December 11, 1988).

business do not know more about the value of freedom than people in the press, academe, the sciences, sports, or entertainment. I would be willing to bet that on the whole about as many people in business lean toward policies hostile to a free market as do people in entertainment. It is just that the latter are more visible and vocal in their campaigning.

But consider that thousands of people in corporate commerce support the left wing of the Democratic Party. Thousands of people in business explicitly reject the ideal of free trade, even while they may give empty lip service to free enterprise. Even among academic economists, who ought to know best, the commitment to a free society is not as widespread as readers of the *Wall Street Journal* might assume.

Granted, at any given time a given segment of society may include a majority or a minority of supporters of anticapitalist ideas. But I would be willing to bet that it all averages out. The consistent support for a free market is lacking just as much within the business community as it is within the academic community.

While it is important to appeal to members of the business community for support of the free society, they should probably not be approached as such, but simply as human beings. Freedom is not just good for those in business; it is good for everyone. It may not be enough for one to get the best possible life, but it certainly is the beginning for such a life. This has been amply demonstrated by the millions of people who have emigrated to the United States from all corners of the globe. They were not from some one economic, social, or professional class. They were and are a very mixed group. Indeed, a free society is the only one that can hold out benefits for the members of any group concerned with genuine, honest self-improvement.

I do not believe that our founding fathers felt that their vision of a free society would benefit business any more than it would benefit farmers, writers, engineers, educators, or artists. I think we should not forget that the liberty of all is what is at stake, and turn to various groups only incidentally to give support to this grand ideal.

HOW NOT TO DEFEND FREE- MARKET CAPITALISM*

The recent controversy about comparable worth—whether women ought to be paid the same wage or salary as men when they hold jobs that are virtually identical to those held by men—touches on a fundamental dispute between free market capitalists and various advocates of a planned or regulated economy.

Marx, for example, in contrast to neoclassical advocates of the free market economy such as Milton Friedman, argued that there is a way to determine whether a price is right or wrong. The free-market economist believes that all a price tells us is where demand and supply intersect, never mind whether the demand or supply is rational, right, good, or whatever. And for these economists the

---

*Originally published in the *Libertarian Party News* (January/February 1987).

free market is essential, not only to learn about the prevailing market price of commodities and services, but also because economic freedom is essential for securing individual freedom. In contrast, Marx denies that "the negation of free competition [is] the negation of individual liberty." He charged that the "free" market embodies a "free development on a limited foundation—that of the dominion of capital." He conviced many people, from Lenin to the Nicaraguan regime and some in the women's movement, that in a free market capitalist system only the rich flourish. The poor, however, must suffer and always to the benefit of the rich. For Marx, free-market capitalist "liberty is . . . the most complete suppression of all individual liberty and total subjugation of individuality to social conditions which take the form of material forces." Karl Marx and millions who follow him deny "that free competition is the final form of the development of productive forces, and thus of human freedom." Rather such free competition "means only . . . the domination of the middle class."

Marx and those influenced by him hold that the prices and wages that are evident on a free market—including the salaries of women working as administrative assistants, nurses, or secretaries—are mostly the expression of the interests of those with property. They can call the shots and they call them in their own favor, exploiting those without property by paying them mere subsistence wages.

Comparable worth is an idea that has resurfaced from Marxian and other elitist critiques of free-market capitalism. It holds that there is a right price for women's work, namely, that which is due them in light of the real worth of their service, one which men are receiving because they command greater power in the marketplace. And public policy should be directed toward adjusting the wages to reflect this "real worth"!

Marxism is not the only source of this elitist critique of the free market. Recently the Roman Catholic bishops have issued drafts of a letter in which they take on free market capitalism for failing to adhere to the proper ranking of social priorities. They argue, in essence, that free market capitalism misallocates resources, including labor, in the pursuit of frivolous and even demeaning ends, while neglecting important objectives that might otherwise be attained. This is how free market capitalism can tolerate poverty, famine, social insecurity, and the like in the midst of opulence for some members of society.

There is some sense in this, contrary to the protestations of many modern economists who hold that there is no place for value judgments in economics. We often do make pretty good guesses about how exorbitant some price is, how overpriced some item is on a given restaurant's menu, how overpaid some people are, and how the salary someone receives is merely nominal and fails to record the real worth of the person's work. We can also intelligibly lament the fact that some objectives go neglected in a free market, e.g., we often find it disappointing how little heed members of the business community pay to educating people about the merits of the market economy itself.

Now such judgments are intimately tied to particular contexts. They can be made mostly only from moment to moment, with full knowledge of the details of the circumstances. The groceries in one store may be overpriced, but this can only be known by those who are familiar with local conditions. The wages of some secretary may be too low, yet this too requires detailed knowledge of the market to determine. Suppose that because some person is disliked by the boss, he or she receives no raise even though others doing the same work have been advanced. And suppose the basis of dislike has nothing to do with performance. If one knows this, one can say, correctly, that the person is underpaid. There is, furthermore, no way to tell without knowing the details whether some corporation is spending its money correctly when it chooses to promote classical plays on the Public Broadcasting System rather than support a think tank that spreads the word about privatization and the virtues of free-market capitialism. Not that these are mysteries, only that they are difficult to know.

And of course these are just simple examples. Attempts to generalize about the situation are futile, however, and this can be shown by considering how difficult it would be to generalize about consumer discrimination against producers—e.g., if people refused to purchase goods from blacks, or women, or Southeast Asians, and patronized only stores run by others. This could certainly go on but it would be impossible to trace and to remedy via the powers of the state.

It is one thing to know that such cases are possible, quite another to be able to demonstate specific cases. Without the detailed knowledge, no such demonstation is possible. Still, those who protest the idea of injustice in the marketplace overstate their case when they say that the idea is nonsense. It is nonsense only from the point of view of economic science, which aims to explain, describe, and predict events in the marketplace, not to evaluate them.

But economic scientists are not the only ones who can make intelligent, informative comments about what happens in markets. No more so than physiologists being the only people who can say what happens to one's body when one is in pain—there is also the person who can feel the agony from a bruise, which the physiologists describe in tedious value-free terms.

Consider why many people find value judgments about market transactions significant. Why do they reject the idea that all consensual capitalist acts are equally deserving of moral respect or even indifference? Why do they confidently voice value judgments regarding free transactions?

Clearly, some elements of free-market capitalism can irk even the most libertarian of us. Think of its frivolity and trivia, such as the pet rock fad of a few years ago or the Michael Jackson glove craze of more recent times. And those are just the wildest cases. People keep flocking to shops purchasing frivolous and even disgusting merchandise—e.g., Cabbage Patch dolls, Perrier water, pornography, cigarettes, hard liquor, and the like, not to mention useless diet pills, pointless cosmetics, or breakfast cereals.

Such enterprises clearly siphon off a good amount of the productive energies of a community, energies that could have gone toward the creation of genuinely vital goods and services. A very productive system is geared away from what is important and useful toward what is trivial, silly, and even foul. There is a great deal that is more important than to satisfy such desires, even if it is sometimes difficult to tell from afar what it is. We have to admit that millions waste a lot of their income on stuff they could do without.

In a society of millions of working people, such reckless spending is surely going to be extremely influential. When people decry low wages and high prices, they are implicitly extending their awareness of the market's ability to make room for all this kind of nonsense. They are saying, in effect, "Yes, we know that all this is partly the result of individual choices, but those choices stink." And that they sometimes do stink is evident to us even when economists try to dismiss the idea as a medieval concept. Their response to that in many people's minds is, "What your science says, our common sense tells us better."

What is disturbing in all this is not that people can perceive that the market makes mistakes—e.g., that people are often wrong as they go shopping and spend their earnings. That is plain common sense and everyone who has ever regretted throwing good money away on some silly product knows it. But critics of free-market capitalism go much further and are willing to promise that they will put into place the right political and legal checks against wasteful extravagance, injustice, imprudence, and all the other human foibles that admittedly make an impact on the behavior of markets.

The problem, contrary to economic supporters of free-market capitalism, is not that no evaluations can be made about the way markets behave. The problem lies with the promise of fixing it by way of state intervention. This is simply a promise that *cannot* be fulfilled. Marx at least knew this. For him communism was not a better alternative to free-market capitalism but a system that would arrive some future day, of its own accord, whether we like it or not, because the world just happens to move that way. (To Marx, capitalism is to communism as the caterpillar is to the butterfly: a necessary ugly prerequisite!)

But since communism is an ugly nightmare, the question remains: What is really the best system for us now in this world? The belief that some special class of leaders—the likes of Ralph Nader, Mother Teresa, or Walter Mondale—should take power and guard us against the human foibles we are all capable of in a free society, just produces the Lenins, Stalins, Hitlers, Gadhaffis, and other little and big dictators of human history, as well as a population unwilling to guard itself against some of life's adversities—e.g., shyster lawyers, lying used car salespeople, unscrupulous brokers, quacks, etc. There is no escape from the fact that human beings can do wrong, but the free market copes better with human fallibility than do socialism and related efforts to wish our problems away by counting on firm outside help.

No, the marketplace is in fact our best tool for resolving the problems we face in our economic lives. We know that things can go wrong there, and to pretend otherwise is self-delusion. Some economists, unfortunately, claim that the marketplace is a perfect instrument for securing the good and right things in human society. It is not. Human beings enjoying freedom are also capable of misusing it. But giving some people political power to remedy matters only worsens the problem.

In a free market, errors get corrected more readily than in any planned society.

They do not become entrenched or petrified but can (though may not always) be erased when and where people think clearly and promptly.

Finally, features of the market often deemed to be trivial, useless, unjust, unkind, and so forth, are not what they seem to be. There is a lot of hasty judgment about matters of commerce—about who is getting his or her share, who is paid well or badly, etc. That infamous pet rock, which became a fad, may very well have been the most touching gift for an old Colorado miner on his eighty-fifth birthday, and brought a warm smile to his face as it reminded him of his life spent digging in the Rockies. When the large group of women employees marched in protest of low wages at Yale University, they kept saying they should get paid as much as Yale's truck drivers did. They were of comparable worth, they claimed. Upon closer inspection it turned out that, among other things, Yale paid its truckers higher wages but gave them only a week's vacation, in contrast to the three weeks received by the administrative staff. And there were all sorts of perks that were conveniently forgotten about. The fight appears to have been in terms of high-sounding moral notions not because these really applied but because that seemed the best strategy for getting what some people wanted. But the fact that moral categories can be corrupted in the heat of argument and the urgency of desire does not invalidate them.

Of course, it is one thing to defend free-market capitalism and another to claim that any society enjoys one today. But even if no such system is in place, and even if those societies historically associated with the idea have enormous distortions in their midst, the merits of the theory need to be clearly articulated, not overstated, in order to know in which direction we should be making progress, toward or away from free-market capitalism.

In the end only utopian perfectionists will disregard such matters and make the futile and tragic attempt to impose some perfect vision on us all. They should heed the words of Herbert Spencer: "The ultimate result of shielding men from the effects of folly is to fill the world with fools."

TELEVISION NEWS VERSUS ECONOMIC REALITY*

The reporters on CBS News and their counterparts throughout the news business are in a tizzy. The networks are cutting back on the staff and money devoted to news. And this dubbed as a betrayal of journalism for the sake of business.

First of all, there are plenty of alternative sources for obtaining news. Second, is television the best way for us to get news? Sure, it is quick and prompt, but is it thorough? Does it afford us a chance to look and read closely, to double-check the reports? Third, is the star system that seems to be inherent in broadcasting conducive to news reporting? Dan Rather, Mike Wallace, Tom Brokaw, Leslie Stahl—why do we know these people's names so well? Because they have become more newsworthy than what they report. And that is a distraction. In short,

---

*Originally published in the *Orange County Register* (circa 1986).

I am not sure that television should be so involved in broadcasting news—it seems to cheapen the result. A little cutback is not such a bad thing.

Furthermore, with all this hoopla, the public is once again subjected to a fallacious bifurcation—money *or* professionalism. When ABC News covered the topic of economization in the network news departments, the report was one of those pleas that bad reporting is all about—never mind the various facts, just cry for your favorite projects. And this was of course a clear case of special pleading—even forgivable, perhaps, since the newscasters were pleading the case for their own colleagues. Like cops, doctors, and other professionals, newscasters are not likely to be saying bad things about each other. They see themselves as a team, and when experiencing setbacks its members seem to care less for truth and reality than for solidarity in the fight for collective success.

Is there really a conflict between the great professions of our time and business? Virtually every profession outside of politics and the bureaucracy must make its way through the market in order to suceed. Must this intrude on the quality of the professions involved?

We often see matters put in terms of schisms, dichotomies; but let us not be fooled. The simple fact is that every activity human beings engage in, from science, art, and education to religion and law, must come to terms with economics. (No doubt, economics must come to terms with other aspects of human life, too, such as ethics, laws, and science.) The point is that to cry about the fact that news reporting must not ignore money matters is really to protest an insurmountable fact of nature: Not everything is possible.

If there is a need for economization in some profession, e.g., broadcasting, it is not because those who handle the economic aspects of the profession do not see the value of the profession. Artists are indeed respected by those who run galleries, as are scientists by those who earn their living from technology, and comedy by those who build and run clubs. More often than not the reason the managers enter the firm that handles these professions is that they find value in them, not only because there is a chance of making money. But one cannot ignore the fact that there are costs involved in all professional activities, even those that are very precious.

Newscasters are in an excellent position to promote themselves and their field. Used-car sellers do not generally have access to the forums or enjoy the kind of respect that newscasters covet, even though there is a great deal of good that used-car sellers do for us all. Of course, the people selling those cars are compensated for their work. But the same is true of professional broadcasters. Some of them earn a great deal. Most of them get a decent salary. Some become celebrities and earn enormous sums—e.g., the folks on "60 Minutes," Barbara Walters, and others.

When, however, the belt must be tightened, newscasters suffer from the illusion—or want to create one—that their work should be impervious to economic reality. They are engaged in a public service. Aren't we all! Arguably Johnny Carson does as much of a public service as a Dan Rather or a Peter Jennings. If by "public service" we mean "good for the people in our society," there can be no question about this. Certainly entertainment, transportation, farming, and other occupations are all worthy matters. No one has a monopoly on serving the public. In each of those cases, however, there can be shifts of fortune. Yet those in the field often refuse to come to terms with this fact.

One of the worst things a person in the news profession can do is to lose his credibility. Misreporting the news, selective presentation of ideas, and so forth are the ways that newscasters can become untrustworthy and violate their professional ethics. Those professionals in newscasting who fail to be honest about their own professional predicament by refusing to see that economics must impinge on their work, betray their loyalty to their profession. They are willing to sacrifice objectivity to special pleading, to vested interest lobbying. They are the ones who sacrifice their own professonal integrity to economic concerns!

This is what is happening just now at network broadcast news departments. All the hue and cry about how journalism is a profession, not a business, misses the point that there is a business side to every profession and vocation, even the priesthood! To deny this fact, to omit it from consideration, to fail to present the side of the field—that is plainly biased broadcasting. And for those who engage in such unprofessional conduct at the various networks there should be no forgiveness; viewers should take heed and refuse to continue to trust these men and women when they broadcast the news! Apparently they are not willing to do this with integrity and are willing to sell out to sentimentalism, to favoritism. And that is a good lesson for us all: Just because people on network television news have the skill to sound righteous, indignant, moral, ethical, and holier than thou about virtually every subject, they certainly should not be mistaken for anything but plain folks who are no more immune to vice that are the rest of us.

The current economizing in network television news departments is a good lesson for us. It helps us to demythologize the newscasters whom we usually see not at their worst but at their most favorable—the way stars like to be perceived. But stars are in the business of deception, newscasters are not.

DON'T TURN EMPLOYEES INTO POLICE INFORMANTS*

The prospect of crime exists wherever there are human beings. So an attempt to combat corporate crime could be considered wise and noble. However, a federal bill designed to combat "crime in the suites" is a peculiar approach to combating crime anywhere.

The bill, under consideration by the House Judiciary Committee's subcommittee on crime, which has been conducting hearings, proposes to fine or imprison anyone in business who as a manager or production supervisor with significant responsibility for the safety of a product or business practice knowingly permits or tolerates the production or sale of dangerous products or services without notifying federal authorities and potentially affected employees.

---

*Originally published in the *New York Times* (April 16, 1980).

This effort seems to be benign enough, but let's look again.

First, it imposes the duties of a police informant on business employees and managers. Yet that is clearly neither what these people were hired for, nor something they can be considered competent to engage in. A policeman's duties include developing expertise in adhering to due process of law. Accusations, charges, and suspicions must be handled carefully and conform to the letter and spirit of the law when informants engage in their extremely sensitive and potentially police-related harmful work.

Second, this bill imposes on business firms the burden of carrying out the law-enforcement work for which the taxpayers have already been forced to pay. It is against the law to produce goods and services that are demonstrably harmful to consumers, especially when consumers are not permitted to become aware of this fact and could have been made so aware. Any firm that perpetrates such action can be taken to court. But it would be entirely unjust—a violation of due process—to require firms to bear the cost of discovery and disclosure. It would of course violate principles of being innocent until proved guilty.

Third, although it may appear that the proposed legislation would go a long way toward eliminating some harmful business practices, there is nothing to prove that this will happen. The bill presupposes widespread carelessness of managers—indeed, it presupposes their willful disregard of serious dangers. If this assumption is correct, it must be made to apply not only to managers in business firms but also to everyone else in a decision-making position—inside or outside the business community.

To pick on business people as a special class is extremely discriminatory. Consider, for example, that teachers at universities can abuse their work as much as any manager of a production line or business practice. This bill would open the door to a more general piece of legislation that would require that members of every profession be fined unless they also acted as police informants. Thus, it would be punishable for professors not to inform the United States Department of Education if they were to discover that one of their colleagues was engaging in indoctrination rather than teaching. The writing of books that contain falsehoods would have to be reported since there is not question that reading these books could lead people to order their lives in dangerous, harmful ways.

This proposed piece of legislation continues a very sorry trend in recent history: the abandonment of due process when it comes to dealing with members of the business community. More and more, people in business are regarded as guilty without having been found guilty.

The size, frequently very visible success, and the plain wealth of some members of the business community, considered in light of the crimes found in this group, have led to their being treated as second- or third-class citizens. But their crimes are by no means proportionately greater than those of any other group.

I am not defending all these people, but members of all groups must have their basic rights protected and preserved. Bills such as this one involving concealment of known hazards aim to rob members of the business community of the need to think for themselves, to make morally responsible decisions.

To believe that one can regulate all the potentially harmful practices of the business community is foolish and unjustified. What remains is the motivation to do something, anything to prevent some future harm. Such a desire should not suffice as grounds for such discriminatory and onerous legislation as the bill before the crime subcommittee.

In short, there is no room for preventive justice in a free society—and in any kind of society the practice is impossible to carry out successfully.

8

Law

LEGAL POSITIVISM AND JUSTICE*

The doctrine of legal positivism maintains that the authority of government to force citizens to do as its says comes from the written law alone. As Judge Robert Bork puts it, "If the Constitution is not law, what authorizes a judge if not the judgment of the representatives of the American people? If the Constitution is not law, why is the judge's authority superior to that of the president, Congress, the armed forces, the departments and the agencies, and that of everyone else in the nation?" (*The Detroit News,* July 12, 1987).

Oddly, even if opponents of legal positivism believe in some conception of law that is mistaken, wrong, even pernicious, this alone will not invalidate their objection to positivism. So, for example, when Judge Bork's positivism was opposed by Senators Joseph Biden, Edward Kennedy, and Howard Metzenbaum—all of whom claimed that they spoke for the founding fathers' moral vision but in fact distorted that vision by stressing not individual freedom but entitlements to social welfare—what made the objections credible is not their particular viewpoints on what the law should say but their expressed view that they wanted the law to have some moral content. Indeed, they referred to individual liberty or individual rights as that moral component they said the U.S. Constitution contained.

By denying that there is such a component in the U.S. Constitution, Judge Bork lost his credibility. This is true even if the practical effect of his role on the Court, given the Constitution's existing ties to justice, might have been very beneficial.

Many legal theorists find the positivist conception of the authority of law enforcers too limited because established law might not give expression to the requisite morality that would render legal authority nonarbitrary. Clearly, for example, a basic legal document—even the constitution of a government—could

---

*Originally published in the *Orange County Register* (1987).

be the result of dictatorship. A powerful ruler could draft a constitution and set it up as "the law of the land." It is obvious in such a case that this document would not be able to authorize its own enforcement by anyone! It would be sheer arbitrary power to enforce it, a power backed by brute force, nothing else, even though it was called "law"!

What of a constitution that is established—drafted, debated, and finally adopted—by a relatively democratic assembly? What if this assembly itself represents a substantial segment of the public that would later have to live with the established law? Is that by itself sufficient to make the law binding on them and to authorize a selected group to enforce that law? Clearly, if we take seriously the idea that all individuals are sovereign persons who ought to govern their own lives and whose consent is required for others to take over that task, then even this representative democratic or republican form of lawmaking is insufficient to command full respect and obedience. Those who did not give their consent to being represented by the persons who then produced the constitution certainly could complain.

But perhaps this is only so if the resulting document requires that the nonconsenting parties act in ways that they ought not to act or act only on their own initiative. Clearly, if I am forced to respect your rights to life, liberty, and property, for example, my consent to be so forced is not required. (It is arguable that my consent is required for selecting *who* will do the enforcement.) But if I am forced to sacrifice my life for a goal that is unrelated to me or to what I have chosen, any enforcement could again be construed as arbitrary, unjustified. Surely, just having the majority prefer some laws does not give those laws any moral standing, any conviction over and above fear, any *authority* over those who are not members of that majority.

This is the main problem with legal positivism, even in a relatively democratic society. The enactment of the legal system—establishing the Constitution, for example—could very well require majority backing, simply to ensure its practical viability. Without majority support the system is unstable, lacks power, and thus even its legitimate authority would be ineffective. But if all that the system has is majority support, its moral force and legality itself may be in serious question. Opponents can argue that lacking moral support, it has only physical might backing it.

Legal philosophers have sometimes argued that some minimal moral content must be part of a legal system that confers authority. In practical terms this means that if the judgment of a court is to carry conviction—inducing compliance out of something other than mere fear—then the court needs to be backed by laws that also possess this attribute, i.e., some intimate connection with justice. And the most prominent suggestion is that widespread agreement with or acceptance of the legal system secures this element. Yet this again contains the flaw of unchecked democracy. The majority may obliterate with its law the basic rights of minority members. So something else is necessary.

This something else would be what Judge Bork and others reject in the law, namely, its moral support, its presumed ties to justice. That idea has usually been labeled the "natural law conception of legality." Some connection with what by nature is right and just must be seen within established law, otherwise this written law lacks full authority to command compliance. The reason it has to be "by nature" is that it is only the natural world that can be studied by everyone, i.e., any member of a human community who is not crucially incapacitated. Natural law and natural rights are therefore indispensable background supports for the authority of a legal system.

By refusing to admit that morality is an integral part of law—and by treating law as if it were merely an instrument for engineering what the majority or the king wants, positivists, including Judge Bork, leave the high ground to people who are in fact willing to have their own moral feelings commandeer the law.

Once again the Republicans have shown their ineptness in defending what is in essence a glorious cause, namely, the protection of the integrity of our legal system. They failed to put their trust in someone who has more than a mere economic agenda for our Constitution, namely, the protection of individual rights and thus a just, rather than merely an efficient or prosperous, society.

A JUDICIAL IMPERIALIST*

Those who love liberty and the U.S. Constitution's support of it should be careful about the nomination of Robert Bork to the Supreme Court.

Is Judge Bork a strick constructionist, one famous for judicial restraint, as many claim? Is he someone, in other words, who reads the Constitution for what its wording means when rendering judgment? Since that is the duty of a Supreme Court justice, no one can object to a strict constructionist nominee.

In the recent past the court has been led by judicial imperialists, judges who hold, basically, that if the U.S. Constitution does not say what we want it to, justices should ignore it and pass judgments in light of our personal conscience.

If Judge Bork were indeed a strict constructionist, he should be nominated. But he may himself be a kind of judicial imperialist, at least judging by his views of the First Amendment or rather that portion of it that states that "Congress shall make no law . . . abridging the freedom of speech, or of the press. . . ." Judge Bork wrote in 1971 that consitutional protection should be accorded only to speech that is explicitly political. There is no basis for judicial intervention to protect any other form of expression, be it scientific, literary, or that variety of expression we call obscene or pornographic. Moreover, within that category of speech we ordinarily call political, there should be no constitutional obstruction to laws making criminal any speech that advocates forcible overthrow of the government or the violation of any law (*Indiana Law Journal,* vol. 47).

Notice that by reference to the actual meaning of the First Amendment, the U.S. Constitution does not permit Congress to legislate any sort of speech or press, period. Any qualification on "speech" is an invention, a form of judicial imperialism that Judge Bork has condemned in recent interviews.

---

*Originally published in the *Orange County Register* (1987).

When one hears reference to original intent, the danger arises that the views of some of the framers will be favored over against others. But the U.S. Constitution as a document is mainly a protector of human liberty. That is its distinctive meaning, whatever various framers had intended for it during its drafting. A conservative bias in reading it is no better than a liberal one. Both are hostile to human liberty.

It is not *intent* but *meaning* that needs to be paid attention in the Constitution, and the implications of that meaning. Those who would substitute "subjective meaning" are also wrong. Meaning is conveyed in words, sentences, and the context in which these are made, and that is true about a legal document. Meaning is the only non-arbitrary, concrete guide to the Constitution, what we must do by the terms in which it is stated. We speak English and we know of the English spoken by the framers and that gives us common ground and continuity. We cannot consult the intentions of the framers any more than we can consult the intentions of all lawmakers whenever we wish to know what laws tell us and how to apply them to new issues that arise that the original authors of the law cannot be expected to have known about. Nor do we need to do this. We know their final intent best when we understand what they said to us, when we know their meaning.

As to the First Amendment, for instance, some who framed the U.S. Constitution may have intended to refer only to political speech when they agreed to protect speech and press. But this is not what they ended up doing. They actually *said* that when someone speaks or uses the presses to say something, that person's actions may not be interfered with by Congress. The rest is added law.

For many conservatives, the Bill of Rights is an obstacle to government. They see the idea of restraining Congress from dictating speech and press, outside the very limited sphere of not intruding on our strictly political activities—e.g., voting, running for office, speaking out on the issues—a serious limitation on the elitism they endorse for governing the weak people of society—to do what conservative columnist George Will calls "soulcraft" as they carry on with "statecraft." They want legislators who engage in spiritual—in contrast to the liberals who want economic—regimentation.

One can only hope that Judge Robert Bork does not support any kind of distortion of the Constitution. The American system was designed to restrict the power of government, especially its power to control our thinking, never mind what the subject matter happens to be—political, scientific, literary, philosophical, or artistic. The Supreme Court is to ensure that this happens. Judge Bork's 1971 discussion of how the First Amendment should be interpreted does not promise the best guide for the Supreme Court regarding respect for a constitution of human liberty.

Perhaps Judge Bork has changed his views. That would be welcome. He should be scrutinized by the Senate not for whether he likes this or that political agenda, but for whether he is loyal to the only judicial ideal in human history that has upheld the dignity and freedom of individual human beings—including their freedom to speak or write on any subject they choose.

MORAL EUNUCHS CANNOT DEFEND THE U.S. CONSTITUTION*

When Ronald Reagan nominated Judge Robert Bork for the Supreme Court, a furor began that culminated in a bitter political war and yet another defeat for Reagan's embattled presidency. The reasons for that defeat, and the lessons to be drawn from it, go to the core of the role of law in a free society.

As depicted by Reagan, Judge Bork was the forthright defender of the integrity of the U.S. Constitution as a federalist document. He championed "states' rights," a limited federal government, and the freedom of the fifty states to enact laws they deemed necessary, provided the Constitution is not directly contradicted.

But Judge Bork turned out to be a jurisprudential theorist who regarded the Constitution as expressing only the will of early Colonialists. He believes that a state power may be exercised only when the Constitution explicitly authorizes that power and that, alternatively, individual rights ought to be protected only when this document explicitly protects those rights. The Bork view contradicts the idea that the U.S. Constitution contains certain moral and political truths that reinforce the (more or less) democratic process.

Judge Bork, however, adheres to a school of legal theory that discounts the importance of moral and political principles. He testified, for example, that he sees no general protection of individual rights in the Constitution and so cannot justify the 1965 decision in *Griswold* v. *Connecticut* that the State of Connecticut violated the right to privacy of persons wanting to use condoms in their bedrooms. In several other cases he said that, lacking a general right in the Constitution, the Court decided improperly even if by some other route of reasoning the same decision might have been justified.

Bork no longer sees any connection between the Constitution and some moral and political precepts—for example, natural rights (which he in 1968 thought to back this document). Rather, he now holds to a version of legal positivism: the idea that government authority comes from the written law alone, because that law expresses the will of the majority. "If the Constitution is not the law, what authorizes a judge if not the judgment of the representatives of the American people?" he said recently in the *Detroit News*.

This view holds that the Constitution should be treated respectfully because it emerged from a largely democratic process and therefore embodies majority opinion. But majorities can be dead wrong about a lot of things. Indeed, it is clear enough that the founding fathers and framers of the Constitution recognized the danger of majoritarianism and thus combined respect for democracy with individual rights—limits on how far the people's power, via the executive and legislative branches of government, may reach.

The Constitution's authority in fact derives from two conditions: It contains political principles that ought to govern a just society, and the majority of the people of the United States have consented to the legal protection of those prin-

---

*Originally published in the *Orange County Register* (February 1988).

ciples. Neither of these conditions alone suffices to authorize enforcement of the law. Both are necessary for moral government.

By refusing to give credit to the moral dimension of America's legal history, Bork swept away a major tool by which the Reagan presidency might have recaptured the Supreme Court for a good and noble cause, namely, the Constitution. By insisting on a narrow reading of the Constitution, Bork left it to the reformers and radical opponents of that document's moral and political philosophy to advance their moral doctrines and so capture the high ground.

People require a moral justification for a legal system that they are asked to respect and obey. Bork denied this to them and so a substantially fraudulent account of the American Constitution—at the hands of moral sentimentalists such as Senators Joseph Biden, Edward Kennedy, and Howard Metzenbaum—succeeded against his arid, morally relativistic viewpoint.

The lesson is that those who defend the American system of limited government must emphasize not just its efficiency and usefulness for producing prosperity but also its moral superiority. The liberal senators played it very well. They produced their sham rhetoric favoring individual rights as the moral component of the Constitution, even if in practice they support legislation that abridges individual liberty.

Yet that fraudulent language still rings more credible than the doctrines of majoritarianism, utilitarianism, and economic efficiency advanced by Judge Bork. Consider his response to the question, Why would you like to join the U.S. Supreme Court? He said it would be an intellectual feast. But surely, the sentimentalists responded, there is more to being on the Court, namely, a concern with justice and rights. And thus they ensured their victory.

PUBLIC SUPPORT AND THE FREE PRESS

The U.S. Supreme Court was hearing arguments in late 1987 in the case of *Hazelwood School District* v. *Kuhlmeier*. The issue was whether Hazelwood East High School of St. Louis violated the First Amendment rights of Cathy Kuhlmeier and her editorial staff at the school's student newspaper, which is associated with the school's journalism program. The Court ultimately decided against the high school paper, arguing that the school authorities, as publishers, could exercise final editorial jurisdiction over the publication.

There have been similar cases in the past and what is interesting is not so much which way the Supreme Court decides them. (Previously, in 1969, the Supreme Court ruled, in *Tinker* v. *Des Moines Independent Community School District,* that school interference is justified only if what is published "materially disrupts classwork or involves substantial disorder or invasion of the rights of others." This is hardly a principled decision, guided by the U.S. Constitution!) A very similar problem surfaces whenever radio and television stations come up for their license renewal. Since the electromagnetic spectrum is "owned" by the people— i.e., the airwaves were nationalized in 1927 and the federal government took over their management via the Federal Radio and later the Federal Communications Commission—the public retains ultimate authority over how it is to be used. This is why broadcasting is not fully and unambiguously protected by the First Amendment.

The much more vital issue is whether a free press can coexist with widespread public or government involvement in the society. Both kinds of cases—those involving newspapers at public high schools, colleges, or universities, and publicly licensed broadcast media—point to something rather frightening. They demonstrate the incompatibility between the growing public realm in the United States and the rights and freedoms protected by the U.S. Constitution through the Bill of Rights.

The plainest way to put the matter is that when the public pays the bills, it will insist on having a hand in the use of what it underwrites. If I am a member of a school district that pays for a high school newspaper, I will certainly want to have some say about the editorial policies of that publication—e.g., I would not tolerate the transformation of the paper into communist or Nazi propaganda or a sleezy sexploitation rag. I would regard any attempt to restrain my efforts to influence the publication as abridgment of the principle of "No taxation without representation." In other words, I would insist that the school district represent the public sentiment about the matter and not allow the students to do what they please. No freedom of the press here!

Similarly, if I am a member of the public that owns the airways and I believe a broadcaster who leases a frequency is engaging in misconduct of some sort, I will want my representatives, namely, the Federal Communications Commission, to do something about it.

To put it bluntly, there is no freedom of the press when the bills are paid by the public at large. The government, representing the tax-paying public, must have an influence, otherwise democracy goes down the drain.

The only solution is the one that follows in the footsteps of the founding fathers. This is to reduce the public realm as much as possible. Allow governments to do the most limited number of jobs for us, namely, what we are not capable of doing for ourselves: e.g., the running of the courts, the defense of the country, and the development of the law through legislation.

A free high school, college, or university press is incompatible with the public funding of high schools, colleges, and universities. A free broadcast media is also incompatible with the public ownership of the airways. And the story can be extended to the use of public facilities for the advocacy of viewpoints. The famous incident in Skokie, Illinois—in which Nazis insisted on their right to parade their views on the public streets in a neighborhood of predominantly Jewish residents—also illustrates the point. The streets are under public jurisdiction, their upkeep is publicly financed. So how could it be expected that Jewish citizens should simply accept the use of this public property for the insidious purpose of advocating nazism?

If we respect the principle of free expression of ideas—a free press and freedom of speech—we must not allow the public realm to grow. We must make sure that it contracts farther and farther, so that more and more of the resources that may support the expressions of diverse viewpoints are privately owned. Then no public action could be legally brought against those who express unwelcome views.

If Hazelwood High School were a private institution, there would be no issue to be brought to court. The high school would be in charge of its journalism school and newspaper. Students would clearly be operating the paper at the discretion of the owners of the school. This is clear from the way in-house publications of varioius firms such as IBM and United Airlines are edited. They are under the jurisdiction of the owners—the stockholders and their representatives who manage these companies. If the editors refuse to comply with the wishes of the owners, they are fired. And the same is true with major newspapers. Editorial policy is ultimately under the direction of the owners of the publications.

Of course, editors of magazines, newspapers, news departments of broadcasting companies, and the like are always beholden to the owners. But two factors ensure the independence of the press. First, the government may not dictate what will or will not be printed. Second, there is ample diversity of ownership in a free society so that even if some owners might wish to hush up some topics, others will not wish to do so. This, plus competition for readers and viewers, leads to a free, independent media.

Furthermore, in a free country if an editor is fed up with the dictates of the publisher, he or she can always save up some money, borrow more, and start a new publication. So long as we are not dependent for support on the central government of our community, the freedom to publish various viewpoints on the innumerable topics of interest to members of our society will remain relatively safe.

We can see the difference between our kind of press and that of such totalitarian systems as the Soviet Union, Cuba, Nicaragua, or authoritarian systems such as Saudi Arabia, Chile, and South Africa. A free society keeps a clear distinction between public matters and matters of private and social interest. Freedom requires the divorce of the public purse from the activity that is worth keeping free.

SMOKERS STAND ALONE IN BLAME*

It is puzzling to what lengths some people will go to deny their own humanity. A good case in point is the recent rash of lawsuits against the various tobacco companies by people who have smoked and have then been diagnosed to have lung cancer. In some cases the plaintiff has already died but the case is still being adjudicated. In all these cases the central claim is that the tobacco companies are responsible for the plaintiff's ailment.

Let no one think that I have any great stake in this issue. I smoke about one cigarette a month, if that much. My wife smokes a pack of one of those tasteless brands every two or three days. And I own no tobacco stocks. But I am appalled at how glibly people will maintain the line—and how readily the

---

*Originally published in the *Los Angeles Times* (March 5, 1988).

country's news media will fall for it—that not they but those who sell them products are to be blamed for what befalls them as a result of their consumption of the harmful products.

The point to be made is not the same that some of the lawyers defending the tobacco companies have argued. They have tended to focus on the technical scientific issue of whether any clear-cut causal relationship may be established between heavy smoking of their tobacco products and the presence of the plaintiff's debilitating disease. That is not the major concern—it can be granted that for many people tobacco smoking is unhealthy, if not eventually fatal. One can, of course, reasonably doubt this idea.

It is possible, based on current scientific knowledge, that only those with a special genetic make-up are hurt from smoking. Some people in their eighties have smoked all their lives and have experienced no discernible adverse health effects from this. And even if people do experience adverse health effects from it, this does not clinch the case against smoking—one can benefit from unhealthy or risky activities. Mountain climbers may die younger than the rest of us but presumably they get enough of a benefit from what they are doing so that it's worth the risk to them.

But what if smoking is all wrong? Why should it be those who sell cigarettes rather than those who use them who should shoulder the blame? Many who also have a higher-than-average cholesterol count crave ice cream. Eating ice cream is, therefore, risky for them. They could, given what is the most recent medical/nutritional information on this topic, suffer a heart attack because of their consumption of ice cream. And in the case of eating ice cream—or drinking spirits or eating potato chips—there is nothing terribly positive that these persons gain, outside the satisfaction of the taste. And yet people carry on, and it is not the producers' fault.

Cigarettes are widely known to be capable of causing serious harm to people. Alas, even without the U.S. Surgeon General, who forced the companies to announce that fact on each tobacco product being sold in the United States, we would be amply informed. Even in Europe, where it is much more widespread than here, we all grew up knowing well enough that smoking could hurt us, especially if we wanted to engage in a physical sport.

To suggest that people are persuaded by tobacco advertising that cigarette smoking is good for them is utter nonsense. They are not dumb. They just like to smoke, whether or not it is good for them, whether it is a high risk or not. And they decide to do it, and to continue it, and do not seek help in trying to quit if it is difficult for them to do it on their own. And this is their responsibility, no one else's. That is what is true, and the claims of the plaintiffs, as reported in the national media, seem to be so much denial of personal responsibility for their actions, choices, and decisions throughout their lives.

But if you go by the news reporters—e.g., Mike Wallace on CBS television's famous "60 Minutes," on January 3, 1988—you would think that the idea of self-responsibility simply has never surfaced in this land. In their coverage of the litigation they never even mention that possibility. All we learn is how rich the tobacco companies are, how much they must prevent plaintiffs from winning any of their lawsuits, and how unfair the legal system is for allowing the companies to hire those expensive attorneys to defend them.

No doubt, there are cases when various people selling a product exploit the weak-minded and do so perhaps even knowingly. But why not simply admit that millions of smokers want to smoke, whatever the risks. They keep it up despite all the chances to stop, to gain help, or to receive treatment. Never mind all the information hurled at them about the hazards of excessive smoking.

The U.S. Surgeon General wants to make this country smoke free. But he would have to become a dictator to do it. Nor will it help to thoroughly distort the legal system by blaming not the perpetrators of risky activities but those who accept that consumers know what they want and proceed to provide it to them.

BHOPAL, MEXICAN DISASTERS: WHAT A DIFFERENCE CAPITALISM CAN MAKE*

Some months ago, when Melvin Belli and several other attorneys departed for India, Belli accused American businessmen of being "obsessed with profit and not with safety," and charged U.S. companies with "dumping inferior produce on poor Third World countries." He lashed out against American businesses as such, in the wake of the Bhopal disaster, even before anybody knew exactly what happened and who was responsible.

During his scolding of business, Belli also observed that "If you bring hazards to a community, you're responsible, even if you don't intend to do harm. You're guilty simply because the disaster happened." This is roughly correct, as far as standard tort law goes. Yet, even here, Belli exaggerated a bit: in our legal system it isn't attorneys for the plaintiff but juries who determine the nature and extent of liability.

In any case, certain oddities appear when we compare Bhopal to another recent industrial accident. In the State of Mexico, near Mexico City, storage facilities exploded and killed nearly 500 persons. They were owned by Pamex, a government service monopoly under the authority of Mexico's Ministry of Natural Assets.

A Crucial Difference Between Disasters

There is still a lot of controversy about what started the oil fires in Mexico City. Pamex is claiming that the leak which precipitated the fire was started in an adjoining (Mexican) private facility, while the owners of the latter are making a counterclaim. In any case, there is a lot of bureaucratic haggling going on about who started what, who is responsible for what, and so on. As to who will pay what amount, that remains to be seen.

---

*Originally published in the Los Angeles *Metropolitan News* (1984).

This disaster, as will be recalled, did not arouse the outrage of the likes of Belli. Belatedly, however, a lawsuit asking nearly $2.4 million—far short of the $50 billion Belli is asking from Union Carbide—was filed with the Mexican government.

A major difference between the plants is that the one in India is partly owned by American capitalists, while the plant near Mexico City is owned by the State of Mexico. With this in mind, not hearing from Belli back when the Mexican disaster occurred suggests several ideas.

When the Mexican government pursues the same objective Union Carbide seeks, namely, the production of goods that people want, Belli and Co. seem to consider it quite okay. Is this because Mexico is a political state—a government—not private individuals seeking some measure of prosperity through the marketplace?

Humanitarian Advantages of One Scenario

Is it permissible for government to do what profit-making firms should not do? Why? What is so noble about an institution of armies and police doing something that men and women wishing to prosper ought not to do? Why is Belli so indignant when disasters occur in the combined pursuit of profit and the public interest—but not when they occur in the bureaucratic pursuit of the public interest? Is there something inherently good about bureaucracies or inherently bad about business? Does this not condemn his own profession?

Actually, it seems the profit-making approach has many humanitarian advantages. We should seriously consider the difference between the way disasters are handled in cases where the owners are "the people," as may be the case in Mexico. It would be interesting to explore this issue fully. On its face the results promise to be very instructive and to serve to put an end to much irresponsible babble by the likes of Belli.

Consider that where even partial private ownership is involved, the processes of obtaining some, albeit incomplete, restitution—when compared to the tremendous losses—can get under way rather smoothly. As noted already, Belli and his fellow pleaders of the case for the aggrieved can file a lawsuit, and an independent judicial process can begin to determine the extent of responsibility and the appropriate compensation and penalty.

Even when the case is settled out of court, as is now likely with the Union Carbide case, a very sizable settlement is probable. Except when firms go bankrupt and no insurance is in force, private companies, found liable for causing harm to people, can be forced to pay. Of course, in some cases companies are unfairly protected by the government. But that need not be the case: It is usually government policy to establish limited liability, for the sake of encouraging the "free flow of commerce."

Generally, in a relatively free marketplace—when one is party to a disaster such as those in Bhopal or Mexico City—the law makes possible many roads of restitution and recovery. Is this true in the cases where government plants are involved? Is it true in the Soviet Union, for example? No doubt, some policy of making restitution to victims will be in force, but in such cases policy is forged by the perpetrators of the "accident"—which could hardly be regarded as procedurally fair.

A conflict of interest is hardly avoidable when the same party is both responsible and sets the terms of rectification.

Needed: A Concern for Individual Rights

In the Mexican situation, the concern for the rights of the individuals who were harmed may play a role, of course. The state will try to alleviate the immediate hardship which fell upon the victims who survived. Lawsuits may be filed "for compensation ranging from $17 to more than $24,000," as the Associated Press recently reported—a pittance compared to what is being sought in the Bhopal case.

It seems that in India, which along with Mexico is a Third World country, the rights of the individual victims and their kin will be fully considered. That is because where a private firm is involved, harmful byproducts of manufacturing processes must be paid for whenever possible.

A society that values individual human rights will infuse its laws with provisions to rectify any violation of those rights. It is questionable whether a society that discourages the right to private property can retain this concern about individual welfare in its legal system.

SEPARATION OF CHURCH AND STATE *

There has been much concern lately about the doctrine of the separation of church and state. Most people understand that law must rest on certain moral convictions and that most of our moral convictions are taught to us by our religions. So how could there be substance to this doctrine, after all? There is a way to appreciate the doctrine without denying the simple fact of the connection between religion and morality in most people's lives, as well as in most cultures.

Let us consider a pertinent story that turned up in several newspapers recently. A judge sentences a couple to five years in prison for letting their child die of pneumonia without medical treatment. The parents argued that as members of the Faith Assembly Church, they were required not to seek medical help; convicting them for what they did would involve a violation of their freedom of worship.

Gary and Margaret Hall of Columbia City, Indiana, were told by the judge that "We can't tolerate human sacrifice in the name of religion." According to the *Fort Wayne News-Sentinel,* there have been eighty-eight deaths among sect families because of this doctor-shunning practice.

The incident brings up an interesting aspect of the current controversy. There are those who maintain that a legal system depends on religion for its very content.

---

*Originally published in the Los Angeles *Metropolitan News* (November 17, 1984).

Joseph Sobran, an editor of the *National Review* and an astute conservative pundit, has defended a substantial connection between religion and government. In a recent column he approvingly cites President Franklin Roosevelt, who observed:

> An ordering of society which relegates religion, democracy, and good faith to the background can find no place within it for the ideals of the Prince of Peace. The United States rejects such an ordering and retains its ancient faith.

Sobran also quotes FDR as saying that "three institutions (are) indispensable to Americans, now as always. The first is religion."

FDR aside, this is difficult to uphold. There are at least 750 different religions in the United States alone, and clearly one reason for this large number is that they disagree on numerous issues. So while for Americans religion and its tenets may be of the first importance, they differ drastically on which religion should be accepted and practiced.

Is there a way to admit that religion plays a vital role in people's lives and yet also pinpoint some of the topics on which they must all agree despite their different religious convictions? The judge ruled against the parents who engaged in negligent infanticide—thus refusing to let them practice some of their religious views with impunity—and in so doing, appears to have found a way out of our dilemma.

Religions are important to Americans and are indeed the source of many of their beliefs and practices. Yet, there must be some other source of rules and laws that is of greater general importance, otherwise we could not live among each other without constant warring.

The basic law of the land must transcend the special focus of religions and spell out whatever human beings as such must obey so as to live in each others' company with a high probability of success. Interestingly enough, the Declaration of Independence, in mentioning the basic rights of human beings—to life, liberty, and the pursuit of happiness—lays down certain requirements of civilized life that anyone is supposed to be able to appreciate, just by being human.

John Locke, the English political thinker and founding grandfather of this country, noted that there are natural laws that human reason—if one but consults it—can demonstrate, and from these certain basic human rights can be derived. Jefferson, as well as other influential members of the prerevolutionary American culture who read Locke, proceeded to affirm the transcendent significance of these basic human rights. What is remarkable about these rights is that they are not founded on religious belief. They are founded upon everyone's normal awareness of human nature. These rights are evident—even self-evident—to people as people, plain and simple.

But how would all this solve the controversy about the relationship between religion and law? Mainly by reminding us that any moral law that cannot be demonstrated without reference to one's special faith must not be imposed upon others as a requirement of their lives. Of course, not everything that can so be demonstrated need become part of law. But if it is to become part of law, it must be demonstrable to general human understanding.

Consider the abortion issue. Roman Catholics and many fundamentalists hold that by their faith the zygote, embryo, and fetus are persons with the same rights as children. But this derives not from a simple awareness of the way human beings emerge into the world but by way of special religious interpretation of the natural phenomenon.

Birth dates are normally recorded when people emerge from the womb, begin to breath, take in the world, and form their own ideas about it. That is when they gain a name and begin their history. But this is not what Roman Catholics and other religious opponents of abortion hold. Thus they want the law changed so that abortion is regarded as homicide. They wish to impose this on nonbelievers and different faithful who depend on their secular understanding for accepting the society's laws as binding.

The couple convicted of negligent infanticide would have wanted it to be part of the law that medical treatment for children with pneumonia may be sidestepped by parents who adhere to their religious convictions. Such a curious doctrine arises from the special interpretation of health gained from their faith. Normal human awareness would not be able to demonstrate such a view, quite the contrary. By all commonsense accounts, available to anyone who cares to check, a child with pneumonia needs medical care.

It is not that religion and ordinary moral understanding do not often overlap. Nor is it that most people don't gain their moral sensibilities from religion, even when they might have gained them from secular sources. Only when it comes to public policy, where cooperation and agreement are vital, specifically religious or faith-dependent conceptions of how to live are insufficient. We must here depend on what so many sincere religious believers dislike, namely, a secular and naturalistic understanding of our world.

STATISM AT THE HIGH COURT*

The rhetoric of the Reagan administration is famous for attacking big government and calling for returning power to individuals, for both private enterprise and the efficiency of the free marketplace. The Reagan revolution is supposed to be one that will restore liberty to its proper place as our national priority. The Soviet Union is our enemy and we need to boost our defenses because communists despise human freedom and wish to enslave us all.

Meanwhile, the highest courts of the United States have unanimously affirmed the supreme power of the federal government in a recent ruling. Edwin D. Lee, an Amish farmer, resisted the collection of Social Security taxes from his employees on grounds that his religion forbids him to do this. The U.S. Supreme

*Originally published in the Los Angeles *Metropolitan News* (July 9, 1982).

Court unanimously upheld the efforts of the IRS to force Mr. Lee to collect the taxes for them.

This is perhaps to be expected, what with the nine justices all dependent for their income on the U.S. taxpayer. But the arguments the Court offered should forever put to rest the claim that these United States are dedicated to the ideal of human liberty in this world. Chief Justice Warren E. Burger, the well-known "conservative" leader of the court, appointed by former President Richard Nixon, another "conservative," put the case for supreme state power quite neatly:

> Not all burdens on religion are unconstitutional. . . . Because the broad public interest in maintaining a sound tax system is of such a high order, religious belief in conflict with the payment of taxes affords no basis for resisting the tax. . . . Mandatory participation is indispensable to the fiscal vitality of the social system. . . . A comprehensive national Social Security system providing for voluntary participation would be almost a contradiction in terms and difficult, if not impossible, to administer. . . . The tax system could not function if denominations were allowed to challenge the tax system because tax payments were spent in a manner that violates their religious belief. (*U.S.* v. *Lee*, 80–767.)

It is rare that one encounters such an unambiguous endorsement of the ideal of state supremacy. Only from the propagandists of the Soviet Union could one expect to hear anything comparable. It was *Pravda,* the Kremlin's mouthpiece, that justified the jailing and mental hospitalization of dissidents by proclaiming, back in 1977, that "legal action is taken in conformity with Society law in the case of individuals who engage in anti-Soviet propaganda and agitation, designed to undermine or weaken the established social and political system in our country, or who systematically spread deliberate falsifications vilifying the Soviet state and social system" (*New Times,* February 1977).

Pravda and former Chief Justice Burger agree that any threat against the state must be resisted, never mind the means. The U.S. Supreme Court has not yet declared published attacks on the tax system as open to legal censure. But this is clearly not a principled difference.

Why shouldn't the high court eventually move against publishers who print books aiming to persuade citizens to engage in tax resistance? If the maintenance of the tax system is indeed such a "high order" of public interest, surely other portions of the First Amendment could be sacrificed for it? If not even the constitutional right of freedom of worship and belief associated with religion "affords [a] basis for resisting the tax," what on earth could? Why should the Court not reject even a fair and square congressional vote on the subject?

In addition to the blatant rejection by the U.S. Supreme Court of the distinctive tradition of tax resistance in the name of individual liberty, we also have here a clear case of outright contradiction of fact. The way the Social Security system is run has now been found to be nothing less than fraud, affording anything but social security to working people in this country. The value of the funds placed into that system (at the point of the state's guns) had been progressively eroded throughout the system's few decades of existence. The future of the system appeared doomed, but after some revamping, officials have found ways of meeting the legal obligations that government has assumed. So, although a voluntary social security system on the order of the idea of a mandatory one is, of course, a contradiction in terms, there is no evidence at all to support Burger's claim that a voluntary system "would be . . . difficult, if not impossible, to administer."

The system as it stood was a flop. In terms of its very own objectives, the alternatives of permitting people, especially those who are philosophically and religiously committed to this, to attempt to fend for themselves certainly offers a better prospect than we now face. It may be true that "our system of taxation would be seriously jeopardized," as claimed in the Justice Department brief in opposition to Mr. Lee's case. But why should this be decisive in a supposedly free country? Why, moreover, is this country arming itself against Soviet communism, whose alleged distinguishing mark is that individual rights can at any time be crushed when the state interest demands it? In a free country the tax system is as open to the challenge of the people as anything except every individual's sacred right to liberty. Contrary to Burger, it is not the "sound(?) tax system" but the individual's right to liberty that is a "broad public interest . . . of such a high order" that nothing, not even the collection of revenues for state purposes "affords [a] basis for resisting" it.

Simply put, the ruling of the U.S. Supreme Court in the case of Edwin D. Lee stands as a complete indictment of the United States for its hypocrisy concerning its alleged status as the protector of freedom in the world. Certainly the value of liberty is upheld, helter-skelter, in this country—probably more so than elsewhere. But the Burger Court's unanimous ruling must be seen as the ominous signal to the world: We, too, have come to join those who worship state power over everything else.

THE PARADOXES OF EXPANDED STATISM*

For some time now, the U.S. Supreme Court has been hard put to make up its mind on the proper relationship between church and state. In 1982, the Court didn't think that Nebraska's having a salaried chaplain for its legislature violated the First Amendment to the U.S. Constitution. Against those who tried to oppose Minnesota's tuition tax deduction on grounds that this, too, violates the principle of the separation of church and state, the Court also ruled that the law could stand.

Of course, the Minnesota case is easy to handle outside the scope of any state-church controversy. When students receive their education from church-related schools, they are still receiving education, not mainly religious training. Of course, some of the latter may also be infused, but what is crucial is that the Minnesota case involves an educational tuition tax credit, nothing else.

---

*Originally published in the Los Angeles *Metropolitan News* (March 3, 1984).

The question of the Nebraska legislature's chaplain is a bit more tricky. Here, there is nothing to remove it from the state-church controversy and the Court's ruling is clearly partial to some connection, however ineffectual, between church and state. True, according to the three-part test the Court has been applying since 1971, a law will not be declared unconstitutional if (a) it reflects solely a secular legislative purpose; (b) it does not either promote or retard religion as its main result; and (c) it does not permit extensive involvement between state and church, the Nebraska law may manage to slide by. Chaplains are sort of an ornament and nothing much more these days. Yet, this could change. And a consistent church-state separation would not allow even the suggestion that the people as a whole can be served loyally by giving special preference to a representative of the clergy (however nondenominational).

But now the Reagan administration wishes to go further. In the case of the Pawtucket, Rhode Island, effort to keep on display a Christmas crèche, the Justice Department has joined the dispute in support of keeping the display intact, not because it meets the three-part test, but because Christmas is rooted in religion "as a matter of undeniable historical fact" and to try to wipe it "from our national consciousness is nothing less than intellectual and historical dishonesty." So declared Solicitor General Rex E. Lee.

Now, there is something to this argument: Both from a simple interpretation of the spirit of the political tradition, which has to some degree and ought to guide America's legal practices, and from the viewpoint of strict constructionism, there is no requirement for the U.S. Supreme Court to root out Christianity from the American culture. That would be, as Lee has called it, "cultural censorship."

But the problem is that when a culture has become as fully engulfed by its government, when it has become statist to a very large degree, as the United States has by now, a paradox arises. Virtually everything is done by governments these days, either directly or by way of some subsidy, grant, regulation, vital interest, whatever. Guided by that wonderfully dangerous view that is today promulgated by George Will—regular "conservative" columnist for *Newsweek,* author, and regular television commentator—namely, that statecraft is soulcraft, government touches everything. But then it is impossible for it to say "no" to anything without becoming a censor.

Take the Pawtucket case. The city displays the nativity scene on municipal property or some public park or at the public high school, or perhaps the local college makes room for it in its parking lot. Maybe some private mansion puts it in front of its "private" property, exposed to zoning ordinances. Can you escape public involvement in this matter at all? And why not? Because no private realm remains where the diverse cultural patterns that characterize the American melting pot could manifest themselves without encroaching upon the interests and concerns of unwilling participants.

When government does something, it is supposed to do it on everyone's behalf. In a pluralistic culture, that means government can do mighty little in the first place, since hardly anything can be done in such a way that it really does either serve everyone's interest or expresses everyone's view.

For this reason, among others, it is extremely useful to have a very large private realm within a pluralistic society. All kinds of things can then be done, on behalf of all sorts of traditions, majority ones or minority ones, and no one will encroach on anyone else's rightful dominion.

But with the current trend toward nationalization of the culture, the encroachment of some factions' concerns on those of others is inevitable. This is not something our culture can easily come to grips with—not, as least, without taking a fundamental and fresh look at the situation.

Any society that prizes both the adherence to values and practices—including religious ones—as well as the toleration of innumerable sets of values and practices, cannot afford the yoke of centralization. In such a society of free minds and free markets the government must content itself with the role of peacekeeper and not embark on soulcraft. This latter vocation must be left to the people themselves, which, all things considered, is a far more productive idea than all the alternatives that have been thought up throughout human history, from right to left and back again.

FREE PRESS VERSUS FAIR TRIAL*

A serious debate is developing over whether the traditional freedom of the press does damage to the recently emphasized rights of the accused. Since the First Amendment of the Constitution explicitly guarantees the right of free press, and since the Sixth Amendment requires that an accused be given a speedy trial by an impartial jury, many consider the issue of "free press vs. fair trial" a serious contradiction in the U.S. Constitution.

The fact is, however, that underlying this debate rests a very far-reaching assumption that has not been clarified. Those who have lined up on either side of the controversy have emphasized the social or moral importance of one of the constitutional provisions over and above the other, hoping that this approach would win them the required constitutional revisions (by limiting the right of the press), or the retention of the status quo (at the acknowledged expense of the accused, however). What is rarely, if ever, realized in this controversy is that it is not the Constitution that embodies a contradiction but the claim that "given a free press, a fair and impartial jury is impossible." Before I explore in just what way this claim embodies a contradiction, let us see how it happens that it has been taken seriously by so many.

Newspapers being what they are, on the occasion of a crime they will explore whatever is newsworthy about the crime, the suspects, and its varying dimensions. Very often information will be offered by newspapers that would not necessarily be admissible in a court of law, as for instance the criminal record of a person who is accused of a crime. Given this sort of information in the press (and other news media), it is assumed there could not be anyone who would be fair and

*Originally published in *Reason* magazine (September 1976).

impartial for purposes of serving on the jury. Since the newspapers print their news before a jury is selected, and since most people in the areas read the newspapers (or come in contact with other news sources) by the time jury selection rolls around, "the minds of the prospective jurors will be conditioned to pass judgment in certain ways."

What is assumed in all this? It is simply that people are incapable of confining their judgments to what is relevant in the situation of a courtroom. In effect, then, the whole controversy of "free press versus fair trial" is based on the premise that "if a member of a jury knows anything about the accused which has not been admitted into evidence, he cannot pass judgment over the guilt or innocence of the accused in accordance with the law." This strikes at the very heart of the claim that man has the capacity to be objective.

In ordinary life, we tend to take it for granted that there are prejudiced people to whom it is a waste of time to present facts and arguments, and that there are those who are willing and able to listen to a set of facts and base their judgment on this, exclusively. This is what gives us our general confidence in our jury system. We hold, implicitly, that when a number of carefully selected people are asked to judge certain facts in accordance with a set of standards—that is, the law—these people will, through diligence and conscientiousness, apply themselves to this task and accomplish what is expected of them. The controversy I am considering denies this common understanding. It holds that if people are confronted with facts that may lead to certain conclusions, they will not be able to disassociate themselves from these conclusions and facts when so asked, and that they will not be able to pass judgment upon a (legally) relevant set of facts without prejudice. Notice that this is not a claim about what people often fail to do but should do; it is a claim about what people cannot accomplish by their very natures. So the claim itself goes far beyond the issue of securing a fair trial. It is an indictment of our ability to rid ourselves of prejudice, false beliefs, and irrelevancies in given situations. The very possibility of objectivity in all matters, including the matter of judging the guilt or innocence of a person accused of a crime, is at stake in this controversy.

With the Constitution as it stands, it is assumed that despite free access to information, prospective jurors will be capable, if willing, to confine their judgments to the case and setting (the trial) at hand. The newly sparked controversy denies this possibility; but it does more than that: It denies that any human being is capable of offering objective judgments on anything once he has been exposed to facts that may be related (or may seem to be related) to the situation about which judgment is required.

And here is where the claim indicting human judgment and objectivity runs into serious difficulties. The claim itself, or so its proponents would like to maintain, is objective, unprejudiced, pure, etc. But how can it be? If all human judgments, ranging from those of jurors to those made by all others, are necessarily fettered by irrelevant facts, prejudices, and the like, would not the judgment that arrived at this conclusion also be so fettered? And if it is a hampered, disturbed, prejudiced judgment, why should we accept it at all? Is it not the aim of this indictment of the human capacity to make objective judgments to show that such judgments are unreliable precisely because they could not be objective? But if so, then the indictment itself is unreliable and cannot be accepted as valid. So the basis of the whole controversy is dissolved since it rests on a contradiction. If the indictment is valid, then it is invalid; only if it is invalid could it hope to be valid. Thus the indictment cannot be supported at all.

The controversy about free press versus fair trial is sham. It rests on a mistake or misrepresentation of facts. Let us hope that those who could act on such mistakes will not be moved to act on this one.

Let me now add that there is something that should be of concern to those who are interested in maximum justice within the criminal law. This concerns the appropriateness of police and court authorities to supply newspaper reporters with information not related to the crime in question. Is it right for clerks to release the information on the accused that concerns the accused's record of previous arrests? Should other personal data be at the disposal of the public? Should legal authorities supply reports with any kind of information pertaining to a crime?

These questions require lengthy answers. But they do not pertain to questions of free press versus fair trial. A newspaper reporter should be allowed to print anything he can get his hands on. Whether a police or court official should be able to release to newspeople any information that happens to be in his trust is an entirely different question. It relates to that other touchy problem of "open versus closed public files."

PROSPECTS FOR FREEDOM*

The awareness among people in our society of the need for radical answers to pressing social questions is growing. Since most of the major political movements connected with the last few decades of America's history have shown themselves to have been inept in their efforts to provide good answers, the people apparently are looking for "new" ideas. The modern welfare state is not working. Socialism is a failure. Communism is an impossible and irrational dream. Nationalism, expounded by many on the American Right, breeds hostilities and inauthentic confidence in one's culture to the detriment of real solutions to problems. Where, then, can we go in search for answers?

The radical ideas I referred to at the outset are those of pure laissez-faire capitalism and the morality of human, rational self-interest. The former has been part of the American tradition in a somewhat inadequate form: American capitalism or free enterprise has been something of an ideal whose workability even its strongest proponents failed to take seriously. American capitalism has been plagued by such obvious flaws as the institution of taxation without the consent of the governed; governmental regulation of industry and trade; interventionism in foreign trade;

---

*Originally published in the *Orange County Register* (February 1971).

the granting of monopolistic, privilege status to selected businesses and individuals; the protection of exclusive unions; governmental instead of market control of money; and, of course, the evil of slavery. While the vague notion that freedom of trade is good for people has been given lip-service far more than it has been instituted in practice, a truly free economic system has never been accepted in this country. (Of course, it was much more a part of our economic life than that of any other culture's, which is why America is a better place materially and in many other ways than other countries.)

What undercut America's progress toward freedom has been our culture's infection with an evil system of values. Children and adults have, on the whole, been told that it is bad for them to want to improve their lives. They must, the ethic went on to prescribe, promote the welfare of others. America, therefore, is a country with a population that suffers from constant guilt. Even though people will be better off with it than without it, in their personal lives what is good for one is to be rejected in preference to what is good for others. Since, however, we cannot make others' lives good for them, in our feeble and insincere efforts to secure the good for other people we proceed to ruin their lives rather than help them. Enforced charity is a contradiction in terms, and yet the present American welfare state is based on that concept.

At first, unfortunately, those who founded this country concerned themselves only with politics. They believed in doing the right thing politically because it more or less secured the general welfare. So having a free economic system was fine, at first, by the morality of doing things for others. Even this was frowned upon by some who claimed that the founders were too "selfish" when they came out for property rights.

But the culture was unprepared for the responsibility of coping with freedom. In freedom the individual must be convinced of the rightness of taking care of himself, for none can be forced to care for him, nor can he be forced to care for others. Yet most people believed that others had a right to be taken care of and actually wanted some laws that would force them and everyone to achieve this kind of forced charity. Thus the culture was based on a legal system that contradicted its moral atmosphere. People had the right to be free, in law, but did not believe that they or others could make use of this freedom to their own advantage. Yet the freedom itself was demanded in order to serve each person's advantage—the advantage of being able to pursue his own happiness without interference from others or the state (represented by the government).

Today there is a political philosophy that brings together the concepts of a free society and the moral rightness of pursuing one's own happiness. It is the philosophy of objectivism and the political philosophy of libertarianism. The former was founded by Ayn Rand, in her novels such as *Atlas Shrugged* and *The Fountainhead* and in her nonfiction books *Capitalism: The Unknown Ideal* and *The Virtue of Selfishness*. (Rand's major philosophical contribution, however, has been the difficult but important work *An Introduction to Objectivist Epistemology*.)

Recently (January 10, 1971) the *New York Times Magazine* printed an article describing and chronicling the libertarian movement. I believe the *Times* essay marks an important step in the right direction for American culture. I hope it will inspire people to examine libertarianism and help restore people's confidence in the ideas upon which our country has been partly built, however inadequately. Those ideas have made it possible for America to be the most sought-after place for millions. Perhaps now it will be possible for Americans to desire and seek the upgrading of these ideas and the continued improvement of both their personal and political existence.

TO PROFIT IS NOT EVIL*

Making profit in a business depends on producing something for which there is a demand, for which people will pay, i.e., exchange the earnings of their own work. Business accomplishes progress by addressing itself to the economic needs of people.

Those who criticize American business on the grounds that business activity is profit-oriented want governmental activity to be nonprofit-oriented either in itself or in its regulation of the activities of people in business. Presumably when this happens, the public is better satisfied. But is that true?

One should not suppose that free-market economic theory assumes that people always know what is good for them so they will spend money only rightly, well, wisely. This is not the case and free-market economics would be crazy to suppose it. All that free market economics supposes is that people ought to be left alone in making choices, that is, in what they want to buy from others. This will bring about optimal satisfaction, at least, though not necessarily utopia. The political theory of the free society holds that freedom of choice reaps fewer casualties than does full or semi-slavery.

There are more reasons, of course, to suggest that a regulated or socialist economy and its legal framework will not be good for people generally, and will be unjust to them individually. Such a system imposes the wisdom of a few whose mistakes will be suffered by everyone and whose contributions will be a direct subtraction from people's lives. Rulers can, on occasion, support something that is good—thus, even a Hitler built Germany an Autobahn. The cost is the legal system that makes one man's rule over another a common practice in the community and subjugates individual and voluntary group efforts to improve their lives in line with the best judgments. Collectivism imposes the average on us all, and the more pervasive the collectivism, the more centralized the decision making for everyone, the greater the degree of subjugation.

In a free society all men can aspire to become great and are primarily responsible for their own failures but not for those of others. In freedom there exists the limited sphere of influence one's inadequacies can have, while the adoption of elevating practices can be encouraged, not through force but through voluntary cooperation. When peoples' efforts to improve themselves are removed from their

---

*Originally published in the *Orange County Register* (circa 1972).

own sphere of influence and voluntary associations, the connection with their own actions is severed drastically. The impetus for self-improvement diminishes and the community's quality of life suffers correspondingly.

The profit motive that operates in the market provides a forum for competition; alternative ways of improving one's life compete for each person's attention and achievement through trading and exchanging; the goods to be traded go far beyond those of washing machines, cars, and stereo records. They include heart pacemakers, hearing aids, nutritious food, safer home appliances, different varieties of educational programs, and more—provided there is competition. Competition makes possible the satisfaction of people's unique needs, whether it be the tall man's need for a longer car or a shortsighted person's need for the appropriate eyeglasses.

In a centralized system no real competition exists, even though with less regulation, the opportunity for competition is greater and vice versa.

The defenders of the regulated marketplace really have no argument in their claim that the profit motive leads to evils. Well carried out, the profit motive leads to action that satisfies the needs of people and also respects their considered judgment in how they want to live their lives, which is something that justly casts upon each individual the moral responsibility to develop his own life.

ENVIRONMENTAL CRISIS*

During the last decades this country has been shocked into awareness about the bad quality of its environment. The air, waters, and even wildlife are seriously polluted. Big cities are slowly becoming unlivable, while the plains cannot support life economically. The phenomenon has created a "crisis condition" on radio and television; news programs abound with documentaries and commentaries about various aspects of the problem. "Population biologist" Dr. Paul Ehrlich from Stanford University gets top billing on both college campuses and the very middle-class "Johnny Carson Show."

It would be silly to deny that something is seriously wrong and that our environmental pollution is part of it. Unfortunately this time, as so often before, most people jump on the bandwagon not so much to do something about (maybe solve) the problem but to join in with blaming something or someone else for its presence. Thus, Dr. Ehrlich outlines the problem quite reasonably in his book *The Population Bomb* but then jumps to the conclusion that what we need is greater governmental involvement with the environment and with the problem of population. He, like so many others, is turning to government to fix things. And since the problem is quite real—even if badly analyzed—the Nixon administration is quite willing to play along. Congress was asked by the president for some $10 billion to handle matters—$6 billion more than it would cost to maintain a voluntary military service; Ronald Reagan first asked for $3 billion and later moved down to $1 billion. In both cases the humor of the situation is tragic.

---

*Originally published in the *Orange County Register* (1972).

It has, of course, been the governmental system of planned economics, of interventionism, of favoritism to people with lots of children, etc., that brought the problem to its present catastrophic state. How could the government do anything about the problem other than repeal those measures that fostered it? Neither $3 billion nor $10 billion will be spent, or useful, for that matter, in behalf of the solution of the problem. Governments cannot do anything productive; they can only order, constrain, interfere with, shift burdens, take from Peter and give to Paul (while they eat up some of it themselves), and in the main disturb the peace whenever they stray away from their job of keeping peace. And keeping the peace is not a productive job—it creates nothing; it merely sustains a condition in which production and creation may be pursued.

People, now as before, still believe that if one only calls upon Uncle Sam, allows him to steal and spend more, things will get done. Unfortunately, the college students who bury cars and go off into the wilderness with their transistor radios have no idea what caused the ecological situation or how to solve it. As before, neither those in power nor their most violent opponents have a solution, though they cry a lot about the problem.

The environmental crisis, like all crises that involve some people harming others whether through negligence or intention, is essentially a moral-legal one. For decades the legal system of the United States has fostered the view that people can simply transfer the burdens they have assumed whenever they like. Thus beaches, education, parks, forests, freeways, and the like can all be had without the realization that to obtain these things someone will have to pay for them. And so everybody keeps acting irresponsibly. This means over-population (more people than goods needed to support them), pollution of beaches and waters, student upheaval (since the quality of education is faltering drastically), traffic jams, urban and farm disasters, increasing prices, and so forth.

And after all this has been produced by the proliferation of immoral governmental activity, people still think that Uncle Sam will do it for us—put down the revolution, build more highways, keep the forests green, assure the air is pure, see that the oceans are filled with healthy fish, restrain prices, maintain high levels of income, eliminate drug consumption, provide universal education, and so forth.

Why don't we wake up and realize that only individual human beings can solve problems; only we have minds and can really go to work on the problems. We just have to do it!

TOPLESS BUT FREE*

California's Orange County is noted for its so-called ultra-conservatism. What precisely is meant by this I have not the vaguest idea; but, among other things, the characterization aims to indicate that the majority of the citizens, organizations, politically active institutions, news media, etc., in this part of the country are

---

*Originally published in the *Orange County Register* (1971).

out of line in their thinking with the fundamental precepts of the rampant national political philosophy of welfare-statism, socialism, etc. People who are called "ultraconservatives" usually oppose the federal income tax, support greater liberty for businesses, dislike the United Nations, consider liberals to be "soft on communism," and in general want less of the federal government and more of the individual in our way of life.

Not surprisingly, what I said thus far is not very clear. After all, liberals aren't very clear with their accusations aimed at conservatives, nor are conservatives too clear about what they stand for. I want to point out that while this is a situation for which the liberals are not to be blamed (except when they misrepresent some specific view of someone, like Barry Goldwater), conservatives themselves are indeed guilty of some of the most embarrassing contradictions and thus are responsible for the major part of the confusion.

One of the most blatant examples of this indulgence in inconsistencies is the recent flood of demands within Orange County that the topless bars and restaurants be outlawed. While on the one hand the majority of conservatives, politicians and nonpoliticians alike, make exasperating use of the word *freedom* in their discussion of political ideas and institutions, they seem at the same time to discard the necessary attention that should be paid to the application of that term in all fields where freedom becomes important.

When in 1964 the federal government was pushing for a civil rights bill that included the "public accommodations" clause, conservatives throughout this nation were up in arms about the authority of the state to interfere with the owner of an eating or lodging establishment in the management of his business. The theory, a correct one I might mention, asserted that since the business is the property of the owner, and since property rights are the social expression of each man's right to be free, to force a businessman to manage his business in line with the edicts of the federal government was a serious limitation of individual rights. I was on the side of the conservatives in this battle, though more often than not they managed to bring up the issue of state "rights" in this connection, an issue the introduction of which did considerable damage to their thesis. And this is where the conservatives run amuck with respect to the matter of topless bars and restaurants.

Asserting that the federal government should not expand its powers, conservatives manage to evade the fact that the only sound reason for the containment of the federal government is that its expansion tramples over individual rights. The concept of individual rights is the only source of a sound defense against oppression—whether the oppression comes from the federal, state, county, or city government. The reason it is wrong to force someone to serve a black person—more so than the fact that the person is a racist—is that to do so is to eliminate the concept of property rights from the law of the land. Once one allows the federal government to interfere with property rights, there is no stopping this practice (as is well demonstrated by the use of the interstate commerce clause of the Constitution). But this does not apply only to the federal government; it applies to all institutions that have the legal power to enforce their edicts.

Some communities are flooded with topless bars. They are considered immoral, obscene, or just "offensive" to a number of the people in these communities. Politicians, representing the people, are always eager to come to the aid
of the offended. Thus they originate proposals for laws that would eliminate topless bars, girly magazines, and the like from the community. And this flagrant
statism is perpetrated upon us not by liberals, communists, leftists, or socialists
but by our most freedom-oriented (in lip-service, at least) local conservatives. Of
course this flagrant statism is done in the name of "local control." No doubt,
some of the intentions behind the statist measures are good, noble, and moral,
as is the intention behind the Rumford Law, which, in behalf of decency to minority groups, manages to evade the property rights of individuals.

It appears that neither conservatives nor liberals are quite clear about just
what the proper, consistent, noncontradictory (i.e., correct) meaning of the term
freedom is. But liberals do not usually pretend to be for freedom. They prefer
"freedoms" and welfare, not individual liberty, as that applies within the context
of a free society. They talk of a "Great Society" or an "open society," and have
managed to drop the pretense of speaking about a free society. Not so, however,
with conservatives. They preach of freedom, urge freedom, defend freedom, and
do everything with the mouth as far as freedom is concerned—they simply forget
to practice freedom. Thus they want to deprive a man of his right to feature
any kind of entertainment on his own property; they want to deprive a man
of his freedom to trade his magazines with people who are willing go buy it
on the free market. They want, in the name of local control (small-scale statism),
to regulate the management of local small businesses, just like the federal government wants to regulate the management of the big businesses of the country.

It even appears that (former) State Senator John G. Schmitz, the only politician in the State of California who ran on the platform that he will not initiate
any legislation but will work for the repeal of many antiliberty laws, supports
the idea that local communities, cities, districts, counties, ought to have control
over the affairs of their citizens. According to the *Register,* Schmitz urged city
officials to write to Governor Ronald Reagan and urge him to return control
over crime and "morality" laws to local communities. One has to argue with
the contention of those who hold that these "conservative" politicians are pro-
liberty when one recognizes just what sort of action they want to take once something happens in their communities that is an expression of individual liberty,
property rights, and self-determination, even though it is a fact that other members of the community might not agree with the kind of self-determination and
activities performed by some others. But it is precisely in just these circumstances
that the issue of liberty versus control becomes clear-cut. If Joe's bar has topless
dancers and I am revolted by the prospect of viewing such a sight, I ought to
be free to stay away (individual freedom), while Joe ought to be free to offer
this kind of entertainment (individual freedom and property rights). The same
goes for discrimination: If Bill does not want to serve blacks he ought to be
free to refuse (individual freedom and property rights), while if I am revolted

by this act of irrationalism, I ought to be free to stay away from Bill's bar (individual freedom).

I suggest that the conservatives who scream and yell about federal infringements upon our freedom do a little soul-searching and note just how they are quite frequently willing to limit the freedom of their fellow citizens. If they would rather continue to censor magazines, put bars off limits, and burn books, then they should stop their lip-service to liberty and join the liberals who are equally willing to abridge the freedom of those whose aims are not consonant with theirs. Thus, while the conservatives will run around eliminating nudity and topless entertainment, liberals will make sure that all of us will have to support the fine arts (their style), their type of education, their charity ventures, etc.

To paraphrase an old cliché, "Birds of a feather should flock together." Those of us who are for freedom in all realms of life, those of us who want to protect every person's liberty—including the black's, the man who wants to discriminate against blacks, the owner of the topless bar, and the person who wants to stay away from such bars—those who want freedom for all those citizens will have a chance to present our position without the odd bedfellows surrounding us who are willing to compromise the principles of freedom at every turn of the political road—whether in Austin; Costa Mesa; Sacramento; or Washington, D.C.

SENATOR INOUYE ON THE NUREMBERG TRIALS*

When Senator Daniel Inouye, chairman of the Select Committee on the Iran-Contra diversion of funds, spoke at the conclusion of Lieutenant Colonel Oliver North's testimony in the summer of 1987, he mentioned that the United States Uniform Code of Military Justice (UCMJ) had been used as the model penal code at the Nuremberg trials where the leaders of Adolf Hitler's Third Reich were prosecuted for their inhuman deeds against the millions they murdered. Inouye believes that the provision of the UCMJ that requires a soldier to disobey an unlawful order served as the main theme of those trials.

During his testimony Colonel North had gained the admiration of many Americans. Senator Inouye wanted to counter this because he regards North as a law-breaker. Inouye thinks North also violated the provision of the UCMJ that requires that a soldier disobey unlawful orders. By stressing that Colonel North in fact obeyed an order he was legally prohibited from obeying (by the Boland Amendment), the senator tried to discredit North and discourage the growing admiration for him. Inouye probably sincerely believes that doing this was imperative; it would be encouraging idolatry, the admiration of false heroes, to do less.

Yet there is a better way of understanding this. First, the defendants at Nuremberg were charged with something different from the complaint against Oliver North. They *wrongfully* obeyed certain *lawful* orders of the Third Reich.

---

*Originally published in the *Orange County Register* (1987).

They could not be charged under the laws of the Third Reich precisely because those laws required them to act in the morally intolerable way they in fact did act. But because they were charged under unwritten or moral "laws" rather than the written or enacted laws of their country that they could have consulted, they could be convicted.

There remains considerable controversy in jurisprudential circles as to whether that trial did not lay a dangerous precedent by prosecuting defendants not because they violated but because they obeyed their country's admittedly unjust laws. If one must obey the law, surely it is the law of one's country that one must obey. But if this is so, how could it be just to prosecute someone for having done what one ought to do? Presumably since some laws ought not to be obeyed.

But the problem now is, if it is right to disobey some laws, just when should one do this? Must one rely on one's moral conscience? Is there some higher law to which one must defer?

Perhaps, though, when laws are enacted via the democratic process—that is, in accordance with the provision that the law must have the consent of at least the majority of those who will be governed by it—then they certainly must be obeyed, and violating them is inexcusable. Yet Adolf Hitler's Third Reich came into being via the semi-democratic process of the Weimar Republic. The subsequent anti-democratic character of many of its laws continues to remind us that out of democratic processes one may find the development of anti-democratic institutions.

But there is a remedy for this, especially from the American viewpoint of limited democracy. I want to once again recall what the Supreme Court has argued in *West Virginia State Board of Education* v. *Barnette* (1943), namely, that "The very purpose of the Bill of Rights was to withdraw certain subjects from the vicissitudes of political controversy, to place them beyond the reach of majorities and officials. . . ."

It seems then that even in the United States one ought to perhaps disobey some democratically enacted laws, i.e., those that bear on subjects that have been placed "beyond the reach of majorities and officials." And this imperative could apply to the duties of the executive branch of our government. In which case, Colonel North might well argue that what he was doing is just what the spirit and even the letter of the Nuremberg trials would require anyone to do, namely, disobey certain laws on moral grounds.

The grandfather of our legal system, philosopher John Locke, agreed with this when he noted that "it is fit that the laws themselves should in some cases give way to the executive power, or rather to this fundamental law of Nature and government—viz., that as much as may be all the members of society are to be preserved."

Contrary to Senator Inouye's opinion, Colonel North may have done right not to obey the spirt—he said he did obey the letter—of the Boland Amendment. Inouye himself agrees that the UCMJ required him to disobey orders that are "unlawful."

The problem is that "unlawful" is ambiguous—if one is invoking Nuremberg, then one must mean "not following the higher laws of humanity." But if one is invoking written law, then one must mean the principles spelled out in the U.S. Constitution. As far as Oliver North's conduct is concerned, one can make a plausible case that the Boland Amendment has been either (a) a violation of higher law (by requiring someone to abandon the Contras to a humanly intolerable fate) or (b) a violation of the U.S. Constitution because it contradicted executive prerogative.

In either case, Lieutenant Colonel North may have to be regarded as having conducted himself more in accord with proper citizenship than Senator Inouye and some of his colleagues suggested. That, of course, teaches us the lesson that ultimately we cannot rely blindly on any laws, even in a democratic society, to guide our conduct. We must rely on our awareness of sound moral principles. But that is exactly the lesson that many of us learned from some of our political leaders during the civil rights upheavals, the antiwar movement during the Viet Nam debacle, and the anti-establishment furor accompanying both these periods in recent U.S. history. We were told that when the laws are unjust, when they are intolerable from the moral point of view, we are obligated to fight them and at times even to disobey them.

In a democratic society, where accountability of public officials is such a vital matter, such morally sanctioned law-breaking must, of course, be examined, at least after the fact. Even the executive's prerogative to go against the law when necessary must be justified to the people. And the Iran-Contra hearings may be said to be the current forum in which such accountability is demonstrated.

It is crucial, however, that the law is not always the court of last resort. The real question is this: What are the higher moral laws that we must all be accountable to in the last analysis?

SOVIET BOY SHOULD STAY*

Do parents have unconditional authority over their children? This is the impression given by some who have discussed the case of twelve-year-old Walter Polovchak, the Ukrainian boy who ran away from his emigrant parents when they decided to return to the Soviet Union after a brief stay in this country. Walter and his seventeen-year-old sister, Natalie, don't want to go back. The sister has her own visa and isn't meeting with any resistance, but Walter will have to go to court and face the Chicago chapter of the American Civil Liberties Union, which is representing his parents in a suit to get custody of Walter and take him back to the Soviet Union.

With regard to the hearing to "reassess the family situation," let me offer some reasons supporting the claim that Walter Polovchak should not be sent back to the Soviet Union if he does not wish to go.

Children normally have the right to be cared for by their parents, at least

---

*Originally published in the *New York Times* (August 28, 1980).

until they reach adulthood. Parents brought them into this world as extremely young and dependent human beings. Dependence is built into the nature of childhood, so that those embarking on parenthood ought to know a good deal about their obligations to their children.

In many cases, of course, the government has usurped parental responsibilities. But at heart it is still parents, not others, who are obligated to care for their offspring.

As it stands, Walter Polovchak claims the right to remain in the United States. There are those who would gladly care for him until he learns to do for himself. But Walter's parents claim that they have the right to take him to the Soviet Union against his will.

Ordinarily, parents have the right to take their children anywhere they go. Ordinarily, however, parents are not marching off to a totalitarian dictatorship. In such a world, children are commandeered from birth. Certainly they have no legal protection against such commandeering. Walter Polovchak's parents are claiming civil rights that make sense in a free society. As it is, their plan is to eliminate any chance of Walter ever claiming any rights and having them protected.

Suppose a child ran away from home because his parents decided to take him on a suicide mission. Have parents the right to take their child with them? It would be unheard of for anyone to take this line seriously. Parents have the obligation to take care of their children, not use them as they desire.

A child is a young human being, entitled to protection by the legal system. In Walter's case, his parents refuse to accord him what they are obligated to, namely, reasonable child care. They want to deliver him into a society where children have no rights now or when they grow up.

Taking a child to such a place is bad enough. But when the child is capable of showing to a court in a free society that he does not wish to go, then to send him anyway would be gross injustice. It would be to deny this young person what would be his right in but a few years and could, through judicial discretion, easily be granted to him now.

Childhood is a provisional period in anyone's life, and between it and adulthood there is considerable gray area. Once it is demonstrated that Walter does not want to go to the Soviet Union, his parents should not be given protection against Walter's attempt to leave them.

The courts of a free society should not be confused, not even by an organization calling itself the American Civil Liberties Union, into believing that granting the claims of the parents to their parental rights in this case is like granting such a claim in the case of a child who wishes to run off to go hunting in the jungle or to steal a motorcycle. Walter Polovchak is engaging in no mere child's play in running away. He is giving himself a chance to live the life of a free person.

REFLECTIONS ON AUTHORITY AND LIBERTY*

A constant theme of recent discussions among conservative intellectuals has been the relationship between authority and liberty. It would be convenient to discuss the topic by way of precise definitions, but the problem with definitions is that they require elaborate support, especially when they pertain to such high-level abstractions as those involved in this issue.

Now, in the space provided I cannot embark on complete discussions of issues such as the one on which I wish to focus. What can be achieved here is the presentation of some ideas, coupled with certain arguments that may show where answers might be found.

The concept of authority, as concerns the issues on which many conservatives have focused (namely, social and political relationships among human beings), means something akin to having a justified superior status concerning decisions to be made and actions to be taken. One who has authority in teaching, for example, is supposed to have satisfied certain nonarbitrary standards that qualify him to educate others in a subject matter. Similarly, someone who has authority in government is supposed to have satisfied certain nonarbitrary standards that qualify him to set binding public policy (or enforce the same, depending upon his type of political authority).

The concept of liberty, in turn, pertains to the status of persons vis-à-vis each other, so that if people should live in liberty, others should not interfere in their conduct, at least no via physical force or threat of force. (Liberty can, of course, mean other kinds of relationships, e.g., that between a person's proper ends in life and his ability to pursue them.) Thus, if I have the liberty to pursue a career in teaching, no one should interfere with my efforts to seek an education and position toward this goal. (This kind of interference does not include not doing something for me as I seek my goals! That conception of liberty is different, albeit often confused with what I have just specified.)

Why is it often thought that authority and liberty conflict with each other? Mostly because, at a certain level of analysis, it appears that if someone has the authority to judge what another should do, it is held that the other has no liberty to act differently. In social relationships this problem does not seem to arise except when matters are not clearly understood. For, although my physician has the authority to judge what I should do concerning my health, yet I may also be at full liberty to do differently. That is, if my physician is not also someone who has proper political authority to set binding policy for me (as he might be if he were a judge responsible for authorizing a court order that would prevent a communicable disease from spreading in the community).

Yet this point is often ignored and there are many who would reject the very idea of authority simply so as to preserve liberty, mainly because they understand the pertinence of authority in social relations. The very act of judgment— of saying something critical or approving—is thought at times to imply a claim

---

*Originally published in the *New American Review* (November 1977).

to have this judgment binding in more than a rational, moral, or practical sense. "You have no right to tell me what to do" is the obviously ambiguous outburst, since it confuses judgment ("telling") with imposition ("ordering").

As a result of the immense fear that supporters of liberty have of unauthorized interference with people's lives, they have often gone all the way toward denying the very possibility of any kind of authoritative judgment. (This tendency by classical liberals and libertarians has actually aided the current egalitarian trend in social and political philosophy in that it is felt that no one's judgment can be better than another's!) Indeed, it is classical liberal philosophies that have given aid and comfort to subjectivism and relativism in ethics, leading to subjectivism and relativism in everything else—e.g., what counts as science, art, education, love, happiness, value, and much more.

Paradoxically, this result has also given support to unlimited democracy, whereby the very idea of fundamental, absolute political principles (e.g., natural law, natural rights) is denied, just to keep things consistent. Democracy concerning political values—not methods of selecting administrators—arises from complete subjectivism, as the only plausible alternative to complete chaos on the public front. (There are, of course, the subjectivist anarchists, such as Max Stirner, who take the position to its strict logical extreme, denying any possible role for public, policy, as such.) So the initial denial of proper authority is the creator of the monster of the tyranny of the majority, the rule of gray mediocracy.

The solution seems to require a distinction between different kinds of authority, both possible but yielding different results. It is quite possible, by this view, that some people really are justified in passing judgment on the quality of education, music, film, dress, wine, love, marriage, and so on without it being the case that these same people can claim any justification for wielding power over those who reject their perfectly sound judgments. On the other hand, in matters political, where the issue is who may set binding edicts and enforce the same in a human community, the possibility of authority also exists. If some individuals have been appropriately selected by others to concern themselves with the protection and preservation of the rights everyone has (including liberty), then these individuals are justified in ordering others to act in certain ways and in having their orders properly enforced.

9

Morality

No one can reasonably deny that throughout our culture there is and has probably always been extensive concern with ethics. Yet this concern seems to conflict with a commitment to view the world scientifically.

Ethics arises in response to the question, "How should I conduct myself?" It can be focused on specific tasks (e.g., politics, parenting, or a profession) or very broadly, on the most general approach people will have occasion to consider taking toward living their lives.

We encounter ethics through thousands of personal problems and through such widely publicized controversies as the Iran-Contra affair, the abortive Bork nomination, and Ed Meese's alleged wrongful behavior, and the insider trading scandals on Wall Street. More significant is the case of someone like President Kurt Waldheim of Austria, who is suspected of taking part in Nazi war crimes. Presumably, if wrongful conduct faces us we ought to hold responsible the person who acted wrongfully because persons are supposed to be able to choose and could have done otherwise.

I don't wish to raise any ethical issue here. But I do want to remind us all of the presence of ethical issues in our society. My main question is: Can all this concern about ethics be squared with the scientific view of human nature, which enjoys much respect?

There is no doubt that ours is a "scientific age." The answers we give to our questions are often deemed adequate only if they are backed by the findings of the special sciences. Standards of theoretical and intellectual adequacy are set by the sciences. This is at least true for the community of persons who work with ideas: academics, pundits, authors, theorists, consultants, and advisers.

So what is the problem? Many pit morality against science because the latter

---

*Originally published in the *Orange County Register* (November 20, 1988).

would seem to require abandoning the individual's unique role in producing his conduct and goals. As Harvard psychologist B. F. Skinner puts it in his *Science and Human Behavior,* "The hypothesis that man is not free is essential to the application of scientific method to the study of human behavior." Skinner has been perhaps the most outspoken on this issue, yet many others also believe that if all realms of nature are open to scientific understanding, then there is no place for morality in human life. Certainly a good deal of social science follows Skinner here, what with crime, delinquency, drug abuse, family mismanagement and the lot all being explained in terms of various factors that determine how people will behave.

Why does this rule out ethics? Because morality requires that human beings be free and responsible, capable of choosing their actions. If we do not cause our behavior, if we cannot choose what we will do, we aren't the sort of creatures that could be responsible for doing things rightly or wrongly. In that case it would be wholly grotesque to blame or praise any of us.

What has been missing for there to be some concrete possibility for morality is the capacity of persons to determine or cause their own behavior. This is rejected in the dominant mechanistic idea of causation, which holds that causes and effects form an exhaustive daisy chain throughout the universe, without beginning or end. Human behavior is just a link in this infinite chain.

The skeptic's pull is considerable. Many people try to explain their own "immoral" conduct, and sometimes that of others, by reference to facts they cannot control. We blame not ourselves for our bad habits but the childhood traumas we had experienced. We look to our environment, our social surroundings, our economic circumstances, our biological or genetic make-up and the like in order to explain what we do. And if we didn't carry on exactly like this in earlier times, some similar idea—the devil made me do it, the gods are responsible, demons got into him, etc.—prevailed. When all else failed, we threw up our hands and declared human affairs mysterious.

Yet, surprisingly perhaps, there is reason to think that morality can indeed coexist with science. Mainly this reason emerges from a reconsideration of our understanding of science as a general area of human concern.

First, science is not identical with mechanistic physics. This obsolete view does require that the behavior of everything conform to just one finite set of laws. It also proposes that ultimately everything is to be accounted for in terms of just one kind of thing, physical matter-in-motion. As Nobel prize-winning neurophysicist Roger Sperry notes in his book *Science and Moral Priority,* "the advances of the last half-century in our understanding of the neural mechanism of mind and conscious awareness clear the way for a rational approach in the realm of values." He explains that his recently

> . . . proposed brain model provides in large measure the mental forces and abilities
> to determine one's own actions. It provides a high degree of freedom from outside
> forces as well as mastery over the inner molecular and atomic forces of the body.
> In other words, it provides plenty of free will as long as we think of free will as

self-determination. A person does indeed determine with his own mind what he is going to do and often from among a large series of alternative possibilities.

It appears that science, properly conceived, does not pit itself against morality. Rather the science of human life shows that human beings are, when not crucially incapacitated, correctly conceived as self-responsible, moral agents. Of course, this still leaves a lot to be explored about the exact way for us to reconcile the findings of various special sciences—physiology, neurophysics, perceptual psychology, organic chemistry, and so on—with the moral sciences, so called, such as economics, sociology, politics, and ethics. What is promising, however, is that two concerns that seem to persist in human life, an organized understanding of the world and the imperative to act properly within that world, do not seem to be at odds with each other.

THE PITFALLS OF HUMANISM*

Humanism is a kind of secular religion that many American intellectuals have adopted as their non-ideological commitment to ideals. The latter are discussed and often developed in the *Humanist,* a magazine edited (at one time) by philosopher Paul Kurtz at the State University of New York at Buffalo.

There is a crucial feature of humanism that renders it both unworkable and dangerous. To explore it, let me briefly characterize what humanism is. The philosopher Ludwig Feuerbach was an early critic of Hegel's mystically inspired idealist (religious) philosophy. Feuerbach initially admired Hegel but later chided the towering German thinker for getting matters backward. Hegel put the transcendent mind or spirit, namely God, ahead of all the rest of existence or nature. Starting with a highly complex idea about how pure spirit will produce its antithesis, concrete matter—and thus start the dialectical process in reality—Hegel accepted God or Absolute Spirit as metaphysically, logically, and existentially prior to material reality.

Feuerbach did not see Hegel's theory as a viable means by which to make sense of reality. He argued that material reality must come prior to ideas and ideals, including consciousness itself. He moved on from this to criticize theology in general, demanding, in turn, that theology's subject matter be studied within anthropology or, as now understood, the social sciences.

Marx, who drew on both Hegel and Feuerbach, accepted the latter's materialistic framework but tried to combine this with the dialectical principle he learned from Hegel. For Feuerbach and Marx not deity but humanity comprised the proper realm of philosophical investigation, including the field of political economy. In Marx's hand, however, the investigation of humanity could benefit greatly from the Hegelian system of dialectics. Both Marx and Engels believed that although there is no *apriori* metaphysical case to be made for a dialectical

---

*Originally published in the *New Guard* (March 1975).

process throughout nature, a straightforward empirical study of nature yields the conclusion that dialectical laws permeate all of reality.

The effects of this conviction are evident throughout the Marxian system of thought—dialectics assumed both an analytic and explanatory role in Marxist philosophizing. This is evident, also, in Marx's concept of humanity. To wit, the ideals to be aspired to in life are not to be accepted from religion, which is based on mysticism and is throughout bound up with class-consciousness; instead the scientific approach, employing the method of dialectical reasoning, can serve to demonstrate the proper ideals for humanity.

It is my view that this general evolution of human thought has culminated in a humanistic outlook of philosophy. One reason I am confident in this conclusion is that humanism is often taken to be a more rationalistic, scientific acknowledgment of certain ideals and goals (others have) found emphasized through religion. Many religious humanists accept a sort of parallelism between the ideals of meaningful religion and humanism. Moreover, there was in Marx a definite concern with how mankind could achieve the realization of man's essential nature, how imperfect man could become truly human. And his basic response to this query was that the dialectical development of human society will eventually produce the new man who will be truly, essentially human.

Now my point about all this is that humanism rests, in part, on an extrapolation from certain sorts of ideal cases to a general theory of human relationships. In short, I want to claim that humanism commits what I call the "blow up" fallacy— the mistake of taking a principle applicable in one realm of reality and attempting to interpret some other or all other realms of reality with the aid of the principle. (For more on that fallacy, see my *The Pseudo-Science of B. F. Skinner* [1974].)

There are certain general ideals that hardly anyone will construe to be unrealistic. The love of someone for his or her children; a mutually satisfying friendship; the trust between friends; the love of lovers, siblings, members of families (when these are at their best); solidarity of various communities; loyalty to one another; and many other elements of human life that have existed and could exist if only we made the effort. The immense power of feeling and realization of same that go hand in hand with only a brief reflection on these features of people's lives can certainly elevate the human soul. To work for ideals reflecting the circumstances that surround the concrete cases that one knows involve the above-listed human capacities is assuredly inspiring.

But now I must raise some cautionary points. These, however, should not be taken to demean the ideals I have been talking about. What I am concerned with is some of the leaps of judgment that can be made once one is inspired by the ideals in question. Can it be accepted that the ideals realized between lovers, siblings, members of a certain kind of community, friends, and even comrades in work are (a) appropriate to how one can be expected to relate to all of humanity and (b) capable of being not just imposed (e.g., by political means) but even taught? It seems to me clear that the ideals are realizable only in those circumstances where knowledge of individuals is possible—just knowing that another is human, and no more, cannot lead to the love of that person, or a friendship with that person. The dynamics of family life, even to the point of temporal and special factors, is well suited for the realization of fraternal bonds. Yet it would be unrealistic—impossible—to have such ideals manifest themselves between persons not in these circumstances.

But that takes care of *a* only. Concerning *b* we have another problem. I am not unfair, I think, to claim that there are humanists who want to bring about the consequences of these ideals by political means—frankly, through force. Now, within the Marxist framework the function of force has to be accepted, at least when we focus on the prominent aspects of Marx's political economy, his theory of revolution, and his belief in the incommensurability of opposing class ideas. But humanism is not now bound to Marxism, and where force had an intrinsic, systematic role in Marxist humanism—seeing that it promised the realization of humanistic ideals only from a culmination of the social dialectical processes—it is not so tied to contemporary, democratic humanism. Once Marxism is not the system out of which humanism derives its main tenets, and the freedom of the individual is acknowledged in humanism (granting some prominent exceptions), force is entirely incompatible with humanistic ideals. Forced love is no love at all, and so with friendship, fraternity, camaraderie, etc. Yet it seems to me that many of the large political aspirations of contemporary humanism fail to take these matter into consideration.

But *a* and *b* are not unrelated. By making the extrapolation from human ideals—as these can be realized, however rarely, in individual, intimate relationships among persons who know each other not merely as human beings but also as the unique persons they are—to the larger circumstances of societies, the inclination of forcing the situation becomes more and more frequent. B. F. Skinner, who does have a number of valuable ideas to offer about personalized education, training, and the like, illustrates only too well how easily such extrapolation can lead one to the advocacy and support of oppressive measures for realizing certain ideals. Impatience with the realization of impossible goals, their evident absence in the broad social arena (for if they are impossible, they will be absent), and the suspicion that others are actually working to suppress the great goals will lead many with humanitarian motives to propose coercive measures toward others!

My purpose has not been to indict all humanists. For those among self-admitted humanists who are concerned with why the humanist point of view is not more widely adopted and implemented, the above considerations may be of some value. I actually made an attempt to have these points voiced in the *Humanist* itself, but it appears that the editors could not see their way clear to giving them a forum just now. Let us hope that some of the self-proclaimed humanists are sufficiently concerned to take up these issues even if that are offered in a forum other than their own.

PRIVATE PROPERTY AS A PREREQUISITE OF HUMAN MORALITY*

A central tenet of any morality is that we are responsible to choose our course of conduct correctly. We ought to choose what we will do in a way that accords with the moral standards applicable to human life. Concretely this means we ought to guide ourselves properly with respect to the reality that we encounter.

Such a minimum idea is implied by all genuine moral systems and by our commonsense understanding of what it is to blame and praise persons for how they conduct themselves regardless of place or historical period. All the details of morality must ultimately presuppose this element of personal responsibility, regardless of whether they were elaborated in modern or in ancient times. The assumption of voluntary, self-responsible conduct can be found in ethics from Aristotle to the most recent moral philosophy, from hedonism to rational altruism.

This also means that we are committed to the exercise of rationality, which will enable us to identify our moral responsibilities. I have in mind "rationality" not in a Cartesian or economic sense of that term but in the sense that we mean it when we refer to thinking clearly, being perceptive and aware of what we should do, how we should act. We are committed to being thoughtful, to applying ourselves to concrete living tasks in a basically principled fashion. Work, communication, integration of goals, choice of friends and country, concern for long-range tasks, etc., are all part of a concrete and varied moral task of every individual capable of rationality.

One characteristic of rational living is the conscientious consideration of available alternatives. A person should choose the right course of conduct and this means that he or she must know what alternatives and choices are open to them. For example, the question may be: Should I attend church or go to the golf course; should I purchase a car or a new encyclopedia; should I invest my earnings in stocks or CARE packages; should I spend my time with my children or doing extra work at the office; should I move from my present quarters to new ones? In each case the availability of the alternatives is presupposed: Going to church or to the golf course would both have to be available for the question to arise, etc., and, of course, often numerous options are available. Should I take swimming lessons, send my child to dancing school, purchase a new tire for the family car, contribute to the homeless children's welfare fund, write a philosophy paper, or send a gift to my parents? Given that at any time I have a fixed "budget" or other resources, I would have specific options.

In any case, as any conception of human moral life supposes, if persons are responsible for the decisions or choices they make, the alternatives would have to be clearly available to them. To put it another way, they would require jurisdiction over them so as to make a determinate choice about them. In the absence of such jurisdiction, the moral situation is systematically ambiguous and just what a person ought to or ought not to do is impossible to specify clearly. While approximation may be possible, the possibility of clear assignment of blame or praise will be rare.

---

*Originally published in the *Freeman* (1987).

We can put it another way: Without a clear idea of what is ours, what belongs to someone else, and so forth, we must remain morally confused and ultimately lose confidence in our ability to live a moral life. That in turn can produce a demoralized society.

All this should begin to indicate the moral significance of private property rights. Suppose that my available options are unclear. I do not own memberships in the church and the golf club. Whether I may—that is, am authorized to— select either as an alternative is indeterminate: Membership is largely at the discretion of the congregation and the city athletic association, respectively. Then whether I will go to one or the other is not something I *can* decide. "Ought implies can." If it is not up to me whether I will be going to one or the other place, I cannot be responsible for where I shall go—and so forth, down the line with every option involving two or more alternatives.

One way of interpreting the famous doctrine of "the tragedy of the commons" is to realize that when common ownership *and* authority attach to some valuable option, individuals who are responsible to make morally right choices cannot make them. They are unable to determine what they *should* do because the various alternatives are not theirs to select. With this goes the more widely recognized problem that when no individual authority is recognized with respect to some alternative—e.g., the choice of going to the club does not impose responsibilities of doing this carefully, prudently, and so forth—the ramifications, consequences, implications, etc. will be unattended.

Suppose I may personally select some portion of land with no obligation to admit others to share it, at least for a given time period. Now it is also clearly my responsibility if I take good care of or neglect this land while using it. But if "we all" or some other indeterminate group has this authority, it becomes inherently ambiguous whose responsibility it is to take care. As Aristotle observed,

> For that which is common to the greatest number has the least care bestowed upon it. Every one thinks chiefly of his own, hardly at all of the common interest; and only when he is himself concerned as an individual. For besides other considerations, everybody is more inclined to neglect the duty which he expects another to fulfill; as in families many attendants are often less useful than a few. (*Politics*, Bk. II, 1234ff)

Yet even Aristotle missed the full story. What is ultimately tragic in "the tragedy of the commons" is that even if one were determined not to neglect any of one's responsibilities *it cannot be clear what one's responsibilities are.*

One might suppose there is a way out of this problem. By finding an overriding common interest, so that when no personal sphere of authority is evident, one would know to aim at this common concrete goal.

But no such alternative is possible. The common or public interest, though capable of being specified, takes care of only a minimal of the concerns human beings have in life. The common interest or good is limited to values people in fact share, based on their nature as human beings. But all alternatives must be linked to actual or actually possible outcomes, only a few of which can effect the common good.

When considering the public interest apart from the protection of the rights of everyone—for example, the upkeep of what are called "public" parks or beaches— it might be thought that it is clear enough what our duties are. They must be used with proper care. They should be kept clean. Or, when we administer so-called public education, it often sounds as if there is a very clear purpose at hand. Appearances to the contrary notwithstanding, attempting to deal with societies along these lines poses insurmountable difficulties.

In anyone's life, sound decisions are required pertaining to what will be attended to, what will be cared for considerably, and what will be neglected. No one has infinite time and resources. For example, during any timespan any parent may have to choose between attending fully to a baby, to work, or to other responsibilities. Because of the fully dependent status of the baby, its care will rate most attention, with other matters having to be relegated to lesser significance.

When, however, we do not have full authority over our sphere of activity and a choice presents itself—say, we are suddenly called away from a public beach because our child needs us, and we do not clean up after our area—we cannot determine what we should do about the common sphere. We might, of course, spend time cleaning up before we rush away, but that could turn out to be irresponsible in light of the parental obligations we would thus neglect. If we do this with our very own bathroom, there we have jurisdiction and impose our decision only on those within its sphere, for instance, our family. The beach is left for others, unrelated to us, to care for. But they, too, have pressing matters calling on them, so eventually collective spheres become neglected, not because people fail to do their duty but because in public places their duties are indeterminable.

These have also been called "uninternalizable negative externalities," meaning that apparently legitimate activities taking place in or adjacent to the commons have negative impact on others who have not agreed to suffer them. All this may appear to be quite manageable by electing politicians and appointing bureaucrats to take care of collective affairs. Yet they administer these matters with others' resources, some of whom sincerely—and possibly rightly—judge the allegedly collective purpose morally or otherwise objectionable and thus will resist it. Accordingly, discord is inherent in the management of virtually all but the most specific and determinate sort of collective affairs.

Even the most conscientious individuals will find it impossible to avoid the tragedy of the commons. But if one also considers that few individuals will be morally perfect and consistently responsible, then exacerbation of the problem is unavoidable without the establishment of a sphere of individual dominion and the corresponding legal machinery to keep track of it for purposes of making self-responsible conduct possible, as well as for resolving disputes among human beings.

The right to private property is indispensable for a decent human community, one in which the moral life of individuals can fully flourish. Individuals literally cannot conduct themselves morally without a determinate sphere of authority.

ETHICS AND VESTED INTERESTS*

Two facts today demonstrate that vested interest motivation is widely taken to be the only viable ground for action in the social world. One is the widespread phenomenon of vested interest-group activity in the legal and political arenas, the other the widespread employment of the vested interest concept to explain social, economic, and political events.

In both cases the ethical factor emerges only from critics. In other words, those who criticize the activities of, for example, members of labor unions, professional organizations, or Congress frequently point to the general improprieties involved in attempts to obtain the goals being sought. And critics of the methods of, for example, economics, sociology, or political science often note that no room is left for considerations of right and wrong, justice, decency, human rights, and other ethical factors in the academic explanation of human behavior.

Clearly, the critics may mention these lacks, but the fact that they criticize does not imply that they possess a better approach either to the practical problem of conducting one's life or the theoretical issue of gaining an understanding of human behavior. And in some respects the activity and the concept reinforce each other: Without a different and better understanding of human behavior, people are not likely to govern their own behavior differently and better; and when they do govern their lives in terms of the vested interest model, the social sciences—which often aim for hard-core empiricism—will gladly record the behavior as conforming to the model of vested interest motivation.

Part of what accounts for this development is the recent history of epistemology and, consequently, ethics. The possibility of identifying the nature of things— to demonstrate what things are essentially or necessarily—has been denied by most philosophers since the rise of Christianity and, later, the materialist/nominalist philosophies of Thomas Hobbes, David Hume, modern positivists, and pragmatists such as Harvard University philosopher Willard van Orman Quine.

The view of these thinkers is either that nature is fundamentally mysterious and the essence of things is hidden, known only to God and communicated only to select individuals or groups, or that nature is fundamentally unknowable and the essence of things is (at best) something we impose on reality to serve convenient goals. In neither approach is it possible to know the nature of things.

In human affairs, the guidelines governing personal, professional, artistic, or public conduct are often associated with certain ideas as to what role a person has assumed in these various areas. A medical doctor has presumably decided to engage in those practices that are linked to medicine, and so with a teacher, a union leader, or a member of Congress. The idea of a designated role is linked, furthermore, to some notion of the ethics of these various human activities. When one chooses to be a medical doctor, a promise is made to do well at the profession, to act in accordance with its principles. And underlying these special fields of human conduct there is often thought to be an even broader set of principles,

---

*Originally published in the *New American Review* (December 1977).

namely morality or ethics as such, which is binding on people simply as living human beings carrying out the business of life.

But to know the ethics of the medical, political, or teaching professions it is necessary first to have a reasonably clear idea of what these fields are; i.e., the nature of medicine, politics, or education. Thus, quacks are distinguished from doctors, in part, by reference to the general idea of medicine or our knowledge of the essentials of medicine. The same goes for education and all other fields. How can one know the proper conduct for those in commerce, politics, or education unless one has a well-defined idea of these areas of human activity?

It is also clear that the numerous endeavors change quite rapidly. Even in professions that experience only gradual change—mathematics, for example—new discoveries and elaborations of old ideas and practices will occur. But despite this there is an underlying notion that something or some elements render a person a mathematician, doctor, teacher, or public servant. So while the capacity for change is ordinarily admitted, so is the idea of certain basic unifying features that justify the special groupings to which we refer.

But if epistemologists deny any foundation for such groupings, why believe that any basic guidelines should be invoked to govern one's behavior in these various areas of human conduct? Only convention or human decisions are admitted as the basis for these groupings, and if some people can create them by a decision, others can surely destroy them by decision. No one's decision is any better founded according to this position, since all decisions are, ultimately, arbitrary.

When objective guidelines are dismissed, the gap can be filled only by the desires, emotions, interests, or concern of the individuals in these professions. Doctors may not know what medicine is, essentially, but they probably have a clear enough idea of what they want. And one thing they probably want is to earn a decent living from their professional activities. What that means for them is, by this account, a subjective matter—as economists of all varieties will tell us. So it is not unreasonable, the epistemologists would argue, for us to both strive to advance our own vested interest and explain the actions of others in line with this model of behavior.

The trouble is, of course, that in the final analysis this kind of thinking and acting must lead to absurdity (and the concrete expression of absurdity: continued human conflict). Any understanding presupposes that something exists to be understood, which in turn presupposes that things are of one kind or another: that A is A and B is B. By giving up all forms of essentialism we give up understanding and, in concrete result, the slightest prospect for peace; but understanding this much demonstrates that things are not beyond understanding, or beyond the prospect of peace, which in turn indicates that the current trends discussed above are wrongheaded.

OUR MORAL CLIMATE CREATES DESTRUCTION*

The moral climate of a culture is equally, if not more, important than any factor that influences the development of human events. This has been obscured by the stress placed on environmental determinants by behaviorist psychologists, on the unconscious by Freudians, on economic forces by economists, and on the productive arrangements of one's historical epoch by Marxists.

Many of the analyses of personal and social change omit from consideration the moral element. Yet, in human affairs, morality is decisive because anything about which something can be done by human beings, and anything that might have been done differently, is primarily a matter of human character, of morality. Where there is choice, there is the opening for evaluation, achievement, irresponsibility, blame, and progress.

The moral climate, in turn, consists of the opinions held by people of influence concerning the standards to be used in evaluating people, of appraising institutions, of judging ourselves. This climate generates its various currents through the media, including university classrooms, editorial pages, books, and television dramas or situation comedies. It is in these "forms" that praise and blame make their way into the consciousness of the citizenry, either explicitly or, more often, by subtle, implicit means.

In our time two main currents are prominent concerning matters of morality. These are altruism and nihilism. Both are enemies of human happiness. It is tragic that in a country built on the idea that each has the natural rights to pursue happiness, the moral climate would renounce precisely that goal or, in the alternative, any goal at all. We're taught the moral imperative that others' happiness is what we ought to pursue or the denial that anything ought to be pursued at all.

Perhaps the second prominent view on morality, namely nihilism, can be explained as a result of the hopelessness of the first. If one is constantly told that one's duty in life is to live for other people, but in fact one just cannot live with that principle as one's standard, one will either have to change the principle or give up morality completely. Those who have been most harshly assaulted with the altruistic outlook have been the members of the business community. They have worked hardest to produce, to seek profit, to achieve values that are obvious and widely desired. So they are the people who have been preached to about their duty to the world, to the needy, to the poor, to the helpless, etc. From the Right and from the Left, the bourgeoisie has been denounced. Both Charles Baudelaire and Karl Marx thought business vile. The former believed, "Commerce is satanic, because it is the basest and vilest form of egoism"; the latter held, "It has resolved personal worth into exchange value."

With this kind of harangue against them, the members of the business community and those who study it, economists, have turned their backs on morality. Economists claim that all of us are simply ruled by private interest. There is really nothing else but our personal preference that accounts for our behavior. As Milton Friedman

---

*Originally published in the *Orange County Register* (June 7, 1981).

put it recently, "The great Saints of history have served their 'private interest' just as the most money-grubbing miser has served his interest. The private interest is whatever it is that drives an individual" (*Encounter,* November 1976). Not in the business of figuring out whether the moralizers and moral philosophers who support the altruistic doctrines are really correct, it is not surprising that those involved in business and most economists simply regard morality as meaningless. If science tells us that we are all moved by self-interest, well then moralizing has no impact anyway. The explanation for this faulty reasoning could well be the cynicism that comes from having tried to live by an impossible moral code.

For that is what altruism is. The view doesn't just claim that there is virtue in kindness and generosity but that charity is the first virtue we must practice. But that is absurd. For if this were true, not even those being helped could accept the help. Mankind would have to be a never-ending daisy chain of self-sacrifice. No one would be aided if altruism were true and consistently implemented. It is not even an impossible ideal but an impossible nightmare.

The truth is that human beings need a morality that can make living both good and possible. This morality would involve a substantial dose of self-interest. But the self-interest would differ from that which many take it to be—sheer callousness, selfishness emphasizing thrills and quick pleasures. Yet pleasures and well-being would be part of this morality. Indeed we should seek these, in moderation.

Most important to human life, however, would turn out to be the pursuit of happiness. This would come by pursuing those goals that are proper for any human being—e.g., success in one's family life, career, and other general ventures—and for the individual one, e.g., teaching for those so inclined, tennis for those with the talent, and business with those who are good at this profession. There need be no fear that murder or cruelty can be personal goals because these violate the human virtues of honesty, productivity, and the respect for everyone's rights as human beings.

This is a moral code in which pursuing health and personal welfare is considered not just tolerable but imperative. It would back up those who want to make it in life, to succeed, to profit.

But the likelihood of this morality becoming prominent soon is minuscule. Too many people like to live off the sweat and labor of others, especially among those who are in the business of talking about morality, of writing on ethics and how people should live their lives. Nevertheless, it is imperative that a morality that encourages human success and survival, as opposed to one preaching constant self-sacrifice, become the main current in our moral climate. Evading it for much longer will produce just the results that can be expected, namely, the sacrifice of the best in all of us, our concern with success as human beings.

ABORTION MAY NOT BE DESIRABLE, BUT IT IS NOT HOMICIDE*

The crucial question surrounding abortion is the moral one: Should abortion be prevented by the state, on the grounds that it is the murder of young human beings, or should the state protect those who want abortions because they have a right to terminate pregnancy?

Right-to-life groups have argued, in essence, that the state has as much interest in preventing abortions as it has in preventing any other form of homicide. No one quarrels with the view, they point out, that it is the business of government to protect individual rights. But what is not often discussed is whether abortion is actually a form of homicide. The closest that we come to discussing the issue is when right-to-lifers insist on displaying photographs of fetuses and even embryos that, as they point out, closely resemble infant human beings. Thus, it is argued (at least implicitly), that the killing of these fetuses and embryos amounts to nothing less than murder. Pro-choice people answer mostly in terms of the right of a woman to control what grows in her body or, alternatively, the horrors of being an unwanted child.

Just what is a human being? And when does something that grows out of a sperm cell and an egg cell turn into one? These are the crucial, if thorny, questions. After all, right-to-lifers might note that the fetuses of monkeys, too, look very much like human infants. Yet no one wants to charge monkey-killers with homicide. Meanwhile, pro-choicers who insist that a woman has rights over what grows in her body simply decline to consider that, if it is a human being that is growing in the womb, killing it would be murder. If I have a right to what is in my home and someone visits me, I cannot then kill my guest with impunity—even if the guest is helpless, just as a fetus is.

No, the real issue is whether fetuses, embryos, and zygotes are human beings. If the answer is affirmative, the right-to-lifers clearly have their case. Abortion would constitute murder or some variety of homicide, entirely open to state jurisdiction.

The problem is that the nature of a human being is in great dispute, especially among those who ultimately look into these issues—philosophers. Admittedly, biologists also study the matter, but the biological data usually enter the philosopher's artillery to be used only when other ways of determining the nature of human beings have been exhausted. More important, in our times most philosophers seem to reject the very idea of speaking of "the nature" of something. Instead, they accept something on the order of an indeterminate group of characteristics establishing what something is.

As one well-known English philosopher, Margaret Macdonald, said some years ago in connection with the issue of human rights, " 'Man equals rational animal' is the fossil preserved in logic textbooks since Aristotle." In other words, the idea that human beings share a fixed nature is wrong.

This is very important. Many issues in medicine and law, to name just two

---

*Originally published in the *Los Angeles Times* (July 27, 1981).

areas, depend on some conception of human nature—whether, for example, the death of the brain of a person qualifies as the demise of the human being in that case. The issue of abortion also hinges squarely on this matter.

If by "fixed nature" Macdonald means fixed forever, she may be right. But we must cope with the world as best we can in our own era. And for now it seems clear enough that what distinguishes human beings from other living creatures is that they are capable of rational thought. Even if this capacity can manifest itself only in the slightest degree, only hinting at greater performance in the future, we are justified in holding that we have a human being before us.

Of fetuses, embryos, and zygotes—at least barring the last weeks of pregnancy—the same cannot be said. These are only potential human beings, not actual ones with actual rational capacities. Their biological-mental functions are not sufficiently developed for any degree of rational thought and perception.

What follows from this is that, barring very late abortions when questions about rational thought can legitimately arise, abortion is not homicide. This does not make it desirable, but not something that a civilized society should prohibit.

REFLECTIONS ON OSTRACISM*

You live in a small community. From your encounters with business or social contacts, you learn that Harry Blomer is a racist. Harry works with you in an engineering firm. He is, say, a draftsman. On and off, during coffee breaks and occasional lunches taken together, he makes offensive references to blacks. And he clearly makes them just because they are blacks, not because the particular people he has in mind have behaved badly or have treated him unkindly. Harry is, for all his charm and professional talents, and out-and-out racist.

You, on the other hand, are unequivocal about the moral shortcomings of racism. For a while you make attempts to talk to Harry, to goad him out of his detestable disposition, to disabuse him of his odious attitude. But he is stubborn; he won't budge; indeed, he begins to demean you for your efforts. Finally, you give up. You begin to avoid Harry. You ostracize him. Yet you also see that he is an effective racist. He manages to sway some people through devious, clever means, so that certain blacks are adversely affected. His position in the community as a person of high professional talent helps to make him the effective racist he is, which reveals to you the need to take some action that may silence Harry or, at least, render his racism impotent.

From the time you decide to do something, you continually advise your friends and colleagues of Harry's moral deficiency. You don't deny his competence as a draftsman. You don't disparage his qualities as a dancer, dresser, or family man. You simply put it on notice that Harry is a racist, and a very clever one at that. Slowly your words make their way through the community, and Harry's influence begins to wane. Eventually, when time for promotion comes, Harry

---

Originally published in *New American Review* (January 1978).

is overlooked, in part because your trustworthy message has reached the firm's heads, who acknowledge Harry's professional competence but would rather choose a more worthwhile human being to promote. In the end, Harry is fired, for his company is not wanted. And Harry cannot find another position matching his talent. His life starts to decline, his family suffers as a result, and Harry ends up, as it were, in the gutter. He never recants and firmly believes that a gross injustice was done to him.

Now, I submit that, aside from the improprieties and falsehoods that accompany many such efforts, the actions taken to discredit such individuals are not only excusable but possibly quite proper. A person's moral character does not always have its influence on everything he does, and sometimes morally blameworthy individuals can be proficient artists, entertainers, engineers, or even parents. Some of the worst people are nevertheless very sincere. Cowards can be honest. Unjust people can be generous; generous people, unjust. In fact, one of the signs of moral degradation is character-inconsistency. If people were thoroughly worthwhile or thoroughly horrid, how could the behavior of an acquaintance shock us into saying, "I didn't know Charles was like that"?

Yet, as the above scenario illustrates, we may be justified in excluding that partly immoral person from our professional and social activities. In short, it is plausible that blacklisting is quite proper practice—something we all do to some extent and something we can often be better off for doing.

Recently, there has been a lot of talk about blacklisting, mostly in a tone of righteous indignation. Even those who believe that both overt and covert advocates of communism, especially of the Stalinist variety, had a lot to answer for, at least in moral terms, tend to disassociate themselves from the practice of blacklisting. Yet if the communist sympathizers did have a lot to answer for, morally, then they are comparable to my Harry Blomer, racist. It simply is immoral to favor a system or ideology that (with all the evidence needed to verify this) has consistently disregarded crucial human values—indeed, destroyed the lives of millions of innocent people. It would have been just as proper to blacklist Nazi sympathizers, and today we find it perfectly proper to ostracize those among us who offend many of our more recently acquired sensibilities.

While there can be misdirected blacklistings, no doubt, and some trivial or hasty ones, it is surely quite unreasonable to hold that advocating Stalinism is just a minor aberration. I do not personally consider it a compelling objection to someone that he or she is homosexual or has joined the army, although I know conservatives who would blacklist (in their small ways) the former; liberals the latter. But these and many other widespread practices that are, in effect, blacklistings (e.g., boycotts), are far less justifiable than those practiced against supporters of one of history's worst tyrannies—supporters who, not insignificantly, could give that regime ample play via their particular professional platforms.

None of this justifies the government's harassment of people who were guilty of moral shortcomings that warrant social and professional ostracism. If and where that occurred, the law was subverted to ends that should have been accomplished via personal moral vigilance. When governmental muzzling enters the picture, the abridgment of people's liberty also enters. Not so with private actions expressing moral outrage. When a television network or motion picture firm, for example, refuses to aid and abet those who so badly default on their responsibilities, one should be grateful that some businesses uphold moral principles even at the expense of some temporary commercial gains. Granted, some of the businesses yielded not so much to moral insight as to public pressure. But why should that be demeaned? Is not "violence" on television today being combatted in part via public pressure on sponsors of "violent" programs? Was not racism in the media combatted in part by such public pressure?

Congress only subverted its own function when its members attempted to run up political mileage by exploiting justified public outrage against communist sympathizers; the resultant side show was reprehensible. But it seems to me that spontaneous private blacklisting needs to be announced as a very decent—even courageous—aspect of American history. Why make feeble apologies about it, as if the onus of proof were on the blacklisters, not on those who professed and practiced the horrid and irrational emulation of a bloody tyranny?

WHAT IF IT'S PUBLISH *AND* PERISH?*

Most people know of the standard charge leveled against commercial newspapers and magazines. If they accept advertising, how could they ever be objective in their reporting and discussion of the business community? But do we fully realize that noncommercial—educational, scholarly, scientific—enterprises are just as vulnerable to a similar problem: If they accept support from the government or other subsidizing bodies, how can they report objectively or critically on matters relating to them?

Journalistic ethics normally requires that one report and discuss matters of significance to members of the reading, listening, or viewing community whom one has chosen to serve. Anything else would seem to be an evasion of professional responsibilities. Scholarship faces a similar task. Of course, there are obvious cases where the journalistic posturing is mere sham, as in trade publications, e.g., the education profession's *Chronicles of Higher Education,* IBM's *Think* in-house magazine, etc. But these publications are so obviously partisan, interested in promotion rather than news reporting, that no one expects adherence to the normal standards of journalistic ethics. Nor do we usually think of government pub-lications—even those of the United States Information Agency, which is supposedly dedicated to informing the deceived of the truth about America—as paragons of objectivity. Yet the responsible professional conduct by bona fide journalists and scholars has its pitfalls. Usually it is advertisers who are said to be capable of intimidating a paper or magazine. But there is the further charge that when a publication is owned by some huge corporation, one that is involved not only in local or even domestic but international business and political affairs, the

---

*Originally published in *Liberty* (July 1988).

publication won't be free to discuss matters of vital interest to its readers. Indeed, those rationalizing censorship in various countries throughout the world—in the Soviet Union, Israel, Mozambique, etc.—usually claim that the idea of a free Western press is a myth anyway, since corporate ownership skews journalistic focus. It is not easy to defend freedom of the press by denying this claim. It takes a sophisticated political analysis to bail out freedom here.

Yet nonprofit publications face the possibility of similar conflicts of interest. Consider that such publications rely on the support of foundations, among which many are well established and influential organizations. (When these are some government body such as the Navy or the National Endowment for the Humanities, ethical problems multiply.) The Ford, Rockefeller, Earhart, Olin, and Carnegie foundations are not neutral bodies. They are presided over by numerous important individuals, some whose ideological and business commitments are far-reaching.

It is not at all difficult to imagine that some news item or topic of general lasting concern would emerge involving a foundation that is a vital source of support for a magazine or broadcast project. "Firing Line" is sponsored by several major corporations, and Mr. Buckley could well find himself with a guest whose book is a sustained, serious, and telling attack on one of these. *Ms.* magazine is the recipient of foundation support. Various progressive, libertarian, conservative, and other publications, programs, or projects are in the same position. And virtually all those little centers or institutes involved in the study of professional ethics, business ethics, values and society or whatnot—ones usually affiliated with universities, of which there are too many to list here—receive support not just from foundations and corporations but also, very often, from the government. Numerous scholarly papers devote their first footnote to thanking the Lilly Fund, the Rand Corporation, or the National Science Foundation, National Endowment for the Humanities, or some other private or government granting body for funds that made possible the research leading to the piece. In each of these instances it could be problematic if the scholar were to focus his or her attention on the source of the support. In fact, it is rare to find anything along those lines.

Of course there is a clear distinction between obtaining private funding and support from the government, mainly because the presumption in the former case is that the support is voluntarily given and was not stolen from anyone, while the presumption in the latter is just the opposite. This itself points up an interesting aspect of the ethics involved.

There are special problems associated with advocating government funding. But I don't want to dwell here on the problems associated with these but with professional ethical problems related to the sort of journalism and scholarship that gains its funding from corporations or foundations. What about the charge that these create ethically insurmountable problems, e.g., in the way of easily imagined conflicts of interest?

The main response to this charge has two parts. First, as far as the consumer of publishing—in journalism or in scholarship—is concerned, the most important thing for him or her is the existence of a free, competitive market. There is no doubt that the practitioners of these professions will often refuse to stick out their own necks just to scrutinize and perhaps expose the misdeeds of their funders. So the consumer has to rely on the existence of an open market.

It is true, as the rationalizers of government censorship argue, that the Western-style free press is not altogether at liberty to do just anything, if it wishes to stay alive. I can imagine that even the impeccable *Wall Street Journal* would have some trouble directly attacking Dow Jones, even if the editors felt it journalistically justified. Oddly, a former employee of the *Journal* reports that the publication is required to print all of the parent company's news releases— verbatim! One might have thought that with such eminent and secure publications there is less likelihood of the acquiescence to pressure of that kind. But in any case, the consumer is better off in a free, capitalist society because competition ensures variety of sources. If this broadcast network won't report something because it involves badmouthing its parent company's president, the other will.

The main danger to the consumer is monopoly or oligopoly, and as anyone not wholly ignorant of economics knows, those are more likely within an economy that enjoys extensive government intervention than in free markets.

Second, what about the practicing scholar or journalist? Sure the consumer may be protected, but does this vindicate the professional who succumbs to the pressure? If a major funding agent for a scholarly or public policy foundation does something of interest to the scholars or researchers, should not the organization study and report on this?

Well, the first point to note here is that while professional ethics is every bit the objective (but more narrowly focused) code of conduct that one should expect from a sound ethical system, it is certainly not on the level of fundamentality as are the basic ethical principles that everyone should invoke in life. In short, a principle of professional ethics is not anything on the order of an absolute moral principle. Rather it is contingent on the impact the adherence to other moral principles will require.

This may be illustrated with business ethics, in which it is a moral responsibility of an executive to further the economic well-being of his or her firm. But since this executive is also a citizen, a friend, a mother (father), and/or a spouse, surely other moral responsibilities will also guide his or her conduct. Total devotion to work will itself be irresponsible, since parenthood, too, requires attention to one's children, and marriage devotion to one's spouse.

Of course, in emergencies one must use discretion and maybe put in abeyance what is ordinarily required in these other roles in one's life. Normally, however, the whole thing is a grand balancing act.

Now the same applies in journalism or scholarship. One may find an interesting story about some major supporter, but because it would be suicidal to run it, one should choose some other topic. If the story is vital enough, it may be wise to point this out to some competitor. Total silence could be immoral, especially if the story itself involves immorality—say the funder is betraying the cause, violating some ethical precept or breaking a just law. And there is a point at which one may have to forgo the benefits of the support—e.g., if the funder is stealing the funds it contributes or is making demands on the journalist or scholar that would require betraying professional ethics.

As with most ethical problems, the difficulties one faces in a conflict-of-interest situation can only be hinted at in abstract discussions. They must ultimately be dealt with in concrete situations, and they may be distorted if dealt with sketchily. One needs to consider the details. The principles involved are not the very general ones that a sound ethical theory will propose for virtually every situation faced by human beings. Rather these are hypothetical principles: If you face these situations, then act in such and such a way! Principles of journalistic ethics are not similar to the prohibition against murder or theft but more like edicts about therapist-client or doctor-patient relations. In too many cases, outside the most basic and simple ones, the right thing to do will have to be determined from a very rich context of background information. But it is clear that the simple charge is false that because there is the potential of conflict of interest there is something inherently problematic in the practice of the profession itself—a charge made by some reckless idealists whenever economic interests are involved in some undertaking (that is, in virtually any aspect of human life).

It can be seen, even from this much, that conflict-of-interest situations may be handled in a variety of ways, including simply shelving them or passing on the problem to those who can discuss it more effectively, with less risk of severe costs. The idea that martyrdom is noble belongs to a very dubious ethical outlook, one that certainly was not developed with an eye to making one a success at living a human life. (Rather the point was to attain success in another world!) It would be wrong, from a sane ethical viewpoint, to seek out actions for oneself that lead to the destruction of one's values and projects, unless there is something very fundamental at stake, in which case one is still preserving what counts the most for oneself, one's integrity.

Journalistic or scholarly ethics requires no suicide. Courage, of course, requires taking some risks, weighing values, choosing sides when conflicts occur. But courage is not the only virtue—so is prudence, moderation, thrift, honesty, and the rest. Each must be attended to, and being reasonable in this task is the ultimate ethical responsibility of every human being, one that is prior to the more specialized ethical responsibilities related to one's profession, including journalism.

RECONSIDERING ENVY

Envy has not been a favorite subject for discussion in recent moral philosophy. Except for Robert Nozick in philosophy and Helmut Schoeck in speculative sociology, there has been little written on the topic. It is perhaps telling in this connection that envy is a touchy idea in an era when egalitarianism is a favorite moral stance. In our time justice is supposed to consist mainly of fairness, the thesis defended by John Rawls, the most important contemporary academic political philosopher. Thus envy, which by tradition is a vice or certainly at least a sordid emotion, changes into something on the order of moral indignation.

Yet fairness in most moral systems is but a subordinate virtue (so that one can be a thief but perfectly fair by stealing from all the available rich with equal enthusiasm). Which is right? That is not what I wish to address here, though in my view the justice-as-fairness thesis rests on faulty methodology and reflects it by transforming a common sentiment, which itself rests on bad ethical theory, into a paramount moral claim.

During a recent lecture the question arose why the possession of wealth so readily infuriates people and why has an entire moral industry, both religious and secular, grown up around the denunciation of it. Someone said that the cause must be envy. This is not an unfamiliar thesis, often espoused by conservative thinkers, such as Helmut Schoeck. The idea is that if only people did not feel envious, they would not resent the wealthy and would therefore support public policies that place limits on their liberty.

Envy certainly is a tempting explanation but it has its pitfalls. One of these is that envy is a feeling reserved mainly for those enjoying superior conditions that have no redeeming moral merit. Let me explain.

Unless the subject of envy is also morally suspect for holding the status that is being envied, the envy itself comes under moral censure. It is not unproblematic to envy the superior status of someone who has reached it honestly and in a field that is itself morally legitimate. For example, if someone has received the Nobel Prize in Literature or Chemistry by honest means, surely it is possible to be jealous but hardly to be envious. Blatant envy would at least show that one's values are perverse. Not that no one is envious of such individuals, but envy in such cases is evidence of moral shortsightedness. Of course, if one seriously suspects that the recipient has reached the heights by devious means, then envy can be righteous. But this is because the envy is accompanied by moral rebuke.

Before unashamed and thus widespread envy can be felt, its object must already have become morally tainted. Thus, for example, it is easy to be envious of the wealthy if by its very nature wealth is supposed to be morally suspect, as surely it is within almost any religious, and certainly our Christian, heritage.

If indeed sooner will the camel pass through the eye of the needle than the rich man enter the gates of heaven, then little nobility or honor may be associated with riches and those who possess them seem to stand justly indicted, without any other vice needing to be associated with them. Then, of course, the ill feeling of envy may with impunity be harbored toward those who are wealthy, since their wealth itself makes them morally besmirched.

So the feeling of envy cannot be a primary explanation for the bad reputation of wealth and prosperity, even though it can be a strong supporting or sustaining element of the bad reputation of riches. But first of all there must be the value judgment that something must be wrong with the possession of wealth. And this, of course, is just what is the case: Being wealthy is associated with something morally evil. From Aristotle to Rawls, the advantages of wealth have been decried by moralists as immoderate or unfair, either because higher aims were put in jeopardy by its pursuit or because no morally relevant trait in the person was thought to contribute to the attainment of wealth.

Now it might be tempting to leave the matter at this and simply lament the moral error of the ages. But in fact there is some reason to suspect most wealth. Throughout much of human history the acquisition of wealth has been associated with conquest, looting, robbery, exploitation, and oppression. Even in our time it is difficult to tell what exactly differentiates those who came by their wealth without moral liability from those who did. There is, of course, a model of society that suggests the difference is real and knowable, but this model has hardly been in contention for more than two hundred years in the intellectual history of the West. One can hardly suggest that it has been approximated as a reality within any society, except perhaps in the United States, although even that is questionable. Given, for example, the origins of the great trusts and many major industrial empires—e.g., the three broadcast networks, the three big automakers, which all had their positions in the marketplace shielded from honest competition for several decades of their existence—it is hardly surprising that the bulk of the people mistrust any allusion to wealth gained through merit alone.

The feeling of envy—or at least the feeling that much of the envy felt is justified, just as one's envy of the success of a charlatan in any profession seems perfectly justified—seems then to rest on certain historical facts that support it, give it a sense of genuine justice, without any such bloated thesis as that fairness itself is the essence of justice. It is unjust to be wealthy in most cases not because it is unfair but because the wealth has been acquired by theft, conquest, oppression, etc. It is unfair that so many millions should have ended up without wealth while those with it have largely obtained it by means having little to do with merit.

Of course, the more basic issue is whether it is possible to obtain wealth through merit. It is. And that fact needs serious discussion. Perhaps then we can change people's attitudes and then fewer will feel envy and influence by this the moral and political climate.

ON NEGLECTING ETHICS*

It is not unusual in our era to explain what people do by reference to their vested interests. Thus, when a doctor tells us we should consider his cure for what ails us, we are tempted to say, "No wonder; he's a doctor, and it will benefit him to have us take his treatment." Never mind that the doctor has perfectly good reasons for his recommendation. They are treated as rationalizations.

There is no doubt that many people act from motives that are best classified in terms of vested interests. In an age when the very idea of having good reasons for acting is widely debunked, when ethics, especially, is regarded as a myth, perhaps most people who make up our society have difficulty being confident about any other reasons besides their vested interests—that is, reasons having to do with perpetuating their own function as doctors, politicians, bureaucrats, teachers, steel workers, and the like.

---

*Originally published in *Reason* magazine (March 1978).

But the very idea of vested interest gains its meaningfulness from the possibility of other interests that could motivate a person. The typical idea voiced by economists, namely, that all of us always act because we prefer to do what we do, also makes the concept of preference meaningless; it makes sense only when it is contrasted to desires, wants, purposes, plans, obligations, responsibilities, and so forth.

So, contrary to widespread opinion, there are very different motives to account for what people do. Among the many, we should not lose sight of people's moral convictions, whether right or wrong. Granted, for example, that many bureaucrats, politicians, and citizens in general act from motives such as preserving their status as powerbrokers, employees, patrons of special groups, or beneficiaries of favors, some of them actually act as they do, especially in matters of public concern, because they believe that as human beings they ought to act that way. (We need also to keep in mind that people do not always act on the same motives. Thus Ralph Nader may at one time press for certain governmental policies because they will perpetuate his power, and at other times because he thinks them to be the morally right course to pursue.)

It is a favorite claim of some economists, including those who advocate free-market policies, that even moral exhortation is necessarily motivated from vested or "self"interest. (In a recent essay for *Encounter,* Milton Friedman made just this claim about all the saints, namely, that they are pursuing their private interests.) And in view of the fact that economists tend to operate or reason on the basis of statistical generalizations—or assumptions that are useful even if false—this claim is not without analytical value to them in their effort to make very general predictions about human behavior. (For instance, they base on this belief their prediction that bureaucrats administering regulatory agencies will oppose efforts to deregulate. Since the ethics of government regulation are necessarily internally inconsistent, like those of thieves and liars, this claim probably fits them better than ordinary persons.)

Still, one reason that moral exhortations are often effective is that many believe in the morality being relied upon. As hypocrisy is the compliment vice pays to virtue, so phony moral exhortation is the compliment baloney pays to sincerity. Both, however, assume the reality of their polar opposites. Unless some credible adherence to certain moral positions exists, faking adherence to the position could have no point at all.

Now the moral position that still permeates the cultures of our epoch is a grab bag of various forms of altruism. There may be cynics who deny this, and millions who fake it, but there are enough of those in influential places who sincerely believe that each person's highest duty is to serve others (which may include gods, neighbors, future generations, the human race, the working people of the world, the whites or the blacks, the women or the men, etc.). When those who find something crucially wrong with this morality simply ignore its influence, or pretend that talk of morality is meaningless—that is, could never be right— the altruist's stance ends up being victorious. This is because some system or code of values, whereby people can guide their choices in terms of some hierarchy, is indispensable for the sort of beings humans are. (Not possessing instincts but minds, they need principles, abstractions, to guide them. And a moral position is aimed at providing the most general system of principles for this purpose.)

The one area that most of the influential people who promote the cause of liberty tend to eschew is moral philosophy. Various foundations and institutes are devoted to the clarification and promotion of the free society. And most of them devote their funds mainly to economic education of varying complexity. Some strive to teach Chicago school of economics, others promote the thought of Adam Smith, others instruct in Austrian economics, and yet others find it important to counsel simple economic common sense. There are such organizations that focus on education, history, and other fields. But hardly any find it important to explore moral philosophy.

The fact is, however, that the most consequential ideas and ideals in society are moral ones. When all the economic reasoning is over, when all the history has been laid out, when all the varieties of educational theory have been explored, there still remains that central question, "What should I do?" And if the answer that is most widely respected remains, "Do whatever you can for others," then considerations of inefficiency, lack of previous success, high cost, or pedagogical ineffectiveness simply will not suffice. When you accept an ideal as binding on you and others, it makes no difference how unrealistic, ephemeral, or illusory it may be, you tend to stick to it.

Why then the widespread avoidance of investment in the exploration of ethics by what are otherwise dedicated groups of individuals?

I suspect that altruism is itself partly to blame. Those who support various foundations tend, in the final analysis, to accept the altruistic ethics (in one or another of its varieties). Perhaps, also, the subject of ethics or morality cuts too deep. Religious issues would, no doubt, come under scrutiny. And this realm is very touchy, even in our so-called secular age. Also, there is the plain fact that ethics is a highly personal matter, yet not easily dealt with verbally or articulately.

What if it were to turn out that a proper ethical code would reflect badly upon those who sponsor a conference on ethics? What if the hedonism some leaders of think-tanks practice were to turn out to be a form of viciousness or immorality?

There is, finally, the point that, while ethics cuts very close to home, those who deal with the field professionally tend to be verbally agile, able to rationalize their form of behavior quite readily, handle their viciousness or immorality with virtuosity, so that it is difficult for those not trained to give clear verbal expression to their ideals and ideas so as to give a good account of their own stance.

Despite these obvious and understandable obstacles, it would be extremely valuable to mount a full attack on the most pressing problem of our age, namely, the lack of sound moral principles. If those who love liberty could come to at least cherish virtue also, their case would be so much stronger, indeed, so much more persuasive. For while they stress liberty, in the sense of the absence of coercion, the bulk of the problems people face concern virtue, in the sense of what one should do, how one should act, what goals one should pursue. I for one am convinced that no virtue is possible where liberty is absent. But this needs to be shown to many more people before they will give liberty a chance. To that end the hard, risky, even frightening task of confronting the serious and basic questions of ethics must be faced squarely.

LIBERAL DEMOCRATS STILL HAVE THE MORAL INITIATIVE*

Ronald Reagan or some other Republican could win the presidency repeatedly, until he is 104, yet he would still not gain the reputation of the late Hubert Humphrey, the epitome of the well-meaning politician. Senator Humphrey made clear throughout his career (e.g., in *The New Republic* several years ago) that what counts most is *hope,* not progress. Giving people hope is more important than ensuring for them what *can* be fulfilled, the modest policy for most people to reach a reasonable standard of economic well-being. Arguably, the Reagan administration has to its credit this modest objective, albeit in a halting, often confused way.

But Conservatives and Republicans have for years been guided by pragmatists, public policy analysts, and others who want to concentrate on immediate results, on pocket-book issues, on the concerns of readers of the *Wall Street Journal* and *Business Week.*

Republicans are guided by the "realists" at the American Enterprise Institute, the Heritage Foundation, and the Hoover Institution. These are the intellectuals of the Republican Party. They see questions of morality as largely irrelevant, the concern of ideologues, and are acute strategists in obtaining political power. They learned their lessons in political economy at the feet of value-free economists. They believe moral talk is mere personal prejudice. As one of them put it: "All that moral talk is music, what we need is science."

Yet it is the party with the moral initiative that has a more profound grasp of this nation's needs. Moral visions have a greater impact in the long run than tactical know-how—Jesus and Marx have proven that. Adam Smith, the creator of scientific economics, has never quite managed to inspire anyone, however powerful his analytical tools have proved to be. And unless the Republican rhetoric of "liberty for all" is given some intellectual footing—aside from the technical policy analysis and advice—the recovery will be a brief one. This may have been the hidden message of former Federal Reserve Chairman Paul Volker when he testified that all the earlier good economic growth signals could soon turn into a Latin American-style disaster for this country. As a Marxist colleague of mine explained, the Republicans' victories these days are the last gasps of capitalism. Without a sustained vision, based on sound political ideals, the future rests on quicksand. Such a vision is needed to pull a nation together.

If the moral imagination of the people is addressed by Democrats, while their pocket-books are kept from draining by Republicans, it will take but a

*Originally published in the *Orange County Register* (November 2, 1986).

short period before pangs of conscience will set in and the Democrats' agenda will be picked up again, indeed, by the Republicans themselves.

This agenda is one that Governor Mario Cuomo put on record with his keynote address during the 1984 Democratic Convention. Its main theme is compassion: Our primary duty in life is to serve the needy, and the way to serve them is to make government everywhere a powerful redistributor of the wealth of the nation, never mind who produces this wealth. It is an old moralistic theme but still the main one in town.

New York Governor Mario Cuomo is only the most brilliant liberal Democrat at capitalizing with story after story on some old people's experience of the hardship "caused" by Republicans, the rich, those who want to prosper rather than have the government waste tax moneys on fruitless efforts to make a utopia. For Cuomo, a Ronald Reagan's only aim in life—e.g., with his tax cuts—has been to benefit the rich, the powerful, the very folk who need no benefits at all since they are doing so well already. The Democrats can cash in on the plight of some farmers, some old folks, some who lack medical support, etc. They make considerable use of the fallacy of appeal to emotions. Logic is not their strong point.

It is clear that some people will always fit those horrible anecdotes. So Cuomo, Edward Kennedy, Walter Mondale and other "compassionists" cannot be refuted on their own terms, not even by inviting refugee West Point graduates to the State of the Union address. Sure, the Democrats' tactic is pure demagoguery. But there is no way to meet this kind of rhetoric effectively by just making people reasonably well off. They need to know that their better lot is not undeserved, not a mere accident of their lives. Otherwise they will begin to feel remorse, shame, and guilt at their well-being in the midst of poverty and famine in the world. Even when compassion isn't deserved—after all, some folks *are* the cause of their own misery—to rebuke those who are calling for it is just bad form.

What is needed is an alternative to compassionism. For compassionists the poor are a moral priority just so long as there are any of them left. And the dominance of such *compassionism* is due to the prevailing moral climate. Most people believe, however inarticulately, that they *should* be altruists, even when they are not! Most of us have been taught that caring for the needy is the noblest of all deeds, even if we cannot really do much for them and thus suffer from guilt (and develop cynicism in the end). This must be replaced with a sensible ethic, one that we can actually practice as well as stand by with pride.

Never mind, also, that the practical consequences for the needy of a policy that initially benefits the well-off may be better than any direct spending programs. As the compassionists would have it, in morality "It is the thought that counts." That is one reason so few are impressed with the kind of argument advanced by Charles Murray against the welfare state in his book *Loosing Ground*. He is talking to the convinced. When the compassionists speak, however, they address everyone's moral conscience and fears of doom. Altruism sells well: *You* may be the other who might need help. That makes more impact than whether the help is for real!

Is there some way the Republicans can grasp the moral initiative? They will need to if they want not only the bellies but the conscience of their constituency satisfied. There is a moral case to be made against the indiscriminate "compassionism" of the Democrats and in support of the effort to help most people attain prosperity in their lives. Life's priority cannot be other people's well-being; one cannot ultimately achieve this goal, and it demeans others' human dignity to always try to obtain it for them. No, one's first task in life is to live as a successful human being. There is room here for compassion, but it isn't the first order of business.

Prudence, as a friend of mine put it, is not the highest virtue, but it isn't the vice so many make it out to be. The Republicans might reaffirm one of the most important and morally noble themes in human history, the call to individual liberty and the right to pursue one's happiness without thwarting the similar pursuit of others. But they will need to know how to make this point clearly and unapologetically.

10

Medicine

LOSS TO MEDICINE AND FREEDOM*

The welfare state is slowly but surely degenerating into the oppressive socialism that has been predicted of it for many years. Robert Finch, Health, Education, and Welfare Secretary, is now threatening to tell doctors just how much they may charge for their work—possibly the most delicate work that man can perform. This is in response to various governmental discoveries that the Medicare program is a bummer—just as was predicted by many at its inception. (That fraud is part of the program should surprise no one: All activities sustained with the aid of the force of government, through taxation, conscription, or the like, must get corrupt after a while.)

To suggest controls of doctors' fees is to deny any semblance of respect for individual liberty and human rights. It is furthermore just another step toward destroying the quality and productivity of the medical profession in the United States.

For a long time the United States has led the world in the doctor-to-patient ratio. On top of it, in this country the kind of care patients could receive has far exceeded the quality to be found anywhere else. In the main, anyone who could get to a doctor's office or to a telephone, could receive help—no questions asked. But with the entry of socialized medicine, doctors have become far more conscious of money and short-cuts than they have been before. Hospitals are known to have turned away patients simply because according to governmental regulations they were not permitted to treat them. Ambulances have refused their services to patients because the bureaucratic rules limited their territories of operation.

On the other hand, more and more people run to hospitals with little or nothing wrong, simply because they know that it costs them nothing to go through

---

*Originally published in the *Orange County Register* (1969).

examinations. I know of a number of hospitals where patients reside not because of any need for special care but because they can charge their residence to the government. The very idea that people should look out for their future needs, especially with regard to medical care, is losing all respectability (young people tend to think of such measures as insurance and savings as stupid, old fashioned, and restrictive). The welfare state has announced the rule: "You live for the state, and the state provides for you." (The New Left wants the latter without the former and has not realized the impossibility of breaking the two apart.)

It is especially sad to see Robert Finch proposing the additional socialist measure. Many of us had hoped that with Nixon in, the runaway welfarism of the Lyndon Baines Johnson–Herbert Horatio Humphrey clan would be halted and the government would embark on the task of restoring to individuals their dignity and self-responsibility by resting the burden of self-support on them. Instead, it appears, Nixon's team is intent on pushing for more controls on us all (just count the number of antitrust suits that have been started and the frequently heard threats of price and wage controls). Now it is the doctors who are going to get it.

When Medicare first appeared, everyone opposed to it warned about the forthcoming controls on doctors. But the proponents of the scheme screamed "foul" and denied that this was on their minds. When their program was called "socialist" they eagerly denied it. Actually, they were right; "socialism" is too good a word to use—under socialism the government *frankly* takes over private industry and robs men of all their rights; it does not pretend that men are free. What we have now is creeping fascism. In Hitler's Germany everyone had title to his property while Hitler's regime simply told everyone how to use that property. It was a grand deception—you both owned *and* did not own your work, property, etc. That is what's happening in the United States now. The doctor appears to be a free agent—yet his work is controlled by the government through the means of wage controls, red tape, etc. Add this to the burden of coping with numerous phony patients and you'll understand why the profession of medicine, with its already existing difficult prerequisites, is ceasing to attract productive-minded students. Why, the thing to do is to become a bureaucrat: From Washington one can be a doctor, philosopher, artist, television broadcaster, meat cutter, and everything else through the mechanism of governmental controls.

Fascism, here we come!

AIDING SUICIDE ATTEMPTS*

Should aiding suicide be illegal? That is the question that faces legislators who are being urged to repeal statutes that state, basically, "Every person who deliberately aids, or advises, or encourages another to commit suicide is guilty of a felony." I will argue, ever so briefly, that not in all cases should aiding suicide be illegal,

---

*Originally published in *Criminal Justice Ethics* (Summer/Fall 1985).

although the severest onus of proof of justification would be required in such cases.

The issue here is fairly clear despite many complexities that surround it. Ordinarily it is wrong and should also be illegal deliberately to take another person's life without a just cause such as self-defense or the defense of one's community. Even in cases in which ultimately the taking of human life is deemed legally justified, the agent of such action is responsible to show that he or she was justified by standards that a just legal system must respect.

But what about aiding suicide? As Joseph Piccione puts it,

> Life, as seen in the context of the documents of the nation's founders, must be affirmed as a bedrock value, and even a foundational right upon which other fundamental rights are based. From the initial words of the Declaration of Independence, the value placed on life in unsurpassed.
>
> It is undoubtedly true that the American political tradition more than any other places paramount value upon each individual human being's right to life. The Fifth and Fourteenth amendments to the U.S. Constitution unambiguously affirm this right and, in the words of the Fifth, no person may be "deprived of life, liberty, or property without due process of law."

Yet there is a clear distinction between affirming the right to life and life itself. The American legal tradition does not so much affirm life as the right to life as a bedrock value. (In this respect Mr. Piccione overstates his otherwise valid point!) It may be true, and I happen to believe that it is true, that the ultimately ethical basis for such a right must be the value of life to the individual who has it. But the law does not have as its central goal to secure such ethical values, only the conditions for their preservation and flourishing. Thus it is clear that the preservation and flourishing of life require a legal protection of the right to life.

But the right does not itself obligate everyone to respect life or preserve it. For example, within the framework of a legal system based on the (natural) human right to life, all individuals must also be protected in their freedom to either enhance or waste their lives. In other words, to value life is an ethical imperative, something one ought to do as a matter of one's moral responsibility. But by law, which should and in the American tradition does recognize the corollary value of (negative) liberty, cannot do for individuals what individuals ought to do for themselves. (The philosophical slogan "ought implies can" also tells us this: If we ought to value and enhance life, we must be free to either do so or not do so. If the law forced us to value life, then it would no longer be possible to achieve moral credit for doing so and moral demerit for failing to do so.)

Now the question is, given that everyone has an inalienable right to life, may the law permit suicide? The answer is that it may, indeed must. In other words, the legal protection of the right to life implies the protection of the exercise of this right, which may be manifest in suicide. The right to life means that the possessor may not be interfered with in his or her choice and action to squander his or her life. (Of course suicide may be made illegal by means of the prospective suicide's prior willing commitment to perform certain actions, to fulfill certain obligations—for instance, to support a family, to repay a debt, to perform any other contractual obligation.)

But what about aiding and abetting suicide? This is a more difficult matter. If there is one thing the right to life means, it is that no person is morally justified in, and any person may be prevented from, intentionally initiating the killing of another person (which, of course, does not mean that one may not intentionally react in a way that leads to another's death, as when one reacts to violent aggression from another person). If this is so, how could one ever consider aiding and abetting a suicide anything but a kind of wrongful killing or murder?

The answer to this is that under certain extraordinary circumstances a person may obtain permission to kill another, which the law should honor and protect against interference. The right to life means not initiating the killing of another, but this could be adequately qualified by being asked to kill another by that other, when that other demonstrably wants to kill himself or herself but is incapable of doing so or could not do so without incurring intolerable hardship and pain.

This point may be made morally plausible by noting that one may obtain permission from another to act in ways that place that other's life in great jeopardy, as when one enters the boxing ring and is permitted to assault another physically in a way that would without such permission be a clear case of assault and battery. Knife throwers, acrobats, mountain climbers, surgeons, and many other persons willingly place other persons at grave risk of losing their lives. When these willing others do lose their lives or suffer injury in part due to the action of others, the main question that faces us is whether consent was involved, and if the answer is in the affirmative, the person partly instrumental is not held liable or responsible for the death or injury (unless negligence or some ulterior motive can be proven).

It seems to me then that, under certain rare circumstances, aiding and abetting suicide can be legally justified. I base this view on the existence of the right of every person to use or dispose of his or her life and to consent to another person's acting in a way that will give the choice to end life practical significance. (I should make clear that I also believe that under very rare circumstances, once one's life by all reasonable estimate can no longer contain any but the most negative meaning—such as pain and agony—the basic moral imperative to maintain and enhance life could only be translated to mean to end it.)

None of this means that involuntary euthanasia should be legal or that someone should be given legal protection when hired simply to kill another who has consented and indeed sought the "service." The law must protect individual human rights, including the right to life. It must not weaken this protection. Only when it is as clear as possible that under the circumstances an individual's choice not to live could only be carried out through another person's solicited aid or support would it be justified for the law to protect such homicide.

RETHINKING THE "DISEASE" OF ALCOHOLISM*

We have all seen the ads on television: "Alcoholism is a disease and has nothing to do with weakness of will. Come to our hospital, call our number, for yourself or a loved one, to be cured of alcoholism. You or your loved one suffers from a disease; come to us and we will apply our cure."

Even in this day of "truth in advertising," there is little concern about whether these claims about alcoholism being a disease are actually true.

One who has studied the matter, Professor Herbert Fingarette of the University of California at Santa Barbara, argues that, in fact, no disease of alcoholism has ever been properly identified and diagnosed. That such a disease exists rests on the assertions of an individual who conducted questionable studies. (Fingarette later published his entire study in *Heavy Drinking* [1988].)

In 1946, E. M. Jellinek wrote the first paper espousing the disease idea and by 1960 he collected his views in a book, *The Disease Concept of Alcoholism*. He argued that alcoholism should not be looked upon as a moral problem; alcoholics suffered from an uncontrollable condition, similar to cancer or diabetes. Jellinek's method for determining all this left much to be desired. Subsequent studies have not managed to confirm any of his suggestions. Fingarette observes. "The classic alcoholic's career (which Jellinek purported to uncover) is—like many other classics—a dramatic myth."

One of Jellinek's contentions is that alcoholics cannot stop drinking once they have started. But experiments with purported alcoholics cast doubt. In one study it was found that when a group was given vodka (unbeknownst to its members), the results contradicted the accepted ideas about alcoholism. Fingarette makes the point clearly: "If it is true that an alcoholic can't stop drinking, at least after a first drink, then those who actually drank vodka—whether they knew it or not—should have continued uncontrollably to drink all of their pitcher." But "no one drank uncontrollably."

Fingarette found that there is nothing on the order of the predictability we find among victims of other illnesses with alcoholics. The fact is that among alcoholics there is notorious diversity. Very different explanations account for their drinking, as well as for their quitting. No pattern is evident. Here is Fingarette's conclusion about curing alcoholism:

> There is no satisfactory evidence that any medical program for alcoholism contributed any more to improvement than any nonmedical program. In fact it's doubtful whether any program, of whatever sort, adds significantly to rates of improvement. If they do, it's a modest effect, so modest as to be very difficult to identify. What we know is that a certain proportion of alcoholics will stop drinking independently of whether they enter a program or not. . . .

---

*Originally published in the *Orange County Register* (January 2, 1985).

That alcoholism amounts to a disease is undefended. It seems simply to be taken for granted. And one can speculate why this is so.

It is always convenient for people to believe that destructive behavior is something they cannot help. People prefer to regard their personality traits as fixed, so that when these make an impact on the world around them, they remain blameless.

Perhaps, in the end, the "alcoholism is a disease" doctrine is one of the more visible consequences of the intellectual trend to deny that people can be in control of themselves, making all of us victims of circumstances. Here is Fingarette again:

> The reality is that we are responsible for our way of life. Of course it's very hard for me to change my way of life. Still—I must take responsibility for what I have made of myself, for the way I live. If not I, who? But you, and I, and those who are alcoholics, are in the same human boat. We ought to have compassion for each other's troubles in changing our lives, even though in the end we must hold ourselves accountable for what we are. We should see the alcoholic not as a sick and defective being, but as a human being whose way of life is self-destructive. The difficulty we face is stubborn human nature, not disease.

THE CRIME OF INSANITY*

The events of the two multiple murders in Chicago and in Austin, Texas, give cause to reflect on certain points of the legal appraisal of such acts.

Psychologists and legal theorists have recently brought about significant changes in the official attitudes regarding the question of responsibility in the law. The horrendous nature of some "criminal" acts have, subsequently, come to be regarded not as crimes, as such, but more as the uncontrollable activities (or, better, behavior) of the parties who commit such acts. Having been classified as uncontrollable, that is, in some sense involuntary, the law has tended to regard the acts not as criminal as such, but more as stemming from causes not in the power of the actors themselves. In short, people who commit such crimes are less and less regarded as criminals, accountable for their actions, but rather "victims" of circumstances and, subsequently, not to be regarded as "responsible" human beings.

What should be pointed out in considering this gradual change in legal and psychological theory is that human responsibility is not always confined to human behavior within the limits of a certain time period. That is, a man, while he may very well be "out of control" at the time he commits a killing, could have brought about his state of uncontrollability himself.

A simple example of this is the drunken driver. Certainly, "accidents," caused by the intoxication of the party whose unlawfulness brought about the mishap, are not to be regarded as deliberate acts of the time period of the accident. Neither could it be held that these accidents are the result of negligence (failure of sufficient

---

*Originally published in the *Orange County Register* (1968).

care) that ensued within the time period of the accident itself. Nevertheless, the person who is intoxicated, and thereby impairs his ability to drive carefully (or do anything else that requires attention and alertness), is properly regarded as responsible for having entered into the state of intoxication. Thus, an act that causes harm performed under drunken conditions is properly regarded as a criminal act, even though it may not have been specifically intended.

In a similar though far more complex fashion, a person who, under conditions of mental distress, commits a killing (or less drastic harmful act), may very well have been the cause of the act—not specifically, however, but rather by having brought himself into the mental state wherein such acts were permissible to him. What this means, more generally, is that people can cause their own mental illness. The process is far more gradual than the process of getting drunk and then committing a harmful act. Psychological deterioration may ensue within periods of years or even decades. The consequences of such deterioration are innumerable: instead of killing another, the person might kill himself; he may commit lesser crimes or simply inflict harm upon himself or his own property.

The error with the current view (that acts committed as a result or in conjunction with psychological distress render a man immune to responsibility for them) is that it limits the context of the crime to the immediate circumstances of the event. The logical conclusion of such limitation is, of course, that no one can, reasonably or justly, be held responsible for the acts he commits that harm others. Since even the most "cold-blooded" criminal is deranged at the time he decides that acts of killing others are permissible, all people must be considered psychologically distressed at the time they commit the "criminal" act, or at the time that they decide to commit such acts.

What would seem a much more sensible way of looking at this matter can only be hinted at here.

Since psychological distress is, for lack of a better term, a mental issue (event?), it is a person's mental operations that are ultimately at the root of his behavior. It is in one's mental operations that the ultimate responsibility for his acts resides. Mental operations, thinking and motivation, can be impaired by physical causes (such as a brain tumor or other limiting bodily events) or by the failure of people to operate on the conceptual level, that is, a failure to think. This failure may grow to drastic proportions gradually or very rapidly. In either case, the failure is the person's *own,* and whatever the consequences of it, the person is the only one who may and must be held responsible for it.

To translate this into legally pertinent terminology, it would follow that a person, though in a psychologically impaired condition at the time of his criminal activities, must be viewed as an integrated organism whose near *or* distant past can have equally significant influence over his present activities. He would, therefore, be legally responsible (for having *brought himself* to a certain psychological state) even if, at the time of his crime, he could be judged insane.

WHY ALL THE FUSS ABOUT SURROGATE PARENTING?*

There is more heat than light surrounding some public issues, and the surrogate parenting topic surpasses most of them. We can glean the situation well from the fact that much of the press loves dwelling on the money matters associated with surrogate parenting. Thus phrases like "baby selling" are bandied about even on the part of state supreme courts—e.g, New Jersey, which invalidated the surrogate mother contract entered into by Mary Beth Whitehead and a couple who wanted but could not produce their own children. Considerations of whether the poor will be breeding babies for the rich are raised in virtually every article dealing with the topic. And the sentimental factor of bonding between baby and biological mother is focused upon.

But what is really at issue? Not wealth, not selling, but the integrity of promises made between human beings and the legal instrument of contract that has been erected to give the more vital of such promises legal protection. We know that human beings can change their minds, even though others may make plans based on their earlier decisions or promises. Because of this knowledge, we have tried to protect ourselves against the eventuality of someone changing his or her mind after assuring us that they will deliver to us something they have promised to deliver. Sometimes the promise concerns something relatively simple, such as some model of car, a dinner in a restaurant, or a performance in a motion picture. Other times the promise concerns something very complicated, such as a symphonic composition, a painting, a novel, a manuscript of poetry, a newspaper column, or a philosophical book. The complexity of the service, product, work, or idea varies, but fulfilling the promise of delivery is vital.

To add surrogate mothering to the kind of activities that may be contracted for is entirely unobjectionable. As an objection some claim that this service is not capable of being captured in a contract. The "service" is too personal, not the sort about which monetary agreements should be attempted.

But the same is often the case with performances by opera stars, athletes, or authors. These all involve highly personal activities, and there is no way to enforce the performance in most of them. Yet the default on the performance can certainly be discouraged by penalizing it through the instrument of contract law. If the default comes about through malice or negligence, it can be punished and the guilty party can be penalized, fined, even jailed.

Having babies is no more or less a personal, sacrosanct activity than writing a symphony, a novel, or a poem. In each of these it makes perfectly good sense that some people offer their talents, skills, or creative activities to others, often for compensation. We cannot all be great artists, writers, singers, or comics, so we pay others for their willingness to provide us with what they can do. This is all that is being done in surrogate motherhood. It is a valuable, dear service, but nothing extraordinary, only something new!

There is a lot of talk about surrogate mothering involving the selling of babies.

---

*Originally published in the *Orange County Register* (1988).

But there is a huge distortion in the stating of the point in such terms. Is an artist not selling himself! And what of a columnist! We sell our skills to those who value it but do not have it. The baby is not being sold, only the labors of the mother, her care and consideration during pregnancy.

Furthermore, in surrogate motherhood the father is co-creator of the baby, so the mother has nothing to "sell" on her own anyway! What the surrogate mother does is choose to carry a child for another person. To characterize this as baby selling is to reach for the seedy or sensational aspects of the situation. No doubt there can be some cases where such a characterization is appropriate. But in fact almost every other performance of a skill or service could be put in such perjorative terms. It takes a pretty suspicious mind to cook up such terms for characterizing the human exchange of skills, services, products, creative energies, etc.

Some, of course, find money at the root of all evil—even if the original idea is that the *love of money* fits that description. In fact, most people who engage in some creative activity have numerous motives for doing so, only one of which is the economic one of earning income from it so they can go out and in turn obtain the benefits of other people's creative work. It is more convenient to exchange goods and services by means of money than by barter, so the money issue is a phony one.

What really is at issue has little to do with the love of or obsession with money. Rather, it has to do with the fact that in our culture and others, making ingenious efforts to advance one's own cause and interests in life is shunned. One commentator complained that surrogate motherhood is not altruistic enough; it should be like giving blood, a purely altruistic act. (This reminded me of a piece in *Time* back in 1969 denouncing the fleshpeddlers who brought refugees from Eastern Europe to the West. Well, I can thank one such awful person for not having had to spend my life in tyranny.)

Never mind that when we "give" blood, one of the benefits we often receive is a promise that in case we need the blood, we will receive it more easily than otherwise. And never mind that raising the blood-giving issue simply begs the question: It may well be cruel to forbid people who have plenty of it to provide some for others for some economic benefit. After all, artists welcome payment for their (figurative) sweat and blood, as do physicians, broadcasters, columnists, newspaper reporters, politicians, and priests. To obtain economic benefits from even the most noble work should not be looked upon as something low. It is especially irritating and nasty when this is being urged upon us by well-paid heads of various special interest organizations.

The surrogate mother phenomenon is once again something new that people without imagination but with a lot of phony moral notions on their minds would like to resist. A good piece of evidence in support of this claim is the Roman Catholic church's opposition to it. The pope represents the most organized opposition to it in the modern world. (The Catholic objection is really not to be taken very seriously. Why not object to pain killers, organ transplants, artificial limbs, or anything else that does not simply come to us from raw nature? The pope, perhaps, should go without clothes, since that too was added to nature by the human imagination)!

It seems to me most reasonable to leave the surrogate mother situation to the contracting parties and the courts that will adjudicate the occasional discontentments associated with it. Of course, this is too much to hope for. Already many politicians advocate regulating it. Does anyone still suffer from the illusion that politicians are more virtuous and wise than the rest of us?

AMERICA AND HEALTH CARE

For decades now some Americans have clamored for a national health care system. Actually, most of these Americans—including Governor Michael Dukakis of Massachusetts and 1988 Democratic Party candidate for the presidency—would like a great deal of our society to be encumbered by government. Frankly, and why don't they admit it for once, these people are socialists. And certainly they ought not to be intellectually ashamed of that; virtually all of academe, outside of some economists, leans toward socialism.

At any rate, the health care issue is a particularly good one for the socialists. They can count on the fear we all have of being struck down by some debilitating illness, especially in our senior years. They can pretty much assume that some people will not have made adequate preparations for such an eventuality, what with the myriad of governmental programs, it may not even occur to some that they are ultimately responsible for the maintenance of their own health care, not someone else who might possibly have some projects of his or her own to attend to. The suggestion, therefore, that here is a serious problem that needs solution by way of reaching into someone else's pocketbook carries much persuasive weight.

The problem is that the experience with national health care systems has not been wonderful at all. Great Britain is suffering from the overburdening of its health care facilities, with a brain drain (emigrating doctors) and with back-breaking budgets for its government. Margaret Thatcher is slowly moving toward disengagement and privatization, although in the health area even she is a bit reluctant to make a move, lest even more intellectuals join in on denouncing her as a monster lady.

Lately on our very own shores the national health idea has been gaining some headway, despite the bad experiences of Great Britain and other nations. (Need it be noted that in Eastern Europe, the Soviet Union, India, and other socialist and near-socialist countries the health care system, advances in medicine, and the service to the sick are depressingly poor? I grew up under one such system in Hungary and I would not wish it on anyone, despite its phony promise of universal availability!)

In Massachusetts Governor Dukakis has instituted something on the order of socialized medicine, of course it is not exactly like that offered in Marxist socialist systems (which are now all doubting the adequacy of their policies and will soon come to doubt even the socialist medical establishment). In Massachusetts all businesses are now legally coerced to offer health insurance to their employees. In April 1988, a health security act was signed into law that commits the state's business to provide for their employees who are not otherwise covered by health insurance. The act mandates a medical security surcharge on private sector employees. (Senator Edward Kennedy of Massachusetts and Representative Henry Waxman of California have been trying to get such a system established nationwide!)

Let me make clear that the Massachusetts health plan is merely nominally different from outright socialized medicine. Indeed, it is less honest than that kind of system. Here the provisions remain nominally or legally private, but those who do not comply go to jail, and, for example, they pay higher wages rather than offer health insurance to their employees. We might call the Massachusetts program fascist medicine: It follows the fascist practice of leaving society legally tied to private property and freedom of contract, but it severely regulates all this to conform to the state's judgment of what is right and good!

It is easy enough to tell why the fascist and socialist medicine alternatives are morally insidious: They coerce behavior from people who have done no wrong to anyone; they penalize persons who are innocent of any crime; they regiment the conduct of persons who should be left free to live their own lives.

But there is more to this than first appears. Such coercion, regimentation, and penalization turns out to be bad for people. It does not actually deliver the goods (i.e., health care) to those to whom it is promised. That should not surprise us. Slavery, coercive labor, violation of the rights of persons has never resulted in anything but the shortest-term benefits, and then usually to the undeserving few, including those who administer the programs.

For example, in Massachusetts, according to the study "The Massachusetts Health Plan: The Right Prescription?" conducted by professors Attiat F. Ott and Professor Wayne B. Gray (both economists at Clark University) at the Boston-based Pioneer Institute, 60 percent of those uninsured in Massachusetts in 1986 were from families earning more than $20,000 per year. As the authors note, "Presumably this uninsured population could have paid for health insurance, but chose[!] not to select it."

Those without insurance in Massachusetts comprise 10 percent of the population, a lower percentage than elsewhere in the Northeast. Yet the uninsured do not come only from the poor: 11.3 percent are from families with less than $5,000 family income per annum, 30.7 percent come from the $5,000 to $19,999 annual family income levels, and notice, 42.6 percent come from the $20,000 to $49,999 annual family income levels. Finally, 15.5 percent of those earning $50,000 or more are uninsured.

It would have to take a truly blind bleeding-heart statist to construe these statistics to be so dire as to institute policies that rob people of the most precious condition that a government might help them to secure, namely, liberty.

The Tea Party in Boston Harbor—did it all happen in vain? Will the country follow suit or regain its good sense and separate medicine from politics once again?

Culture

ON THE DECLINE OF GOOD THINGS*

My efforts have usually been aimed at analysis, at understanding, at reaching a rational solution to the problems we face. But this time I want to express my feelings. I am no poet and my efforts here have no precedent. But I think that emotions should at times be expressed in public, even by those of us who haven't mastered the ways to do it beautifully.

What I want to express is my immense sadness at the present decline of the quality of our culture. At times it hits me. I get all bunched up inside. I feel terrible sadness, usually at the sight of something simple, forgotten, or rarely mentioned: a well-built office building, a superhighway, a great-looking automobile, a hamburger stand, or a supermarket. Yes, walking by these or just seeing one on television gets to me. These are the forgotten objects of our culture: what no one hails or compliments, but what everyone seems either to take for granted or demean by fancy ideological hogwash.

I came to America in 1956. I liked what I saw. As I traveled through Europe in recent years, I could not keep from my mind how great this country I have chose to live in actually is. How marvelous life here can be. Oh, I know about the horror people can experience in America. But that is not my point here. I am simply crushed at the prospect of destroying all the great but "unremarkable" things we find around us. My car works so well, the gas I put into it is such a benefit. My home is full of items invented by forgotten heroes. Everywhere I go I meet up with these items that some people demean, denigrate, condemn, and debase. I feel pain and sometimes indignation when I perceive all the hostility unleashed at the things that make up this great industrial, capitalist, productive, and intense country I have chosen to live in and would not trade, even now, for anything else I know of on the face of the globe.

---

*Originally published in *Reason* magazine (May 1976).

Don't you sometimes feel this emotion? I swell up with tears. Yes, tears. I feel sadness and anger. I find it incredible that the Galbraiths and Naders of our land hate the things I love so much (or at least like), often without even noticing them. The movies, songs, cars, gadgetry, science, art, music, and all the rest—nothing anywhere matches the array of "goods and services" that have been produced in the United States. I am overwhelmed at times.

No, this is not a scientific sample. Common sense dictates these observations. And my emotions are responses to what I perceive, helter-skelter, off and on, here and there and everywhere. It is just incredible that there are folks who want to destroy it all. But there are such people. They hail other cultures, other values, other styles, other ways. The "American way" is not a precise term but such components as "Yankee ingenuity," "confidence," "ambition," "arrogance," "inventiveness," "hustling," and the lot make up a good portion of it. (My ex-wife, Marty Zupan, once remarked that in Europe she missed the "clean young executive types" who can be seen everywhere in America. I shared the feeling of loss, which was especially acute when we visited Hungary to see my youngest sister. The country was indescribably drab.)

Sure, I have my "system" within which I can understand why so many want to do away with the values and results of our distinctive culture. But when I perceive these values and results, when I learn of the vehement attacks, then I am amazed. Why would anyone want to do away with all this? Why are our products, our great achievements, our minor improvements on life and culture so despised? Why, why would anyone allow themselves to work for the destruction of it all? No, I don't think it is a mystery. But I am baffled, in those moments of unreflective perception, about the irrationality, the stupidity, the callousness that must go into such nihilism.

These are outpourings, which are neither elegant, nor even moving. But I do not see much poetry devoted to the theme of my emotions. So I thought it worth expressing them in just the way I am doing here. To what purpose? I am not sure. Perhaps only to record that a rational person can feel the impact of irrationality around him. I feel sad at the destruction, the insensitivity, and the pointlessness of what is being done to a great culture.

THE CORRUPTION OF IDEAS*

Some say that ideas have no consequences. They do. But often shabby ones take the limelight, and so the consequences are less than glorious. More frequently the consequences are confused and indirect, rather than horrid and easily traceable as in the case of nazism or communism.

Moreover, there are good ideas that can become corrupted. Consider "democracy." What can be understood by the concept in the best and most consistent way is quite valuable: a method of selecting between political alternatives based

---

*Originally published in *Reason* magazine (February 1982).

on the legal right of citizens to participate in a vote. Thus, constitutional democracy whereby the violation of people's rights is not open to a vote is far more valuable than wholesale democracy.

Yet wholesale democracy is not the worst rendition of this idea when in the hands of corrupters. Consider the rendition it has received at the hands of Marxists. Poland was a "democracy" all along, with its one-party dictatorship. The USSR is a "democracy"—or, actually, a republic, along with China! What a cruel joke that is.

A similar thing has come to pass with rights. When understood as meaning the sphere of authority of moral beings, as the freedom of conduct to be respected by others, then it is a valuable thing indeed to pinpoint rights, especially the basic human, natural rights that we are all entitled to. But the idea is as open to abuse as any other.

A drastic abuse is that perpetrated by the Soviet legal quacks who declaim that rights are whatever the State approves: e.g., the right to vote for the Communist Party or to praise the great Soviet leaders. Thus, by coercing people to do whatever it deems proper, this marvelous monument to Karl Marx's version of *Alice in Wonderland*'s more bizarre scenes has made itself out to be a defender of human rights.

Less tortuous corruptions of the concept of rights are evident as well. The right to live without fear, for instance, is just one such relatively harmless yet corrupt application of a fair and good thing. And the right to read. And animal rights: more confusing but perhaps somewhat more benignly motivated, inasmuch as one can hardly blame those who wish well for animals to grab at an abused but catchy idea to make their point.

Sure enough, if folks have the "right" to read—if we should grant the desirability of reading the status such that it is coercible for and by people—then animals have rights. Don't we find it unseemly for animals to be treated with cruelty and callousness? And are there not instances when this could well be avoided? Certainly. But to call this a "right" of animals against being used by humans for food and pleasure and even entertainment is something else again. Yet given what has happened with some of our best ideas in human history, how they have been twisted by confused and sometimes evil people, is it any wonder?

There is "freedom," too. What does this term mean now for thousands of intellectuals? To be free means, for these wise folks, to be without need, without any impediments to automatic progress toward health, knowledge, pleasure, love, virtue, and whatever else one might desire. Freedom is not seen, as it should be, as the absence of obstacles to action thrown up by other people's willful or negligent intervention.

Why? Because whoever heard recently of any such capacity as willfulness, on choice, in human life? That was killed off by science, wasn't it? Well, so it seemed, from all the propaganda we have heard. Now that kind of freedom seems to have been all but lost to our consciousness, especially along the corridors of academe. It is the free state of being, the unimpeded existence, that concerns most of our social and political gurus, even if we have to bring it about by the whip. This is the state that is brought about in the spirit of "You will be free, like it or not!"

Is it hopeless, then, to set any store by ideas? No. Eternal vigilance is not just freedom's price but the price to be paid for truth, virtue, even beauty. One must keep checking, clearing things up, making sure not to buy some phony rendition of a good idea, yet not to miss out on improvements either. Conservatives are right enough about many developments being better left to traditional motivations, because new ones often are hopelessly muddled while the old ones have survived much harsh weather. Yet, unless we keep our minds on them, all too often the traditions can get worse, and we might miss some of the good ideas not yet thought of.

So I would not despair completely when I hear about the "freedom" of the Albanian people, or the "rights" of pigs, or even the "democratic" economic plan of a Tom Hayden. It is more vital to keep up the pressure in support of good things than to recoil at the junk. As Shakespeare observed through King Lear, "Wisdom and goodness to the vile seem vile." Likewise, freedom and rights to the confused will become confusing. The point is, like the lesson in the story of the three little pigs, it is how well a house is *built* that matters.

PARADOX IN THE "AMERICAN MIND"*

When Allan Bloom's book *The Closing of the American Mind* was published, it promised to be just another criticism of American intellectual culture, only this time from the Right wing instead of the Left wing. Nothing new about that: In the United States intellectual self-flagellation is the norm. The press loves it, politicians love it, and intellectuals are absolutely addicted to it. I have done a bit of it myself.

This is such a rich culture, so filled with diverse points of view, that criticism of one aspect of it from those who are hoping to advance their own agenda is quite understandable. More monolithic, homogeneous cultures are not so filled with self-criticism—the figurative self of the culture is too united and also too fragile to be able to turn on itself all the time. But this country has encouraged it and is managing to survive it.

Bloom's book turned out to be a bit more prominent and popular than most such critical volumes. After all, it took on an institution that is thought to be the backbone of the whole culture—higher education. He condemned it as frivolous, narrow, and, most of all, under the spell of moral relativism. That is, most universities are homes to intellectuals who tend to think that no fundamental, basic, absolute values are worth seeking, never mind whether they are to be found in the first place. Bloom presents a penetrating diagnosis, although some of the symptoms that disturb seem to be idiosyncratic and have little to do with basic malaise. Take, for example, rock music: His hatred of it induces him to engage in a lot

---

*Originally published in the *Georgia Journal* (Summer 1988).

of pseudopsychology, most of it embarrassingly self-justificatory. But when he turns to the problem of the general philosophical views of many educators—especially those teaching in the humanities—Bloom is often on target.

Essentially Bloom's lament is that the search for excellence has disappeared from the bulk of the academic world. We live now in a wholly politicized and, therefore, democratized and egalitarian or "uniformitarian" educational climate. Seeking to be better than others is thought of as a kind of political power trip and therefore feared. Similar themes had been put forth in the past—e.g., by Ayn Rand (whom Bloom carelessly dismisses, even though she had said much of what he says much earlier and often much better). The idea that democracy is dangerous when it is extended to all aspects of culture is not all that novel. But Bloom shows how awful it is when the mind of human beings is democratized, if only implicitly. Grayness permeates the culture: Mediocrity becomes good and just and right.

Bloom might have pointed to one particularly fervent and explicit defender of this idea, namely, Professor Paul Feyerabend, a philosopher at the University of California at Berkeley, who has just published his latest relativist treatise, *Farewell to Reason*. Feyerabend would actually extend democracy to science and medicine: For him, the witch doctor's dance is of no less merit as a means by which to heal than is the brain surgeon's skill! And there are other prominent and well-paid scholars who advocate such balderdash.

So Bloom's thesis about the degeneration of culture into a uniformity of democratic rule is very much on target. But his own book contains two vital anomalies.

First, Bloom never challenges the politization of education, its public or political character. In a democratic political system it is inevitable that public education would follow the theme of politics, namely, democracy, thus catering to the lowest common denominator. Second, Bloom fails to engage in some constructive philosophy himself, that is, in arguing for the fundamental principles he believes we ought to seek.

The first failing is quite revealing. Even one who focuses so much on basics fails to pay heed to a fundamental issue about education. Bloom's criticism is validated by his own oversight.

The second failing is more subtle. Bloom is a student of Plato, the Greek philosopher whose dramatic protagonist was Socrates. Plato is an idealist philosopher who does not like the real world very much. He also believes that while we must constantly pay homage to the ideal world—to ideals of justice, knowledge, virtue, beauty, love, etc.—we are never quite able to reach those ideals in our earthly lives. So the prescription to carry forth with this vital search ultimately produces cynicism: Forget it since we can never succeed anyway! Bloom belongs to a school of philosophical thought that mystically wishes for things to be more noble, more elevated than they are, but has no practical, workable way to make it happen. And this is a significant failing.

Impossible dreams have produced most of the disappointment in human existence. Absolutism that is impossible to reach is a cruel joke. Basic standards of right and wrong, good and evil, truth and falsehood, beauty and ugliness are useless if they are unattainable dreams.

In my view, the Blooms of the world share the responsibility for the very malaise they lament. If they kept their eyes on what is possible—not even necessarily highly probable—then higher ground might be sought and now and then even reached. As it is, higher ground fades away in a dream, giving way to acceptance of the mediocre.

EDUCATION THE "PUBLIC" WAY*

Teachers in California and other sections of the nation are rebelling. They want more money—not just for salaries but for the support of various services the schools think valuable to offer to their pupils.

On the other hand, taxpayers are, in the main, refusing to support bond measures toward the raising of the monies in question. In Los Angeles, for example, the taxpayers consistently defeat bonds while the State of California, to which the superintendent of public schools wants to turn, cannot muster up the votes to supply the extra funds.

This disenchantment with education, which is not restricted to elementary and high school levels, is widespread indeed.

Thinking about the matter, one ought to consider the basis of publicly financed, compulsory education, in general.

The idea that the "private sector" cannot provide education for the people, that is, that education cannot be supplied on a profitable basis, originated in the United States in the mid-1800s. It was thought that since education is such a vital portion of our lives, it cannot be left in the hands of private individuals or groups; instead, it must be taken over by the coercive body of the state. This meant that education was provided more and more through political means. The financing and the student attendance of public schools was secured with coercion by the government, which was used precisely because it was coercive, because it forced people to pay for education and forced parents to send their children to school.

But as with all government services, this method of providing education did not turn out to be the flawless and valuable thing the supporters of the system had thought it would become. Instead, education itself became progressively less excellent, while teachers who worked for publicly financed educational institutions became more and more dissatisfied with their lot.

It should be noted that when a particular service or good is taken out of private hands; when education, for instance, is made into a nonprofit enterprise, then those who are part of this way of providing the services and goods cannot expect to enjoy the benefits of profit-making endeavors. Neither the revenue received from taxes, nor the lives of people who are paid out of such revenues should be expected to be so high and full of rewards—especially material rewards—

---

*Originally published in the *Orange County Register* (October 4, 1969).

as those enjoyed by profit-making enteprises. Those who join the ranks of people engaged in supplying "free" education therefore, cannot, make demands upon their field of work as can people who are engaged in work for which there is a voluntary, uncoerced demand in the society. In short, teachers who strike are refusing to face the fact that, in a sense, they are engaged in a charitable endeavor, one that requires their support without the usual remuneration to be had by other, profit-making ventures.

Strikes by governmental employees are strange affairs for other reasons, too. In a profitable business the strikers can withhold their work, but so can those who buy the goods or services the strikers produce. When something is provided by government, those who pay for the goods are forced to do so under penalty of law. If I were to refuse to pay my property taxes, I'd be put in jail. Yet, the striking government workers want to strike in the same manner as workers who are engaged in production of goods that I may or may not want and that I can refuse to purchase if I so choose. To have it their way imposes totally unequal treatment of the citizenry by the law. Government workers should be able to strike only if taxpayers, who must support their work, are also allowed to withhold their funds from the work these workers perform. In other words, if teachers want to strike, I should be free to withhold my school taxes.

The situation today is very messy. And this is to be expected after a rational consideration of the case. In an economic climate that mixes force with freedom, it is only logical that those involved in the coercive aspect will experience serious adverse consequences. Let us admit that what the private sector is not supporting cannot be supported better by any other means. We should gradually decrease the involvement of government in education and other areas not related to its proper function: the protection of the rights of its citizens to life, liberty, and the pursuit of happiness.

MURDER IN THE SCHOOLROOM*

Just a few years ago a popular object of ridicule used to be, of all things, public schools. But no one has the right to smile anymore, not even out of sheer ignorance. Finally, even the "experts" have realized that public education is a sham. Today, people make plans to keep their children out of school, at least people who care for their children. After reading John Holt's *How Children Fail* and *How Children Learn,* plus hundreds of other horror stories about what is happening in the politically run school systems, any self-respecting parent will do all he or she can to choose alternate modes of raising a child. . . .

Education run by the state must be less than what education could otherwise amount to. This is because education requires full attention and care, not the half-way dedication that political projects are blessed with. Part of the effort that

---

*Originally published in the *Orange County Register* (circa 1970).

ought to go into discovering what education is and how to accomplish it well must be spent on securing the funds and the pupils.

Unlike private educational endeavors, the public school collects its monies by force. It gets its pupils with the threat of jail sentences. And under these circumstances it is logically impossible to educate.

When a child needs an education, his need must be carefully examined and the attempt to satisfy the need must be extremely delicate and well understood. Anything less will cause the gravest damage to the child, sometimes lasting for the whole of his life. The "murder in the schoolroom" is just this sort: A carelessness and thoughtlessness that is criminal. The negligence with which education is being run, due to its essentially political nature, is indeed criminal negligence; if a doctor treated his patient comparably, he'd be sent to jail. Yet our teachers and school administrators are well paid, allowed to strike even though their customers cannot refrain from using their services, and are impervious to the adverse consequences of the evil system in which they partake.

The Register has long opposed public schools at the risk of alienating its readers and the respect of the leaders of the community. For this it should get an award. But the *Register* was not doing this out of a sense of duty but out of a sense of reality and honesty—public schools must be exposed by rational people. They are deadly.

My friends and I will never send our children to public schools. In order to escape the injustice of the law in this regard, we have secured for ourselves teacher credentials. Those who have them need not send their kids into the arms of politicians.

In the process of getting the credentials it became even more obvious what terrible shape education is in. Most schools and departments of education are rotten. The courses are of no substance. Virtually anyone can get through them without doing a stitch of work. It is embarrassing to let anyone know that you are getting a degree in education: Everyone knows that it involves no scholastic or intellectual effort.

Education in the United States is in a mess. So is educational theory. The hundreds of scholarly journals in education contain essays of fantastically diverse points of view. And no wonder; they deal in something that is very difficult to generalize about: How should a person be educated?

But adults and children are different, with different interests, different capacities, ambitions, circumstances, etc. Education requires precisely the kind of diversity that state-run educational systems cannot provide. It must be something provided by free men and women to other free men and women voluntarily, with value for value instead of with guns and at gunpoint.

Perhaps now that the public school system is falling apart, both at the elementary and the highest levels, with students breaking out in frustration and in desperation, with boredom and disinterested submission, at best, and criminal rebellion in many cases—maybe now critics will not be ridiculed. And perhaps public (political and politically run) schools will gradually disappear. It all depends on you and me.

STATE "EDUCATION" AND THE FREE SOCIETY*

In a free society, education of the young (and old) must be left in private hands. Education is a service that requires creativity, production, labor, management, and related skills just as any other enterprise does. By making it a "public" venture, education becomes one more area in which severe limitations on personal and economic freedom become possible. The most obvious of these limitations is the fact that the enterprise must be financed out of taxes, and since taxes are collected from all citizens, many must pay who simply do not derive any benefit. The next most obvious limitation is the compulsory character of some levels of "public education." This imposes on children and parents an educational system that, as free people, they should not have to accept; laboring under such a financial burden it is often impossible or highly impractical for these parents to send their children to quality private schools.

But there are some rather more drastic controls that are direct consequences of our particular school system. But before I discuss them, I want to counter a possible objection to what I have already said. Some might object to my claim that childless couples or individuals who must finance public education do not derive the benefits of the service for which they pay. After all, critics might say, the general conditions of society stem from the level of education enjoyed by its people. The fact is that under this sort of reasoning one could force everyone to contribute to every single venture that is considered of general social benefit. For instance, a society would probably benefit from the beautification of its inhabitants. Thus, it could be reasoned, we taxpayers should pay for everyone's clothing, hairstyling, dieting, and the like. The same benefits might be derived from improving architecture, the theater, sports, or nearly every human endeavor. Should we, therefore, have tax funds furnish the money to achieve all these improvements? Lest we forget, there is still the question, yet unanswered, concerning whether anyone's conception of the needed improvements is correct? In this connection beautification programs are highly presumptuous ventures that assume their supporters are wise enough to tell all of us what beauty is! The point is, whatever is good about anything, be it education, landscaping, sports, or whatnot must be chosen by the individuals who will have to spend their earnings for the venture.

To return now to education, let me examine the numerous ways in which state-controlled education necessarily obstructs some of the most basic and personal freedoms in a free society. As mentioned before, the most obvious infringements are: (1) those who do not have children must finance the education of those with children attending public schools, and (2) people are deprived of their full opportunity to give their children the kind of education they judge to be fitting (since they are taxed to finance public education already). A much more blatant exercise of control arises from the "equal protection" clause of the Constitution. This clause is interpreted to demand that all tax-supported services

---

*Originally published in the *Orange County Register* (circa 1969).

or projects must be completely equal in their methods of furnishing and dispensing the service to the public. This, of course, is the ideal goal of that provision.

In its original context such a provision was fully justified: since government was established to settle differences among people, since its primary concern was to provide a just administration of laws in instances where people were accused of breaking laws, it was absolutely necessary that the Constitution assure equal legal protection to all of its citizens be they rich or poor, white or black, intelligent or less than brilliant. This was equal protection from infringements on one's rights. In other words, an American citizen is entitled to equal protection against any private or public measure that would infringe on his life, his liberty, and his pursuit of happiness. It is hardly possible to list the innumerable cases in which these three rights are ignored by the very agency that should protect us against their infringement. To name only one for each of these, the draft laws infringed on our right to life most directly by putting citizens in direct danger of death against their will; the antitrust laws limit liberty by prohibiting people from engaging freely in business transactions; the anti-sex laws forbid people to seek their own conception of pleasure or happiness by putting legal limits on free sexual behavior. And these three cases are indeed too few to show the impact of government on those areas of life in which it is supposed to guard against infringements.

Instead of offering "equal protection" against the infringement of actual rights, the government has changed its role considerably. By designating themselves, via a democratic process, as society's caretakers, like it or not, the several governments (local state, and federal) have elected to change "equal protection" to "equal distribution." Of course, the object of the measure also has changed. Initially, citizens were to be protected equally against infringements of their individual rights. Now, however, government distributes privileges: e.g., schooling, welfare, housing, subsidies, health insurance, social security, and the like. Since all citizens are supposed to have an equal share of all of this, the ultimate goal of "equal distribution" has to be total equalization.

THE FREE MARKET AND EDUCATION*

None can dispute that most academicians are suspicious of the free market, of capitalism. Their reasons may vary but the main one is perhaps that they regard the noble ends of education as incompatible with the crass goals of business. They find it incongruous that a system that accommodates the unconstrained, rampant pursuit of profit could serve the conscientious cultivation of knowledge.

Recently the main professional journal of American educators, *The Chronicle of Higher Education,* published a very hostile attack on the idea of private enterprise in education. The piece, run as an opinion article but consonant with the kind of legislation and political causes championed by the publication, upheld

---

*Originally published in the *Orange County Register*.

the old myth that this particular enterprise is so very important that free men and women cannot be trusted to secure it for themselves. Rather, we must trust the politicians to help us out. (Put this way—as it should be—it does sound silly, does it not?)

Letters opposing this article were not published by the editors, and a subsequent submission of an opposing view was turned away on very feeble grounds—the editors could not agree whether to run it!

The idea of a free flow of ideas in the hands of promoters of special interst is not received very favorably. The same story is part of most professions or vocations held in esteem. Doctors often protest profit-making hospitals on grounds that medicine is too important to leave to business. Artists are often heard downgrading any suggestion that it might be better to leave the support and cultivation of the arts to the operation of the free market.

Scientists, attorneys, engineers, and postal workers regard it as an unsavory idea that the system of free trade could take adequate care of their professions. Certainly state licensing is needed, often state support, but more often state regulation and even management—compulsory support and bureaucratization.

So, the commercialization of the professions is feared by many, especially some of the more respected and honored members of these professions. Education is no different, except that it tends to be more accommodated. Other than some nominally private but actually state-supported educational institutions, most of which are called independent colleges and universities, the rest of academia feeds off taxes, not funds earned in a system of free exchange. (Of course, this is often defended by denying that the exchange in a market is "truly free," because, well, the rich are freer than the poor. But the point is that in market exchanges no organized, legal aid is supposed to be provided to any of the parties.)

The central point to be made in favor of the market is that perhaps it best reflects institutional arrangements of the human condition. It is not an ideal arrangement, but ideal renditions are never what make human life what it is. The mannequins at Bloomingdales; the models in *Vogue* or *Gent;* the muscle-boys in Venice, California; the "artist's renditions" of the planned hospitals or service stations; or the women in *Playboy*—none of these highly idealized representations serve to reflect the usual human condition. They are images that help most of us aim high or at least fantasize.

The market, instead, is more akin to actual people, those who go about their tasks in life, or of the actual marriages that are certainly not the stuff of Harlequin romances. The market embodies just what one would generally and ordinarily expect of the make-up of free men and women. Horses can be trained, slaves regimented up to a point, but free persons are going to be largely subject to the multifariousness embodied in human existence. We can do well, badly, or somewhere on that continuum in between. Any effort to coerce us to be perfect is most likely going to land us in worse trouble than what comes to us naturally, from our own assets and liabilities.

Does this apply to education? It seems quite clear, at least in any reasonable frame of mind. Consider that all the bureaucrats—including all of us professional educators and scholars who are involved in the running of our school systems, from elementary to post-graduate education—are "mere" human beings. We are no less subject to vices (or virtues) than are the pros of commerce.

Admittedly, the economists overstate the case when they claim that bureaucrats are as much motivated by greed as are professionals committed to that pursuit, merchants, executives, advertisers, and the lot. So, indeed, greed may not be their undoing when they are undone. But whoever came up with the incredible notion that greed is the only vice that can upset our ideals?

In fact, there are quite a few vices that are probably more odious than greed. At least greed, as lust, is somewhat understandable in our civilization, which still recalls the poverty and abstinence that have afflicted Europe and still afflicts so much of the world. Fear of being left penniless, as the fear of living without some thrilling emotional experiences, may generate greed, or lust, and thus lead some of us to lose sight of the oaths of our professional office. It isn't noble, but neither is it all base.

But pride, jealousy, envy, intemperance, imprudence, lust for power, and the rest of the vices that we can succumb to are no less capable of intruding upon our lives with extremely damaging consequences. To believe that if the market produces certain failures, the politicians can somehow remedy them is to believe that political life lacks its own pitfalls, that the dynamics of politics or bureaucracy are less susceptible to corruption than are the dynamics of commerce.

This, in general, is the point that counts most against those who distrust the free society's institutions in their concern for the value of education. But there is more.

A free market in education is not only no more vulnerable to corruption than is a bureaucratized, politicized educational system, it is actually likely to foster some of the many values that education itself is committed to seeking. A free market can lead to diversity. It can encourage innovation. It can encourage excellence in scholarship and teaching. It can fend off orthodoxy and lethargy. It can reduce the likelihood of educators turning into indoctrinators who are promoting some ideology under the protection of the civil service regulations that usually apply to teachers. It can also reduce the likelihood of educators kowtowing to the state with their beliefs, the main source of their perks. No doubt, the market makes such kowtowing possible as well, but because of its diversity the free market educational system is less likely to give just one line of thought continuous, sustained, and legally protected dominance.

There is, of course, the point about what would happen to the needy and poor if one had to buy and sell education as one buys and sells corn and shoes. The first reply is, whatever the members of the population will do for the poor will be done for them. All the arguments about how collectivizing charity will make it more efficient seems to be based on myth and wish. Why should it be expected that conscripting people or seizing part of their wealth and assigning some group to redistribute it fairly will really carry greater beneficial impact than trusting their free judgments and working as well as one can to encourage their good will toward those who are less fortunate than they are? No one has managed to make a case against this line; certainly not in practice.

Free market forces in education would be no worse (or better) than they are in the freest markets in our culture, namely, magazine and book publishing. There are excellent products in these, rotten ones, and a whole lot of mediocrity. That kind of fate would seem to me to bode better for education than what we now have—constant, relentless dissatisfaction, complaining and bickering, self-doubt, and self-flagellation.

I don't think the above should clinch the case for letting free trade reign in the educational marketplace. But I do think that these and related considerations deserve greater respect and more attention than they are being given in the forums of dispute concerning how education might best be handled in a civilized society.

ASSAULT ON THE PASSIONS*

One of humanity's least-heralded traits is passion. Sexual passion, especially, is held in low esteem. Those who doubt this statement might point to the popularity of *Playboy, Penthouse,* and peep shows. And therapists certainly do tend to champion sexual liberation. But when it comes to serious, intellectually respectable advocacy, the passions take a back seat to our spiritual and intellectual nature.

Lust, next to greed, is perhaps the most grievous sin in most moralists' books. Just ask poor Jimmy Carter, who confessed to lusting only in his heart and came in for a harsh round of criticism and ridicule. From Plato to the Bible all the way to contemporary feminism, sexual passion has received very bad press indeed. Plato found spiritual or intellectual (platonic!) love far superior to the sort that gives room for sexual pleasure and excitement. The Bible is filled with sex, yet several of the major contributors, such as Paul, found it less than completely noble. And many feminists today are joining with ultra-conservatives in making sexual pleasure a central political target.

Most recently Hollywood seems to be waging a somewhat oblique war against sexual passion. Several films, some of them remakes—just to make sure old taboos never die—have promulgated a message of guilt by association so far as sexual passion and joy are concerned. Three of these are especially noteworthy: *Body Heat, The Postman Always Rings Twice,* and *Breathless.* What is common to these three films is that each depicts exciting and enthusiastic sexual encounters between their main characters. The intense desire and joy the partners experience, the intimacy, and the relaxed abandon that they demonstrate are perhaps unmatched in the history of cinema. But in each of these films the parties to such exceptionally pleasure-filled and robust sexuality are out-and-out criminals, murderers all!

In *Body Heat,* for example, we see some of the most passionate and unconstrained lovemaking ever shown on the screen, short of inviting an "X" rating.

---

*Originally published in *Reason* magazine (January 1986).

William Hurt and Kathleen Turner depict a couple who thoroughly appreciate each other and give this appreciation passionate physical expression. Jessica Lange and Jack Nicholson, in *The Postman Always Rings Twice,* are no less intense in their sexual feelings, and they are perhaps even more sensual. And in *Breathless,* Richard Gere and his lover, Valerie Kaprisky, exude a pulsating eroticism as they share each other through the medium of sexual involvement. Yet in each case sex is denigrated by linking it with the most horrible of human evils, by having the same person or persons also unabashedly commit murder.

Other movies, plays, and even music videos also brandish this guilt by association. They link sexual passion with obvious, undeniable human evils: greed, cruelty, callousness, obsession, or just plain irresponsibility. Despite some exceptions—for instance, *In Praise of Older Women,* in which good sex goes hand in hand with admirable, albeit promiscuous, protagonists—most popular drama depicts sex in a schizophrenic fashion: When it is very good, very bad people are doing it. (Let us not forget all the gory slasher films of recent years, in which nubile teen-age girls are rewarded for their pleasure with an ax in the face.)

And this is just the tip of the iceberg. Throughout most of the history of Western civilization, philosophical and theological systems have given short shrift to the actual world, only to favor ideals that are outright impossible (Plato) or otherworldly and to be attained once life has been completed (Christianity).

These ideals have always been separate from what faces most of us in our everyday lives, i.e., this messy real world with its myriad possibilities. Instead of finding joy in the world, we are told to seek it in God or in utopian dreams, such as Marx's communism. The spiritual, intellectual world has always tended to eclipse the real one, at least as far as the intellectuals, theoreticians, and moralists are concerned. Since these people are trusted, and since much of what they have given us makes good sense, their attitudes toward sex have gained credibility.

In turn, another trend has been evident, the other side of the coin when mind and spirit are split from body and matter and elevated to great heights—materialism. Cynicism sets in as people realize how futile it is to try to pursue only the ideal set forth by those hostile to the passions. All ideals begin to be rejected. Only raw reality, and none of its rich nonmaterial possibilities, are said to hold promise. Materialists, pragmatists, existentialists, empiricists, and so-called realists fit within this group in Western intellectual history. Since ideals are impossible dreams, they argue, let us turn our back on ideals altogether.

This materialism leads to the depressing kind of raw sex found all around us today. Romance is frowned upon; those who hope for more than the simple joys of life are regarded as snobs; concern with morality, principles, and other lofty matters is dismissed as so much prescientific nonsense. Whereas in the idealist tradition priests, teachers, scholars, and other purveyors of spiritual and intellectual goods and services monopolized the respect of Western cultures, in this flip side it is engineers, technicians, physicians, and other practical individuals who have captured our adoration. In the sexual realm this is matched by the advocacy of raw sex, free love, promiscuity, and callous disregard for others.

But the materialists have not managed to unseat the idealist tradition, and for good reason. Human beings do need to be concerned with higher possibilities; they are essential to human existence. Morality or values may be distorted, misrepresented, or corrupted, but never abandoned. Economists and social scientists may preach forever that value judgments are sheer music, that they are arbitrary biases caused by who knows what in a person's background. But ultimately we cannot escape making such value judgments, even in the marketplace.

However understandable promiscuity may be, no one really believes that all there is to sex can be gotten from a hooker. This is one reason the sexual revolution has precipitated a backlash: Human beings need to find greater values in life, and they need to distinguish between the rotten, the so-so, and the excellent, whatever the endeavor.

But the answer is not to return to puritanism, as, for example, some feminists are clearly doing with their anti-pornography crusade. Instead, we need to explore the full joy of responsible human sexuality.

Neither the idealist nor the materialist tradition pays heed to people as complex beings, with mental, biological, chemical, anatomical, moral, economic, social, political, and aesthetic dimensions. None of these has a monopoly on what is important about a person. As novelist Somerset Maugham perceptively noted, a human being "shares growth with the plants and perception with the beasts, and alone has a rational element." So, isn't the best approach to facing the challenges of human existence to "cultivate the three forms of activity," as Maugham suggested, rather than "only that which is special" to humans?

A fulfilled human life pays heed to all of what an individual is and makes the most of all those genuine human capacities that are peaceable, nondestructive, and nonaggressive. The new puritanism that seems to be infecting our culture is not respectful of these capacities and must be resisted.

We need to reject the crass dichotomy between spirit and body and the corresponding denigration of the human passions. Perhaps then our children will not have to suffer as some of us did who were raised on the old adage that "sex is dirty." We must teach our children that joy is both a desirable and a noble possibility. Passion is not just for murderers.

NOW LIBERALS ARE PORN-AGAIN*

Conservatives have argued for decades that pornography is degrading and demeaning, a soiler of souls. What used to be the answer from liberals? Simply that conservatives were sexual fascists and that lewd is in the eye of the beholder.

There was a time when *Hustler* and *Screw* magazines enjoyed the solid support of Left liberal intellectuals and social scientific establishment. But then came feminism. This view holds that women are a victimized "minority" and men are the oppressors. One sign of oppression is pornographic depiction of sex.

There is no secret about the fact that much of pornography is aimed at

---

*Originally published in the *Orange County Register* (October 12, 1986).

men. So it is mostly women who are made to show and do all, while men tend to be portrayed as objects of lustful feminine yearning. It is all a matter of catering to the oppressor's fantasies, after all, so anything is permitted, regardless of how degrading it is to women.

Now there is some truth in all this. No doubt, the position of males as heads of households, leaders of society, breadwinners, and so on, yielded certain results in the corruption and vice departments as well, which were not shared by women. Yet a good deal of this truth is hidden and what takes centerstage is some hefty political ax-grinding. In the thinking of the Left, most issues take on collective, class, or group significance. The degradation of pornography is never going to be convincing enough unless it can be used as a means to show some kind of class warfare, this time between men and women. After all Karl Marx, the guru of the Left, saw all personal relations in capitalism as a variation of economic class struggle.

But what now of the Left's "free speech" stand of the past? Surely our memory of leftist cries about the First Amendment and freedom of expression is intact. Some people might ask, in the search for a "foolish" consistency, "What about freedom of expression now? How can a sacred principle all of a sudden be cast to the winds?"

The answer is simple: Social science has come to the rescue. One Dr. Gail Stevenson, a psychologist from Los Angeles, recently supplied the needed rationale. Dr. Stevenson explains:

> Pornography has been around for a long time, but only recently has it become problematic for women. The reason for this is twofold: First, women no longer subscribe to the notion that they are inferior to men; as women's sense of worth and power rises, pornographic humiliation becomes less tolerable to them. Second, pornography is becoming more graphic and more violent, and is far more pervasive in the public marketplace; women cannot avoid extensive exposure to the degradation that it breeds, as they could in years past. (*Los Angeles Times*), [May 28, 1985])

Well, here we have it. Now we have a psychological disease that has only recently begun to disable people. Now that women have gained self-respect, pornography harms them more than before. That it should perhaps be the other way around is not even considered worthy of exploration. Yet it seems far more plausible: Surely persons of strength of character are less vulnerable to insult and offense than those who are unaware of their own value.

But, of course, this social science stuff is all very desperate and unscientific. Pornography has always been demeaning, whether depicted graphically or not. Women were always offended by it, directly or not, e.g., through the disrespect many men have shown them. Neither have men escaped the impact of this nauseating cultural byproduct of centuries of official clerical and political denigration of human sexuality. Once women gain their self-respect, surely they should be less vulnerable to offensive material than when they lacked psychological strength.

One reason for the belated endorsement of censorship of pornography is not difficult to discern. It now pays, ideologically, to bring yet another part of the culture under the legal jurisdiction of the Left. When conservatives were the only ones to decry pornography, so that they might have gained political power by having it legally controlled, it was important to pretend that pornography was benign or at least harmless, Now, however, with feminism added to the various political causes cornered by the Left, pornography offers a new field of opportunity. Asking to have it censored or to make the depiction of the disgusting treatment of women declared actionable in court as civil rights violations—a contorted scheme to make this appear to be a liberal, freedom-loving cause—has now become useful for purposes of gaining additional power.

One point is clear. The Left has no moral or political principles. The First Amendment will be praised and invoked while it does duty for the Left. Now, however, the constituency of the Left has changed. It is the much larger women's movement that needs to be cajoled into its ranks. So they must be offered a utopian world, free of vice and free of a blemished environment. Since this world is not about to come into being on its own, the state is invited to build it for us.

We know that in those instances where the Left has gained political power, there is no use for freedom of political expression any longer. In nations such as the Soviet Union, Cuba, and Nicaragua, the revolutionary progress of the people demands that dissidents be jailed or shot. We can be sure that this will soon be the rallying cry in the United States; just as soon as the Left gains political power, it will be declared injurious to social health to speak out in support of "wrong" ideas. Just consider that already, in support of affirmative action measures, the secret ballot has been rejected in favor of making sure that no one gets away with having a bad idea guiding his or her voting habits.

No sensible person can think that, in general, pornography is a wonderful thing. But all sensible persons must know that a free culture must accept the presence of all kinds of offensive features in the environment. In such a culture disgusting, offensive, and immoral ways must be tolerated, so long as they are not physically imposed upon people, even if they must also be combatted in every peaceful way possible. The Left's newly found hatred of pornography is but a Machiavellian grab for power.

EQUALITY AND THE SEXES*

I bet everyone has thought about the proposition that there is natural equality between the sexes. Most educated people pay lip service to the idea that women and men are not necessarily different as far as mental capacities are concerned. Sure, men and women are different; but so are individuals of the same sex. Yet the notion that the nature of womanhood differs essentially from that of manhood in matters of the mind (we know about the body, of course) strikes our liberal sentiments off center. If only women try hard, they can be just as brilliant, rational,

---

*Originally published in *Reason* magazine (December 1971).

and creative as men have managed to be. And, of course, men could be just as emotional, gullible, and temperamental as women are reputed to be. The recurring and predominant difference is thought to be accidental.

This is what we think, or say we think, when we are being watched. But deep down most of us believe otherwise. We feel certain that there is something, must be something, different about women and men other than what makes us mothers and fathers, respectively. Excepting a few freak cases, e.g., Margaret Mead, we feel, though we will say so only privately, that men are the superior sex; we feel—especially we males—that the advantages gained on us by women are due to devious methods, lack of virtue, or whatnot but by no means due to superior intellect. At least most of us believe this. Lately even some experts—psychologists and sociologists, the "methodless scientists"—have come forth with elaborate theses as to the biological and psychological basis of this difference. The deep-seated prejudice in favor of fundamental intellectual differences between the sexes has conquered some of our intellectuals to the point where the feeling is now assuming scientific respectability. Needless to say, the scientific jargon does not permit terms such as *superior* and *inferior*. It puts the matter differently, namely, in terms of "intellectual versus emotional." But of course this amounts to the same thing: Men are more suited to cope with the world than are women, which means men are superior.

But has anyone gone beyond attempting to justify the prejudice: first, our democratic prejudice in favor of equality, then our "romantic" prejudice in favor of inequality? Not really. The biological and statistical bases for upholding either dogma are absent. Biology alone can offer no grounds for embracing either thesis, and statistics cannot be provided due to the immensity of the relevant variables. Since the influence of religion, law, and custom—all of which have much to do with arbitrariness and fiat—carries more than its share of responsibility for the way social habits and roles develop, we are not in a position to consider the matter statistically (our most favored tool in popular sociology and in the not-so-popular sociologies also). We are, therefore, left with armchair speculation, philosophical reasoning, or musing. And I shall embark on these now in an attempt to get clear on this supposed difference or equality between the sexes.

Man has sought out woman, and vice versa, for centuries, so the attraction of the sexes to one another hasn't changed much. Some form of companionship, brief or lengthy, has always been the object of the search. But in the course of these periods of companionship, decisions affecting both parties have had to be made. Who shall have the tail of the beast, and who the head? Such used to be the questions way back. Now it sounds more like: Will we go to Canada or Mexico next year? Or, should Johnny go to Harvard or Yale? In all cases, companionship breeds the need for answers to questions, solutions to problems.

At any rate, since men and women get together, and since togetherness brings a need for answers, decisions have to be made. And here is where the problem arises. Who's going to make the decisions? Oh, yes, we will decide on the basis of evidence, reason, rational argument, or science. Fine. this would be just dandy, provided we knew what these are all about. Clearly, human history is replete with failures at trying to find standards for good judgment. What is good? What is right? Who is good? What makes for evil? Surely none of these questions has been handled scientifically; and surely none appears to be open to rational consideration, at least not just yet.

In the companionship of men and women, the problems that arise and the questions that have to be answered are mostly of the above form. Because man has failed at providing himself with reasonable standards for answering such questions, companionships get undermined in their attempts at harmony whenever matters of this sort are confronted. But the decisions still have to be made. So who will decide: the stronger, the bigger, the more threatening? Since reasonable agreement is not likely with conditions being what they are in the intellectual department, decisions must be made in accordance with the capacity to enforce them.

In our history we see numerous inequalities between men; these inequalities are usually between segments of the population that must cooperate in some areas of their lives. Thus, for example, in the military the planners rule those who must carry out the plans; in the clergy similar popular positions can be detected; in government we can see how people on various levels assume roles that necessitate final judgment in some areas. In short, as long as the basis of human decision cannot be found in reason—in our ability to come to a rational agreement or understanding of what has to be done—in most situations involving cooperation there will be the rulers and the ruled.

Since in man's history there have been periodic upheavals of rationality, the ground for equality does, on these occasions, become firmer. At these upheavals there occurs a breakdown of the ruler/ruled relationship. All kinds of slavery dissolve: Groups, united by racial, sexual, religious, economic, or other characteristics demand equal treatment as to their capacity to make decisions. This demand meets with a level of success that is directly proportionate to the degree of respect that rationality—the adherence to standards of judgment that are justified logically—is gaining. On these occasions those who have been judged (prejudged, actually) inferior can demonstrate their intellectual abilities; since the standards of excellence are objective (not decreed by God or the king), the fact of sexual, racial, or other kinds of equality becomes empirically evident. Since the physical sciences have long relied on such objective standards, this equality has gained its respect from those involved in science, those who see members of the "inferior" groups perform.

So, when we get to the area of values, an area where most people proclaim the impotence of reason, the need for the ancient inequalities remains. Here, where decisions still have to be made—decisions affecting parties in cooperation and companionship—the possibility of objective standards for judgment has been viewed with pessimism for as long as man has existed. Today, especially, values are all said to be the province of individual, subjective feelings. As the saying goes, "You do your thing and I'll do mine," which means, don't presume that your standard of right, good, and the like applies to anyone but you. Absolutism in ethics is confused with authoritarianism. Therefore, since all of us have had enough of authoritarianism in the past few decades, we must reject the suggestion that morality is universal, applicable to all.

But morality enters into the daily decisions of every companionship. Wherever men and women are found, there will be plenty of chances for answering moral questions and solving moral problems. So long, however, as these problems cannot be approached reasonably, so long as each question has a different answer by the various parties involved, the need to provide an answer or a solution that is fitting for all involved can only be met by the application of authority backed up by force or its threat. This is why in all man/woman relations we immediately look for the boss. We know that the situation calls for moral decisions; we "know" (firmly believe) that these decisions cannot be agreed upon; so we conclude that someone has to be the arbitrary ruler, the person whose moral sentiments can be enforced.

In effect, then, the authoritarianism we feared from moral absolutism (the view that there is a standard of morality applicable to all members of the species) pops up as a result of relativism and subjectivism. This is true even in governmental systems: Where no one can know (or prove) what is right, someone will simply get the physical strength to enforce his feelings, his subjective views. Dictatorships are born out of moral uncertainty, moral "agnosticism."

No, it is not true that by nature men and women are intellectually different; neither is superior to the other by virtue of sex, though, to be sure, individual differences in intellect do exist. Our feeling that men are superior is derived from a tradition of male authority; our lack of a deep, rationally based conviction that the sexes are equal stems from the absence of a standard to demonstrate this equality in the areas where we have most to do with one another, romance and family. While in business, education, science women may indeed have demonstrated their equality, in the home, in crises involving morals, they cannot do so, simply because few of us recognize any standards of excellence in moral reasoning.

When deep "in our guts" we think that women are inferior, that they are more emotionally disposed, that they have lesser intellectual capacity than men, it would be good to check the grounds for such thinking. Where do the examples of women's inferiority arise? In what circumstances do women find themselves helpless? How does it happen that they give in at times?

Perhaps, after rethinking the matter in its full context, we will work on those areas that prevent us from making the equality of capacity work to the fullest. In fact, we might see to it that moral decisions need not be made by fiat but in accordance with reason. There is little question in my mind that under such conditions women will be able to demonstrate their equality without threatening the position of the male—a position that he has gained by default through his superior strength and that he is losing not to reason but to the social power women are slowly acquiring. Instead of switching the role of superior/inferior, it is hoped that we might do away with these categories altogether in favor of rationality.

THE NEW PROHIBITIONISM

Have you noticed? Prohibition is back in fashion. It is a reaction to extremism.

On the one hand, we have those who indulge in and treat most pleasures as if they were vital needs. On the other hand are those who want to legislate a ban on all these pleasures. With these two forces going strong, those who are moderate are besieged with extremism.

Take smoking. What about those of us who like a smoke now and then and never would consider becoming fanatically committed to the practice? Lighting up once in a while, after a special meal in a restaurant or at home, perhaps on the road to enjoy the drive we are taking, or at a party, with a nice drink that can use the contrast of the smoke—what about those of us who handle smoking in this way? Well, we are to be liquidated by the zealous prohibitionists, who campaign for smoking bans in restaurants, even when the proprietor would not wish to exclude us as patrons. They would even ban ads for cigarettes, thinking that free speech does not apply in support of causes that are dubious! (Next: banning unwise political advocacy!? If you think it can't happen here, think again. It is happening in Nicaragua and many folks just love the Ortega regime that instituted the policy. This suggests that they do not regard such deeds as a bad thing *when necessary!*)

All this prohibition is excused because it is supposed to help those many silly persons who have "mistakenly" made a small pleasure of life into an obsession. The abuses of some people are serving as the excuse to ban the pleasures of the rest.

Is this not a very bad policy? Is it right to stop people from doing what they want even when it harms them? Suppose a lot of people took to skiing, surfboard riding, mountain-climbing, etc., all of which entail dangers, hazards, and could certainly lead to calamities. Suppose some people became fanatics, so that they would break their legs repeatedly, nearly drown, or perish in deadly falls. Would this then warrant prohibiting the practice? Would it entitle the zealous Ralph Naders of the world to rush in with their politicians and forbid the practices even though careful and moderate persons would have to forego the small pleasure? Surely not.

The abuse of certain practices by some or even a lot of people is no sound reason for general prohibition. The moral authority simply does not exist for that kind of intervention in the lives of other people, their personal sphere of jurisdiction, even if the law sanctions such tyranny. It is no less tyrannical just because the majority of the people support it. Here is another example of how democracy can be carried to extremes, making even personal bad habits subject to democratic political regimentation. No wonder our founding fathers feared the process two hundred years ago almost as much as they feared a monarchy! To counter it they tried to erect a defense in the form of a Bill of Rights. But in our time, conservatives as well as liberals are arguing themselves blue in the face to tear down that defense for the sake of their agenda!

Ralph Nader and his band of raiders are perhaps most responsible for having made heroes out of zealots. They are far worse, in fact, than all the phony religious or moral reformers who are content to achieve their goals by way of persuasion, not legislation. The Nader model of helping people should be held in contempt by anyone who respects human dignity and independence. It is an insult to presume to treat us as if we were children in need of perpetual parental discipline. The fact is that adult human beings should be respected for their capacity to make their own decisions, even the life and death ones, regardless of how many of them in fact fail to do a good job of it.

There is, of course, the frequent result of any attempt to legislate away bad habits: The law will simply be evaded and a black market will result. That in turn will produce a real disaster, not merely occasional self-abuse.

An underground economy will develop when people want to obtain something that they know very well does not violate anyone's rights. They will want pornography, liquor, coke, grass, or crack wherever these are under prohibition, simply because they will say, "Well, it's my neck that I'm risking, so who are those politicians to say I can't do it!?" And from this grows the black marketers who say, "Well, I just want to supply perfectly willing, adult human beings with something they deem to be worthwhile to them, so who am I to argue with them? It is their business to figure out what is good for them and what is not."

Once driven underground, the enterprises supplying forbidden goods no longer have due process of law to guide them in case of promise breaking, contract violations, and the like. So enforcement will commence, which is where real crime begins. The zealots are largely responsible, let's not forget that!

WHAT THE FUNDAMENTALISTS UNDERSTAND, INTELLECUTALS HAVE FORGOTTEN*

When in recent years fundamentalists have announced that they would fund and support anti-homosexual crusades it was another reminder that the organization has outlived the 1980 presidential campaign.

Certainly, liberal organizations and activists seem convinced of the group's staying power. Indeed, liberals—convinced that the Reverend Jerry Falwell and his supporters are a threat to the constitutional separation of church and state—have turned the issue of fundamentalism into a rallying point. The American Civil Liberties Union, for example, now prominently features warnings against such views in its fund-raising campaigns. Similarly, producer Norman Lear has formed People for the American Way, dedicated to making television safe from the Moral Majority.

In fact, this conflict obscures the issue at hand. Actually, both conservative religious leaders—from Cotton Mather to Cardinal Francis Spellman—and liberal secular leaders—from Woodrow Wilson to Lyndon B. Johnson—have "legislated morality."

---

*Originally published in the *Los Angeles Times* (March 1, 1981).

The true significance of the Moral Majority is that it speaks to each human being's need for moral awareness, something left unsatisfied by contemporary secular currents. Intellectuals tend to be relativists and in the public schools and universities they direct, moral education is legally—and properly—prohibited.

However, the First Amendment is no communist trick or an underhanded way of suppressing religion. It is, instead, a realization that in a country of free men and women, no government has the authority to impose a general set of personal beliefs.

Yet morality remains an indispensable part of human life. Every day we ask what we should do, when several alternatives face us. And often, picking the right one involves more than simply taste and preference.

Contemporary academic intellectuals and those whom they influence— including most lawyers, writers, politicians, and other influential citizens—reject the relevance of morality in human life. Most psychologists for instance, do not believe in free will, holding instead that choice is an illusion. Sociologists see things pretty much the same, though they would substitute social class for the unconscious. Economists believe, in the main, that we are all automatically seeking to satisfy desires or tastes that are themselves not of our choosing.

Since the seventeenth century, most influential philosophers also have viewed human beings as molded by forces other than themselves. This outlook has been encouraged by a narrow view of science, which demanded that everything in nature, including human affairs, be modeled on machines. The great discoveries of Isaac Newton, which concerned the movements of physical objects, were freely adopted to help understand human affairs. Since in a Newtonian universe everything is passive unless acted on by something that moves, human behavior, too, was ultimately explained in this fashion.

Indeed, by the early twentieth century, many Anglo-American philosophers claimed that moral judgments are actually nothing but expressions of feelings and thus contain nothing meaningful, let alone true. Philosophy gave up trying to do what it had tried to do in ancient Greece and as the handmaiden of theology in the Middle Ages, namely, to identify the nature of the good life and the good human community. Instead, philosophy was restricted to examining language, to clarifying the meaning of the words we use.

Following the Southeast Asian war, many graduate students and young philosophy professors began to take another look at philosophy's abandonment of morality and politics. The earlier concern with language held out some suggestions: Perhaps by studying language we could learn what is morally significant, at least to the bulk of people. After all, people do express themselves in moral terms: "You ought to listen to your father." "You shouldn't treat him like that simply because he is black." "Everyone deserves some help when in need." These and similar expressions contain clues to people's moral convictions. And when they sampled such statements, philosophers tended to sample their own beliefs, their own feelings about morality.

This led to a moral philosophy that states, in essence, that what you feel very firmly about, when coordinated with what others feel very firmly about, should count as morally true. But the examples used were chosen by people involved in the discussion—academic philosophers and other intellectuals. Ordinary people were entirely left out. The moral viewpoint that is accepted, therefore, by most academicians, pundits, magazines, editors, and televison commentators tends to reflect the subjective tastes and inclinations of these people and cannot make any claim to universal, objective applicability.

All along, however, the ordinary people who haven't been to college, or who don't remember much from it, have been left without moral guidance. And the intelligentsia really cannot claim more validity for its point of view than to say that its members feel strongly that it is true. When questions arise about "abortion, the equal rights amendment, homosexuality, and pornography," to quote a list given by Falwell in the *Los Angeles Times* last fall (1980), philosophers have nowhere to point, in the last analysis, but to their "considered moral judgments."

And in the contest between traditional Judeo-Christian ethics, which the Reverend Falwell and his followers invoke in support of their views, and the sophisticated prejudices of contemporary philosophers, there is good reason to think that the former have a claim to precedence. At least they are older, more resilient, and more general in impact, throughout the ages and in our time.

The sad part of all this is that most people will still be left at sea when it comes to personal moral choices. In our time—at least in this country—both religious and secular moralities suffer from lack of grounding. Reason is left aside and, instead, intuition and tradition are invoked. Only when we recover the commitment to search for ethics in the nature of reality and in human nature itself will there be at least some promise of finding moral "truth" rather than moral prejudice and dogma.

THE CREATION DEBATE OBSCURES THE REAL PROBLEM*

I am definitely not a creationist. Admittedly, I do not know for certain that Darwin was correct, nor again whether there might not be some better way of explaining the development of human life on earth than Darwin's evolutionary theory, as taught by many biologists in our schools. But I don't believe for a moment that the world was created in one of the several ways proposed in the Bible. (Yes, Virginia, the Bible suggests more than one such way, including what has been called Three World Creationism! For this, see Delos B. McKown, *With Faith and Fury* [Prometheus 1985].)

Yet there is something quite wrong about teaching a given version of humanity's development to children whose parents basically disagree with it. In a free society, parents have the responsibility to educate their children, even if they don't do it right. That is what freedom means! They public schools have usurped this responsibility and that is what is causing all the trouble, not the clash between creationism and Darwinism.

---

*Originally published in the *Orange County Register* (January 25, 1987).

There are those who claim that democracy overrides all this, that we must yield to majority rule, and since the majority of the people believe in one thing and not another, our schools should teach what they believe, not something else.

But this is taking democracy outside its proper limits. Surely the people who believe in the Bible would hate it if an agnostic or atheist majority would deprive them of the liberty to teach their kids as they judge fit. Truth is not a matter of majority rule: It would be entirely illogical to hold that view, since members of the majority may know the truth not knowing that they are in the majority. Science, medicine, and all that we care about follow the most advanced standards developed throughout the ages, by those who have become competent in these fields, not some current majority's view on things.

Even in politics there has to be a limit to majority rule. The idea was that our public officials would be subject to democratic vote, but once they are elected, they would make intelligent judgments on their own. That is what a republican form of government requires. Furthermore, there is the Constitution, with its Bill of Rights, which strictly limits the powers of government. Finally, one has those unalienable rights delineated in the Declaration of Independence. Majority rule cannot enjoin what will happen to people's lives, liberties, and ways of pursuing happiness, including how they rear their children, provided they are not abusive toward them.

Among the protections against majority rule that we need to keep in mind in this debate about creationism is protection against the majority's view of the development of the human species. Neither a majority's nor a minority's idea should be made law! Yet the public education system makes it unavoidable that majoritarianism be the guide to education. That is sad. It is also quite unjust. Instead, we should open up the sphere of education to all sorts of input from intellectual, religious, and related communities. We should have a free market in education, just as we have a free market in ideas and the press. This does not mean teaching every doctrine to everyone. That would be irresponsible and utterly confusing. It means that there should be no barriers to people sending their children to schools that they find most suitable to their children's well-being. If there are no legal barriers to this, soon a free market in education would develop.

But here again politicians are the main obstacle to progress. With the feeble excuse that a free market would mean that poor children would get no education—which in some cases would not be such a tragedy, judging by human history—they cling to the monopoly they have over the minds and hearts of our children. They won't allow diversity. They want to be in power!

The answer to the controversy over creationism versus evolution is not the imposition of one or the other doctrine, nor even both of them in the name of fairness, an idea that should be irrelevant in both education and science. The answer is to put the whole matter to the test in the marketplace of ideas. I am certain that this would do full justice to all parties and may even forestall the kind of insidious court battles we have witnessed in Alabama and elsewhere in the country.

So long as education remains the province of politics, however democratic the process, it will not be possible to approach this issue without someone or some group believing, rightly, that it is being coerced into having its ideas rejected. Parents, who know in their bones if not in some intellectually impressive way that they must be responsible for the moral and intellectual rearing of their children, will not sit still for such tyranny.

With education removed from the hands of politicians, it may appear first that some of the poorer children will not receive a good education. However, this is a myth and easily overcome with some ingenuity, especially in a free society where the creative energies of people can explore various ways to solve problems. So the road should be open to the solution of the controversy about what to teach to whom in our schools. Let there be a wide-open educational marketplace, just as there is such a marketplace in the publishing of magazines, books, newspapers, in the establishment of churches, and in the development of scientific theories. Then, under the protection of the First Amendment, the search for the truth about the development of the human species can continue in peace.

IF THERE IS A GOD, IS HE CAPRICIOUS?

At the outset I have to admit to being faithless. My position on that score is that before I will believe something and, especially, take action based on what I believe, I want it backed with reasonably good evidence and sound argument. How insistent I am on this depends on the nature of the issue at stake. For example, in the matter of whether God exists, I want the best case I can find. Thus far I have not found good grounds to believe there is a God.

This is not a position I have taken lightly. I was raised in a prominent church and learned many of the tenets of Christianity. Those who taught me answered the questions I had about them quite unsatisfactorily. Eventually I realized that my belief rested entirely on hearsay, on my trust in those who told me what to believe. That was not enough so I studied most of the arguments bearing on the topic in the history of philosophy and theology. In the end I gave up my belief in God, quite consciously and with considerable trepidation. There is too much trouble from people accepting their ideas on other's authority alone, too much misunderstanding and confusion, not to mention deadly hostility.

I no longer think constantly about this issue. But now and then my eye comes across something that rejuvenates the topic for me, and that is just what happened recently.

A while back the Associated Press ran a story about the fortunes of several people who for one or another reason missed a flight that crashed on takeoff in the summer of 1987. One group had an automobile mishap—a radiator hose broke and they could not find a replacement, so they missed the plane. Another family decided to extend a stay in Michigan. It is the remarks of the man in this family that shocked me into reconsidering some issues concerning the existence and nature of God. I approached this from a simple, commonsense viewpoint.

Pete Mandley, who is a wide receiver for the Detroit Lions, made the following comment, quoted in the AP story: "It had to be the work of the Lord protecting my family like that." Reading this I thought of all those people who lost loved ones in that awful crash and asked myself, how could Mr. Mandley make such a terribly callous remark? After all, if there is a Lord and the Lord selected his family for protection, He would have had to select all those other families for annihilation. An omnipotent, omniscient being surely would have had to know about the coming crash and could have done something about it, just as Mr. Mandley suggests. But then, could we say with any degree of confidence that such a being is also most benevolent, all good? No, I don't believe we could.

Of course here believers will often say that God's ways are mysterious. No mere mortal ought to presume to understand and, especially, criticize them. Yet this reply cuts too deep; it makes all religious subjects impossible to discuss, even for ministers, popes, and priests. We should just never say anything about the supernatural: It is beyond us, and the unbeliever, such as I am, cannot be faulted for not believing, at least by the believer who says that God is too mysterious to be the subject of a mere human reflection or understanding.

All this would be of no great public interest if we did not live in a world in which so much concern centers around religion. Despite the prevalence of science and the secular outlook among intellectuals—e.g., the teachers of most of our children—many of the world's events revolve around religiously inspired topics. Islam versus the "satanic" West, the Protestant Irish versus the Catholic Irish, abortion supporters versus opponents, fundamentalist Christians versus practically everyone else—all this and more appears to stem from our involvement with belief in supernatural, mysterious gods.

And of course the pope—his posture throughout the world seems to be every bit as prominent these days as it was several centuries ago, if not more, given the instant spread of his presence via the secular electronic media. Why is he honored so much? Why does he deserve any greater respect than, say, some African or Malaysian witch doctor? Why do even the most erudite of men and women revere him? Why do gays care about whether the pope accepts them?

I suppose it has a lot to do with people wishing to have answers to questions for which there are none as yet. They choose to trust someone who pretends to offer them rather than admit that much work needs to be done before answers are forthcoming.

But there is probably a lot more to it. Is it not appalling, nevertheless, that some have the sheer gall to claim that God saved their family from death but chose to send hundreds of others to their demise even though He could have helped them too! Doesn't this upset even those who believe in God?

MEANINGS OF CHRISTMAS: SPARE ME THE SCOLDING*

I have this wish that we be spared this year all the talk about how Christmas is turning into a commercial orgy, how people so shamelessly indulge their desires, whims and materialistic concerns and thus forget the true, spiritual meaning of the season.

When the world is clamoring for a better life, when we are wringing our hands about unemployment, hunger, destitution, and sickness, let us for once admit that what we really want is for everyone to buy a great deal and produce a lot. Why shouldn't Christmas be a time to want more and better and to resolve to do what is necessary to get it—earn more, work harder, produce, and create.

The spirituality of Christmas is mysterious and it should be private, intimate. But the wish for nice gifts, the desire to please, the search for a good buy, these can be quite public. If there is more of it everywhere, the country and perhaps the world can look forward to deflecting an economic depression.

Americans have for decades been the main hope of the world. That great revolutionary society, the Soviet Union, counts on America to feed its people, even as it condemns capitalism. The rest of the world sells us cars, oil, shoes, coffee, and more, while we sell them some of what we make. We buy more than they do because we produce more and can afford more.

Except for a few, foreigners admire America, mainly because they know the value of freedom better than we do. That is why they wish to come here and why the dollar is so strong; they know which country is most likely to keep up its productivity, its economic prudence, which creates jobs and good investments.

We should keep it up. A Christmas brimming with goodies encourages people to do more for themselves. That is how progress can be maintained. We discover more, we learn more, we want more and better, of course. A new piece of software, a new car, a new dress, a new book, even a new heart, and on and on. All of that is wonderful, even though it isn't all there is to life.

Wishing to be surrounded with interesting things, with sources of pleasure and satisfaction, is quite what everyone would like. It is a matter of how much folks will do about it.

As an ex-European, I know that Americans work harder, more productively. They like the idea of fulfillment in life. They are practical, pragmatic, utilitarian; yet they are also generous, joyful, cheerful. Everywhere in America one sees people walking about laughing, sitting about smiling, kidding, showing that above all they tend to enjoy life rather than regard it a great pain.

So at Christmas, let us relax about our interest in all the goodies people want to sell us. We should enjoy shopping, and defy the calls to feel guilt and shame. We should flaunt the fact that we like life here on earth. We should indulge, sensibly, but unashamedly. We should enjoy all there is to give, to take, to play with, to use, and think of what we might have next. That is the way the world

---

*Originally published in the *Orange County Register* (December 24, 1984).

can be better fed and housed, become more healthy and even wiser, since the time required to gain wisdom is affordable only when one has some wealth.

Christmas could have far worse uses than running about to chase good times, good buys, good gifts, and good cheer. It could pit us against one another. It could make us feel resentful, envious, and jealous. Isn't it far better that it prompts us to cheer, to seek pleasure? We should not be denied such innocent hedonism. We are creatures of this earth and our nature is creative, inventive, exploratory, adventurous. Why be surprised, then, that we would seek and make newer and better things? That is most human of us, indeed.

SELF-MEDICATION AGAINST GUILT-INDUCING MORALIZERS*

It was Christmas Day, in the afternoon. I was sitting in my den, reading a novel. It was a very leisurely moment, just the sort one dreams of for a holiday. I assume, from what I hear from many others, that most of us wish for a few such days in our busy years. My two children were bustling about the house, testing the new toys they found under the tree that morning. My wife was puttering around the house, including the kitchen. She had succeeded, on her first try, to make a pie crust—and from memory, to boot.

All in all, it was the kind of atmosphere I expect from a pleasant holiday. And then it hit me. Our many moralists throughout the ages and in our own time would find me a selfish, callous, vicious bastard. I dared to enjoy myself while there are millions over the world who suffer. How dare I delight in my peaceful day while victims of crime, grief-stricken relatives of air crashes, a propane tank explosion, and the awful earthquake in Soviet Armenia were experiencing terrible blows in their lives?

Are we not constantly bombarded by this kind of harangue? Aren't our moral leaders always telling us, in serious books on ethics as well as at commencement exercises and in novels, plays, and poems, that truly good men and women— Mother Teresa, for instance—love everyone and worry about everyone's happiness and don't settle into their own before they make sure everyone can be included? And don't our pop culture critics—most editorial writers of the various dailies and weeklies, magazine free-lancers, op ed columnists, the Phils and Oprahs of television and radio—constantly exhort us to think of others, to consider the plight of the needy, to stop being so selfish, so commercial, or so materialistic as we carry on with our lives?

Exactly. Even as we run around to find that perfect gift for gramps or that last little item for the stocking to give an added bit of joy to our daughter or grandson, the abstract ideals that bombard us say, "No, you must abandon this petty bourgeois concern for those near you and reach out to everyone, everywhere. Unless you do that, you are not a good person, not a decent human being."

In my constant reading of moral philosophers this is the dominant message.

*Originally published in the *Orange County Register* (January 8, 1989).

If you like the people you try to please, especially if you love them, your doing good deeds for them is morally meaningless. What counts is doing things for people you don't care for, don't even know, perhaps actively dislike! That is what a good human being does. And this is indeed what many conventional moral teachings embody as well.

When I remember this as I sit and enjoy my few days of calm and reflect on the fact that millions of other people are probably torn a bit about whether their enjoyment is deserved, decent, or, as the moralists tend to claim, wicked and selfish, I do find myself saddened. Oh, sure, I feel for the victims of accidents, for grief-stricken relatives, and all the others. I do have a flicker of emotion to spend on them, but I also guard against extensive involvement lest I am emotionally spent and have no room for those near me, those I have chosen to spend my life with, those who are indeed part of my life.

But my sadness in this instance goes out to all those decent folks who are not casualties of disasters or some extraordinary events but to those whom you might call normal, hardworking, simple folks whose minds are being cluttered with the nonsense that makes it difficult for them to enjoy their holidays, not to mention their very lives. I feel sad that they have to feel guilty for not being self-sacrificial saints. I suspect very strongly that all this lamenting about our inhumanity to others—based on our willingness, albeit in fear of everlasting damnation, to do well for ourselves and those close to us—is not only unjustified but unjust.

The dreams of moralists and those who propagandize for them have wrought emotional misery on millions. They have perpetrated a kind of schizophrenic mentality in a great portion of humankind. Millions of people are not able to feel pleasure with what they have done for themselves and for their loved ones. Instead they seek their small and great satisfactions in a state of confusion, with mixed emotions, wondering whether it is right but unwilling to abandon their search because bewilderment isn't sufficient to detract us from what seems such a natural course.

Should I really love the children in India; the Sudan; Ethiopia; Lockerbie, Scotland; Soviet Armenia; etc. as I love my own? Must I be devoted to the happiness of all men and women as I am to the happiness of my wife, friends, family? Can't I be a decent human being, a good person, unless I "rise" to these supposed heights of nobility?

I am convinced that it is not necessary to strive for such a state of being in order to live a decent human life. But it took me decades to discover that. It must torment many people, who may not have the kind of life wherein they can spend ample time on figuring out such matters. I feel sad for them. I only hope they have some moments during Christmas—and other holidays, vacations, hours of their days—when they can feel comfortably at home with their hard-earned peace and calm. I hope they do not ruin it all by focusing on the confusing preachings of gangs of guilt-inducing moralizers whose messages—which are impossible and unnatural to fulfill—could make us all miserable and help no one very much.

RICH UNCLE GUILT*

Television and magazines—not newspapers—are my main sources of current popular opinion on the variety of problems that we face these days. I watch talk shows, both the intellectual variety and those designed to be more entertaining. I also watch the popular weekly new programs.

One of the big items concerns food. Doom-sayers everywhere—and only doom-sayers seem to get on the air or find space in the major magazines—predict virtual universal famine in the coming decades. More important—because doom-saying is a standard feature of any human epoch—it is usually Americans who get the flack about this situation. We consume "too much," waste "too much," are too greedy, exploit the rest of the world, and so forth; no one else, no other nation ever does anything wrong! And so it is up to Americans to remedy this (or any other) malady on the face of the globe.

Not that American political policy did not manage to ask for these absurd indictments. Unfortunately American foreign policy has always been developed in response to the charge that Americans owe the world everything. Whether these policies managed to help anyone is beside the point. (Or perhaps some of the foreign policy measures taken by the government were meant to help others.) The point is that most of our politicians have accepted and advocated that Americans must be guilty for being rather well off, in the main.

But, if generalizations are allowed about such things, we can (and more and more of us better do so quickly) affirm that Americans are not guilty. Yes, the American people do consume more per capita than do the people of other nations. But people forget that Americans also produce far more and better, on the average, than does the rest of the world. When we hear that Americans are always in a hurry while other people take it easy, it is well to remember that Americans are in a hurry to work and produce. (One of the features of America I miss whenever I am abroad is the clean-cut business-type person, the hustler, that group whose members keep the wheels of commerce, industry, and other productive activities moving at the highest speed in history.)

What about other nations? Are the people abroad doing everything they could to avoid famine? Are the Italians, the French, the Spaniards, the Indians (on the average again) working hard to improve their lives? What about all their religious taboos against earthly well-being? What about the taboo against killing cattle in India? What about the time spent on rituals at various times of the day, week, month, and year in virtually every country that is now facing disaster? So Americans go to football and baseball games and indulge in a lot of entertainment and rituals. But that's nothing compared to what other people in the world do.

The central guilt of America is that people here refuse to assert their right to what they produce. They work hard but then refuse to defend the fruits of their work. Instead, most Americans have allowed, even supported, the proliferation of political programs, both here and abroad, that signal the message that

---

*Originally published in the *Dunkirk-Fredonia Observer* (January 27, 1975).

people need not work for their well-being but can rely on the productive members of the world community to carry the burden of everyone's welfare. With these messages beamed out for decades—through word and deed—it is no wonder that many throughout the world are not producing the needed and wanted goods and services. As with the rich-uncle/kept-nephew syndrome, those who are kept eventually find it unbelievable that they, too, could improve on the general situation.

Doom-sayers can, of course, bring about doom. But that is different from a correct assessment of what must happen. Famines, shortages, and the like need not occur. But current policies, whereby Americans are playing rich uncle to the rest of the globe, will contribute to them even more than they have thus far.

GOVERNMENT AND SELF-ESTEEM

To what lengths will governments go to dehumanize their citizens? One example of going a very long way to produce that result occurred some time ago in California. That state established a Task Force to Promote Self-Esteem and Personal and Social Responsibility! Only in California, perhaps, but in some way a promising, if wholly ironic, effort!

The United States has recently celebrated the two hundredth anniversary of its basic legal document, the Constitution. What may have escaped most of those who celebrated this event is that our Constitution is human history's quintessential political instrument for the promotion of self-esteem, but not the way the folks in Sacramento would most likely understand it.

When the law of the land leaves the bulk of society's problems for individuals to solve on their own, without resort to government and coercion, then that society is already in the business of promoting self-esteem. Why? Because self-esteem is the psychological-moral condition enjoyed by those individuals who, upon examining their own lives, realize that they are largely in charge and manage to exercise their responsibilities in a proper, productive, honorable—in short, virtuous—manner. What is it to esteem oneself? It is to think of oneself highly from the moral point of view. It is to consider oneself to be good at the task of living one's life as an all around individual: citizen, friend, parent, neighbor, professional, playmate, or whatever. And this is only possible in a society that can secure for each of its citizens the mastery of their own fate to the maximum possible degree.

A society that gives the state the task of running the lives of those it governs, a paternalistic government that takes over the management of individual affairs—in that kind of system self-esteem becomes impossible. The reason is simple: If people have little to do, they have little at which to excel, and experience diminished pride. Wards of the state cannot acquire self-esteem unless they do so from battling the state with all their willpower and ingenuity. Those who acquiesce in their enslavement cannot acquire self-esteem; only rebels against the forces of oppression and tyranny can achieve self-worth in a society that fails to protect the liberty of its citizens.

Similarly, it has been only two hundred years that some people in the world finally went on record with the idea that self-government—not dictatorship, paternalism, or some other kind of oppressive rule—is the best politics for a society. Government is best suited for handling the relatively modest though formidable task of adjudicating disputes among those who feel aggrieved by their fellows.

Even in the United States this idea has not had much of a career, what with all sorts of people betraying it from the very start. And the world can hardly be said to have learned from the discovery, given its shoddy record in this century alone—with Hitlers, Mao Tse-tungs, Stalins, and the group of lesser maniacs setting about to regiment their fellow human beings—always, of course, for the good of all!

So the dreamers in Sacramento may perhaps be looked upon with more sadness than indignation. They are trying to square the circle, and will probably continue trying for years. Yet is it not an attractive fantasy that they might all resign and write a declaration of resignation along the following lines:

Citizens of California! We, the members of the Task Force to Promote Self-Esteem and Personal and Social Responsibility, have reached a startling conclusion. We have come to understand that the first step in the direction of fulfilling our mandate is to set a marvelous example to fellow politicians and bureaucrats. This example should be followed not only in California but especially in Washington, D.C. We are speaking, of course, of a most courageous, honest, just, and, yes, generous act. We are speaking of our mass resignation. We have to realize that the main obstacle to the encouragement of self-esteem—the condition whereby individuals can fully realize and acknowledge their own worth as human beings—is a government that pretends to take care of everyone's problems. The welfare state—no less than a paternalistic or matriarchal monarchy, a dictatorship of the working class (lead by the party, as it is everywhere), the military regimentation of society (as we find them in many countries to the south of us), and the rest—is a fraud. It does not establish welfare: Where it does for a few, it extracts the heavy price of creating more misery for others. The welfare state is an insult; it dares to suggest that you, the people, are inept in handling problems unless you lean on politicians who will use their legal power, ultimately backed by the guns of the police and military, to strive for welfare. The welfare state is, finally, a major psychological impediment to health. It takes away from you, the people, the possibility and opportunity to fend for yourself, to make use of your own minds and bodies and good will to flourish in life.

So, having realized that we were established to accomplish something that only individuals can accomplish for themselves, in voluntary cooperation with each other, we are resigning and setting an example. The only way in which government can promote self-esteem is by getting down to its own business of administering laws that protect and maintain individual rights along the lines spelled out in the U.S. Constitution. We want to reaffirm the spirit of that great document and leave it to the rest of society to carry forth with its various peaceful objectives. By this act we can hope for the maximum that governments can do in the fulfillment of our mandate, namely, not usurping each person's task of the attaining self-esteem.

But whoever heard of a governmental body with power to wield resigning and returning the power to the people? The shining example of that occurred when George Washington, the father of this country, refused to accept an invitation to become king of America! Since then our governments have been going largely downhill. It will remain for those of us still clinging to the fundamental message of our founding fathers—that securing self-esteem is the job of every individual in peaceful company of others—to reestablish progress in the direction they conceived for us. We cannot count on governmental commissions, especially those aiming at *giving* us self-esteem, to do this for us.

UTOPIAN AMERICANS AND FALSE GUILT ABOUT THE POOR*

I have been an enthusiastic supporter of the free society for as long as I can remember taking an interest in politics. When I came to the United States from Europe I was politically ignorant.

What I did have was a sense of America's psychological atmosphere, based on reading novels by Zane Gray, Mark Twain, Erle Stanley Gardner, and Max Brand. I read these works in Hungarian; they were traded on the black market even during the reign of the Soviet and local Communists. These works conveyed that in America it was accepted that free men and women are more likely to live a life of personal initiative and responsibility. When I arrived on these shores I realized this acceptance was tacit and without intellectual respectability. Those Americans who gave some modicum of assent to this idea often embarrassed themselves when making their case.

In contrast, those who ridiculed the spirit of liberty and individualism had sophistication. They wrote for most of the polished political magazines, the columns in the dailies, and gave the commentaries on cultured broadcasting stations. In the main, the defense of the basic ideals of America occurred at the level of *Reader's Digest,* while the attack was at the level of the *New York Review of Books.* And it has only changed a little bit since then.

I wanted to explore this situation, and the best way seemed to me to get educated in political philosophy. But there was no such thing in the early 1960s, so I had to find out why. And the answer could only come from studying philosophy itself, which is why I finally majored in the subject in college. I became ever more convinced that there is something extremely basically right about the

---

*Originally published in the *Orange County Register* (December 27, 1987).

American idea but that Americans are woefully inept at stating what it is. And the reason is that they are stuck with a fundamental dilemma in their lives.

Americans are politically wedded to individualism—the idea that each person is sovereign in his life. This is the basic message of the Declaration of Independence and it gains substantial legal support through the U.S. Constitution. But as far as the personal moral ideals of most Americans are concerned, they provide no backing for the political viewpoint.

In matters of personal politics most Americans are stuck with the idea that striving to live a happy and prosperous life is a lowly goal, something not really worthy of pride and glory. They like being well off, they enjoy economic success, but they have little confidence in the moral righteousness of these objectives. American culture is beset with the legacy that from the moral viewpoint, as long as there is one poor person left on the face of the world, no one is justified in being happy with his or her economic achievements. In other societies this attitude rules almost everything. But in America the political realm had gotten away from the idea—we all have the right to the pursuit of happiness, even while others are not so well off.

Why does this attitude prevail? Because of the way supporters of utopianism—the view that politics must aim for the achievement of perfect happiness for all persons—capitalize on one of the virtues of any decent person, generosity or compassion. We all realize that when we can, and we know the situation clearly enough, those who meet with mishaps in life deserve our support, our help. We tend to know this even when we do not act on it consistently.

So the idea that there are poor persons in our midst is naturally disturbing to most people. They will try to make provisions for such persons if they can, although more often than not they do not know how to help those among us who are helpless and remote. In these kinds of cases all we tend to be able to do is trust some people. And here we become extremely vulnerable to being conned.

For centuries those who have insisted that citizens who enjoy freedom are better at forging a successful society than those who are subjugated (whether by some elite or king or even a majority) have been rebuffed by the remark, "But what about the poor?" Of all the questions asked in connection with sociopolitical or economic matters, this one is packed with the greatest amount of guilt.

If you have no political provision for education, what about the poor? If you have no political provision for unemployment insurance, what about the poor? If no public beaches and parks, governmental inspection of health and safety at the workplace, etc., what about the poor? The poor have had the great burden of being invoked as the standard excuse for limiting people's liberty in society. This is so even though the freer a society has been, the lower the percentage the poor people in it.

What, though, is the result of the customary decision of Americans to yield to this outcry about the lot of the poor? We have had the most extensive welfare state in the history of the nation for the last fifty years—New Deals, Fair Deals, New Frontiers, Great Societies, etc., and what is the most visible result of this?

Well, it is the spectacle of the homeless throughout the nation, people who qualify about as well as anyone could for being poor. Yet has the welfare state—which is the result of the progressive compromise on our freedoms—brought anything to the poor? Not without violence to liberty and wealth.

The poor have served as the excuse for a bloated bureaucracy in all the state capitals and in Washington, D.C. They have set the precedent for ushering in the enormous public realm, with its public broadcasting on radio and television, public education from elementary to graduate schools, public wildlife preserves, symphony orchestras, museums, and subsidies to big business in virtually every major and minor city of this nation.

The poor have served as the ground for a compromise on the free society, yet the compromise has done nothing for them. But it made many in the middle class well off, creating an elite corps of social engineers. Is it not about time that the American people recognize what kind of grand con they have been the victims of? Is it not about time we get off the backs of the poor and build a free society in which the poor will have as good a chance as they could ever have of removing themselves from their dire straits?

DEMYTHOLOGIZING THE POOR*

It is a common precept that the poor shall inherit the earth. But it is a widespread dogma that they are deserving of it. Why should we accept and live with this point of view? This dogma of the inherent virtue of the have-nots may be widely propounded but its truth is not beyond question. In almost any discussion with those who want the state to assume greater power to regulate human life, the basic premise is that the poor must be helped—not some of them but all of them.

Surely if their ranks included some evil folks, the call for helping the poor would have to be modified. And the thought that they must be helped—that we must all be forced to help them—would have to be absurd. We might be told that the deserving poor should be helped. But from shallow calls for unlimited government programs to "assist" them to complex philosophical treatises on justice, the assumption that all of the poor deserve help is clearly evident in our culture. Even on television programs criminals are rich and greedy, while the good and innocent folks are penniless. Should a poor individual happen to do something wrong, one is certain to find that he had to do the deed: His poverty drove him to it. This is also the idea in politics when theft, glorified as taxation, is justified by reference to the plight of the poor. And most newscasters never miss a chance to renounce any social or political event that contributes to the welfare and goals of the haves, while they constantly and diligently proclaim their dedication for and sensitivity toward the cause of the have-nots.

Virtually all efforts to reverse America's economic tendencies toward bankruptcy are met by cries about the fate of the poor. Everything the poor needs

---

*Originally published in the *American Spectator* (May 1975).

is accepted as their natural right, to be supplied by others without question. When Alan Greenspan, as President Gerald Ford's chief economic advisor, remarked on the relatively huge losses suffered by Wall Street brokers in an inflationary period, his audience booed and jeered him roundly. When brokers suffer losses the bulk of the socially concerned seem to respond without the slightest care or compassion, as if people on Wall Street had no capacity for suffering and couldn't possibly deserve a helping hand. But the notion of cutting out some federal programs aimed at helping the poor is generally considered to be criminal. Never mind for a moment that the bulk of such federal programs as minimum-wage legislation, advocated as a means to eliminate poverty and to promote the "general well-being of workers . . . without substantially curtailing employment or earning power," actually hurt the very poor and unskilled whom they were designed to assist. (Of course some people are helped by all such programs, aside from the bureaucrats who run them. But millions are hurt by them.)

If we grant that being poor automatically renders someone worthy, the point of helping those in poverty has to be self-defeating. Why should anyone contribute, even voluntarily, to the degradation of a human life, in this case the life of a poor and, therefore, virtuous individual? If the poor are so virtuous, and if virtue deserves support, the most appropriate support the poor could receive would have to be support for their poverty. Judging by prevailing dogma, the wealthy simply cannot be deserving (except, perhaps, if the wealth came about entirely by accident and is consistently demeaned by the person struck by such cruel fortune). This is not simply an impression one receives from the popular media. It is an intellectual creed, propagated at fancy scholarly conferences. If it has any merit whatsoever, the poor, who are already granted virtue, ought to avoid riches with all their might. For theirs would be the greatest sin: having known virtue, to leave it aside for the evil of riches.

There is not a shred of evidence to support the view that the poor are any more virtuous than those who are not poor. Economic condition has nothing to do with moral character. We all have our own particular condition to contend with as moral gents. Rich and poor alike must make the choices that can turn out good or bad, and the poor as well as the rich can neglect to make the right choices. To confer virtue on the poor because they are poor is to rob them of human dignity. Any self-respecting person of meager means would find it appalling for others to judge his moral character on the basis of his poverty. Moreover, I have personally been poor, quite poor, in my life, and I have lived with others who were very poor. I can testify that the poor have no monopoly on virtue. Some are decent, while others are pretty rotten, and most just vacillate in between.

Under certain circumstances, however, it is not unjustified to suspect the poor of less than complete virtue. I have in mind a marketplace where government does not interfere to restrict mobility or opportunity. Clearly when the state meddles with the economy, too many folks gain unearned advantages in the business world. Subsidies, special "rights," close ties between firms and regulatory agencies, exclusionary laws, protection from foreign competition, and the like make it possible for some to maintain economic security with no real effort other than hiring the government's widely available gun.

Under conditions of a free market, however, it is often reasonable to suspect that those who are really destitute have neglected their own care. I am not making a purely historical point, one that is easily researched. My point is that when people neglect their well-being, permit their future to rush in while they have given it no thought, produce children but take little care to ensure their economic security, refuse to prepare for their old age, and otherwise contribute to their own poverty, it is not unreasonable to suggest that their actions betray a character flaw, moral negligence, and thus deserve no rewards at all. Clearly, even in the free marketplace, poverty does not always betoken irresponsibility: Artists, scholars, scientists, teachers, and many others pursue values that do not show up in the Gross National Product figures. But on the whole, when people neglect their economic welfare, fail to retrain after a job becomes obsolete, become inattentive to their own and their family's needs and wants, this is nothing to be admired. There are, even now, among the poor many who have no one else but themselves to blame for their poverty. And to sell the rest of the people on the familiar tale of the virtue of poverty will simply make this lamentable state of affairs continue beyond its natural course.

It won't do here to talk about the incredible advantage of "initial endowments," a favored argument of modern egalitarians. In a free society one's responsibilities tend to match one's initial circumstances: A poor man need not cope with setting up parties for foreign ambassadors, while the wealthy do not have to keep the grocery budget under close scrutiny. The rich, the poor, and those in-between can do better or worse with what they have at any point. It may be trite to say, but happiness is not guaranteed by wealth, although wealth certainly does contribute to the fulfillment of our material, biological, aesthetic, and other needs and wants.

Another favorite argument of those who reject the free society for some well-managed state (well managed by whom, if people in freedom are so vicious and such bunglers?) concerns the morality of successful business folks. When it is proposed that the market be freed and there be a sustained, peaceful marathon race (not a boxing match, as most conceive of market transactions), egalitarians protest that when some get rich, they will only suppress the poor: Economic liberty may last a while, but soon the successful will step on those who would challenge their stance. So the poor stay poor quite independent of effort, ambition, and the like. The poor are kept poor, period.

First of all, if becoming rich is a sufficient condition for becoming mean and heartless, then the poor should certainly be best off, seeing as they are the least callous. But the egalitarian does not see the logic of his dogma, so he continues advocating (and trying, once he's been given a post in the state) in an effort to make the poor richer and make the rich poorer.

Second, all of this may miss the crucial point about the concern with the poor. It has always seemed to me to follow from one's desire for some goal that effort to achieve it will be forthcoming. It is, for instance, one thing to wish that there were no poverty, and quite another to want to eliminate it. The latter would call for action, and the action to be taken to help the poor is rarely forbidden. Unlike spending money on illegal activities, there is no law to prevent any of us from giving half or all his wealth to another person. While here and there some of my egalitarian acquaintances do send off a check or two to the United Way, the Red Cross, and other charities, most of them send their checks to political pressure groups that help only the goal of egalitarian power. I have never known of an egalitarian who actually, voluntarily practiced his own doctrine of redistribution of wealth. And this is quite understandable: Those who invoke the egalitarian argument do not seriously believe it. These people are often very bright. They are not barred from economic reality: they know of it only too well, so they avoid consideration of it like they avoid reading some economic history books about capitalism. It is all wrong to believe that egalitarians are generally well meaning, decent, compassionate people; if this were so, there would be no poverty anywhere, since the egalitarians would have eliminated it through sustained private, voluntary effort. No, the point is that their concern for the poor is largely a pose and their real goal is political power. The motivation, although quite difficult to generalize, seems to be envy. Why do those businessmen, engineering dropouts, entrepreneurs, and the like, with no finesse, no sophistication, no appreciation for the nuances of language and life—why do these people have so much to say about what goes on in the world? Why should barbers, bakers, insurance agents, bankers, building constructors, and the like have so much say about the things filling department stores, the content of television shows, the style of furniture, the color of the local drive-in restaurant? Who are these people who get away with such vulgarities, in the face of so much talent, i.e., all the intellectuals, scholars, educators, and artists, who obviously could construct a more beautiful and worthwhile world?

Now I am not making a case for the neglect of those with whom egalitarians are supposedly concerned. It does seem unjustified to lay that much stress on the lot of the poor simply because they are poor. On the contrary, I think we should help those who have met with misfortune or handicap through no fault of their own; but I ground such assistance not on a duty to the helpless but in the natural generosity and benevolence characteristic of those who value successful life—a sort of fraternity of the living, of those bent on "making it." Egalitarian solutions to the conditions of the unfortunate do not embody such generosity. When charity and benevolence are politicized it can only reap neglect of and hostility toward those who would be made the parasites of a productive society, instead of the beneficiaries of those who have chosen to lend a helping hand.

Even those who argue that charity is a moral duty must reject the egalitarian's approach: There cannot be anything virtuous in observing a duty because one is threatened with jail. (Kant, the supreme altruist, never sanctioned force in producing virtue.) Egalitarians have argued that general political reforms would be more helpful than private charity, so we might as well concentrate on remaking the world. That will be charitable enough. But this won't do. There is no evidence that general political reforms have ever helped the poor, even those who have deserved help, to offset the drastic harm in their wake. Welfare measures, socialization, and similar egalitarian approaches are demonstrable flops. By now most advocates of such reforms cling to their last but highly dubious argument: By making the state even more responsible for distributing wealth, perhaps, as at least a logical possibility, things will get better! This is not an argument but a confession of ignorance.

In the final analysis, our entire moral atmosphere needs serious revision. Those who are concerned with reassuring a free society must rigorously reemphasize the value of liberty and the moral and economic bases for a free society. It won't do simply to dismiss the enemy as a group of fools ignorant of economic theory and caught up in blind homage to misfortune. Ignorance is part of the problem, but evasion is its most frequent cause. It is not that egalitarians could not know that the poor are not all that nice and that the rich aren't all that nasty—they don't want to know. It is not that they could not know that the free market is best for the fortunate and unfortunate alike—no effort is made to acquire that knowledge. By refusing to come to terms with these facts about the opposition, the supporter of the free market may feel sophisticated and beyond petty moralism. Yet it will prove to be his undoing.

HOORAY FOR HOLLYWOOD, SOME LESSONS OF SHOW BIZ*

Perhaps one of the most vulnerable parts of American culture is its preoccupation with show business. Of course, the world has been perfectly willing to follow suit here, but the blame is usually laid at the feet of Hollywood. Indeed, one reason that many orthodox religious cultures such as Iran refer to the United States as a satanic power is that, by the lights of their leaders, all this public exhibitionism surrounding show business leads to decadence.

Yet there is an element of show business I have never seen praised. Economists have coined the term *positive externality,* and surely here is a positive externality if there ever was one. It is the enormous educational benefit we gain by seeing people in show business carry on with their careers in public. Where else would we be able to learn of the ups and downs of professional careers than by seeing the likes of Joey Bishop, Dick Cavett, et al., go through the agony and ecstasy of finding and losing lucrative jobs on television? Who would teach our kids all about blowing a great career through drug and alcohol abuse if it were not for all those rock stars who have gone under as a result of seeking ever more far-out trips via artificial substances?

Most children tend to listen with boredom to inept parental exhortations about the wisdom of getting a steady job, of learning something in school, of moderation and temperance. Yet they can see the rising and falling stardoms of their idols and the personal miseries of publicly successful celebrities, from

---

*Originally published in the *Orange County Register* (July 20, 1988).

which they could well learn some hard lessons of life that otherwise would not reach them.

I am always grateful to gossip columnists, the tabloids, the show-biz spots on television and radio when they tell us about all the deals being made in the business. Most big business events are only discussed in the *Wall Street Journal, Barron's,* the *Economist,* or the business pages of the better dailies. These are certainly not read by most people, not to mention our youngsters. Yet they are well aware of how some enormously expensive Hollywood movie flopped at the box office.

These are small, incremental lessons in economics. They also learn about what it takes to stay on top: coming out with innovative songs, diversifying in one's stardom, and other, career-oriented moves. These are valuable lessons. But there is more. By way of the scrutiny of the people in show business, we also learn about many possibilities within family life, some very bad and some quite commendable. We learn about the delicate balance between career and friendship and love and family and citizenship. Jane Fonda has had to explain her political foibles to a group of Vietnam veterans, thereby showing that while one can succeed in some area and be a star, in another area one may have to eat crow and remain humble.

Personally I am grateful for show business. It is not just directed to the public at large as a matter of its professional purposes. It also achieves a kind of public service by keeping us aware of the diversity of the lives of others, many of them competent, admirable, or at least notorious. By this means many of us find that the events we face in our lives are not all that unique. We may even learn how to cope with them better, having seen some of the celebrities do this under the microscope of public scrutiny. But more than anything else, the public nature of the lives of people in show business can help us appreciate just how diverse human life can be, how many variations there can be on how people live, work, cope with problems, deal with tragedies, succeed, fail, or remain rather mediocre.

BUSINESS AND THE MOVIE BUSINESS

In my case going to the movies is a risky undertaking. Well, I know other people have trepidations about paying for some bomb, but for me there is a real danger of serious irritation. The reason is that I have respect for the profession of business.

You can imagine that *Wall Street* was not my favorite film. I would only see it as a lesson in cultural anthropology; certainly not as entertainment, let alone a source of artistic elevation.

In virtually every medium of fiction—stage, screen, television, the novel—business is getting badly treated. I have written about this before, and it is no mystery to me that this is so. After all, Western culture has been very seriously influenced by the idea that what matters most to everyone is spirit, not this world, and business has as its distinctive task to satisfy our worldly desires. How could we then admit its honorable nature? So, even though we depend on the institution and we seek it out all the time, we nonetheless scoff at it. Even the old rich (who inherited their wealth) get better treatment from moralists than the nouveau riche, those who actually earned their money!

To see how pervasive this line of thinking is, one might take a look at a recent essay by Janet Maslin, one of the film critics for the *New York Times.* In early January 1989, she went to town on the movie *Working Girl,* one of my current favorites, a bright and delightful romantic comedy involving professionals in New York's financial district. I won't spoil your enjoyment of the film by dwelling on details. What is interesting is that the film actually does not dump on the money business as an institution but simply focuses on the actions of some decent and some indecent members of the profession.

Our Ms. Maslin, however, does not like this. She complains: "So where is this [the movie] headed? Not to a renunciation of grasping, striving and getting ahead, even though the film has spent much of its time gently satirizing these pursuits. *Working Girl* assigns its heroine the kind of reward that makes her part of the very system she set out to skewer."

And these remarks are made as criticism of the film as a movie, as an entertainment vehicle, even as an art form. Ms. Maslin would have liked it better if *Working Girl* damned business all the way through, no mercy, no holds barred. Never mind that the film is actually much more profound in its underlying approach to its theme than such categorical dismissals of business, a profession that even Ms. Maslin seems to depend on for her well-being and progress in life.

Working Girl, much like the film *Big,* simply picked some thriving business as the setting for a confrontation between some decent and some not so decent people. It did not condemn the profession they chose for themselves but warned, at least implicitly, that one can become corrupt in it. The heroine was rewarded with advance in her field precisely because whe had talent and brains and integrity, while her boss fell from grace because she lacked all these traits.

What a good, old-fashioned reason to reward people, unless you think badly of business as such, unless you harbor prejudices of the sort that are only too evident throughout Hollywood's writing community. These folks are only too willing to put the smoking gun into the hands of some corporate executive, some man or woman of business, who is supposed to have no scruples and will do anything to climb the ladder of economic success.

But this stereotype is entirely silly. It is no more accurate when it comes to business than it would be to charge all professors with being deadbeats, or all journalists as practicing plagiarism. We might as well stereotype film critics as jealous for not being in the movies but only commenting on them, all doctors for wanting people to be sick just to perpetuate the influx of patients.

But then while there are prejudices around—against the military, attorneys, politicians—no profession gets it as hard or as often as business. The prejudice is so powerful that it even clouds the artistic judgments of those who hold to it, leading them to confuse the art of film making with the messages conveyed by that art—messages that they do not happen to find ideologically sound.

INSULTING MOVIE-GOERS*

Bull Durham was a nice little movie, about minor league baseball and love and good times and friendship. Probably about more than all this. But recently it has come in for a strange criticism.

This and other movies, including television shows, are being charged with a kind of deceitful—i.e., subliminal—advertising. The charge is that Hollywood movie makers peddle various brand products. (In *Bull Durham* it was some kind of beer and some other products, none of which I remembered after I saw the movie or even noticed as I watched it.)

Of course, movies that deal with contemporary life would be entirely artificial if they disguised brand products used in the course of the action. Since I have been going to the movies I have always felt cheated when someone picks up a pack of cigarettes or a can of beer and hides the label. Mind you, I never remember it when the label is visible, but I do remember when it is artificially hidden from view.

What are these critics complaining about anyway? They are insulting us by implicitly accusing us of being passive robots who simply cannot keep from going out and buying what is presented to us in use on the screen. Imagine it. Movie-goers are being conceived of not as people with wills of their own, not as individuals who know what they do and do not want, but as mechanisms that respond automatically to subtle stimulation. And, of course, the movie makers are accused, by implication, of being manipulative and exploitative.

The evidence for both of these charges is utterly feeble. People are hardly robots available for such easy exploitation. One thing the advertising industry has learned is that you simply cannot sell people things they do not want. Of course, people may want silly and useless things, but they have to want them before they pay attention to the brand ads that invite them to go out and purchase what the producer has to sell. If this were not so, advertising campaigns would not flop as often as they in fact do. (Even ads we love do not always manage to sell the products we are invited to buy. We like the jokes, the characters, the themes, the scenery but not necessarily the product).

Furthermore, why must these critics assume that movie makers have nothing else in mind when they include various brand name products in their films? Why not assume that they simply wish to be realistic? Why not consider the possibility that they see the phoniness of pretending that, while everything else in the film manages to fit the picture, those disguised products do not?

Consider, also, that every movie "advertises" the actors who appear in it, not simply the artistic product or story. Movies are also "advertising" the cities in which they appear, the newspapers people read in them, the kind of clothing worn by the characters, and on and on.

I am confident that this special attack on the movies is yet another way in which the critics express their hatred for the marketplace and invite yet another

---

*Originally published in the *Freeman* (1989).

reason for it to be hated and feared by others and handed over to the bureaucrats to be regulated and managed. These critics are power seekers even though they have convinced themselves that their motives are sincere and virtuous.

Only these motives are not virtues, however sincere they may be. They are dangerous and should be pointed out as such. They are the subtle messages to the public that people are generally inept and need the wise guidance of intellectual kings who will populate various seats of power and issue orders as to what film makers and television producers may do.

Let us respond to these folks forcefully and tell them to take care of their own problems and leave us to cope with ours. We are quite able to handle anything offered us on the screen—we can even walk out if we find something offensive or pushy.

MEDIA INTELLECTUALS AND OBJECTIVE REALITY*

It is worth exploring the way many intellectuals who write for various magazines fall short of the very standards they often invoke when criticizing various segments of our society. Isn't it rather hypocritical of many of these people to have it both ways: On the one hand they invoke very firm standards of behavior for people in the worlds of business, politics, diplomacy, and other fields, yet the critics declare these very same standards to be mere myths or entirely transitory?

It was Allan Bloom in his book *The Closing of the American Mind* who got word around about the way most American educators deny the very possibility of truth. For example, many who write and teach about the political ideals of American society claim that these were mere figments of the imagination. When discussing the Declaration of Independence, they are all to eager to dismiss its "self-evident truths" as nothing but "important historical myths." This way they can pay some homage to that document of American history but also justify why they do not champion its tenets. So while the Declaration of Independence speaks only of life, liberty, and the pursuit of happiness as our basic rights, most modern political thinkers want to dismiss those rights. They would block the all-powerful state they advocate since these rights imply the restriction of government to a very limited job. Declaring these rights to be myths serves these political thinkers very nicely: They want to invent new rights—to education, health care, vacation, job, and even (if we are to believe former President Jimmy Carter) the right to be free of suffering from disease—and denying the permanence of the basic rights of the Declaration and even the Consitution makes this intellectually easy to do.

This historical—as well as cultural, ethnic, sexual, national—relativism is far more widespread than most people would suspect. It is usually invoked when Americans criticize other cultures or other political systems. While our system

---

*Originally published in the *Orange County Register* (1989).

might suit us, surely things are relative and others might be better off with a different system (e.g., socialism).

Some people—very influential ones—generalize this relativism even to such scientific pursuits as astronomy, physics, biology, and psychology. This means that the laws of these sciences are not actually aspects of reality but merely invented by scientists to suit their purposes, which change in different epochs.

Indeed, there are serious books in print arguing that all of our sciences are constructions of the human mind and no actual reality corresponds to what these sciences produce as their findings. This constructivism is being advocated by all kinds of professors—most recently I saw it defended in a magazine called *Marriage and Family Networker* (September/October 1988). Earlier, the book *The Anthropic Cosmological Principle* argued that we construct all reality out of our minds.

In essence, this notion gives us carte blanche regarding what we want to believe. Ultimately it isn't even important to be consistent in our beliefs, since even the need for consistency is a mere invention of human beings. Professor Paul Feyerabend of the University of California at Berkeley argues along these lines. (He also holds that whether one adheres to the theories of modern medicine or the African witch doctor really is of no significance; it's all a matter of one's point of view!) His most recent book is aptly called *Farewell to Reason!*

Now of course this kind of outlook implies that, for example, whether or not Lieutenant Colonel Oliver North was correct to act as he did must also be a matter of one's point of view. Or whether the press treated George Bush or Michael Dukakis in line with journalistic standards is also a matter of how one looks at it. There is no truth in such a view, but often the same intellectuals who espouse relativism quickly jump over to champion transcendent truth and standards of right and wrong when it comes to their pet political or social causes. Are champions of affirmative action, full economic equality for all, destruction of South Africa's apartheid policies, or national health care willing to be relativist and let everyone be equally right about his or her viewpoint? Certainly not. For example, in a recent issue of the *New York Review of Books,* two articles— one by author Theodore Draper, the other by *New York Times* columnist Anthony Lewis—show unhesitating loyalty to ultimate truth.

Draper goes after Oliver North, good and hard, and there is no question in his mind that only one ultimate truth on that topic is possible. Scholarship is produced aplenty to indict North's character, actions, and anything else Draper can drag out for examination. It is all supposed to show, without a shadow of doubt, that North is a crook. Anthony Lewis, in turn, indicts virtually all of the Amerian press for not chiding Bush and Dan Quayle much harder than it did during the 1988 presidential campaign. Again, there is no hint of relativism here. Indeed, Lewis invokes "the framers of the First Amendment," who "would scarcely have understood the idea of a 'balanced' press." Lewis says this in an effort to remind the press that its job is to go after the *facts*—and he italicizes this word—not to advance a balanced presentation of various points of view about these alledged facts. He does not see that in a relativist intellectual climate there are no facts, only different opinions. And then the press can do no more than be balanced and fair!

When it serves their purpose these folks will quickly adhere to truths and standards that indict what they do not like. Just the other day, on "This Week With David Brinkley," Sam Donaldson argued that Gadhaffi is mad "from our perspective, but not mad from the Arab perspective." Yet when Oliver North was being interrogated in Washington, Donaldson was upholding honesty and lawfulness as moral absolutes that should hold for all time, all circumstances, everywhere.

When it does not serve their purpose—say, when the property rights of people in business or home owners, or citizens (to their earned income) is concerned—some people are quick to abandon the ideal of truth and invoke relativism and its political cohort, majority rule. (Just try criticizing a homeless person for not working and you'll see how quickly ultimate standards of right and wrong get dropped.)

That these are the folks who provide our culture with most of its leading ideas is a frightening thought.

DID BUSH UNFAIRLY ATTACK THE PRESS?*

During the second debate between George Bush and Mike Dukakis the Vice President was asked about why the campaign is such a poor one, why the candidates don't address the issues, why is there so much negative campaigning.

Bush responded by first blaming the Democrats for having started it in Atlanta when they ridiculed him roundly and over and over again ("Where's George?"). And then he claimed that he and Dukakis are in fact dealing with issues, putting out policy positions, but the media is interested in focusing on the occasional barbs and jibes instead of doing the more demanding reporting of the candidate's positions.

Following the debate the Cable News Network conducted various interviews and finally got to Bernard Shaw, the moderator from its own news team, and this question came about regarding Bush's complaint. Shaw, whom I usually like and find one of the most professional newscasters and interviewers, made one of the most pious responses. He said, "When I hear this I always get angry," or something along those lines, and then proceeded to lambaste the candidates for complaining about the press. Finally, he went so far as to use the term "phony" with reference to Bush's complaint, clearly implying that he thought Bush was advancing a phony thesis. When Shaw was asked whether the panelists asked any questions that favored one candidate over another, he instantly dismissed the suggestion.

In fact, Shaw was being entirely disingenuous on both counts. While sometimes politicians like to pick on the press with little or nothing to back it up, in this

---

*Originally published in the *Orange County Register* (October 19, 1988).

case Bush at least had a plausible case that could use some serious attention. I have read the major newspapers and many magazines of opinion and have watched the broadcast news and analyses for as long as the 1988 election has been covered. There is no doubt in my mind that the media picks those elements of the campaign for special emphasis and highlights them with contentiousness, sham controversy, flashy trivia, and ill will.

The Dan Quayle matter is a clear case in point. Then Dukakis's alleged lack of heart. Then the matter of the flag factory. What about Lloyd Bentsen's quip, "You're no John Kennedy"? And on and on. Maybe this is inevitable in a medium that requires its topics to be amenable to quick and dirty treatment and can only feature lengthy coverage in specials that the networks probably rightly believe too few people will watch to make it financially feasible. All in all, the proposition advanced by Bush was not one that should have been dismissed so readily. Bernard Shaw, thou dost protest too much!

Indeed, there is a general principle of American life that is noteworthy in this connection. The media is perhaps the most protected industry in this country—and rightly so. The First Amendment to the Constitution protects the press—even the broadcast media, although not all facets of it—more than any other industry is protected from government intrusion, regulation, supervision, intervention, etc. Moreover, it is also the one industry that is relatively free of popular criticism—since it is the industry where criticism would have to be produced and aired. In short, self-criticism is not one of the strong-points of the press, e.g., "60 Minutes" rarely does pieces on newspapers, radio commentators, television news or the Public Broadcasting System's method of producing a documentary, while it constantly attacks the rest of the business community.

I would love to see Mike Wallace go after some new director or managing editor of a major daily newpaper. But, no, these folks are largely shielded from criticism, no matter how evident it is to all of us that they, too, can commit professional malpractice.

If they engaged in such self-criticism, they would have to ask themselves how it is that they are not asking the government to come in and help solve the problem with the press! Which brings me to Shaw's second piece of dishonesty. The panelists at all three debates asked questions favoring, largely, Dukakis. Why? Because in many cases their questions went, "What would government do about this problem?" or "How would your administration deal with this issue?" The presumption in such questions is outright statism. The government is taken to be the source of solution.

Can you imagine asking the question, "Governor Dukakis, there is too much sensationalism and bad reporting in the nation's media. What will your administration do about this?" I would challenge Bernard Shaw to consider whether it would not have been unique, yet quite on the mark for someone to ask one of the candidates, "Don't you believe that by taking on so many problems to solve, your administration will contribute to the gradual erosion of liberty in this free country of ours?" Surely, anyone would have to admit that asking this kind of question would have favored Mr. Bush's "thousand points of light" approach more than the questions they did ask, which generally helped Dukakis's "one bright light in Washington" theory.

SPORT IN AMERICA*

When I arrived in America the first time, back in 1956, one of my laments had been that Americans didn't do as well as they could in the Olympic games. The Soviet Union and its Eastern bloc countries did comparatively better, as anyone who was familiar with the record could tell.

Everyone in my family had been involved in sports. My father was a oarsman and achieved some fame as one of Europe's better rowing coaches. He even coached here in the United States for a while, at Philadelphia's renowned Vesper Boat Club. My mother was 1942 foils champion in Hungary and is still a coach in Salzburg, Austria. My stepfather was a saber fencer in Budapest and is today the U.S. Olympic fencing coach. My sisters were top swimmers in Budapest. I myself did a little of everything for a while, until I decided that I had other priorities in my life and confined myself to mere exercise, not serious athletics.

One advantage of being an athlete in communist Hungary had been that if one showed talent and perseverance, one's life was made much better by the state. Under most statist political systems sports becomes a kind of public exhibition of collective excellence. That was especially true in Hungary and is still true in most Soviet-bloc countries, as well as in China and in some of the Right-wing states such as South Korea. If someone demonstrates ability and willingness to become a world-class athlete, he is freed from all normal responsibilities of life and kept in considerable luxury and privilege. For this he sells his soul and, especially, his body (as long as it holds up) to the state.

In my ignorance of the American political tradition, I was appalled at how little investment the American government made in amateur athletics. I noted that, with all its fabulous talent, America could win at virtually any of the Olympic events, if only sufficient resources and discipline were invested in that goal.

But of course here is the rub. American society may include some of the greatest talent for practically any task, including any facet of athletics. But it is not primarily a statist system. Government in this society is—or at least was supposed to be—a servant of the people. Individuals and their own goals are of paramount importance, not showing off the system or proving to the world how fabulous the social organism happens to be.

Therefore, in American society many of the Olympic sporting events are truly amateur sports. Of course, there are exceptions and there are gray areas—e.g., tennis and basketball, respectively. But in the main the athletes compete because that is what they want to do, as individuals or as uncoerced members of teams and clubs. And these athletes tend to have a variety of goals in their lives. Unlike the East German swimmers, for example, American swimmers will devote con-

---

*Originally published in the *Freeman* (1989).

siderable time to training for their sport but a good deal of time, as well, to studying, family, and fun. Why not? Life has much more to offer most of us than being a single-minded athlete. Sport, after all, is supposed to be something of an enjoyment in one's life, not a mission of slave labor.

But I did not understand this when I first came to the United States. I was something of a convert nationalist and did not realize that what made this nation worthy of respect had little to do with winning the most medals at the Olympics, having the most productive economic system, being first in space, or any other single purpose that some people might prefer to take as a sign of collective success. What was vital for this nation—and there are signs that this has not been entirely forgotten even now, except perhaps by most of our intellectuals and politicians—is that each individual had the liberty to strive for his or her own goals in life, provided he or she did not trample on the efforts of others.

Now when I watch the Olympics my thinking and emotional reactions are very different from that first time. I scoff at the nationalism injected into the commentary. I am usually bemused and even elated, in contrast to the network commentators, when it is noted that American's are not doing as well as the Soviet-bloc athletes, who usually appear glum even after delivering a 9.95 performance in gymnastics!

Free people do not put all their energy into a showy project such as the Olympics, except spontaneously. Thus the 1984 Los Angeles Olympics disturbed me, although I realized that most people were celebrating the rejuvenation of the country, of which the American athletes' success in Los Angeles tended to be something of a symbol.

I am a refugee to this country, not because it manufactures Olympic winners or the greatest technology in the world or any other single achievement found in it, but because it is the best environment for individuals to pursue their own happiness, according to their own individual talents, abilities, and choices.